WALT WHITMAN'S MRS. G

WALT WHITMAN'S MRS. G

A Biography of Anne Gilchrist

Marion Walker Alcaro

Rutherford • Madison • Teaneck
Fairleigh Dickinson University Press
London and Toronto: Associated University Presses

© 1991 by Associated University Presses, Inc.

All rights reserved. Authorization to photocopy items for internal or personal use, or the internal or personal use of specific clients, is granted by the copyright owner, provided that a base fee of $10.00, plus eight cents per page, per copy is paid directly to the Copyright Clearance Center, 27 Congress Street, Salem, Massachusetts 01970. [0-8386-3381-1/91 $10.00 + 8¢ pp, pc.]

Associated University Presses
440 Forsgate Drive
Cranbury, NJ 08512

Associated University Presses
25 Sicilian Avenue
London WC1A 2QH, England

Associated University Presses
P.O. Box 39, Clarkson Pstl. Stn.
Mississauga, Ontario
Canada L5J 3X9

The paper used in this publication meets the requirements
of the American National Standard for Permanence of Paper
for Printed Library Materials Z39.48-1984.

Library of Congress Cataloging-in-Publication Data

Alcaro, Marion Walker, 1922–
   Walt Whitman's Mrs. G: a biography of Anne Gilchrist/Marion Walker Alcaro.
      p.   cm.
   Includes bibliographical references and index.
   ISBN 0-8386-3381-1 (alk. paper)
   1. Gilchrist, Anne Burrows, 1828-1885—Biography. 2. Whitman, Walt, 1819—1892-Friends and associates. 3. Authors. English—19th century—Biography. I. Title.
PR4715.G5Z65   1991
828'.809—dc20
[B]   89-46136
                                                                      CIP

Parts of chapters 10 and 11 have
been published in an essay, "Walt Whitman
and Mrs. G," in the Walt Whitman Quarterly
Review, spring 1989.

PRINTED IN THE UNITED STATES OF AMERICA

For those who gave me wings

*And in memory of
James Gilchrist, M.A.
Canon Emeritus
1910—1988
great-grandson of Anne Gilchrist*

CONTENTS

Acknowledgments — 9

1. O Pioneer! — 13
2. Clergy, Gentry, Weavers of Fine Cloath — 25
3. A Child Went Forth — 34
4. Alex — 47
5. Guildford — 63
6. 6 Cheyne Row — 73
7. Brookbank — 92
8. Godiva — 116
9. My Dearest Friend — 140
10. Mrs. G — 158
11. A British Lioness — 187
12. Dark Mother — 203
Epilogue — 229

Notes — 232
Bibliography — 269
Index — 275

ACKNOWLEDGMENTS

A biography is a search for someone—a search that one hopes will reveal at least a glimpse of a living person. My search for Anne Gilchrist has been a great adventure, shared and made possible by many persons in England as well as in the United States.

Although I never met the late Charles E. Feinberg, whose magnificent Whitman collection is in the Library of Congress, I was privileged to have his advice and continuing interest during the research and writing of this book. I shall always be grateful.

With a great deal of amateur detective work and enormous good fortune, early in my research I was able to find a number of persons in England who have become my friends as well as co-researchers. The material that they have generously and enthusiastically provided has given *Walt Whitman's Mrs. G* a scope and quantity of detail that would not otherwise have been possible. I would like to thank the following English friends whose contributions to the writing of this book cannot be overestimated: Bronwen Tickner of Shottermill; H. Clifford Stacey of Saffron Walden; Canon A. Stuart Holden, formerly vicar of Saint Andrew's Church, Earls Colne; Richard Harlakenden Carwardine Probert, laterally descended cousin of Anne Gilchrist, and his wife, Elizabeth; Canon James Gilchrist, great-grandson of Anne Gilchrist, and his wife, Norah; and their daughter Anne Gilchrist, named for her great-great-grandmother.

Walt Whitman's Mrs. G began as a doctoral dissertation at Drew University. It could not have been written without the resources of the Drew University Library and the kindness of its staff, especially Bruce Lancaster and the Interlibrary Loan Department under Josepha Cook. I am also grateful to the staff of the Musselman Library at Gettysburg College for allowing me to use its facilities. Working with the special collections in the following libraries and institutions has been a great privilege: the Department of Manuscripts, British Museum; the Feinberg Collection, Library of Congress; the Special Collections Department, Charles Van Pelt Library, University of Pennsylvania; the Ferdinand J. Dreer Collection and the Microfilm Department, Historical Society of Pennsylvania; the Carl H. Pforzheimer Library, New York City; the Berg and Oscar Lion Collections, New York Public Library; and the Harry Ransom Humanities Research Center, University of Texas at Austin. I also thank the following libraries and institutions for sending me photocopies of the Gilchrist material in their special collections: The Royal Academy of Arts, London; the Whitman House, Camden; the Archives and Special Collections on Women in Medicine, Medical College of Pennsylvania; the Manuscript Department, Alderman Library, University of Virginia; the Special Collections of the University Libraries, University of Iowa; and the Beinecke Rare Book and Manuscript Library, Yale University Library.

It is impossible to list all of those who have given me information, material, and help of many kinds, but I would like to list at least a few: Jennifer Railing, Marion Scharf, Eleanor Ray of the Whitman House, Frank Paluka of the University of Iowa, Frederic Carter, Idda-Marie Rossi, Oscar Kruesi, Georgianna Ziegler of the Charles Van Pelt Library, Susan Schubart, Eleanor Mittendorf, Betty Martin, Chris Fick, and Kay Hollabaugh. I am deeply indebted to Jerome Loving for his careful and critical reading of my manuscript and detailed commentary. *Walt Whitman's Mrs. G* could not have been undertaken without the support and encouragement of Bard Thompson, former dean of the Graduate School of Drew University; he will always be remembered with affectionate gratitude. I am also grateful to my family, especially my husband, for their forbearance during the many months that Anne and her children—and even Walt himself—have been, in a very literal sense, guests in our house.

Most of all, I would like to thank Professors Arthur Jones and John Warner of Drew University, and Barry Qualls of Rutgers University, who shared my search for Anne Gilchrist all the way. I thank them for their unflagging interest, invaluable advice, and challenging criticism; for the time and thought that they have given so generously, and for their continuing friendship.

WALT WHITMAN'S MRS. G

1
O PIONEER!

Loud! loud! loud!
Loud I call to you, my love!
High and clear I shoot my voice over the waves,
Surely you must know who is here, is here,
You must know who I am, my love.

Walt Whitman

On 10 September, 1876, the steamship *Ohio* arrived from Liverpool at the port of Philadelphia. An Englishwoman in her midforties—with a light, firm step and a lovely and unusually expressive face—was undoubtedly among the passengers who crowded the rails to watch the ship's docking.

It was her first glimpse of America. Fond of long, brisk walks over the fields and down the lanes of Essex and Surrey, during the eleven-day voyage she must have walked the deck daily, her eyes, like her heart, turning eagerly westward. Unlike the other passengers—most of whom must have been businessmen, Centennial visitors, ordinary immigrants, or Americans returning from a European tour—her reason for making the voyage was extraordinary. Even in the twentieth century it would cause comment; in 1876, for a woman of refinement and impeccable social position, it bordered on the out-and-out scandalous. She had come to America to marry a man she had never met; a man with whom, through the power of his published words, she had fallen passionately in love.

"O come. Come, my darling: look into these eyes and see the loving ardent aspiring soul in them—easily, easily will you learn to love all the rest of me for the sake of that and take me to your breast forever and ever," she had written to him in 1871.[1] Although he tried gently but firmly to dissuade her, five years later she made the long voyage to Philadelphia, confident that once they met he too would be convinced that theirs would be a perfect union.

Unfortunately for Anne Gilchrist's ardent dreams, the man was Walt Whitman. And Walt—for one or possibly all of the many explanations that have been offered by critics and scholars—throughout his life never married.

Anne had not planned a short visit to America. So certain she was that Whitman would respond in kind to her fervent love—and would allow her to comfort and tend him in the infirmity that had followed his paralytic stroke in 1873—that she had brought with her the beautifully carved furniture that she and her husband had collected, her pianoforte, her music, pictures, china, silver, and books. She also brought with her the three youngest of her four children: Beatrice, who was twenty-two; Herbert, who was nineteen; and seventeen-year-old Grace. Anne's journey has been seen as an incredibly foolhardy expedition. It has also been seen as an incredibly magnificent gesture of ideal and idealizing love. Either way, when the *Ohio* docked at Philadelphia, Anne Gilchrist not only arrived in America but entered the annals of American literature—as one of its most misunderstood, misrepresented, and consistently underrated figures.

Posterity has often been neither kind nor just to Anne Gilchrist. Unlike many nineteenth-century English women writers—who were not Austens, Brontës, or Eliots, but who somehow, in spite of limited educational opportunities for women and unlimited masculine editorial prejudice against female writers, managed to be published—her name has not been entirely forgotten. In most literary encyclopedias she is listed in a brief entry that follows a much longer account of the life and work of her husband, Alexander Gilchrist, the biographer of Blake; these entries note, in a line or two, that after Alexander's death at the age of thirty-three, his wife finished the biography. In studies of Whitman, Anne's one-sided courtship of the poet is frequently mentioned—not infrequently with a sort of literary snicker. Historically, she has been defined by these two men in her life and often dismissed, even by eminent scholars, as a silly woman who made an international fool of herself.

However, when one reads Anne Gilchrist's letters to her family, her friends, and to Whitman; her biography written by her son Herbert; comments by the many distinguished persons who knew her; and the miscellany of her own writings, a very different picture of Anne Gilchrist comes into view.

She was charming and vivacious, a gracious hostess, a spirited talker, a woman of culture and intelligence. Endowed with a quick and curious mind, a gentle but awesomely adamant independence of thought, and an avid intellectual appetite, Anne Gilchrist was one of the remarkable women born early in the nineteenth century who, largely through their own efforts, became as well educated as their most privileged masculine peers; who overcame the educational restrictions imposed on them by an era in which the approved curriculum for girls consisted of "accomplishments" and a once-over-lightly smattering of arts and sciences, learned for the most part by rote. After her husband's death in 1861, with the help of his friends Dante Gabriel and William Michael Rossetti, Anne took over the enormous task of completing and supervising the publication of Alexander's scholarly, handsomely illustrated, two-volume *Life of William Blake*, a work that is still a standard reference. In 1880, after her return to England from America in 1879, she edited a second two-volume edition, adding new illustrations and a memoir of her husband. Anne was also a biographer in her own right; her carefully researched and compassionate *Mary Lamb*, published in 1883, is still in print. In addition, she was a translator of Hugo, a writer of short stories and travel sketches, a writer of articles on popular science, a literary critic, and a powerful essayist.

Anne's resolve to leave England for the first time in her life and go to America was not a hasty decision, a spur-of-the-moment impulse. It had been her goal and dream for nearly seven years. In 1869, when she was forty-one and had been a widow for eight years, Ford Madox Brown, the artist, lent her a book of selections from the work of a controversial American poet that William Rossetti had edited. The book was *Poems of Walt Whitman*. Reading this startling new form of poetry—with its new rhythms and line patterns, its powerful emotional undercurrents, and its frank treatment of subjects that had been previously taboo—Anne was enthralled, shaken to the depths of her being. She asked Rossetti to lend her the complete *Leaves of Grass*, which he did, and she was even more deeply moved. It seemed to Anne that "the tenderest lover" was speaking directly to her, and she responded by falling in love with the whole of her passionate nature. She wrote a series of letters to Rossetti, putting into words, charged with emotion, her reactions to this new poetic phenomenon and her analysis of it as a great and valid work of art. Realizing that this was brilliant as well as inspired literary criticism—and eager to help Whitman, whom he greatly admired, and who, in 1869, desperately needed favorable criticism—Rossetti persuaded Anne to allow him to make the letters public in essay form. The essay was published anonymously in the Boston *Radical* in May 1870 as "A Woman's Estimate of Walt Whitman."

Through Rossetti, Walt sent a letter of appreciation to "the lady." A year later their correspondence began. From the first, her letters were frequent and passionate; his were warm and friendly—and infrequent. In 1876 her elderly and invalid mother had died, her older son, Percy, a metallurgist, was established in his profession and engaged to be married, and Anne was free to go to Philadelphia. Walt, alarmed, tried to discourage the "American transsettlement." But go she did. To become not Whitman's wife, as she had hoped, but to be for the rest of her life—and to the end of his much-longer life—in Walt's own words, his "noblest woman-friend." The strong, affectionate, and lasting bond that developed between them, apparently from the moment they met in Philadelphia, made Whitman's relationship with Mrs. G, as he called her, one of the most enduring and all-nurturing relationships that he ever experienced with any woman.

Much has been written about Anne Gilchrist by scholars and biographers of Whitman and in the memoirs and reminiscences of those who knew him. It has been written from widely divergent points of view and with equally divergent conclusions and interpretations. These assessments and studies should be considered in two groups: those written while Whitman was still living or in the twenty-six years after his death; and those written after Anne's letters to him were published, in 1918.

John Burroughs and Edward Carpenter, who wrote two of the early reminiscences of Whitman, had known Anne. Both had been guests at her house in Philadelphia and at 12 Well Road in Hampstead after her return to England. Like Whitman, Burroughs had succumbed to Anne's charm from the moment they met, a day or two after she arrived in Philadelphia. He and Anne maintained a friendly correspondence until her final illness brought it to a close; after her death he wrote to Herbert: "She was the only woman I have ever seen to whose strength of mind and character I humbly bowed."[2] Yet Burroughs does not mention her in his *Whitman: A Study*, published in 1896. In *Days with Walt Whitman*, published in 1906, Carpenter remembers Anne only as "a capable and large-minded woman," and notes briefly that she was the first Englishwoman "to fully and publicly recognize (as she did in some printed letters) the splendid genius of the poet."[3] Perhaps both men were standing too close to Anne, their view of her too limited by its subjectivity, to see that she had been a major contributor to the success of Whitman's career and to his eventual acceptance by the genteel literary establishment.

Dr. Richard Maurice Bucke, superintendent of an insane asylum in London, Ontario, and Whitman' first biographer, may or may not have met Anne when he first visited Walt in Camden in the summer of 1877. There seems to be no record of such a meeting. However, before her return to England, Dr. Bucke called on Anne in Brooklyn in the winter of 1878,[4] and she sent "kindest remembrance to Dr. Bucke" in a letter to Whitman on 22 August, 1880.[5] In his *Walt Whitman*, published in 1883—carefully edited and even written in part by WW himself[6]—Bucke does not mention Anne. He does, however, confirm her position as a distinguished critic of Whitman by including excerpts from her "Estimate" in his book's "Appendix to Part II—Contemporaneous Criticisms, Etc., 1855—1883."[7]

In the last years of his life, Whitman was the center of a group of devoted, mostly young men—lawyers, journalists, businessmen—from Camden and Philadelphia. They came to see him regularly, entertained him in their homes, arranged birthday parties for him, ran errands, managed his business affairs, took care of many of his personal needs, including annual passes on the Delaware River ferries—and sometimes wearied the grateful but ailing old poet with their busy note taking for books about him that they were planning to write. All were pallbearers at his funeral. Among the Camden Disciples were Thomas Harned, a Camden lawyer;[8] Thomas Donaldson, a lawyer from Philadelphia; Talcott Williams and Harrison Morris, journalists; and Horace Traubel, a young bank clerk and aspiring poet who devoted his life to Whitman, visiting him daily and taking the voluminous notes that have been published as the massive, multivolume *With Walt Whitman in Camden*.

The Disciples may not have been overly impressed with Anne Gilchrist's role in Whitman's life. Knowing as little about her as they did—they had only her "Estimate" and her son's understandably myopic biography for reference—they may have seen her as only one of the many, many distinguished persons who wrote about Whitman, became his friends, and traveled long distances to see him. It is probable that none of them ever met her. Traubel was a young boy living in Camden when she lived in Philadelphia; Whitman met Harned, Williams, and Morris after she returned to England; and although Donaldson could have met her, since he and Walt had known each other since 1862, he does not mention having done so.

It is not surprising, therefore, that in two books about Whitman written by Disciples before 1918, Anne is seen only through Whitman's eyes. Donaldson's *Walt Whitman: The Man,* which appeared in 1896, is a stiff little Victorian biography in which Walt—whom Donaldson describes as his intimate friend "in Camden, New Jersey, from the summer of 1873 to his death"—is referred to throughout, and even on his deathbed, as "Mr. Whitman." Its mention of Anne is confined to a single sentence: "When Anne Gilchrist's death in England, December, 1885, was announced, he [Whitman] sat quiet, and finally, in a deeper tone than usual, he answered, 'A sincere and loving friend.' "[9] In *With Walt Whitman in Camden,* Anne—as well as everyone and everything else that Traubel's daily notes recorded—is also seen only through the poet's eyes. Traubel's volumes of transcribed shorthand notes— the first three published before his death in 1919, the others posthumously— are filled with Whitman's reminiscences of Mrs. G: with anecdotes about her, quotations from their conversations, and expressions of his admiration, gratitude, and affection. Traubel gives us these reminiscences with the fidelity of a modern tape recorder, exactly as they were spoken; he seldom offers either comment or embellishment. They are Whitman's view of Anne Gilchrist— and no one else's.

Long after Whitman's death, a third Disciple, Harrison Morris, wrote his memoir of the poet, dedicated to the memory of Horace Traubel. *Walt Whitman: A Brief Biography with Reminiscences*—a delightfully chatty little book by a delightful man—was published in 1929. Since this was eleven years after Anne's letters to Whitman were made public, Morris's interest in her is greater and his view of her more comprehensive than that of the other members of the Camden coterie and should be compared with those of the other post-1918 Whitman biographers rather than with theirs.

Two pre-1918 Whitman scholars, using the same information about Anne that had been available to the Disciples, apparently read between the lines of both "Estimate" and Herbert's biography; they sensed astutely that here was no ordinary literary lady who admired Whitman, but a truly remarkable woman. Anne captured the imaginations of Bliss Perry and Elizabeth Porter Gould. The pictures of her that they created are far more appreciative of her critical acumen, her position in English literary circles, and the importance of her place in Whitman's life than those created by previous writers of Whitman biographies and memoirs. Their pictures of her—even though their view of their model was necessarily limited—are the first attempts at anything more than a thumbnail sketch of Anne Gilchrist by scholars of Whitman.

In *Walt Whitman*, published in 1906, Bliss Perry, editor of the *Atlantic Monthly* at the time, looks at Anne neither as a friend nor through Whitman's eyes, giving us an extended view of her—a pier glass rather than a hand-mirror image. He sees her as "a woman of personal charm, of marked power of character," and, in addition to mentioning her many times in the text, devotes four pages to her, quoting at length from her letters to Rossetti about *Leaves of Grass*; describing the genesis of "Estimate" and its reception; noting that "their intimate friendship continued until her death."[10] Perry was too disciplined a biographer to state as a certainty what he only surmised, but his intuition was obviously telling him that Anne's ecstatic admiration of Whitman was something more than ordinary enthusiasm—that her reaction to *Leaves of Grass* was not only intellectual.

Six years earlier, in 1900, a remarkable study of Anne Gilchrist had been published. *Anne Gilchrist and Walt Whitman* by Elizabeth Porter Gould is an earnest attempt to paint a truly full-length portrait of Anne. It is the only book that has ever been written about her, with the exception of her son Herbert's biography, which, because of its restrictively close-up focus, will be discussed in later chapters.

Elizabeth Porter Gould was a Whitman aficionado from Boston. Walt described her to Traubel as a lady who "bristles with conventions" but "is all right at the core."[11] Whitman had never given permission to anyone except William Rossetti to publish *Leaves of Grass* in any form other than in its entirety; but, mirabile dictu, she had persuaded him to allow her to edit a little book of selections. Walt quickly regretted his capitulation, and his publisher and friends wished that he had "sat down on" her book from the start. "God knows I wished to! Consent? How did I consent?" he fumed to Traubel. "The only thing I really promised was that I would not raise a hell of an objection to it." As a further explanation, he added that he had consented because he hadn't wanted to continue to be, like so many aging men, "a damned hog."[12] Having given his word, Walt would not retract it, and in 1889 David McKay published Miss Gould's *Gems from Walt Whitman*. Even the title made the poet's toes curl. "These gems, extracts, specimens, tid-bits, brilliants, sparkles, chippings—oh, they are all wearisome," he grumbled to Traubel. "Some books fit with them; but *Leaves of Grass* is different—yields nothing to the seeker for sensation."[13]

Miss Gould's "little gratuitous work," as she called it, passed into oblivion and did not prove to be the affliction to his career—"one more added to the rest"[14]—that Walt had feared it would be. He did not live to read her biography of Anne.

In her carefully and lovingly researched *Anne Gilchrist and Walt Whitman*, Elizabeth Porter Gould did wonders with the material available to her. However, her book—although its focus is on Anne's friendship with Walt—

is essentially an expansion of Herbert's biography. Miss Gould adds a few minor details from letters to herself, in response to inquiries about Anne, from Joaquin Miller in 1896 and William Rossetti in 1897; from Tennyson's *Memoirs* and Lady Tennyson's *Journal*; from Donaldson's *Walt Whitman*; from Matilde Blind's biography of George Eliot; and from "Chats with Walt Whitman," a piece by Grace Gilchrist that appeared in *Temple Bar* in 1898. But Herbert's biography—both in content and tone—is her principal source and the spring board for her late-nineteenth-century imagination. Carried away by an almost fatuous admiration of Anne, what Elizabeth Porter Gould creates is not a biography of her but an apotheosis. Hers is a sentimental view of Anne. In her book—which, in its emotional climate, often seems perilously close to the nineteenth century's "domestic" novels—she makes Anne the implausibly noble and selfless heroine of a story of implausibly idealized love, "one of the grandest, purest affections this age or any age has revealed."[15] One wonders how "pure" Miss Gould would have considered Anne's love if she could have known that Anne, in her letters, had urgently offered herself to Walt in body— "I am yet young enough to bear thee children, my darling"[16]—as well as soul.

Another pre-1918 Whitman biographer was an Englishman, Henry Bryan Binns, whose mother was proudly an American. His splendid *A Life of Walt Whitman*, exhaustively researched—and dedicated "To my mother and her mother, the Republic"—was published in London in 1905. Binns never met Whitman. However, in his research, he communicated with an impressive list of Walt's friends on both sides of the Atlantic: Edward Carpenter, William Rossetti, Moncure Conway, John Burroughs, Peter Doyle, Dr. Bucke's son, and many others. In his acknowledgments, he speaks of "my kind friends, Mr. T. B. Harned and Mr. Horace Traubel." If, as this suggests, Binns may have met and conferred with Harned and Traubel, it seems not unlikely that, like Bliss Perry and Elizabeth Porter Gould, he too suspected that "Estimate" was no ordinary appreciative review and the ensuing chain of events no ordinary admiring-reader-meets-poet scenario. At any rate, even though he gives Anne full credit for her contribution to the poet's career and pictures her as a woman of courage and dignity, Binns glides over the Whitman-Gilchrist friendship like a man skating on very thin ice. He does point out, however—and he was the first to do so—the similarity between their friendship and the friendship of Michelangelo and Vittoria Colonna.[17]

During his lifetime, Whitman refused to allow the publication of Anne's letters to him. After her death, when he was collecting material for his mother's memoir, Herbert asked the poet if he might have either her letters to him or extracts from them. Walt replied: "I do not know that I can furnish any good reason, but I feel to keep these utterances exclusively to myself."[18] And there is no evidence that during his lifetime he ever allowed anyone else to read them.[19] However, since he kept them carefully for twenty years, not destroying them as he did so many documents and letters, Whitman apparently did not want Anne's tribute to his poetry and to himself, private as it was, to be lost forever. Her letters were left to Thomas Harned, who, with Dr. Bucke and Traubel, was one of Walt's three literary executors.

On inheriting Anne's letters, Harned was faced with a hard decision. In his preface to *The Letters of Anne Gilchrist and Walt Whitman*, Harned justifies making the letters public by explaining that he had three choices. He could leave them in his will or place them in some public repository and thereby "shift a responsibility which was evidently mine to the shoulders of others who, perhaps, would be in possession of fewer facts in the light of which to discharge the responsibility." He could destroy them, which "Whitman should have done if it was to be done at all," and thereby "erase forever one of the finest tributes that either the man or poet ever received." Or he could "edit and publish them (after keeping them a proper length of time), for the benefit, not only of the general reader, but as an aid to the future biographer who from the proper perspective will write the life of America's great poet and prophet."[20] After his judgment had "been confirmed by that of a few sympathetic friends who, during the twenty-five years that the letters have been in my possession, have been allowed to read them," Harned chose to publish Anne's letters.[21] In 1918 *The Letters of Anne Gilchrist and Walt Whitman* was published in London and New York. It is one of the most illuminating portraits of a lady in literature.

Understandably, the publication of the Gilchrist letters stirred up a brouhaha on both sides of the Atlantic.

In England, in an indignant letter to *The Nation* on 5 October, 1918, Grace Gilchrist Frend—her brother Herbert had died in 1914—bitterly protested the publication of her mother's "love letters" to the poet. "As my attention had been drawn to a paragraph in 'The New York Times Book Review,' announcing from a well-known New York firm of publishers, a book purporting to be the 'Love Letters of Walt Whitman and Anne Gilchrist,' it might be as well to correct in advance some misapprehensions which may arise, especially from the title," she wrote, adding, "As a daughter of the late Anne Gilchrist, and also well acquainted personally at one time with the poet, I am fairly entitled to speak on the subject, and I can safely say that though my mother was a warm admirer of Whitman's writings, the poet himself entertaining a hearty regard and friendship for her, the correspondence which passed between the two would in no sense lend itself to the suggestion of the title of the proposed book."[22] Katherine Anthony, in an article in *The Dial* on 11 January, 1919, defending the publication, responded tartly to Grace: "It was an unfortunate inspiration which led the daughter of Anne Gilchrist to write in advance to the London Nation a letter protesting against the title of the forthcoming publication of her mother's correspondence with Walt Whitman. Her mistake consisted literally in the fact that she was speaking without the book. In the first place the volume is neutrally entitled The Letters of Anne Gilchrist and Walt Whitman (Doubleday, Page; $2), and not the 'Love Letters,' as she has heard it was to be headed; and in the second place, so far as her mother's letters are concerned—and they practically compose the volume—to call them merely 'love-letters' is to understate the case." Anthony followed this with a bit of pointed advice: "The episode might well serve as a warning to all daughters that they can not safely say anything about their mothers' love affairs until all the returns are in. The mothers of this generation are wisely beginning to learn that the adolescent daughter has her own private soul; but it remains for the next generation to learn that middle age too has its secrets."[23]

In the *New York Times Book Review*, Bliss Perry, no longer editor of the *Atlantic Monthly* but a professor of English at Harvard, applauded Harned's decision to publish the letters "as likely to win the approval of those whose judgment counts."[24] Others had reservations. J. W. Wallace, one of Whitman's "Bolton College" group of admirers in Bolton, Lancashire, wrote to Clara Barrus: "I cannot read them [the letters] without feeling that Mrs. Gilchrist would have been deeply shocked and pained."[25] And Kate Buss wrote to Dr. Barrus in April 1919 that, in her opinion, "to have guarded the legend of Whitman Mrs. Gilchrist's letters should not have been published."[26] Kate Buss seems not to have been an all-out admirer of Whitman. In an article in the *Boston Evening Transcript* on 31 May, 1919 "Anne Gilchrist to Walt Whitman: Some Comments on the Love Letters of a Woman to the Great American Poet, Whose Centenary is now Being Observed," she wrote that the publication of the correspondence "may be a disillusion to a discriminating Whitman public" and "its reading will destroy something of the popular Whitman legend." She added sternly that the finger of blame should point nowhere other than directly at the poet himself. "Whitman's was the mistake to have kept the letters," she wrote. "But he was insensitive about the publication of his personal notes and, in at least one other instance, allowed the use of a private letter for his own panegyric. Emerson's courteous resentment is recalled."[27]

Harned doggedly rode out the storm. "I don't care what they say about the Gilchrist book. It is launched, and it will take its place as an important interpretation of the great power of 'L. of G.,' " he wrote to Dr. Barrus. "I have traveled the open road and tried to discharge my duty as a trustee for Walt."[28]

Harned's prediction proved to be true: *The Letters of Anne Gilchrist and Walt Whitman* has indeed taken its place as an important interpretation of *Leaves of Grass*. What's more, it has given new insight into the poet himself, for the letters reveal almost as much about WW—his character and psychological nature—as they do about Anne Gilchrist. In most biographies and many studies of Whitman since 1918, Anne's relationship with the poet is given extensive and thoughtful coverage. Without question she is conceded to be a courageous and perceptive critic of *Leaves of Grass*, whose valiant defense was a milestone in Whitman's career. However, even among post-1918 biographers and critics there have been widely disparate views of Anne herself and of her one-sided courtship of the poet.

In 1919, Edith Wyatt, in a superb article about Anne in the *North American Review*, saw Anne as "the victim of a species of self-hypnotization." But she also saw her as a woman "strong-hearted enough to love the individual reality as deeply in an altered fashion, more in the way of a mother perhaps, as she had loved her fancied idol of another kind of devotion."[29] Clara Barrus in 1931, in *Whitman and Burroughs: Comrades*, found Anne, in her capacity to love and in her self-abnegation, "as great as Walt is in his poems." To her the letters revealed the "beautiful nude soul" of Anne Gilchrist.[30] In 1933, in *Poor Splendid Wings: The Rossettis and Their Circle*, Frances Winwar, in the tradition of Elizabeth Porter Gould, perpetuated the view of Anne as the sob-inspiring heroine of a sentimental love story, who "dwelt three sober years in America, whither she had transported her furniture and pianoforte, and then went back home to grandmotherly peace."[31] Eight years later, in *American Giant: Walt Whitman and His Times*, Winwar still kept the strains of the mighty Wurlitzer playing in the background as she wrote of Anne and Walt: "But it was too late for the love she would have given. Before the beautiful but shipwrecked actuality there could be no thought of bearing any sweet comfort but such as could be found in the sunset glow of their lives," and each "returned to his own."[32]

In contrast, other post-1918 critics and Whitman historians have seen Anne and her passion for Walt from a point exactly a hundred and eighty degrees around the circle. In 1951—in the revised edition of his *Walt Whitman*, first published in 1933—Frederik Schyberg saw Anne's famous friendship with Whitman as "really a pitiful tragedy."[33] In the 1960s, Edwin Haviland Miller referred to Anne as "that pathetic Victorian lady."[34] He found her transatlantic pursuit of the poet "an amazing spectacle, the stuff of tragedy for some writers, of comedy to others."[35] In 1984, Paul Zweig, in *Walt Whitman: The Making of the Poet*, with binoculars reversed, saw Anne only as one "of the women who fluttered around Whitman in later years."[36]

With so many considerations, studies, and assessments of Anne Gilchrist over so many years, which have resulted in so many divergent views, there is one view of her which, amazingly, no one has ever seemed to take: a view of Anne Gilchrist as neither the widow of one distinguished man nor the friend and would-be lover of another. A view of Anne herself—the woman. Anne herself—seen on her own in close-up and quite apart from either man. For as Anne Gilchrist emerges from the modest but scholarly shadow of Alexander Gilchrist and the towering shadow of Whitman, a very different figure from the one biographers and critics have pictured comes into focus.

For one thing, in their preoccupation with Anne's passion for Whitman as the reason for her trip to America, critics have given scant attention to the importance that her visit proved to be as a link between British and American literary circles.

In 1876 American literature had not yet come into its own. Irving, Cooper, Hawthorne, Emerson, Poe, Longfellow, Twain, and Thoreau were the names of lasting prominence on the American roster. Melville was not yet appreciated; and Howells, Henry James, Emily Dickinson, and acceptance of Whitman himself were yet to come. American literature still bowed with colonial deference to the glory of a literature that traced its genealogy back to *Beowulf* and had produced in the nineteenth century alone the work of Wordsworth, Coleridge, Shelley, Byron, Keats, the Brontës, Jane Austen, the Brownings, George Eliot, Dickens, Thackeray, and Scott. The visit of a noted English woman of letters, who had known the Carlyles intimately and who was a friend not only of William Michael, Dante Gabriel, and Christina Rossetti and the other Pre-Raphaelites, but of Tennyson himself, was an event in American literary circles. Athough she described it more reticently in her letters, there is no doubt that Anne was lionized. She returned to England with a new list of literary friends and acquaintances, this time American: John Burroughs, Emerson, Longfellow, Emma Lazarus, Joaquin Miller, Horace Scudder, Frederick Holland, and Jeanette and Richard Watson Gilder, to name a few. Anne Gilchrist was a two-way literary ambassador.

What is even more amazing, however, is that the critics and biographers—and, above all, the twentieth-century feminist writers—have, in spite of a wealth of plain-as-day evidence, missed the fact that Anne Gilchrist was a pioneer, one of the great pioneers, in the crusade for the equality of women.

For, although she designed no liberating "hygienic" clothing for women, like Amelia Bloomer; and although she wrote no scathing diatribe on the status of woman in the nineteenth century, like Margaret Fuller; and although she delivered no fiery speeches on "the woman question," like Annie Besant, Anne Gilchrist, in her own way, made as strong or even a stronger statement. In her own life she demonstrated that the changes that the others were clamoring for could be accomplished without destroying the Victorian way of life, as opponents of the movement for equality predicted direly and with equal passion. She demonstrated, after her husband's death, that a woman could be a devoted mother, an accomplished housekeeper, and an accepted member of refined society—in short, the Victorian ideal woman—and at the same time live independently of relatives, manage her own business affairs, carry through to completion a monumental scholarly task, achieve literary recognition on her own, take an intelligent and informed interest in politics, and maintain warm friendships with many men as well as with women. She also proved, by her quasi-scandalous trip to America, that even in the mid–nineteenth century—and in spite of the rules for female deportment unequivocally spelled out in Mrs. Ellis's popular *Women of England*—a woman could defy convention without sacrificing either her dignity or her status as a lady. By her own example, Anne suggested that one way to expanded freedom for women could be by quiet but determined individual transition—which reassures the opposition instead of alarming it—rather than by violent disruption.

Anne's role as a pioneer in the feminist crusade was not limited to the Q.E.D.'s that her life and accomplishments provided. Far from it. Like

Margaret Fuller, she believed that the curriculum considered suitable for female students in the nineteenth century was little more than farce and that women, like men, should have the opportunity for a challenging education. She championed this cause all her life. She was delighted with Smith College when she visited it in Northampton; after her return to England, she described it enthusiastically in an article in *Blackwood's Magazine* as "a really noble institution," which embodied "the most advanced ideas for giving young women precisely the same educational opportunities as young men."[37] In an even more personal way, Anne was a valiant champion of the cause. Her daughter Beatrice received her medical degree, served a residency, and went into private practice—a herculean feat for a woman in the 1870s. Bee accomplished this with the unfaltering support and encouragement of her mother.

Like Charlotte Brontë and Louisa Alcott, Anne was also deeply concerned with the limited opportunities available to respectable women—especially single women—who needed to earn their own living. In her biography of Mary Lamb, she included a long and bitter essay on the subject written by Mary Lamb herself. The prominent place that Anne gave it in the small volume makes it clear that the essay expressed her own views.

Anne Gilchrist was most truly a pioneer, however, in her championship of the sexual liberation of women. At a time when sex was considered a pleasure for men but a duty for women, she publicly defended the controversial author of *Leaves of Grass*, who proclaimed that physical love should be a joyous experience for both. In addition to being a critique of Whitman's poetry, Anne's "Estimate" is a thinly disguised but poignant plea for the acknowledgment of the reality and normalcy of feminine sexuality. It is a between-the-lines protest against the tenets of nineteenth-century physicians, who held that women were asexual—and that sexual feelings in a woman were a sign of insanity. It speaks out courageously for all women who had denied and stifled their instincts, needs, and desires in the belief that their femaleness was shameful.

What Charlotte Brontë suggested in *Jane Eyre*, Anne Gilchrist dealt with frankly—the validity of a woman's sexual feelings. She may have been the first woman in the nineteenth-century Anglo-American world to declare— publicly in "Estimate" and privately and more explicitly in her letters to Whitman—that sexuality is a beautiful and natural aspect of being a woman.

As Anne Gilchrist comes into focus, she emerges not only from the shadows of Alexander Gilchrist and Walt Whitman but from the confines of her age. She was very much a woman of her own time; yet in both her actions and thinking, she often seems to belong to the twentieth century as much as to Victoria's era. Like Whitman himself, one feels that she would have been wonderfully at home in the modern world; and that, like the poet, she would have delighted in it.

2
CLERGY, GENTRY, WEAVERS OF FINE CLOATH

> Of every human life,
> (The units gather'd, posted, not a thought, emotion, deed, left out,)
> The whole or large or small summ'd, added up,
> In its eidólon.
>
> Walt Whitman

Anne Burrows was born on 25 February, 1828, at 7 Gower Street in London. Her father, John Parker Burrows, was a hardworking and highly successful solicitor. Seven Gower Street, a handsome London town house with white steps and black iron railings leading up to the entrance door, is presently occupied by professional offices. In the early-nineteenth century it would have been an elegant house for a little girl to grow up in. However, much of Anne's childhood was spent in long and frequent visits to the village of Earls Colne on the Colne River in Essex, the ancestral home of her mother's family; these visits would continue throughout her girlhood, after her marriage, and when she had children of her own to accompany her. Earls Colne would always be Anne's second home.

The principal source, indeed the only source, of information about Anne's family background, childhood, and adolescent years has been the biography that her son Herbert lovingly, but hastily, compiled in the ten months following her death.[1] The biography did not receive unqualified praise. When *Anne Gilchrist: Her Life and Writings* was published early in 1887, the review in *The Athenaeum* began: "The materials thrown together by Mr. Herbert Gilchrist might, with proper handling, have furnished a far more satisfactory memoir of his gifted mother than this volume; and it is not doubtful that much matter besides that which he has used would have been easily obtained and worked up without great difficulty into a narrative which need hardly have occupied more space than he has filled with irrelevant and unimportant matter." The review continued: "Many besides the author of 'Leaves of Grass' had, sixteen months ago, reason to mourn the untimely death of a brave, honest woman, and the story of her life and the good work done in it is full of profitable lessons for the outside public. Perhaps it may be told aright some day by a sympathetic, yet critical biographer."[2]

This criticism, harsh as it seems, was not altogether unjustified. Herbert's biography does contain much "irrelevant and unimportant matter" that has nothing to do with Anne: interminable conversations between his father and Carlyle (taken from his father's notebooks); conversations between himself and Whitman (taken from his own notebook); long letters to his father from Carlyle quoted in toto. In addition, as a researcher soon learns, Herbert's attitude toward exact titles and dates of publication could be decidedly cavalier. And his penchant for name-dropping comes close to obsession. However, it must be remembered that Herbert was an artist by profession, not a writer, and he acknowledges this by designating himself as the editor, not the author, of the book. It must be remembered too that he was only twenty-eight when he began compiling the book, and grief stricken by the death of his beloved mother. Exasperating as it often is—exasperating most of all because of what Herbert fails to tell, because of the almost complete lack of personal reminiscences of his mother—*Anne Gilchrist: Her Life and Writings* is an invaluable repository of information that would otherwise have been lost forever. It is also, in spite of its flaws, a charming, gracefully written, and entertaining book. As Whitman would say of Herbert in a letter to Dr. Bucke, "He is very good company."[3]

In one chapter of the biography, Herbert gives a detailed and colorful history of Earls Colne and of the Harlakendens and Carwardines, two old and distinguished families from whom Anne was descended through her mother, Henrietta Carwardine Burrows.

Earls Colne was the home of first the Harlakendens, later the Carwardines. Alberic de Vere, earl of Ghisnes in Normandy, who came over with William the Conqueror, was given William's half sister Beatrix in marriage and the manor of Colne. In 1100 A.D., his son Aubrey de Vere—later the first earl of Oxford—founded Colne Priory, a Benedictine monastery. In the chapel of Colne Priory, at one time, there were three beautifully carved tombs of earls of Oxford: Robert de Vere, fifth earl of Oxford, who died in 1296; Thomas de Vere, eighth earl of Oxford, who died in 1371; and Richard de Vere, eleventh earl of Oxford, who died in 1412. William Harlakenden came over with William the Conqueror as "Esquier" to Alberic de Vere. Some of his descendants lived at Colne and for many years were land stewards to the earls of Oxford. In the late-sixteenth century, the extravagant seventeeth earl sold the Priory estates to the family of Roger Harlakenden, his steward and master of horse. By that time the Harlakenden family was related to the de Veres by marriage.[4] In Saint Andrew's Church in Earls Colne—built in the fourteenth century by the seventh earl, its imposing west tower completed by the fifteenth earl—there is a small stone relief of Roger Harlakenden with his four wives kneeling behind him. One of his daughters, Dorothy, married

Anne Gilchrist's grandfather, the Reverend Thomas Carwardine, painted 1772 by his friend George Romney (1734–1802). Private collection.

Samuel Symonds, who emigrated to America in 1637 and became deputy governor of New England. John Addington Symonds, the English scholar—whose persistent questioning of Whitman about the nature of his personal sexuality distressed and angered the aged poet and prompted Walt's famous claim that he was the father of six children—was collaterally descended from Dorothy.[5]

Herbert gives a delightfully gossipy history of the merging of the Harlakenden and Carwardine families. After the dissolution of the lesser monasteries in England in 1536, Colne Priory had been used as the family residence; and in 1770 the member of the Harlakenden family living there was a young girl, Ann Holgate, born 3 April, 1752, who was the ward of Mary Wale, a curmudgeon of a maiden aunt. "Nancy" was courted by Thomas Carwardine, a young clergyman from Thinghill Court who was descended from Sir Thomas Carwarden, "a gentleman of the Privy Chamber to Henry the Eighth, Master of the Revels, and Keeper of the King's Tents, Hales, and Toyles." They were married at Colne on 9 July, 1771. Miss Wale refused to leave Colne Priory. The young couple considered taking legal action to evict her, but they were advised by Lord Thurlow, a legal friend of Thomas Carwardine, to "lose half your estate, rather than go to law." And so Miss Wale remained in obstinate residence until she died on 30 August, 1786—but not before spitefully burning some family treasures, a bundle of Cromwell's letters, and a lock of his hair.

Thomas Carwardine's first choice of a profession had been art. However, Lord Thurlow, whose opinion was sought on this question too, advised against it. His lordship, apparently not impressed with Thomas's talent, bluntly reminded him "that a friend can only have his portrait painted once" and advised the church as a career. But the Reverend Thomas Carwardine continued to be deeply interested in the arts. He was a friend of Romney and Hayley, and in 1773 the three traveled together in Italy—"the divine being the only one of the trio unaccompanied by a fair but unwedded companion—noticeable rectitude in those days," Herbert notes. Through his sister, who was an accomplished miniature painter, "the amiable Divine" met Sir Joshua Reynolds and marveled at the great artist's speed of execution when he visited his studio. As proof of his great-grandfather's artistic aptitude, Herbert quotes two of his sayings: "the most beautiful eye is of a colour impossible to name," and "green is nature's colour." Lord Thurlow's advice seems to have been judicious.

Ann Carwardine was the practical partner in the marriage. Thanks to her frugal management, Herbert tells us, a small fortune was saved out of the entailed Priory estates that provided an inheritance for which both her daughter and granddaughter—Anne's mother and Anne herself—would be grateful, since both were widowed early. Mistress Carwardine was "somewhat formal, never addressing her husband otherwise than as 'Mr. Carwardine.'" However,

The Reverend Thomas Carwardine, painted ca. 1810 by his friend Thomas Phillips (1770–1845). Private collection.

she would "unbend in the nursery," where she would sing "Auld Robin Gray" in a sweet, clear soprano to her delighted children. Romney painted a charming portrait of her; she is shown in profile holding one of her children tenderly in her arms—an eighteenth-century Madonna. She died on 2 March, 1817, at the age of sixty-six, of cancer. According to family legend, when her coffin was placed in the Colne church, a robin flew in, perched on it, and sang sweetly.[6]

Henrietta Carwardine—one of nine children of Ann and Thomas Carwardine—was born on 11 June, 1786, at Earls Colne.[7] Since Herbert was eighteen when she died in her ninetieth year, he knew his maternal grandmother well and remembered her with affection and admiration:

> Henrietta Burrows, née Carwardine, was a gentlewoman of the old school. Descended from a long line of small squires, she was drilled in the now despised accomplishments, being a mistress of those graceful amenities of life that a daughter learns in a family where bringing up is insisted upon, with its high traditions of conduct and unflinching obedience to self-imposed duties; traditions duly instilled into little Annie. A witty and delightful grand-dame she seemed to us, whose stately manners were reminiscent of the "grand old style."[8]

Herbert did not know his maternal grandfather, since Anne's father died when she was eleven. He tells us little about John Parker Burrows, except that, when walking, he was frequently mistaken for Sir Thomas Lawrence by that gentleman's friends; and that the solicitor's legal practice thrived so rapidly that, to those who watched his progress, "it seemed a pity that such ability should not have been called to the bar."[9] He tells us nothing at all about his grandfather's family or background.

The earliest records of the Burrows family that seem to be extant date back to the seventeenth century. In 1694, John Burrowes, gentleman—the first of several generations to own and farm land in the parish—was buried under a large marble slab, with an English (rather than Latin) inscription, in the chancel of the church at Great Sampford in Essex. By English standards, he was a newcomer to the parish. In the Hearth Tax list of 1671, he was not included as a householder; however, the following year, in 1672, John Burrowes, described as a draper, "was presented to quarter sessions for having in the company of Robert Breens, Giles King, and James Newbourne riotously assaulted John Dench, a parish constable, in the execution of his duty."[10]

According to Gerald Curtis in *The Story of the Sampfords*, John Burrowes had come to Great Sampford from Haverhill, where he had made money in the textile trade. At that time wool was spun and some of it woven into worsted in the villages of northwest Essex, and it was merchanted from the towns of Haverhill and Saffron Walden—the latter named for the saffron crop that produced the yellow weld used to dye the cloth. At Great Sampford, the Burrowes family became one of the two great families of parish gentry. John

Anne Gilchrist's grandmother, Ann Holgate Carwardine, and her son Thomas, painted ca. 1772 by George Romney. Private collection.

Burrowes was succeeded in the textile business by his son William, who, even though his father could claim the title of gentleman, described himself in his will as a "webster"—a weaver. However, Curtis explains that it is most unlikely that he ever did any weaving himself; his function was to buy wool for the spinners, pay them, pass it on to the weavers, pay them, and market the cloth. The Little Sampford Church-wardens Book for this period shows the vestry repeatedly buying "cloath" from "Mr. Burrowes" to be made into garments for the poor.[11]

Richard Burrowes, William's third son—and Anne's great-grandfather—was admitted to Jesus College in 1736 and graduated Bachelor of Arts in 1740. His father had probably intended him to enter the church in order to earn his living, but his elder brothers died and he inherited the family property at Sampford. Richard Burrowes died in 1753, at the age of thirty-five, leaving his widow to bring up two sons, John and Richard, Junior. He also left her three farms, land at Balsham, and a handsome house at Sampford that the local curate described as standing "opposite ye great church in Sampford: it is well-built and furnished; in ye parlour there are some good pieces of painting, especially one of a sea-peice [sic], by Vanderveid, and another of an Arabian Horse by a very eminent Master."[12]

Here there is a hiatus in information about Anne's father's history. In the Probert family genealogical chart, John Parker Burrows, the spelling no longer including an *e*, appears as the husband of Henrietta Carwardine. He is listed as the son of Richard Burrows of Saffron Walden. In a record of "The Treasurers & Chamberlains of the Town Corporate of Walden," the name of Richard Burrows, a cabinetmaker—born in 1751, son of Richard and Elizabeth of Great Sampford—is listed as being an alderman and four times mayor of the town between 1785 and 1813. Since he was not the oldest son of Richard and Elizabeth, Richard, Junior had apparently not inherited the estate at Sampford and had gone to Saffron Walden to live; as a cabinetmaker, he had broken away from the family tradition of involvement with textiles. At least two of his children broke away from the same tradition. His son Henry, who was also an alderman and mayor of Saffron Walden, was a chemist and druggist; another son, John Parker Burrows, was, of course, a solicitor in London. Richard, Junior, Anne's grandfather, died on 23 April, 1832, in his eightieth year.[13]

John Parker Burrows was baptized in Saffron Walden in June 1788. His address at the time of his marriage was Austin Friars, London.[14] But his exact date of birth, educational background, and the reason he came to be in London have vanished into the past, leaving no clues. And we can only guess how he may have met Henrietta Carwardine of Earls Colne: the Probert genealogical chart shows that the Holgate family—Henrietta's mother's family—had roots in Saffron Walden as far back as the sixteenth century. John Parker Burrows, thirty-seven, and Henrietta Carwardine, thirty-nine, were married at Earls

Colne on 15 February, 1825.[15] They had three children: John T. Burrows,[16] Anne, and a second daughter, who died in infancy.

In the meager information about his grandfather that Herbert provides, he tells us that John Parker Burrows could be a hasty disciplinarian. He punished his little daughter only once, but her pride was wounded and she never forgot it. When she had children of her own, Herbert recalls, her credo was that a parent should avoid conflict with a child in small matters and "always resort to gentle means when possible." But aside from this single painful incident, Anne remembered John Parker Burrows as a devoted and companionable father.

He was fond of music and often took little Annie to concerts, encouraging at an early age and doing his best to develop her lifelong love of music. It must have given him great pleasure to hear his five-year-old daughter play her first piece on the piano—"La Petite Surprise." On Sunday afternoons, the two sometimes walked from Gower Street to the Zoological Gardens, a long, long walk for a child. And sometimes, in the evening, before dressing for dinner, Anne's father emptied his pockets of coppers and gave them to her. Little Annie—thrifty Ann Carwardine's grandchild—stashed them away until she had enough to buy a rosewood desk.[17]

3
A CHILD WENT FORTH

> . . . the low and delicious word death,
> And again death, death, death, death,
> Hissing melodious . . .
>
> Walt Whitman

In an early-nineteenth-century family, death was not an uncommon event, especially the death of a child. At midcentury, one of every six children died before the age of five, half of them in infancy.[1] The Burrows family of 7 Gower Street was no exception. When Anne was three, her baby sister died. The memory of her little sister, shrouded in black velvet and lying in her coffin, remained with Anne as long as she lived.[2]

As the two surviving children of older parents, there was, understandably, a close bond between Anne and her brother, John Thomas, who was probably about a year older than she.[3] Herbert describes them as playmates in a single arresting sentence: "Anne has a playmate in John T. Burrows, the typical brother, who burns the dollies of a yielding and half-hearted devotee of dolly."[4] If Johnny, as a doll burner, was a typical Victorian big brother, Annie, young as she was, seems not to have fitted into the pattern of the typical Victorian little girl. As "a half-hearted devotee of dolly" who willingly "yielded" up a dull traditional symbol of femininity—instead of running wailing to Mama—one suspects that she enjoyed the conflagration as much as Johnny did. Like Anne the woman, little Annie seems not to have winced at seeing a match touched to convention.

Anne herself gives us the best picture of Annie and Johnny Burrows as children: playing together, squabbling, sharing joy, excitement, reprimands— even terror. "Lost in the Wood," published in Groombridge's *Magnet Stories* in 1861, is an account of a six-week visit, when Anne was nine or ten years old, with her mother's brother and his family at Tolleshunt Knights in Essex— "a wild country place"—where the Reverend Charles William Carwardine was rector.[5] She and Johnny—excited city children—and their mother traveled by coach, which, even with four horses to draw it and fresh horses every ten miles, took nearly all day to make the sixty-mile journey from London:

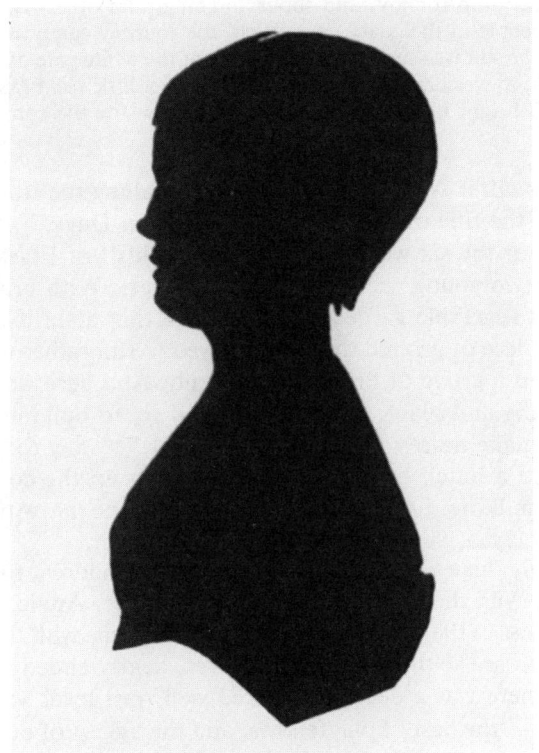

Annie Burrows, 1835. Author's collection.

But oh! were we not wild with delight, I and my brother! When we felt the coach no longer rattling over stones, but bowling along a road with hedges on each side, that seemed scampering away from us instead of we from them; when we passed golden corn fields, sprinkled here and there with beautiful scarlet poppies; and green meadows with dear white woolly sheep nibbling away in them—it was hard to sit still, and not jump for joy, and shout and sing, and otherwise torment the grave grown-up people in the coach. . . . Well, the journey came to an end at last . . . and just as the sun was sinking, we turned in at the white gate of Elmwood Rectory. In the porch, to welcome us, stood my aunt and her little son Frank, a merry-looking fellow, with bright hazel eyes, just the playfellow for the coming six weeks.[6]

Years later, after Anne's death, a friend recalling the story but not its title thought that the title might have been "Halcyon Days."[7] And it might well have been. For the six weeks spent in the "wilds" of Essex were enchanted days for the two young residents of Gower Street. With Frank they explored the fruit and vegetable garden, "and beyond that a shrubbery, and beyond that again a piece of ground that was allowed to run rather wild, with a grassy nut-walk, and a grove of fir-trees at the end. And here we might do just as we pleased, dig and plant, or carpenter, and try to build an arbour, or play games, and make noise to our heart's content."[8] They fed Frank's pets—a tame owl and a hutch of rabbits—helped fetch up the cow from the field, watched the milking, brought windfall apples to the pig. And in the evenings the cousins played games of trap ball on the lawn.

Occasionally there were fallings-out among the children, followed by a sulky hour or two. And there were adventures, of course. Annie, wandering off by herself, was lost in the wood but found her way home with the help of a kindly miller. The most exciting episode, however, nearly ended in tragedy. In the stable yard there was a deep, uncovered well, just level with the ground, in which Grim—"the best of playfellows, and the ugliest of dogs"—had almost drowned. In an argument with Frank, Annie, struggling to get away from him, forgot the well, stepped backward into it—and woke up on a bed with anxious faces bending over her. She had been saved by Johnny, who had grabbed her hair as she came up the second time and managed to hold her nose and mouth above water until the boys' terrified screams brought a gardener running.[9]

The idyll, fondly remembered, ended at last. And Annie, Johnny, and their mother returned in a lumbering hackney coach to London—"to the grand old smoky familiar place."

When she was six years old, Anne was enrolled in the Misses Cahusac's school for girls at Highgate, where, since in those days it was an arduous journey to Highgate from Gower Street, she was a boarding student. It was an evangelical school with a curriculum that at the time was considered very advanced. In contrast to the school that Henrietta Burrows had attended—Mrs. Pugh's at Baddow, where the emphasis was on deportment, with instruction on stepping in and out of a carriage and in "walking magnificently through the school-room once a day, as a lady should walk"[10]—at the Misses Cahusac's school students were given at least a modicum of instruction in mathematics, literature, possibly history, and probably French, since Anne later read and translated the language with ease.

Anne was an eager and talented student. Julia Mary Newton, one of her classmates and a lifelong friend who supplied Herbert with reminiscences of their school days, recalled that "Annie was a favorite with the masters, because of her ability and painstaking application. The 'English Master' would turn to my companion when none of the other pupils could follow him in the problems of Euclid." Learning by rote was an accepted method, and Anne had an unusually retentive memory: "Upon one occasion a page of Boileau's Satires had to be learnt within the space of ten minutes. When my friend's turn came to repeat the lesson, she was able to take up her part in the book at the right time; and twenty years afterwards Anne Gilchrist remembered the lesson, though she had never looked at the book in the interim!"[11]

In spite of the advanced curriculum, however, neither deportment nor "accomplishments" were entirely neglected at the Misses Cahusac's. The young ladies were taught dancing by Tenniel, an eminent dancing master and father of the illustrator. He was a demanding teacher whose stern command "Round your elbows!" taught awkward young arms to make a graceful curve. They were given some instruction in music, and to Annie's delight their teacher sometimes played for them. But, to her sorrow, needlework was required—and Annie, the zealous student, detested sewing. "It was a rule at Miss Cahusac's," Julia remembered, "that we should do some needlework for 'the poor,' two hours a week; a task that was enlivened with reading aloud. The governess's inquiry as to who would like to read, was always answered by Anne. Sometimes Elizabeth Cahusac would say with a smile: 'I think you had better do a little needlework this evening, Anne.'" Anne's inexpert work was always list run upon calico. Julia once asked her why she always chose the same elementary task, and Anne replied, "Because I need not think about it."[12]

While she was a student at the Misses Cahusac's, John Parker Burrows frequently wrote long, news-filled letters to his little daughter—addressed always to "My dearest Annie" and signed "Your affectionate father, John P. Burrows." His letters—which in no way talk down to a child—are a testimony to the bond of love and companionship between them. Three of the letters—written in a firm, authoritative hand, in the gracefully formal style of the early-nineteenth century, and directed to "Miss Burrows"—still exist.

On 10 August, 1836, John P. Burrows wrote to eight-year-old Annie that "much Business" was detaining him in town and preventing him from joining Johnny—home from school on holiday—and "dear Mama," who were visiting at Colne. "The House is now full of Workmen, as the Roof has been taken off," he wrote ruefully, "and I have scarcely room to sit in." He added that Mama had left orders that Elizabeth, a servant, was to bring a cake when she went over to see Annie. He closed with a paternal minisermon: "Therefore you see you are indebted to Mama's never ceasing kindness for this remembrance of you and I feel assured that you will evince your gratitude to her by constantly attending to all her excellent precepts as well as those of the Ladies under whose care you are placed." After his signature, a childish attempt to copy it in pencil is faintly discernible.

A letter of 6 September, 1836 accompanied a brace of birds for the Misses Cahusac and "Buns, Pears, Green Gages, & Apples" for Annie. Her father had spent several days at Colne and reported that Johnny had a pony, hired from a farmer, on which he rode "all over the Neighbourhood, *by himself*" and delivered letters for his Uncle Henry Carwardine.

On 10 December, 1837, John Burrows wrote to Annie, now nine years old, describing at length a business trip to Brighton; he "was obliged to return outside, as all the Coaches were filled inside, with Ladies from the numerous schools at Brighton." A piano, "a nice Instrument," would be waiting for her when she came home for the Christmas holiday, her father told her; he was expecting much pleasure from hearing her play. Elizabeth would not be coming for her, Mama had asked him to inform her; instead she was to be brought home with a schoolmate on the omnibus. "I feel satisfied, my dear Girl," he wrote, "that not only in the subject of Music, but also, as to all your other studies, you will reward the great care and attention, which, we are convinced, the Misses Cahusac bestow upon you, by the proficiency which you will attain in these studies; and I need not say, how much your doing this will gratify & delight myself & your Mama."[13] Anne's father was clearly aware of his daughter's intellectual ability and eager to encourage its development. One doubts that he was deeply distressed by clumsy list run on calico.

When Anne was eleven, there was a second death in the Burrows family—sudden and calamitous. On 18 April, 1839, John Parker Burrows died at the age of fifty-one of an illness that followed a fall from his horse. He was buried in London's vast Kensal Green Cemetery.

After the solicitor's large practice had been closed, Henrietta Burrows and her children—once a family of five, now only three—left Gower Street and moved to a smaller house at Highgate. The move to Highgate, it seems safe to assume, was made to cut down the expense of Anne's attendance at the Misses Cahusac's; perhaps it was no longer necessary for her to be a boarding student. Herbert hints that the school may have made an adjustment in her tuition as well: "School life for Anne at eleven, fortunately was not to receive any check from the break-up of the home in Gower-street, Miss Cahusac being desirous to keep so promising a pupil."[14] In 1844, when she was sixteen, Anne completed the courses offered at the Cahusacs', and her formal education came to an end.

After she left school, Anne continued to be a serious student. She read widely and eclectically. She read Comte, Rousseau, Emerson and other transcendentalists—weighty and controversial material for a young girl to be reading in the 1840s. One day when she was walking on the terrace at Highgate Cemetery[15] reading Rousseau's *Confessions*, the vicar appeared unexpectedly. Herbert relates the denouement: "After the usual salutations, Clericus asked, 'What is your book, Miss Burrows?' Realizing the situation, Annie replied, almost inaudibly, '*Rousseau's Confessions*,' of which the last word only caught the parson's ear. '*St. Augustine's Confessions*. Ah! good reading; a very good book, my dear.' "[16]

In addition to broadening her intellectual horizons with her own discipline of unrestrictive reading, Anne began to develop the critical skill and insight that would culminate in her essay "A Woman's Estimate of Walt Whitman." In a letter to Julia Newton she wrote: "Comte and Emerson are the two opposite poles of the present intellectual world. Comte is, I think, essentially a materialist. Emerson's writings are treated with a good deal of contempt and ridicule now, but I think the next generation will call him a great man. If people would have the patience to study him, in spite of his apparent affectation and mysticism, they would, perhaps, find him a profound thinker." Anne had also read the novels of Maria Edgeworth. In the same letter to Julia, speaking of Miss Edgeworth, she wrote: "She gives us fine deeds and fine talk, but never a human being. She sees only the outside of life, appearances instead of realities, and is evidently one who observed acutely but neither thought nor felt deeply."[17]

In her post-Cahusac years of self-education, without making a great to-do about it, as would always be her way, Anne demonstrated to herself—and to anyone else who might care to notice—that a woman's intellectual capacity is not inferior to a man's. Twenty years later, when she read the work of a poet who proclaimed, "The Female equally with the Male I sing," lines like these would strike a responsive chord in Anne Gilchrist:

> I am the poet of the woman the same as the man,
> And I say it is as great to be a woman as to be a man.[18]

The most significant bit of information in her reminiscences of his mother that Julia Newton sent to Herbert was this: "As early as fifteen my schoolfellow began to think about spiritual questions. With a love of freedom for herself in theology, was combined an anxiety not to unnecessarily shock those who thought orthodoxy essential."[19] For throughout her life nothing illustrated more clearly Anne Gilchrist's quietly uncompromising independence of thought than her attitude toward religion.

There is no question that the Burrows family of Gower Street were members of a parish church in London. Henrietta Burrows was not only the daughter and sister of clergymen, but Convention personified; it would have been unthinkable for church membership and regular attendance not to have been of primary importance in her family's life. After the move to Highgate, she and her children must have transferred their membership to the parish church there, since the vicar and Miss Burrows were well-known to each other. Even at the Misses Cahusac's, an evangelical school, Anne must have been exposed on a daily basis to the tenets of the church—or, one suspects, in spite of the advanced curriculum, Annie Burrows would not have been enrolled as a student.

In the nineteenth century, in England as well as in America, the climate of Protestant theology was a somber one. Sin was a major preoccupation and concern. The slightest deviation from strict observance of the Sabbath, for example, was a Sin. Elsie Dinsmore and Kathie Alston, the pious little heroines of two popular midcentury series of books for girls, were held up as role models for young readers because they bravely risked paternal anger and social ostracism by tearfully, but firmly, refusing to play secular music on Sunday.[20] The first of the six Kathie volumes and the first of the long series of Elsie books were written in the 1860s; but in this moral lesson that they hammered home they reflected rigid standards of theological decorum that had prevailed for years.

The nineteenth century was also an era when theology coexisted, comfortably and compatibly, with fantasy. It was the era of what Ann Douglas calls "the domestication of death"—the attempt to negate its stark reality by prettifying and sentimentalizing it.[21] It was the time of burial in gardenlike cemeteries instead of churchyards, of the appearance of the professional undertaker with an equal emphasis on business and sentimentality, of the rise and enormous popularity of consolatory literature written mostly by women and clergymen—poems, memoirs that Douglas sees as "exercises in necrophilia,"[22] and novels. Consolation literature, in turn, was largely responsible for what Douglas calls "the colonization of the afterlife"[23]—the concept of heaven as a sort of resort area in the sky, where every day is Sunday and residents, alerted by a mysterious earth-to-heaven intercom, stand ready to welcome arriving loved ones.

In the nineteenth century, theology seesawed unperturbed between spiritual and wishful thinking. Small wonder that at an early age Anne Burrows, with her mathematical and scientific mind and her predilection for philosophy, began to ask herself serious questions about sectarian theology as she knew it.

When Julia Newton wrote to Herbert that, as a schoolgirl, although she had loved freedom for herself in theology, Anne had not wanted to unnecessarily shock others, the list of "those to whom orthodoxy was essential" would have included, first of all, Henrietta Burrows. Anne would not have been able to discuss with her mother her reservations about church doctrine and rituals without inflicting great pain. But she could speak frankly to Julia, even though the two seem not to have been in agreement. On 21 July, 1845, seventeen-year-old Anne wrote to her friend: "Rhoda [another schoolmate] and I have already commenced correspondence, and she tells me that she is going to be confirmed. Poor girl, she is very pleased. I never will be cofirmed with my own consent. If I am forced, I must submit, but I trust I shall escape."[24] We do not know if Anne was confirmed. There is no record of her confirmation in the church at Earls Colne, but, to please her mother, she may have "submitted" in a church in London.

One reason for Anne's reluctance to be confirmed may well have been the questions in the catechism, "an instruction to be learned by every person before he be brought to be confirmed by the Bishop," in *The Book of Common Prayer*. One question is: "What is the inward and spiritual grace [in Baptism]?" The answer is: "A death unto sin, and a new birth unto righteousness: for being by nature born in sin, and children of wrath, we are hereby made the children of grace." Anne—whose uncompromising honesty in thought as well as word was one of her salient characteristics all her life—would have rebelled inwardly at having to make this response to the bishop. For she did not, could not, accept the doctrine of original sin. Late in 1847, now nineteen, she wrote to Julia:

> You ask me if I believe in the doctrine of man's total depravity. I do not. I believe that there is much evil in the human heart, and also much that is good; . . . to me it seems [that] our great aim should be to fulfil the ends for which we were created; that is to say, develop to the utmost the nature which God has given us; and I cannot think of Heaven as a place, but as a state of Being.

And in the same letter she wrote:

> I cannot help thinking you attach too much importance to creeds and doctrines. They are mere definitions, after all; and definitions are better calculated to circumscribe truth, and bring it down to the narrow level of our half-awakened understandings, than to raise our minds to deep, elevated, life-giving comprehension of it.[25]

Although she had grave doubts about orthodox rites and theology, Anne had no doubt about the existence of Deity. "The soul pants to worship God," she wrote to Julia.[26] What she could not accept was the narrow, and narrowing, concept of Deity that Protestantism insisted upon. As her independent reading in philosophy progressed, she began to believe that truth might have many theological sources. "Truth is to be found complete in no man's system," she wrote to faithful Julia, "but a portion of it in all systems. It is for the reader to collect it, and reconcile apparent contradictions."[27] These lines in *Leaves of Grass*, when she read them, must have seemed an echo of her own thoughts:

> Magnifying and applying come I,
> Outbidding at the start the old cautious hucksters,
> Taking myself the exact dimensions of Jehovah,
> Lithographing Kronos, Zeus his son, and Hercules his grandson,

> Buying drafts of Osiris, Isis, Belus, Brahma, Buddha,
> In my portfolio placing Manito loose, Allah on a leaf, the crucifix engraved,
> With Odin and the hideous-faced Mexitli and every idol and image,
> Taking them all for what they are worth and not a cent more,
> Admitting they were alive and did the work of their days,
> (They bore mites as for unfledg'd birds who have now to rise and fly and sing for themselves,)
> Accepting the rough deific sketches to fill out better in myself . . .[28]

"No sooner had Annie left school than the sister made herself a perfect companion to the brother," Julia wrote to Herbert in her reminiscences, "giving up her time wholly to him when he was at home; and if 'Johnny' is late in returning from the law-office or opera, Annie will sit up to chat with the amusing, good-natured brother. 'Play me something, Annie,' was a frequent request, readily granted."[29] One senses a bit of embroidery here. Possibly on Julia's part, possibly on Herbert's. Herbert, a Victorian himself, pictured his mother whenever he could as an ideal woman of the era. And the dutiful sister, self-dedicated to an adored brother, was a Victorian ideal. In *Women of England* (1839)—which in the mid–nineteenth century could have been titled *The Gospel According to Mrs. Ellis*—Sarah Stickney Ellis makes very clear what the duties of a sister to her brother should be:

> . . . let the sister possess all that ardor of attachment which young ladis are apt to believe they feel, let her hang about his neck at parting, and bathe his face with her tears; if she has not taken the trouble to rise and prepare his early meal, but has allowed him to depend upon the servant, or to prepare it for himself; it is very questionable whether that brother could be made to believe in her affection. . . . I do not mean that sisters ought to be the servants of their brothers. . . . But no woman should allow her brother to put on linen in a state of dilapidation, to wear gloves or stockings in want of mending, or to return home without finding a neat parlor, a place to sit down without asking for it, and a cheerful invitation to partake of necessary refreshment.[30]

It is difficult to imagine Anne Burrows as an atremble-to-please, Ellisian slave sister. But there can be no doubt that after she left school her brother's companionship meant a great deal to her. In July 1845, the summer after she left the Misses Cahusac's, she wrote to Julia: "I am staying at a very pretty, retired place, within sight of the sea; and we have delightful water parties and picnics. In an excursion of this kind, I fell into the water the other day, and a tall gentleman on the top of me. However, they soon hauled me out."[31] But before long excursions of any kind were impossible for Henrietta Burrows, who suffered increasingly from rheumatism. As her mother, now in her sixties, became more and more disabled, Anne's life must have become more and more restricted—her days filled with care of the invalid, household duties that her mother could no longer perform, and her solitary reading. She must indeed have waited up at night for Johnny, gladly playing for him if he asked her to, preparing a late supper if he needed it, listening sympathetically to his problems and eagerly to his news. Mrs. Ellis to the contrary, one cannot believe that this was a duty that Anne felt obligated to perform or that Johnny expected. Their evenings together must have been happy times for both young people. If Anne was "a perfect companion to the brother," Johnny must have been a delightful, and sorely needed, companion for his sister.

In late September 1846, Henrietta Burrows and her children moved again. This time they moved from Highgate to 10 Heathcote Street, Mecklenburgh Square, in order to be near the law offices where Johnny was studying. Herbert tells us that the house was rented from Mrs. James Gilchrist. Was she Anne's future mother-in-law? Herbert does not say.

Shortly after the move to Heathcote Street, tragedy struck the Burrows family again. Johnny became seriously ill. Herbert tells us that it was "a malignant fever" and that during his illness his sister was not allowed to see him. It seems most likely, since the illness continued for a number of months, that Johnny had consumption, the disease that afflicted so many young adults in the nineteenth century.

The greatest testimony to the bond that existed between Anne and her brother—to their love for and their trust and complete confidence in each other—is a poignant letter that Johnny sent to his sister from his sickbed on 15 January, 1847. It is addressed on the overfold to "Miss Burrows—to be opened—John T. Burrows."

10 Heathcote Street
Mecklenburgh Square

15 January 1847

Lest it should please God to take my life suddenly and without time to prepare myself in this world or for the next, I deem it right to commit this brief explanation to paper of the state of my affairs—that my dearest Mother may be guided in her disposition of them, and to do full justice to those in whose debt I am.

About three years since instead of striving to contain myself within the income which my beloved and indulgent Mother out of her liberality allowed me, I got into careless (and in my circumstances) profuse habits. At different times I applied to my Uncle and Guardian Mr. Henry Burrows to advance me small sums of money amounting in the whole to £50—I believe this to be the exact sum but he has the memoranda. This I am to pay when I attain 21—as I shall then be entitled to some real and personal property now in his hands.[32]

In addition to this, finding myself unable to pay for my clothes, I entered into an arrangement with Mr. Nooke, tailor of Thayer Street, Manchester Square, to pay all monies which might be due to him on my attaining my majority. The exact sum which I now owe him is £58:14 for clothes supplied within the last three years.

This is all I now owe unless there happen to be a few inconsiderable items which I cannot call to mind. For the last year I have endeavoured to break myself of all extravagant habits and have ceased borrowing of my Uncle. As far as I possibly could I have always paid. Unjustifiable as it has been of me to incur these debts, still there is much to be said of me. I have always associated with those better off than myself. From having no father and being my own master I have often been called upon to pay where I otherwise should not. If I am to die suddenly (which God forbid as I am utterly unfit) it will be in the hope and belief that my beloved Mother will forgive me for having acted thus. I would never have concealed it from her had I not felt that the knowledge of it would have caused her pain and unhappiness.

There are many letters in my desk in a well known hand. It is my desire that my dearest Sister should destroy all. They relate to a tender and long cherished attachment.

May the Lord have mercy upon my soul for the sake of his dear Son Jesus Christ.
John T. Burrows

I should much wish £10 to be given to my own dearest Annie Probert for a mourning ring. She may shed a passing tear for her cousin.[33]

In her description of Anne as a perfect sister, Julia added that "there were many little things that she, as a sister, could advise her brother in." In their evenings together, one wonders if Johnny told his sister about his debts. One wonders if she knew about the "tender attachment."

Johnny died on 16 July, 1847. He was buried with his father in Kensal Green. His death was a terrible blow to Anne. In a letter to Julia six months later, she confessed that she was suffering from an "almost unconquerable depression," although "I do not give way to it." Death seemed so encompassing to Anne that she felt surprise at finding any young man that she knew still living.[34]

After Johnny's death, Henrietta Burrows gave Anne a gift—a gift symbolically from her brother. It was an eolophon, a coarse-toned wind instrument played with a keyboard that was invented about 1830.[35] The note that accompanied it is written in a small, exquisite hand on blackbanded notepaper. On the first page is written:

AN ANGEL'S WHISPER

My beloved Sister

My spirit has been holding communion with my poor bereaved Mother's which delights in knowing & fulfilling my wishes. Therefore accept the Eolophon through her affection for us both as a gift of Holy Love from your Brother—and let it be devoted to Sacred Music on the Sabbath that may ascend to Heaven with thoughts that I am There! waiting to be united to all I hold most dear on Earth.

Turn over

And on the second page:

From your Mother

I think my dearest Annie you are aware the money which purchased the Eolophon

Letter to Anne Burrows from her mother, Henrietta Carwardine Burrows, 1847. Private collection.

was saved by me for your beloved brother to spend as he best liked after he had attained the age of twenty-one.[36]

The note is a touching portrait in miniature of Henrietta Burrows—her elegance, her unquestioning belief in consoling concepts of death and the afterlife, her Victorian sentimentality. Anne kept it all her life.

In November 1847, Henry Carwardine, Henrietta Burrow's brother who had inherited the Priory at Earls Colne, wrote to a friend (Herbert makes a point of noting that the friend, James Gillman, was also a friend of Coleridge) that, after the death of her son, his sister had no reason to live in London, "and her daughter not liking it, they are both coming to live at a snug cottage of mine, close to the entrance gate of the Priory. I am going to add a bedroom on the ground-floor; for she cannot mount a stair. She will be near her own family and many of her early friends, and I shall be able in many ways to render her assistance, and minister to her little comforts and requirements; and I think we can get her into a bath-chair in fine weather, and wheel her about the old Priory grounds—a mode of enjoying air and exercise which she cannot obtain in London."[37]

In August 1848, the house at 10 Heathcote Street was closed, and Anne and her mother made the journey—a painful journey for Henrietta Burrows—to Earls Colne and permanent residency there.

4
ALEX

> Fair Annie! the sweet, fair-souled Annie Burrows!
> The dear maid I've seen! in a dream I met her!
> In a sunny dream, before mine eyes she rose . . .
> Alexander Gilchrist

"When I was eighteen I met a lad of nineteen[1] who loved me then, and always for the remainder of his life," Anne wrote to Whitman on 3 September, 1871, in her first letter written directly to the poet. "After we had known each other about a year he asked me to be his wife. But I said that I liked him well as my friend, but could not love him as a wife should love & felt deeply convinced I never should. He was not turned aside, but went on just the same as if that conversation had never passed. After a year he asked me again, and I, deeply moved by his steady love, and so sorry for him, said yes. But next day, terrified at what I had done and painfully conscious of the dreary absence from my heart of any faintest gleam of true, tender, wifely love, said no again."[2] Poor, persistent Alexander Gilchrist. The course of his true love seems to have run anything but smoothly.

Alex was not an unattractive young man. On the other hand, he was not a romantic figure. In his *Reminiscences*, William Michael Rossetti remembers him as "a young man of rather low middle height, of strong build and well-knit figure, with a countenance of much intelligence, not otherwise specially noticeable."[3] In his biography of his mother, Herbert Gilchrist includes a drawing of his father made from an 1851 daguerreotype that illustrates Rossetti's description: a youthfully rounded face that clearly reflects intelligence, the mouth a trifle wide, the jaw determined, at twenty-three the hairline beginning to recede. Not an unpleasing face, but, as Rossetti candidly recalls, not one that would attract attention.

How and where did Anne meet this scholarly, talented, sensitive, outwardly colorless young man? Herbert does not tell us. If they met when Anne was eighteen it would have been in 1846 or 1847, when Anne was living in London. Alex's mother, a widow, was Mrs. James Gilchrist, who at that time was living in London. Perhaps the house at 10 Heathcote Street was hers, and Anne and Alex met through its rental. In 1846 Alex entered the Middle Temple as a

Alexander Gilchrist, drawing by Herbert Gilchrist from a daguerreotype made in 1851. Author's collection.

student of law. Perhaps he and Johnny were fellow students, which brought about both the rental of the house and the acquaintance of Alex and Anne.

Actually Herbert tells us nothing at all about Alexander Gilchrist's background or early life. His first reference to his father in the biography is a quotation from a letter from Anne to Julia Newton in 1848 telling her of their engagement. Anne herself, in a memoir of her husband that she wrote for the second edition of the *Life of Blake* in 1880, gives us the only detailed account of Alex's family, his childhood, his education, and his promising, although tragically short, career.[4]

Alex's father, James Gilchrist, son of a Scottish farmer, attended Edinburgh University and became a minister of the General Baptists, an offshoot of the Presbyterian Church. He was sent out as a preaching missionary to England. After traveling widely in Cumberland, Westmoreland, Lancashire, Shropshire, and Staffordshire and preaching for a while in Birmingham and Derbyshire, he married Deborah Champion of Newbury[5] and settled down in Newington Green, where Alexander, the youngest but one of seven children, was born on 25 April, 1828. James Gilchrist was a writer and a philosopher. His most successful literary work was a little book titled *The Intellectual Patrimony*, published in 1817. His deepest interest, however, was in the use of language as an intellectual tool. He wrote two pamphlets on the subject and began the enormous task of embodying his principles in a new dictionary of the English language, the introduction to which was published separately in 1824 and led to his sometime employment by the publishers of the *Encyclopedia Britannica*. Repelled by both the narrowness of orthodox sects and by what seemed to him the deceitful intellectuality of the Unitarians, Dr. Gilchrist resigned from the ministry. In order to provide for his large family, when Alex was a year old, the newly unordained layman rented an old water mill on the Thames in the village of Mapledurham, near Reading.

Like Anne, as a child Alex was his father's close companion: "Almost as soon as he could walk he became that father's constant companion, the span of years between them bridged by the remarkable gift of sympathetic insight, springing from a great power of loving, which dawned early in the child, grew from day to day, and was hereafter to prove a main source of his strength as critic and biographer. Hand in hand they stood, watching the work go on in the cheerful, busy, old mill . . . or they wandered along the riverside and through the noble beechwoods that crown the surrounding heights, the father musing, the child enjoying."[6] And, like Anne, Alex lost his father when he was very young. Since the former clergyman had neither training nor experience, running the mill was a fiasco. Crushed by his failure, James Gilchrist, who before he left the ministry had suffered a severe attack of "brain-fever" brought on by overwork and mental conflict, succumbed to "a wasting of health and strength without apparent physical cause." In 1835, four years before the death of John Parker Burrows, Alex's father died at the age of

James Gilchrist, Alexander's father, painted ca. 1827. Private collection.

fifty-two. His widow and her children left Mapledurham and, with grief and straitened circumstances combined, went to London to live—"dreariest of places under such conditions," Anne comments understandingly.

Alex's early education began at home. For his older sons, James Gilchrist had devised a rigorous new method of learning reading, spelling, and Latin, based on his theory of the philosophical study of language. The outcome was anything but successful. Whether "the standard of time and attention were fixed too high, or too sternly enforced by the earnest, high-strung, sometimes irritable father; or whether the new system were better in theory than in practice, the progress made was small and the disgust to study great in both the elder brothers." As a result, Alex was spared this trauma and allowed "to travel along the beaten track under the gentle guidance of an elder sister, and the intercourse between father and son was unclouded." At the age of twelve, Alex was sent to London University College School. For four years he was a diligent student there, and something of a loner: seldom frequenting the playground, liking his work and his teachers, winning a number of prizes, and—like Anne at the Misses Cahusac's—"eagerly availing himself of all the opportunities offered to quench his thirst for knowledge."[7]

It was at the London University College School that he was introduced to poetry, and, Anne tells us, he often walked home in the afternoon across Regent's Park in spring reading Wordsworth or Shelley. At an early age, he began to write poems himself. "Lines at Night," written on the back of a page from a school exercise in mathematics when Alex was fifteen, still exists.

LINES AT NIGHT—Sept., 1843

The night is clear & still, the breeze is calm,
And a mild soft light from above is cast,
Diffusing round a soft & gentle balm.
The hours of weary toil & strife have pass'd,
And soothing tranquillity's come at last.
A dim veil o'er past joys & woes is thrown;
All minds are now held in oblivion fast;
And past deeds on the morrow's wings have flown.
Would the regrets & sorrows they have left could flee![8]

Could "Lines at Night" have won its author a schoolboy's prize?

It is likely that the expenses of Alex's education were paid by his two much-older brothers, who were his close and devoted friends. In 1844, when he was sixteen, Alex left school and spent two years studying law. His goal was to be called to the bar. In 1846 he entered the Middle Temple as a student and spent two more years in preparation for examination and eventual practice. However, although he did not dislike the law, he found himself becoming more and more deeply interested in literature and more and more firmly convinced that he would rather have even a modest literary achievement, if it were genuine, than the most brilliant legal career. When he was called to the bar in 1849, he put on the wig and gown for the first and also the last time and, for the rest of his life, devoted himself to literary work. Nevertheless, he took great pride in his legal status. On the title pages of the two books that he wrote, and on his tomb, he is identified as Alexander Gilchrist, of the Middle Temple, Barrister-at-Law.

What were Alex's literary aspirations? For a short time at least, to be a novelist was one. There are a few pages extant of the manuscript of what seems to be a fragment of a novel about "sweet Rhoda," a young girl with a "sylphlike turn of the fair limbs," "fairy feet," and a "swanlike throat," who one fair day "issued early from the cottage" to "meet the rigours of the world" in order to earn a living for herself and her newly widowed mother.[9] Perhaps Alex finished the novel, perhaps he abandoned sweet Rhoda before her story was complete. Anne does not mention the opus in her memoir. His most serious early aspiration seems to have been to be a poet. In October, November, and early December 1848, he compiled a collection of fifty-one poems—some of them revisions of earlier versions dating back to 1846—carefully copied on numbered pages and clearly intended for submission for publication.[10] The collection includes poems to Coleridge and Wordsworth, a long "Lament for Popular Imagination," a monologue dramatizing with typical Victorian bathos the sad lot of the prostitute,[11] and thirty-five sonnets. Speaking of Alex's poetry in her memoir, Anne writes that he was "one who had a poet's heart, if not a poet's gift of utterance." Her gentle critique is charitable. Alex's poetry that was intended to be made public is labored, rigidly conventional, top-heavy with platitudes about Life and Nature and Purity, turgid with "poetic" rhetoric. The poems reflect the tastes and standards of the age, but they reveal almost nothing about the poet himself.

In contrast, another smaller, and never intended for publication, collection of Alex's poems—undated for the most part, but apparently written between 1846 and 1848—are painfully self-revealing. These poems, throbbing with emotion—sonnets, lyrics, passionate exhortations in verse—express the anguish of an ardent but unsuccessful suitor. His mood swings from hopeless adoration of "the sweet, fair-souled Annie Burrows" to self-pity:

> Passionate hath been my love, passionate,
> And painful ever; an unquiet life:
> No gilded Summer, but mere wintry strife;
> No joy-strewn dream, but very sad-cheered fate.

It swings from despondency that he should love one whose heart is "niggard" as "'tis wilful" to querulous reproach: "What knowst *thou*, of love, or loving life?" And from frustration that the best he owned was spent "upon a barren soil" to angry, although short-lived, the-hell-with-her resolutions. "Love's

Baring" ends: "*She* is not *worth* my love, nor loving pain!" And "Love Disdained" concludes:

> On such, my heart! love, waste no longer!
> All boldly, proudly, grasp at once thy fate;
>   Meet pride, with equal pride, and scorn her!
> When she, she too, may learn to love; and love too late!

But his mood soon swings back to poignant yearning.[12]

Because of its directness and simplicity, in one poem in this very private collection—a poem dated 20 June, 1848—Alex came closer to writing good poetry than in the laboriously crafted poems filled with warmed-over emotions that he hoped to have published. One might argue that it is not a poem at all. Ignoring end rhymes and metronomic line lengths, it is a spontaneous outpouring of the shock, the grief, the wounded pride, the bitter pain of a young man who has been adamantly refused:

> *June 20, 1848*
> All my Hopes are ended then; and my Dreams are
>   shattered. Alone, I stand; with naught to cheer;
>   or to which I might trust this aching Brain, and
>   wounded Heart.
> I am mazed, as I had been cast into a strange
>   World. And my eyes are dizzy, with gazing on
>   many faces, to me, purposeless, offenceful.
> I had looked for this lot. And now it is fulfilled,
>   it stuns me; and stupifies.
> Yet in my ear, those Parting Words ring clear—
>   the Parting Hope-knell. Now, with their
>   sense alone; full, decisive, in my mind
>   charged. Now, the very Word-Form shapes itself,
>   in order, before me.
> Ah! Cruel and Unkind! For *this*, I have strived!—
>   for *this*, have bared my soul before Thee:
>   proffered my whole wealth; and *this* attained, for a
>   return![13]

Mercifully, a few months later, Alex's suffering came to an end. Shortly after she and her mother had gone to Earls Colne to live, Anne changed her mind again and, hesitatingly, agreed to marry him.

In her letter to Whitman on 3 September, 1871, she explained her decision. Speaking of her second refusal of Alex, she wrote: "This too he bore without desisting & at the end of some months once more asked me with passionate *entreaties*. Then, dear friend, I prayed very earnestly, and it seemed to me (that) that I should continue to mar & thwart his life so was not right, if he was content to accept what I could give. I knew I could lead a good and wholesome life beside him—his aims were noble—his heart a deep, beautiful, true Poet's heart; but he had not the Poet's great brain. His path was a very arduous one, and I knew I could smooth it for him—cheer him along it. It seemed to me God's will that I should marry him. So I told him the whole truth, and he said he would rather have me on those terms than not have me at all."[14]

This was Anne's explanation, written in confidence, many years later. Critics have persistently questioned it. Alex's account of his long and discouraging courtship, recorded in his private poems, corroborates Anne's account of it to Whitman. However, until now these poems have not been available, and, ever since Anne's letter to the poet was made public in 1918, many Whitman scholars have been skeptical about her claim that she was not in love with Alex when she agreed to marry him. Thomas Harned, for example, in one of his few footnoted comments on Anne's letters, questions the accuracy of her memory twenty years after the event;[15] and Edwin Haviland Miller has suggested that Anne's passion for Whitman led her to "distort reality."[16] The basis for this skepticism has been a letter from Anne to Julia Newton in 1848, announcing her engagement, in which she wrote:

> Do you remember Mr. Gilchrist, and a long conversation we once had about him? Perhaps this question will make you guess the rest—guess that your friend is very happy, for she loves and is beloved by one who can fulfil her aspirations, realize her ideal of a true marriage, one who is her friend and helper, as well as her lover. . . . I know not how to describe him to you, dear Julia, except by telling you that he is altogether, both in intellect and heart, great, noble and beautiful.[17]

But isn't this flimsy evidence that twenty-year-old Anne, in spite of her denial years later, was in love with Alex when they became engaged? Isn't this precisely what a nineteenth-century bride-to-be, brought up in the romantic tradition, would be expected to say to a friend in announcing her engagement? On the other hand, since the announcement is made near the end of the letter—"when I am driven up to the last corner of note-paper, simply because I could not make up my mind to begin"—isn't it apparent that Anne is hardly bursting with eagerness to tell her friend the news? Reading the letter closely, isn't it significant that, although she describes Alex and the advantages that marriage to him will bring, Anne—who was never one to express herself dispassionately about anything—describes her feelings for him only with a perfunctory "she loves"? Isn't it possible that Anne was trying to convince herself, as well as Julia, that she was "very happy"?

Why did she agree to marry him? Paradoxically, agreeing to bind herself in marriage to a man whom she liked as a friend but to whom she was not even slightly romantically attracted may well have been Anne's first attempt to break out of stringent bonds in which, as a woman, both the customs of her age and her own circumstances held her a prisoner.

In London, Anne's life, especially after Johnny's death, had been restricted. In an Essex village, where her immediate family consisted of an invalid mother and her uncle Henry Carwardine, an elderly bachelor living at Colne Priory, her life was even more confining. She was cast in the role of "the daughter at home," a stock character in the nineteenth-century social structure, whose duties and responsibilities were clearly defined. In addition to household duties and care of her mother, as a member of Earls Colne's first family there would be social obligations as well, often as her mother's surrogate: calls to be made and received, tea parties to be given and attended, houseguests to be entertained in the long visits that were the custom of the time. To please her mother, and probably her uncle as well, church attendance would have been mandatory. "To confess the truth, I am in a state of mental starvation," Anne wrote to Julia from Colne on 24 September, 1848, "I am afraid all my cares have been devoted to the body, that is to say, to preparing our new home."[18]

Even after Anne and her mother were settled in the charming cottage with its low-walled flower garden that still stands not far from the entrance to the Priory, Anne's interests outside the domestic mise-en-scène had little priority. In the letter to Julia announcing her engagement, she wrote that she was still pursuing her old studies and general reading—in "the time that is at my own disposal." One guesses that this time was rare, limited, and seldom uninterrupted. Marriage, even if her mother lived with her or next door, as Anne told Julia she would insist, would bring a change of status. Without abandoning her responsibilities to her mother, it would free her from the bondage—and that is what she must often have secretly felt that it was—of being "the daughter at home."

At Colne, twenty-year-old Anne must have been suffering not only from mental starvation but from mental loneliness. She must have been especially starved for masculine intellectual companionship, for all her life Anne enjoyed and was stimulated by communication with the masculine mind. It began with her companionship with her father. It continued in the happy years when, in their evenings together, Johnny must have listened with interest to his sister's accounts of what she had been reading, discussing and debating salient points. In later years, Anne would meet, entertain, and correspond with a number of brilliant and talented women—Jane Carlyle, Christina Rossetti, Emma Lazarus, Jeanette Gilder, to name a few. But it was always a keen, cultivated, boldly creative masculine mind to which her own mind responded most eagerly and which most inspired her. At twenty, Comte, Rousseau, and Emerson already enthralled her. In the years to come, among the men with whom she would share warm and lasting friendships that broadened her horizons and were often enormously helpful in sharpening her own creative skills would be Carlyle, William and Dante Gabriel Rossetti, Tennyson, Samuel Palmer, Ford Madox Brown, John Burroughs, and Alexander Macmillan. And, of course, there would be the most stimulating, profoundly emotional, and intellectually influential friendship of all—her friendship with Walt Whitman. So much for the future. In the mid-nineteenth century, in a small English village, the opportunities for masculine intellectual companionship for a young, unmarried woman would have been very limited indeed. In Earls Colne in the 1840s, Anne must have felt that she was living in intellectual purdah.

Although her uncle Henry Holgate Carwardine, a stately gentleman in the manner that his sister Henrietta Burrows was a stately grande dame, was a friend of a friend of Coleridge, he was apparently not a man of letters himself. In her need for someone to share her interests, Anne turned to another uncle, Thomas Probert of Newport, Essex. He was the widowed husband of her mother's sister Anne and father of Johnny's "own dearest Annie Probert," to whom he wished ten pounds to be given to buy a mourning ring that she might "shed a passing tear for her cousin." In Thomas Probert, in spite of the difference in their ages and a distance between Newport and Earls Colne that made frequent visits impossible, Anne found a sympathetic and knowledgeable companion, and they carried on a spirited correspondence. In a letter of 13 February, 1849—written in part in the elegant hand of a professional amanuensis[19]—before launching into a long discussion of Francois Guizot, the French statesman, Probert paints a charming, perceptive, and wonderfully vivid picture of Anne Burrows a few days before her twenty-first birthday:

> Notwithstanding your very interesting letters my dear Annie, I am a wretched correspondent; you have not however been absent from my thoughts. In my many, many wakeful hours of night, I have mentally written you scores of Epistles etc.: but my fingers are as loth to shed ink, as if it were blood—and luckily for your patience my lucubrations had all vanished with the day light.
>
> I entirely disclaim having "flattered" you which would be an insult to those for whom we have a real regard. I should as soon think of flattering my own Annie. But if I have unconsciously encouraged you in forming a just appreciation of your powers and character, I have done you a service, in which I shall always reflect with much satisfaction.
>
> The fact is, that after some interval of absence I was struck with the singular force of your reasoning faculties, the quick apprehension with which you seemed to grasp the most difficult problems, and a rare avidity and aptitude for studies and pursuits of a highly intellectual nature—coupled with these, I saw, or fancied I saw, symptoms of a decided will—capital associates, if they take, as I confidently predict of yours, a right and safe direction. At present you are perhaps in a state of transition, not unnatural at your early age, to a thinking mind. You determine to use for yourself the faculties with which Providence has gifted you, and I may add for [which] it has made you responsible. You reserve your freedom till more mature consideration.
>
> I picture to my imagination, a young and high-spirited forest Filly, conscious of her strength, impatient of restraint—escaping from the herd—snapping at one plunge, the Drover's cord—and galloping away over the beautiful and heathery plains of Poetry and Literature, fragrant with a thousand sweets—scampering up the mountain, and ascending the heights of science. There she stands, a subject for Landseer—her head and mane erect, every nerve and muscle quivering with delight—gazing around

in ecstasy at the magnificent and boundless prospect—inhaling with delight the free and fresh breezes which blow from every quarter—but not yet stopping to discriminate whether they bring with them "airs from Heaven or blasts from Hell." Have I however any fear of the result? not an atom. I speak from personal experience of the operations of my own mind in early life—and of others in whom it has been ultimately the same. Looking through the vista of years, I exclaim with the Psalmist,

> "The Lord her pasture shall prepare
> And guide her with a Shepherd's care."

Thus ends the first chapter of my Homily—but you are in danger of more. I long to have a little dash at the French Philosophers—audacious, ridiculous presumption! you will say—and truly enough, were it not that I bear about me a Talisman and Shield, of power to "quench the fiery darts of the enemy."

Now for a word of M. Guizot . . . [20]

How understanding he was, this astute and kindly uncle, giving her confidence in both her mental abilities and her ultimate good judgment, sensing the restlessness and chafing against restraint in the "audacious little heretic." However, occasional letters from an elderly uncle, even so delightful an uncle, could not have dispelled Anne's sense of intellectual isolation at Colne. She must indeed have longed to snap "at one plunge, the Drover's cord" and scamper away across the "plains of Poetry and Literature," to ascend "the heights of science." And so when Alexander Gilchrist came wooing once again, begging her "with passionate *entreaties*," it is not surprising that she reconsidered his proposal. For even though he inspired only sisterly affection, his tastes were intellectual and he was deeply interested in the arts. And marrying Alex offered more than respite from intellectual nunhood.

As Anne told Julia in announcing her engagement—in explanation, no doubt, of her change of mind, since in the conversation they once had about "Mr. Gilchrist," she must have told Julia about his proposals and her firm refusals—marriage to Alex would give her the opportunity "to fulfil her aspirations" and "to realize her ideal of a true marriage." In marrying Alex, she would not escape from one bondage of the period only to serve a life sentence in another. She would not have to exchange being "the daughter at home" for the role of "the angel in the house,"[21] the Victorian ideal wife, a vapid creature, both an ornament and a convenience, existing primarily for the comfort and happiness of her husband—the wife that most eligible young men would expect her to be. In contrast, Alex knew that she had a good mind, and he respected it. He knew that her "aspirations" were intellectual, and he encouraged them. And he knew that her "ideal of a true marriage" was one in which a husband was a woman's "friend and helper, as well as her lover," and he concurred. Since he was content to accept what she had told him that she could give him emotionally, and since as compensation for "love as a wife should love" she could be of help to him in his career, it must have seemed to Anne—with or without divine response to praying "very earnestly"—that marrying Alex was the only way open to her to free herself honorably from at least some of the constraints that custom and circumstances imposed on her.

It was a long engagement. This in itself brought a certain freedom; it spared her the attentions of other suitors in whom she would have no interest at all. And Anne would have had other suitors. As a Carwardine, she would be a desirable wife for the ambitious. In addition, she was an attractive young girl. She was not a beauty according to the standards that were fashionable at the time—delicate, oval faced, demure. In a faded, very early photograph of Anne taken at the time of her marriage—that in its crudity contasts sharply with the lovely and often reproduced photograph of her taken much later—the simple dress she is wearing has a narrow white collar, and her dark hair, parted in the center, is looped back severely on either side of a round, young face. The eyes stare with unconcealed interest into the daguerreotypist's lens. In spite of the fact that her neck was probably held in a clamp to keep her head rigid during the several minutes that it took for the likeness to be captured, there is a hint of a smile at the corners of the mouth. It is a photograph not of a pretty girl, but of an obviously strong and healthy one. Years of vigorous exercise in the open air—romping, playing games, swimming, taking the long walks that she enjoyed so much—had left their mark. Whitman would have recognized her at once as belonging to his "race of hardy and well-defined women."

During the two-and-a-half years of the engagement, Alex finished his law studies, became a barrister and immediately abandoned the profession, and determinedly set out to establish himself in a literary career. Except for a few indigestible poems addressed to Anne, with titles like "Love's Realities" and "A Birthday Greeting," he seems to have quickly given up the idea of being a poet. In criticism, particularly criticism of the arts, he found a medium that suited his tastes, his talents, and the duality of his jurisprudent-creative nature. The going was not easy. At first there were even more than the usual number of disappointments and rejections for a neophyte writer. Alex had to radically alter his style, which at first, according to Anne, was "a thicket of adjectives in labyrinthine sentences." "He desired always to treat his subject exhaustively," she explains in her memoir. "No subtlest shade of meaning, no shifting hue of beauty should escape him or his reader if he could help it. Hence the difficulty of obtaining concentration; of making due sacrifice of detail to the force of the whole." Alex honed his style, and the young critic's work was accepted by the *Eclectic Review*, which in the next three or four years published everything he wrote: for the most part, criticisms of poets, reviews of books on art, notices of exhibitions of pictures. In preparation, he spent days in the National Gallery, Hampton Court, and the Dulwich Gallery. He also wrote articles on archeological topics and the restoration of

Anne Burrows, 1851. The Walt Whitman Collection, Department of Special Collections, Van Pelt Library, University of Pennsylvania.

Gothic architecture. Preparing for these, he visited not only Westminster Abbey and other great cathedrals, but old country churches, where, Anne recalls, every stone "was scanned till it yielded up its quota of the history, as well as of the meaning and beauty of the whole." His first recognition came when an article on William Etty, the painter, that had been published in the *Eclectic Review* was republished in pamphlet form by Curdall, and this resulted in a commission from David Bogue to write a book-length life of Etty. Marriage was no longer financially out of the question.

In the nineteenth century, being a sick-nurse was one of a lady's accomplishments.[22] It was also her duty to a member of her family. Late in December 1850, when the news reached Anne that her fiancé was seriously ill in London, she left immediately to take care of him. In a letter to Julia written on 15 January, 1851, after her return to Earls Colne, there is, for the first time in letters from Anne that have been preserved, a note of happy anticipation of her coming marriage:

> Dear Julia little dreamed what sorrow had befallen her friend when her affectionate Christmas greeting reached Colne. The same post brought tidings that Alex was taken suddenly and dangerously ill, and another hour saw me on the road to London. I found him past the worst. My Christmas was spent in nursing him.
> Dear Julia will understand me, I think, when I tell her it was the sweetest Christmas I have yet passed. I left him on the Saturday after, all fear of relapse being then over, and he rapidly regaining his strength, which the severity of the attack had entirely prostrated. And so I left him, with a heart full of gratitude to God, and renewed happiness. And though, of course, his visit to Colne was entirely relinquished, he would not exchange those few days for *months* of our usual happy, serene Colne meetings.[23]

In spite of Alex's illness, it must indeed have been a happy time for both patient and nurse and very different from the time that they usually spent together. In a five-week visit to Colne in the summer of 1849, their time had been spent, Alex wrote to his sister Milly Thomas, in pushing Mrs. Burrows about in her bath chair, walking, strolling, rowing on the river in a boat belonging to Mr. Carwardine, and dining out twice at the Priory.[24] A few days together without the ever-presence of Mrs. Burrows, Henry Carwardine, and the eyes of the entire village of Earls Colne, even though the days were spent in the sickroom, must have been a preview for both of the privilege of privacy, of the freedom from constant consideration of others, that marriage would bring.

In addition to an exhilarating glimpse of future freedom from constraints that stifled her, for Anne her days of nursing Alex must have had another association. Being back in London with a young man her own age—a young man to whose needs she could minister—with whom she could talk freely about the things that interested her, and who talked to her enthusiastically about his own interests, must have seemed like a return to the happy days when

Johnny was living. In her naîveté, she may well have supposed that marriage to Alex would be essentially a continuation of a delightfully compatible brother-and-sister relationship.

For in spite of her wide reading in science and philosophy; and although she knew, probably from reading novels (had she read *Jane Eyre*, the recent sensational novel by Currer Bell?), that there was a feminine emotion, "a true, tender, wifely love," that she did not feel for Alex; and although she must have had some idea of the basic facts of reproduction, Anne Burrows was as naïve about the powerful interplay of the physical and the emotional in the marriage relationship as any other carefully brought up and sheltered young girl of her generation. All her life she had been trained, both by specific direction and strong innuendo, to repress the instincts of her body, to deny her sexuality. The "pure innocence," a highly extolled feminine virtue that Anne, like her contemporaries, brought to marriage, was actually pure self-ignorance. Her sex education may not even have included a prenuptial "talk" with her mother.

Alex was hardly more informed. He too was a child of an era when female sexual feelings were thought to exist only in dark-skinned women with exotic backgrounds, in morally depraved women, or in those who were mentally deranged. William Acton, a respected medical doctor of the time, described the perfect ideal of an English wife as "kind, considerate, self-sacrificing, and sensible, so pure-hearted as to be utterly ignorant of and averse to any sensual indulgence, but so unselfishly attached to the man she loves, as to be willing to give up her own wishes and feelings for his sake."[25] As advice to young men, Dr. Acton wrote:

> Many of the best mothers, wives, and managers of households, know little of or are careless about sexual indulgences. Love of home, of children, and of domestic duties are the only passions they feel.
> As a general rule, a modest woman seldom desires any sexual gratification for herself. She submits to her husband's embraces, but principally to gratify him; and, were it not for the desire of maternity, would far rather be relieved from his attentions. No nervous or feeble young man need, therefore, be deterred from duties required of him. Let him be well assured, on my authority backed by the opinion of many, that the married woman has no wish to be placed on the footing of a mistress.[26]

These were the respected professional opinions to which Alex was exposed. He would have been shocked by the suggestion that there was sexuality as powerful and demanding as his own in the nature of "the sweet, fair-souled Annie Burrows."

Small wonder that after their marriage on Tuesday morning, 4 February, 1851, the months that followed were traumatic for Anne. "The first few months of my marriage were dark and gloomy to me within," she would later write to Whitman, "and sometimes I had misgivings whether I had judged aright."[27] And nearly twenty years after she walked through the covered gate of Colne church as a bride, she would publicly protest—if one reads between the lines of "A Woman's Estimate of Walt Whitman"—the warped "morality," the false modesty, the enforced ignorance that distorted a young woman's sexuality in the same way that steel-stayed corsets distorted her body; the myths, the lies, the quackery that, in macabre orchestration, had produced the concept of "pure innocence" as a desirable feminine possession, when it was, in fact, a hazardous and tragically destructive one.

5
GUILDFORD

A woman waits for me, she contains all, nothing is lacking,
Yet all were lacking if sex were lacking, or if the moisture of the
    right man were lacking.
                                        Walt Whitman

Judging by appearances, it was a perfect marriage. "The marriage was a happy one," Herbert wrote in his biographical sketch of his mother for *The Dictionary of National Biography,* "and she shared her husband's tastes, criticized his writings, and wrote to his dictation."[1] There is no question that Alexander and Anne Gilchrist were well suited to one another intellectually. "Most of all, delightful are our evenings—the reward and crown of the day, when he reads aloud earnest books to me," Anne wrote to Julia the December following her marriage, "and I 'read' music to him. He has selected for me all the music he thinks worth anything."[2] Among the "earnest" books the newlyweds read together were Carlyle's *Life of Sterling*, Elizabeth Browning's *Casa Guidi Windows*, Herbert Spencer's *Social Statics*, and Guyot's *Earth and Man*. What music Alex thought worth anything has not been recorded. "From varied pursuits, ranging over science and literature, the bride and bridegroom were not likely to experience ennui," Herbert comments in his biography of his mother.

The first months of their marriage were spent traveling widely in England from Cumberland to Dorset—by railway, steamer, coach, and sometimes even walking from town to town—with numerous detours to visit old churches and cathedrals. At least once, according to a letter written jointly by Alex and Anne from Keswick, Cumberland, to Milly Thomas, Alex's sister, they were not able to cash a check and had to apply to Milly's husband for an emergency loan.[3] In preparation for Alex's biography of Etty, a good deal of time was spent in Yorkshire, Etty's native county, which Anne recalls in her memoir of Alex as taking "us into some curious old-world nooks and corners, and among people with a fresh flavour of their native soil about them." It also enabled them to see some of Etty's pictures that were privately owned. Their method of gaining entrance was simply to arrive at one of the great houses and announce to whoever opened the door that Mr. and Mrs. Alexander

Gilchrist had come to see the pictures—and nine times out of ten they were invited in and shown around.[4]

"My dear husband most thoroughly enjoys the life we are now leading, and he says I am a very brave little traveller," Anne wrote to Julia from Keswick on 30 July, 1851.[5] However, although the brave little traveler undoubtedly enjoyed the adventure of exploring new places and the novelty of a constantly changing scene, secretly it was not a happy time for her. The sight and sound of the sea at Lyme Regis, the glories of Lincoln and York cathedrals, and walking among real mountains when the highest elevation she had previously seen was Highgate Hill, could not assuage the misery, for her, of the more intimate aspects of the honeymoon. These were the months that "were dark and gloomy to me within," the months when "sometimes I had misgivings whether I had judged aright."[6]

Ten years after her husband's death, Anne would confess—perhaps for the first time even to herself—the unhappiness that the for-men-only concept of sex that prevailed at the time had caused her, not only in the first months but for the duration of her marriage. In 1869, in lines by an American poet who called himself "the tenderest lover," she found assurance that here at last was understanding—and reassurance of what the instincts of her own body and her independent mind had told her.

> Without shame the man I like knows and avows the deliciousness
>   of his sex,
> Without shame the woman I like knows and avows hers.[7]

In her first letter to Whitman, Anne would give a veiled but remarkably lucid picture of what must have been the sexual experience of many, many wives of her generation: strange new emotions half-aroused by the clumsy, and probably apologetic, lovemaking of a young husband, as ignorant about feminine sexuality as she; bewilderment, frustration, self-doubt, and guilt; perhaps even fear in an age when sexuality in a woman was considered a symptom of mental disorder. On 3 September 1871, she would write to Walt in this poignantly confessional letter:

> He said to me many times, "Ah Annie, it is not you who are so loved that is rich; it is I who so love." And I knew this was true, felt as if my nature were poor & barren beside his. But it was not so, it was only slumbering—undeveloped. For, dear Friend, my soul was so passionately aspiring—it so thirsted & pined for light, it had not power to reach alone and he could not help me on my way. And a woman is so made that she cannot give the tender, passionate devotion of her whole nature save to the great conquering soul, stronger in its powers, though not in its aspirations, than her own, that can lead her forever & forever up and on.[8]

Alexander, it would seem, was not only an inhibited but a tepid lover.

Happily, there was to be salvation for Anne. Motherhood. "When I knew there was a dear baby coming my heart grew light," she continues in her letter to Whitman, "and when it was born, such a superb child—all gloom & fear forever vanished. I knew it was God's seal to the marriage, and my heart was full of gratitude and joy." Percy Carlyle Gilchrist was born on 27 December, 1851. He was born at Lyme Regis in a house where his parents had lodged for a time the previous summer. They had liked it so well that they had returned there to spend the last month of Anne's pregnancy and a few months after the baby's birth.[9]

On 28 December, Alexander, a proud new father, wrote to devoted Julia:

>   Marine Parade
>   Lyme-Regis, Dorset
>   Sunday—Dec. 28, 1851
> Dear Miss Newton,
>   You will hear with pleasure, yesterday, about 2 P.M. the long expected little guest arrived in these parts, in good condition, & nowise belated. The young mother is doing remarkably well, though it was a long & trying time. She was taken poorly Friday morning. The doctor did his duty by her; & all around were most kind. I have this moment left her, in repose, comfortably off to sleep. Baby (it is a boy) in like case. She had a good night—a series of little naps, & in every way is in a promising state. You shall hear again from me by the end of the week. The child is a sound & healthful one apparently; a very large one those familiar with babies exclaim.
>   Believe me
>   Yours Truly
>   Alex. Gilchrist
> Annie sends her love.[10]

Alex and Julia had reason for relief and rejoicing. In 1851 childbirth was hazardous; the rate of maternal mortality in England was greater than one in every two hundred births. Even doctor-attended births were not necessarily safer, since doctors knew little about the principles of contagion, the complications of childbirth, and the safe use of forceps.[11] On Monday, 5 January, Alex wrote to Julia again:

> My dear Miss Newton,
>   Dear Wife and Babe are both doing as well as one could wish. The former has felt her weakness, more, the latter half of the week, than the first, but sleeps more; and is free from every abnormal symptom. Our first born is strong & healthy, and decidedly pretty for his years,—I mean *days*! For the last three or four days he has drawn nearly all his nourishment from his mother; with the happiest effects on both sides.
>   Annie's nurse has been most kind: a great happiness this. We keep the dear one very quiet. She is free from all excitement. Tomorrow, she will be lifted onto the sofa awhile. This change will be quite an era in her still Life. Little Percy Carlyle (as we have already named him) is on the whole very quiet: protests vehemently against the operations of the toilette,and proclaims his hungry sensations on first waking,

which latter little noise is soon quieted. He has been otherwise disturbed only twice, during his short span of life.

Dear Annie sends love & all that is most friendly to you: & kind remembrances to your mother & sister: in which allow me to join. Your kind note gave us great pleasure.

Believe me,
Yours Truly
Alex. Gilchrist

Miss Julia Mary Newton[12]

Other "dear babies" followed Percy Carlyle: Beatrice Carwardine, Herbert Harlakenden, and Grace. Anne threw herself into motherhood with all the fervor and energy of her passionate nature. Jane Carlyle would one day observe that she believed "that Mrs. Gilchrist would skin, and bury herself alive for the benefit of her children." It is to Anne's credit as a mother that in an age when the rate of infant and child mortality was even higher than the rate of maternal mortality, when every churchyard and cemetery held many small graves, all four of her children lived to strong and healthy adulthood. She was tender, vigilant, devoted. And she nurtured her children not only physically, but spiritually and intellectually as well. She introduced them early to music and pictures and books. Above all, from the time they were very young, she encouraged their interests and talents in every way that she could.

When Percy was four months old, Alex and Anne left Lyme Regis, where Alex had spent the winter "battling manfully with the plethora of material,— letters, diaries, quality in inverse proportion to quantity—out of which the *Life* [of Etty] was to be constructed."[13] They traveled about for another year, and in 1853 settled in the picturesque town of Guildford in Surrey, a town surrounded by hills of exceptional beauty. Here they found a manorlike old house that Anne describes in her memoir of Alex:

> Our roomy old, gabled, weather-tiled house, standing a little back from the high road, was a home after his [Alex's] own heart. It seemed to have a particularly comfortable, sleepy way of basking in the sun, as a thing it had been used to do on summer afternoons for two or three centuries; but in rough weather it was like a ship at sea, so did the winds, from whatever quarter, buffet it, and surge along the hollows of its many-gabled roof. In the hall, which was the largest room, stood a long oak table, lustrous with age and the polishing of many hands, which must have been made in the house to remain there till both should crumble, for at no door nor window could it have been got in or out; and with it were the high oaken stools on which less luxurious generations had sat at meat. There was a great open fireplace with niched seats in the chimney corner where to rest with a friend over the glowing, fragrant logs when stiff and chill, but in happiest mood, after a twenty-mile walk, was an enjoyment that made a man "o'er all the ills of life victorious."[14]

The young couple had little money. "It was just possible with the most strenuous frugality and industry to pay our way," Anne wrote to Walt in her autobiographical first letter. "I learned to cook & to turn my hand to all household occupation—found it bracing, healthful, cheerful."[15] At Guildford, Anne found another salvation. Hard work.

And living in an old house in the mid-nineteenth century, without means to hire competent servants, was hard work: the endless carrying of wood and water, cooking in a kitchen that must have been primitive even by the standards of the time, herculean tasks of scouring and scrubbing. However, even though all her life she resented and protested the second-class educational and professional opportunities that were available to women, Anne never resented the designation of supposedly menial domestic chores as "woman's work." Iconoclastically, for one of her background and bringing up, she did not believe that doing housework was either beneath a lady's dignity or demeaning to a woman's status. Instead, she believed that, even for a woman of intellect, doing housework, and doing it well, was essential to both her physical and mental well-being. And, as she astutely pointed out in a letter to Whitman on 14 May, 1874, in addition to the healthful aspects of housework and its benefits as a release from the tensions of mental exertion, if women want "to give practical shape to their ardent belief in equality & fair play for all," they must be able to do their share of the bodily work that daily life requires:

> If they would but understand this in schools & colleges for girls & young women. No healthier or more cheerful occupation as a relief from study, could be found than household work—sweeping, scrubbing, washing, ironing, cooking—in the variety of it, & equable development of the muscles, I should think equal to the most elaborate gymnastics. I know very well how I have felt & still feel, the want of having been put to these things when a girl. Then the importance afterwards of doing them easily & well & without undue fatigue, to all who aim to give practical shape to their ardent belief in equality & fair play for all. In domestic life under one roof, at all events, it is already feasible to make the disposals without ignominious distinctions—not all the rough bodily work, never ending, leisure all to the other; but a wholesome interchange and sharing of these. Not least too among the advantages of taking an active share in these duties is the zest, the keen relish, it gives to the hours not too easily secured for reading & music. Besides, I often think that just as the Poem Nature is made up half of rude, rough realities and homely materials & processes, so it is necessary for women to construct their Poem, Home, on a groundwork of homeliest details & occupations, providing for the bodily wants & comforts of their household, and that without putting their own hands to this, their Poem will lack the vital, fresh growing, nature-like quality that alone endures, and that of this soil will grow, with fitting preparation & culture, noble & more vigorous intellectual life in women, fit to embody itself in wider spheres afterwards—if the call comes.[16]

Thus, in 1874, Anne described to Walt the lessons that she learned as a twenty-five-year-old wife and the strong convictions they led to in her maturity.

Beatrice Carwardine, Anne's second child, was born in the old house on Woodbridge Road in Guildford on 18 September 1854. One doubts that this time Anne stayed in bed for ten days after the delivery, "free from all excitement," and then was "lifted onto the sofa awhile."

Although they had to pinch pennies, the Gilchrists were a hospitable couple who delighted in guests, and they had frequent visitors at Guildford. Among them was William Haines, whom Anne described as "my Husband's old and dear friend, almost brother."[17] Another was Walter White, a writer of popular magazine articles on "holiday walks," who came to Guildford often and shared long walks with Alex in the surrounding countryside. "We have kept the two last Saturdays open on purpose for you," Alex chided White in a letter from Guildford on 2 March, 1853. "Last Sunday you could have had a share in a huge leg of mutton such as I can't promise you for next. But next Saturday (to the Monday morning) *make* it."[18] On 18 September, 1854, Alex wrote to him to tell him two pieces of good news. The first was that "I have at last to tell you of the birth of a little girl in our old house, this morning: and that Annie is going on well, also the Child."[19] The second was that David Bogue had promptly accepted *The Life of William Etty* R.A. on Alex's terms of £120.

The Life of Etty was published, in two volumes, early in 1855. It received no critical acclaim whatsoever. "The press was either silent or adverse," Anne writes in her memoir. "The York papers, specially interested in the matter, not for artistic but for local reasons,—Etty having been born in York and ended his days there as a wealthy citizen,—were aggrieved at the author's disparaging comparison of the past grandeurs of their city with its present condition; and, in one journal, an indignant peroration wound up with the scathing inquiry, 'Does he ignore our manufacture of combs?' "[20]

Although Alex's *Life of Etty* was republished in England in 1978 as a standard reference in the history of art,[21] in 1855 it was a disheartening failure. However, in spite of its discouraging initial reception, *The Life of Etty* proved to be of enormous importance in the lives of both Alex and Anne. For Alex, it led to acquaintance with his idol, Thomas Carlyle, an acquaintance that developed into a close friendship between the two men, one in his sixties, the other twenty-seven. For Anne, it prepared her for the physical explicitness of Whitman's poetry, for Walt's celebration of the human body.

Anne had an independent mind, and in many ways she was a rebel, but there was a duality in her nature: she was always very much a child of her time. Although she was a free spirit, she outgrew only gradually some of the attitudes and thinking that had been instilled in her by training and association. Some she never outgrew—part of her was always a Victorian. One cannot help wondering if Anne Gilchrist would have responded so spontaneously and enthusiastically to Walt's ecstatic gloria to every part of the human body and its functions—which outraged the vast majority of her contemporaries on both sides of the Atlantic—if she had not been conditioned by her husband's book to believe that in art the human body, unconcealed by the hypocrisy of draperies, can be pure and beautiful.

A major portion of the work of William Etty (1787–1849), consists of sketches and paintings of magnificent female nudes, usually with classical titles—for example, *Venus and Cupid* and *Venus and her Satellites*. The figures are totally undraped, full, voluptuous; the skin tones in the paintings exquisitely luminous. Like Whitman, Etty was violently attacked by prudish critics:

> Those who knew Etty "only in his Works" often found conclusions of the man sufficiently wide of the mark; accused him, as he says, of being a shocking "and unmoral man": reasoning from the effect faithful renderings of nude form had on eyes unfamiliar to it, on their own unprepared, and so far, uneducated minds,— uneducated to discern the truer aspect and poetic meanings. Even those who had heard of the Painter as, "after all, a decent kind of man," made their own inferences, (reasoning still on the same false data), as to his mind: that it was "a gross one".—&c
> . . .
> Admiration of Woman's form amounted in Etty to devotion. Belief in the purity of the nude when rendered in purity of heart, as in his own case,—with single minded though impassioned worship of its beauties; was a religion with him; a religion innocent and true . . .
> "People may think me lascivious," Etty would protest: "but I have never painted with a lascivious motive, if I had, I might have made great wealth."[22]

And like Whitman, Etty was subjected to "urgent and unremitting remonstrances of friends":

> Clerical acquaintances "take him to task"; express their "disapprobation." Fair monitors tell him:—"You paint ladies *without* dresses, because you don't know *how* to dress them"; &c. The Painter took it all good humouredly enough; smiled and kept on his way. "Very peculiar and obstinate in some of his opinions," they are fain to pronounce him: "not caring what others said on a matter as to which he had once made up his mind,"—and as to which he felt himself in the right. The critics made still less impression on him, with their animadversions to his "recklessness and bad taste," the "grossness of his imagination," &c. For he in time came to be "one of the best abused men in his profession." And to the gross-minded, *he* seemed gross.[23]

"Camerado!" must have been Whitman's comment when he read *The Life of Etty*. He too was "one of the best abused men in his profession."

Posthumously, William Etty had a valiant and skillful champion in Alexander Gilchrist. Alex's defense of Etty's "nymphs with unbound zones" is brilliant. And in its logical presentation of argument, and in its tone, it is startlingly like his wife's impassioned defense of Whitman written fifteen years later. Anne's "A Woman's Estimate of Walt Whitman" unquestionably had its genesis stylistically in her young husband's first, bleakly unsuccessful, book.

In his defense of Etty, Alex, very much the barrister-at-law, strikes down the statement made in a lecture by the painter Leslie, "accomplished Master in a refined and subtle province of his own," that Etty's work sold only because of "the voluptuous treatment of his subjects." If this was so, Alex asks, why was it that his work sold only in the last six or eight years of his career? If

Etty had been less sparing of draperies, he could have sold more readily, the barrister adds, since many of his wealthy friends had "the fear of the respectable" before their eyes. Donning an invisible wig and gown, he warms to the defense:

> The nude forms of Etty are not nearly so alluring as, (to minds untinctured by Art), many a clever female "head," in meretricious style; such as fill the Dealers' and Printsellers' windows. . . . Sir Peter Lely never painted a "Beauty," which is not an intrinsically immodest picture. It is an immodest *soul*,—miserable sight,—which looks forth through the would-be languishing eyes. Yet no English lady refuses Lely admittance into her drawing-room. . . . Happy, who as a youth has learned from them [art like Titian's, Etty's, the Sculpture of Antiquity] that the human form is capable of inspiring other than prurient thoughts. . . . Persons unfamiliar with Art, have been known to be "shocked" by the Antique. The Americans, in their "Great Exhibition," added temporary draperies, where the Sculptor's supply had been insufficient. The authorities at Sydenham have also been compelled, by the sensitive delicacy of the Clergy, to manufacture a large supply of the "usual leaf," for the Antique. Such persons pique themselves on their purity of mind. . . . Not only the creations of a Titian or an Etty, but all poetic realities, lose by exposure to the eyes of some. But are *they* to be consulted? Are we to renounce Art and its ennobling influences, because the thoughts of the multitude are evil? Are we to be guided in this matter by the sentiments of "reformed" satyrs,—or *un*reformed? of respectable fathers of families who have done "sowing their wild oats"? . . . Every study of *his* [Etty's] bears the impress of belief. Believing in the high import of what he painted, his Works teach us something; teach us the beauty and significance of the feminine form.[24]

In biography Alex had indeed found his metier. His *Etty*, with its gracious preface and acknowledgments, is a masterful piece of research and presentation. Although "poetic" language is as abundant in his prose as "nymphs with unbound zones" in his subject's pictures, his style is fluid and his touch sure. He has come a long, long way from the adventures of sweet Rhoda.

Working with Alex on *Etty*—sharing the research, writing at least some of it to his dictation, criticizing, proofreading—was an apprenticeship for Anne for her own future writing. And the book itself undoubtedly freed her from some of the inhibitions that "stiff-necked Propriety" had instilled in her from childhood. But Alex's *Etty* prepared her for Walt's joyous paean to the human body only to a point. For in *Etty* Alex equates sexuality with prurience; to Alex the nude female body is defensibly beautiful and "pure" only if it arouses no sexual feelings in the viewer. In *Leaves of Grass*, Walt's view is the exact opposite. To Walt, "bathing myself, bathing my songs in Sex," "womanhood and all that is woman" is beautiful and pure precisely because it does arouse sexual feelings:

> This is the female form,
> A divine nimbus exhales from it from head to foot,

> It attracts with fierce undeniable attraction,
> I am drawn by its breath as if I were no more than a helpless
>   vapor, all falls aside but myself and it,
> Books, art, religion, time, the visible and solid earth, and what was
>   expected of heaven or fear'd of hell, are now consumed,
> Mad filaments, ungovernable shoots play out of it, the response
>   likewise ungovernable,
> Hair, bosom, hips, bend of legs, negligent falling hands all diffused,
>   mine too diffused.[25]

Anne's response to lines like these, when she read them eight years after Alex's death, was instant, honest, direct, intensely personal, "likewise ungovernable." It was instant recognition as well as instant response. And it owed nothing to Alex's chastely academic, although eloquent, case for Etty's unbound nymphs.

Shortly after its publication, Alex sent a copy of *Etty* to his idol, Thomas Carlyle. Carlyle responded with a gracious note, which was opened, Anne recalls in her memoir, "with eager haste and read with a glow of pleasure." A few months later, Carlyle wrote to Alex: "If you will call here any afternoon about half-past three, you will commonly find me disengaged, and ready for a little speech with a friend."[26] In November 1855, Alex called for the first time at 5 Cheyne Row in Chelsea, a modest house near the river and far from the fashionable section of London. He brought Carlyle a collection of prints that he had found of costumes and portraits pertaining to Frederick the Great, whose history Carlyle was writing. The Sage of Chelsea was overjoyed, "like a wild man" as he looked them over that night, Alex was told.

On a second visit, a few days later, Alex was received by the famous lady of the house—lively, outspoken, freespirited, charming, gossipy, brilliant Jane Welsh Carlyle. Throughout their acquaintance, Jane fascinated, sometimes irritated, and often shocked conservative Alex. She received him that evening in the pink-and-white-papered drawing room on the second floor, where she had received Dickens, Tennyson, Browning, Thackeray, Darwin, Mazzini, and Ruskin. It was the room, once his literary workshop, where Carlyle wrote *The French Revolution*—and to which a distraught John Stuart Mill had rushed to confess the accidental burning of the manuscript of volume one that Carlyle had lent him to read.[27]

In a letter from Guildford to his friend William Haines on 29 November, 1855, Alex describes this second visit to 5 Cheyne Row:

> At half-past seven on Friday evening last, an omnibus set me down in Great Cheyne Row. Shown up into the large, comfortable drawing-room, I found Mrs. Carlyle alone (Carlyle downstairs fetching a short allowance of sleep over night), and was more favourably impressed by her than I had expected. After exchanging a few words, as she was making the tea, Carlyle appeared in his long brown indoors coat, and shook me cordially by the hand; was from that moment to the last *very* kind. . . . Mrs. Carlyle was engaged out to a party. "You must not suppose," she had before

said, "the wife of a philosopher sits at home over the fire in white satin shoes." . . .

After tea, Mrs. Carlyle left. And for the rest of the evening (till twelve) I sat with him alone, he pouring himself out as is his wont; sitting the latter part of the time on a footstool by the fire, smoking, and looking in his old long brown kind of greatcoat, as he was bewailing the pass men and things had come to, and as he thought of it hardly caring to live,—looking like a veritable Prophet, mourning in sackcloth and ashes the sins of the world.[28]

Alex continued to unearth material for *Frederick*, and Carlyle sent him long letters of appreciation. "Beyond doubt you are one of the successfulest hunters up of Old Books now living," Carlyle wrote on 3 February, 1856. And on 16 May, 1856 he wrote, "You surpass all people, of my experience, in the chase of Books!"[29]

Meanwhile Alex had begun a new project of his own. After the publication of *Etty*, he had completed a second commission from Bogue, to write short notices of the artists to be included in a new edition of *Men of the Time*.[30] Then he began a life of the earl of Dundonnald, hoping that it would have more popular appeal than *Etty*. However, Anne tells us, "the enterprise was uncongenial, and relinquished without regret when it came to light that the Earl was preparing an autobiography." Then, in a visit to London, he came upon some of Blake's designs and his *Illustrations of the Book of Job*. Before this, Allan Cunningham's sketch in *Lives of the Painters* and Blake's well-known illustrations for Blair's *Grave* had been Alex's only acquaintance with the artist. He was filled with enthusiasm. He quickly made up his mind to compile as complete a record of the life and work of the artist as possible.

This new project, with all the research that it would require, made living in London both desirable and practical. During a visit to 5 Cheyne Row, Carlyle suggested to Alex that the Gilchrists take the house next door. Soon afterwards Carlyle wrote: "I dare not advise anybody into a house (almost as dangerous as advising him to a wife, except that divorce is easier); but if Heaven should please to rain you accidentally into that house, I should esteem it a kindness."[31]

"And heaven did rain us down there, much to our satisfaction, in the autumn of 1856," Anne writes in the "Memoir." After nearly four years of secluded life in Surrey, the Gilchrists and their two children—Percy, now nearly five, and Beatrice, two—left the rambling old house at Guildford for No. 6 Cheyne Row in London. And a new life with new experiences, new associations, and new achievements opened for Anne as well as for Alex.

6
6 CHEYNE ROW

On eager feet, his heritage to seize,
A traveller speeds towards the promised land;
Afar gloom purple slopes on either hand:
Glad earth is fragrant with the flowering lees;
The green corn stirs in noon's hot slumberous breeze,
And whispering woodlands nigh make answer grand.
That pilgrim's heart, as by a magic wand,
Is swayed: nor, as he gains each height, and sees
A gleaming landscape still and still afar,
Doth Hope abate, nor less a glowing breath
Wake subtle tones from viewless strings within.
But lo! upon his path new aspects win:
Dun sky above, brown wastes around him are;
From yon horizon dim stalks spectral Death!

                                                      Alexander Gilchrist

When Alexander Gilchrist wrote this poem in Guildford in June 1856, a few months before he and Anne moved to London, he must indeed have felt that he was a traveler who "speeds towards the promised land." After surmounting great difficulties, life was opening up to him at last, rich and beautiful on every side. And then, in a long, solitary walk on Hind Head, Anne tells us in her memoir, "a solemn prophetic flash" came to him, and he wrote this sonnet describing the incident. Suddenly the "gleaming landscape" is replaced by "brown wastes," and "from yon horizon dim stalks spectral Death!" Did Alex have a premonition of his own early death? It would seem so. However, the five years following the move to No. 6 Cheyne Row, next door to the Carlyles, were extraordinarily happy and rewarding years for the rising young critic and biographer.

   Some of the most prominent figures in English arts and letters have lived in the neighborhood of Cheyne Row in Chelsea. The roster of illustrious names, in addition to Carlyle, includes Addison, Steele, Swift, Smollett, Leigh Hunt, Henry James, Oscar Wilde, Swinburne, Turner, Whistler, Dante Gabriel Rossetti, and Sargent. In 1834, when he was looking for a house in London, one of the attractions of the neighborhood for Carlyle was that "Chelsea abounds more than any other place in omnibi, and they take you to Coventry Street for sixpence."[1]

No. 5 and No. 6, like the other red brick houses on Cheyne Row,[2] stand shoulder to shoulder, with no space between their adjoining walls. The front entrances, bypassing with two or three stone steps the black-iron railings that guard the windows of the lower-level kitchens, open directly onto the street. The Carlyle house, now No. 24, belongs to the National Trust and has been preserved almost exactly as it was when the Carlyles lived there. The Gilchrist house, now No. 26, is privately owned. Although its handsome white door, with a brass plate and a brass knocker, is clearly a more recent addition, in 1856, when the Gilchrists were tenants, its interior must have been not unlike the interior of its side-by-side neighbor.

On the ground floor of the Carlyle house, which must have been almost as familiar to Alex and Anne as their own, there is the large sitting room pictured in *A Chelsea Interior*, painted by Robert Tait in 1857.[3] In Tait's picture, Jane is seated to the right of the fireplace; Carlyle, in his long brown housecoat, is standing to the left; and Nero, Jane's beloved old black-and-white dog,[4] is lying on the sofa. The picture now hangs in this room above the piano that Chopin played for Jane. It was in this room that Jane jumped up from her chair to welcome Leigh Hunt, who was paying his first visit after a long bout of influenza. Shortly afterward, a little poem titled "Rondeau" was delivered to No. 5.

> Jenny kiss'd me when we met,
>   Jumping from the chair she sat in;
> Time, you thief, who love to get
>   Sweets into your list, put that in!
> Say I'm weary, say I'm sad,
>   Say that health and wealth have miss'd me,
> Say I'm growing old, but add,
>   Jenny kiss'd me.

The dining room is behind the sitting room, and behind that a china room, ample enough to hold Jane's collection of blue-and-white china that was the fashion at the time. The drawing room and Jane's bedroom are on the second floor; Carlyle's bedroom is on the third. The cavernous kitchen is far below in the "sunk-storey." And far above is the most remarkable room in the house—Carlyle's famous attic study. It was built on the roof in 1853 and intended to be soundproof in order to shut out the distracting noises of a young lady practicing on a piano next door, a parrot, and the crowing of a neighbor's "demon fowls."

Behind the Carlyle house there is a long, narrow garden, where, in hot weather, the Sage of Chelsea sometimes wrote at a little table under a sort of awning that Jane made for him with a tablecloth and clothes poles. Carlyle did his own gardening and transformed a once-neglected area into a pleasant retreat filled with lilac bushes, wallflowers, and mint.[5] Behind the house next door there is a parallel long, narrow garden. While Carlyle mowed his grass and rolled his walks, on the other side of a high hedge of shrubbery, for five summers, the Gilchrist children played and Anne undoubtedly tended flower beds of her own.

When the Carlyles took possesion of No. 5 in 1834, water was supplied by a pump from a well under the stone-flagged floor of the kitchen. When the Gilchrists leased No. 6 in 1856, city water had been "laid on" four years before, although their pump and well, like the Carlyles', probably continued to be used for years.[6] City water, when they chose to use it, must have seemed like the height of luxury to Alex and Anne after years in the centuries-old house in Guildford. One of Anne's talents was her ability to make every house that she lived in warm and inviting.[7] With her flair for display and arrangement, the beautifully carved furniture that she and Alex acquired piece by piece, their large collection of fine prints that reflected Alex's knowledge as a critic of art, their many books, Anne's piano, her own collection of blue-and-white china, and the flowering houseplants that she loved must have made No. 6 an attractive setting for a young family and a charming place to welcome guests.

All her life, Anne enjoyed entertaining guests in her own home. She much preferred it to attending "afternoons" or "evenings," those forerunners of the modern cocktail party, where a large crowd gathered and true conversation was lost in the general gabble. In the Chelsea years, although there was never a stream of celebrities in and out of their house, as there was in and out of the house next door, Alex and Anne entertained a number of eminent guests. Anne's first meeting with William Rossetti took place when Rossetti, still a bachelor at the time, spent a long evening with the Gilchrists at No. 6. Later he wrote in his *Reminiscences*: "I liked both him and his wife sincerely from the first. They had many attractive things to show, whether connected with Blake or not, and obviously lived a life of warm affections and solid mental interests, not sodden down into the mere commonplaces of society. They both aspired to do a stroke of good work in their sphere and generation without timorous uneasiness as to how other people might take it."[8] As Alex expanded his acquaintance among London's literati, and as his work on the *Life of Blake* progressed, other distinguished visitors came. Among them were Ford Madox Brown and his gentle wife, Emma, Anne's loyal friends after Alex's death. Alexander Macmillan, the publisher, came to discuss the *Life of Blake*.[9] And the painter Samuel Palmer, a friend and disciple of Blake, with whom Alex carried on a long and increasingly warm and friendly correspondence, was an overnight guest.[10]

But in the Chelsea years, Anne could not have had much time for social life of any kind. Her third child, Herbert Harlakenden, was born on 18 March, 1857, and Grace, her youngest, on 16 January, 1859. After Grace's birth, for a time Anne was seriously ill. Jane Carlyle, deeply concerned, sent "Little Charlotte," her maidservant, next door with a note to Alex:

> Dear Mr. Gilchrist: Your note has shocked and grieved us both extremely. We hadn't a notion of this! Every time I have sent to ask for your wife, the answer has been that she was "doing nicely" or that she was "better" or had had "a better night," except *once*, when Charlotte brought back word of her "having been very poorly the day before, but that she had had a better night."
>
> I trust in God you will soon be out of anxiety about her; nature doing for her restoration what the Drs. don't know to do! Meanwhile, depend on my taking all possible pains to keep things quiet. I have *tied up* our knocker, and the dog shall be *carried* out and in—Indeed it is only his master that has no authority over him to stop his barking. I had been fearing that he might annoy your wife; without knowing how ill she was, and have several times run down to pick him up—after the mischief was done—But he shall be carried quite out of the street.
>
> If I can be of the least use to you in any way—Taking charge of the children—when the servants are busy—going to shops—or anything—I should really take it kind of you to tell me. I have, you know, a great debt of gratitude to your poor wife for very much kindness and help to myself in sickness.
>
> >   Yours very sincerely
> >   Jane W. Carlyle[11]

In the years that the Gilchrists lived at No. 6, as the friendship between Carlyle and Alex grew stronger and stronger in the midnight walks and the long hours of discussion in the attic study that they shared, a similar friendship, warm and mutually rewarding, developed between their wives. It is not surprising that these two women—whose letters were among the most brilliant and famous written by women in the nineteenth century—were drawn to each other from the start. When they met in 1856, Jane was fifty-five and in poor health, and Anne was a radiantly healthy twenty-eight. Jane was an ultra-sophisticated woman of the world; Anne was a naïve young wife and mother. Yet each immediately recognized the exceptional intelligence of the other, and their friendship became a source of comfort and pleasure for both. For Jane it was a joy to have "another intelligent reader otherside the wall."[12] For Anne, in the future, their friendship would prove to be a source of valuable instruction.

Jane and Anne had more in common than they may have known. Jane too, after her marriage, must have had "misgivings whether I had judged aright." The Carlyles' marriage was far from idyllic. When they died, both left records of years of tension, frustration, and misery. Carlyle was a difficult husband. He had a violent temper, especially when he was writing. And, like Ruskin, he was impotent. Nevertheless, Jane loved "Tammas" and, unlike Ruskin's wife, stayed with him. She devoted herself to his comfort, protected him from distractions and interruptions, humored his whims, and even tolerated his infatuation with Lady Ashburton, which, as has been suggested, was as close as he could have come to having an affair.[13] It is not surprising that in 1859, when Jane heard of the engagement of a young friend, she wrote—in her marvelously pungent prose, which some have said may outlast her husband's—a stringently qualified letter of congratulation:

And you are actually going to get married! you! already! And you expect me to congratulate you! or "perhaps not." I admire the judiciousness of that "perhaps not." Frankly, my dear, I wish you all the happiness in the new life that is opening to you; and you are marrying under good auspices, since your father approves of the marriage. But congratulations on such occasions seems to me a tempting of Providence. The triumphal-procession-air which, in our manners and customs, is given to marriage at the outset—that singing of *Te Deum* before the battle has begun—has, ever since I could reflect, struck me as somewhat senseless and somewhat impious. If ever one is to pray—if ever one is to feel grave and anxious—if ever one is to shrink from vain show and vain babble—surely it is just on the occasion of two human beings binding themselves to one another, for better and for worse, till death part them; just on that occasion which it is customary to celebrate only with rejoicings, and congratulations, and *trousseaux*, and white ribbon! Good God!14

In the years when they lived side by side, notes flew back and forth between Jane and Anne, even though only a wall separated them. "My Dear! Behold a cap! Fresh from India—a delicate attention to Mr. Carlyle on the part of a Lady!" Jane wrote in a note delivered by Charlotte. "But the cap fits Mr. C's large head like an inverted tumbler! so I laid it aside to give you when you came as a delicate attention to Percy on the part of *me*!" Carlyle liked Anne's homemade bread, and Anne attempted to teach Jane to make it. At least some of the lessons were given in the Carlyle kitchen, with its stone sink, cast-iron range with a clockwork cooking "jack" suspended over it, and "hastener," a domed portable oven. "Can you conveniently come in and *stand over me* while I make the bread myself today?" Jane pleaded in another note. "If to-day; tell me what hour—and tell me where Emma gets the yeast."15

Even though Jane complained that Anne did not come to see her as often as she would have liked, Anne frequently called on Jane—to chat, to help when Jane was sick, to comfort her when Nero, old and ailing, had to be put out of his misery by a doctor. Alex recorded his own and Anne's visits to the Carlyles with Traubelesque fidelity. His notebooks reveal that he had mixed emotions about his wife's most intimate London friend. His Victorian sense of decorum patently shaken, he reports that Mrs. Carlyle would greet Monckton Milnes and John Forster with a kiss, but, he adds, "given in so natural and unaffected a manner as to cause no surprise." Had he read "Jenny kiss'd me," one wonders? On another occasion he indignantly records that "Mrs. Carlyle asked Annie various questions as to how she first met *me*, etc., etc., to all of which Annie naively replied in full. *Mem*:—This is how Mrs. Carlyle gets possessed of the private biographies of half London."16 Alex may have resented her nosiness, but he enjoyed the tidbits of gossip that sharp-tongued Jane never hesitated to pass along. He regretted that the entrance of Carlyle cut off an anecdote about Skittles, "a very pretty and very wicked lady who rides about the Park—"17 And he must have been amused by Jane's caustic description of George Eliot, whom she met at a party: "I went to see Fechter the other night and found myself between Lewes and Miss

Evans!—by Destiny and *not* by my own Deserving. At least Destiny in the shape of Frederick Chapman who arranged the thing. Poor soul! there never was a more absurd miscalculation than *her* constituting herself an improper *woman*. She looks Propriety personified! Oh so *slow*!"[18]

Carlyle believed that the "true destiny of a woman . . . is to wed a man she can love and esteem, and to lead noiselessly under his protection, with all the wisdom, grace, and heroism that is in her, the life prescribed in consequence."[19] Lonely, childless Jane gladly performed her duties as a wife with all the wisdom, grace, and heroism that was in her. But it is not surprising that she refused to accept sitting "at home over the fire in white satin shoes" while her husband was closeted in the attic study, as the life prescribed for her in consequence of falling love with and marrying a philosopher. She frequently went alone to parties, where she was a vivacious and popular guest.

The social carousel that was Jane's delight, when her health permitted, would never be Anne Gilchrist's greatest interest. But in their years of close association, Anne learned an important lesson from Jane. A lesson in feminine independence. In contradiction to the social edicts of the time, Anne learned that even without a husband at her side a woman of intelligence could function on her own; that she could make a place for herself in a social environment that she enjoyed—a place in which she was both welcome and respected.

To escape the tensions and disappointments of her marriage, Jane turned to gossip, society, and writing letters to her family and friends. Anne found salvation from the frustrations and emotional barrenness of her marriage in motherhood and hard work. And she also had a third refuge. In spite of the arrival of four "dear babies" in eight years, increasing domestic and social duties, and assisting Alex in his work as critic and amanuensis, Anne managed to continue her independent studies. And in the Chelsea years she began to write for publication herself.

From the time she was a schoolgirl, Anne's deepest interest was in science. In this she was quintessentially a child of her time. The Victorians, on both sides of the Atlantic, were enthralled with science and its wonders that were exploding around them. In his ebullient interest in science, Whitman too was most typically a Victorian. In addition to being a celebration of the human body, *Leaves of Grass* is a celebration of every phase and branch of science as it was known in the mid-nineteenth century. His "barbaric yawp over the roofs of the world" sings the praises of medicine, engineering, chemistry, physics, botany, astronomy, phrenology, anthropology, and the marvels that these had produced and were producing in transportation, communications, construction, machinery, exploration, knowledge of the earth and the universe, and the care and healing of the human body. This awareness of the myriad aspects and potentialities of science, and the poet's enthusiastic appreciation of them, was one reason why Anne Gilchrist—whom Walt would one day describe affectionately as "my science-friend"—would respond so instantly and intensely to *Leaves of Grass*.

As a Victorian, it is not surprising that Anne's first published work was a series of articles on scientific subjects. However, as a Victorian woman, it is astonishing. Most Victorian women who cleared the hurdles to publication wrote novels, children's stories, memoirs, poetry, or domestic treatises. And few Victorian women had anything more than the most superficial knowledge of science. Science was considered a man's province. Women might wave their handkerchiefs in applause or clasp their hands in astonishment at the achievements of science, but it was generally believed that women did not have the intellectual capacity to understand its complexities—and certainly not to write acceptably scholarly articles on scientific topics. Anne Gilchrist quietly set out to prove this judgment wrong. Some of the material that she used has been outdated, but in the mid-nineteenth century Anne's knowledge of those fields of science in which she was interested was amazingly wide and comprehensive—knowledge that, after her marriage, must have been acquired late at night or in precious moments between household and maternal chores. Her exhaustively researched essays, which, for the most part, are intended for a popular rather than an academic audience, are written in a smooth, crisp style that is graceful without being unprofessional. She has the journalistic knack of using the colorful, the unusual, or even the bizarre to hold a layman's interest in what might otherwise be very dull material. In 1906, in his *Reminiscences*, William Rossetti would describe her as "a highly competent writer," and that she was. In helping Alex hone his adjective-laden and labyrinthine style, Anne had undoubtedy polished her own.

Two of Anne's early essays were published in *Chambers's Journal of Popular Literature, Science and Arts*. "A Glance at the Vegetable Kingdom," her first published work, appeared in 1857. Using "the distinguished botanist Schleiden" as her source of information and noting that due to the microscope and to advances in analytical chemistry "botany has taken a stride upwards in the scale of the sciences—has become, in fact, physiological instead of merely systematic," she gives a detailed and lucid account of the cellular structure of plants, their means of receiving and utilizing nutrients from the air, earth, and water, and the interdependence of human and plant life. Then, to recapture an English reader whose attention might be straying to the cultivation of his own geraniums, she gives a vivid description of a variety of exotic foreign plants: the four-hundred curious and colorful varieties of South American cactus; and virulently poisonous milk-sap plants, like the upas tree and slender antiar of Java, which grow in primeval forests, where the "melancholy orang-outang wanders gravely about leaning on his staff." She closes by noting that the common English nettle is also "a marvelous little apparatus for mischief," with its nettle so like a snake's tooth in structure that it might be called "the vegetable serpent."[20]

"Whales and Whalemen," published in *Chambers's* on Saturday, 14 April, 1860, is a study of the history of whaling, the anatomy and habits of whales, and the hardships endured by English whalers. Brave English whalemen, Anne tells us, hunt the right, or Greenland, whale in the icy waters of the north, a far more difficult and dangerous undertaking than pursuing the sperm whale, the principal quarry of American whalers: "Brother Jonathan, with his usual 'cuteness, has chosen a field of less risk and more profit—sperm whaling—for the sperm whale has no taste for living among icebergs and polar bears; he likes to float in the tepid waters of the tropics. The right whale shuns these enervating regions."[21] Had Anne read *Moby Dick*, published nine years earlier in 1851? She had indeed. "That clever Yankee, Herman Melville," she writes, "who instructs and befools his reader by turns, but who certainly knows something about whales and whaling, has whimsically classed the great family into three books—folio, octavo, and duodecimo." Anne would seem to have been more indebted to "that clever Yankee" than she acknowledges. Melville's magnificent chapter 32, "Cetology," with its masterful classification of all species of whales, divided according to magnitude—a task on a par with groping "down into the bottom of the sea after them; to have one's hands among the unspeakable foundations, ribs, and very pelvis of the world"[22]—was unquestionably one of her two main sources of information about the great sea mammal. Her other, and more enthusiastically acknowledged, main source of information was "the brave, veracious Scoresby,"[23] an English harpooner and whaleman, whom Melville mentions as one of the few whale authors who ever saw a living whale: "On the separate subject of the Greenland or Right Whale, he [Captain Scoresby] is the best existing authority. But Scoresby knew nothing and says nothing of the great Sperm Whale, compared with which the Greenland Whale is almost unworthy mentioning." This disparagement of the Greenland whale—the English whaler's whale of choice—must have been responsible for Anne's tone of miffed condescension toward both "that clever Yankee" and "Brother Jonathan" as a whaler. Her patriotism must have been further ruffled by Melville's resounding declaration that to the great poets of past days "the Greenland Whale, without one rival, was to them the monarch of the seas. But the time has at last come for a new proclamation. This is Charing Cross; hear ye! good people all,—the Greenland Whale is deposed,—the Great Sperm Whale now reigneth!"[24]

To a twentieth-century reader, the most interesting of Anne's early scientific essays was published on 28 May, 1859, in *All the Year Round*, the periodical conducted by Dickens. It is an article on the recently discovered gorilla. Dickens was pleased with it, Herbert tells us, and showed it to the Carlyles, who also admired it. "You know, my dear," Jane commented to Anne, "you write very nicely!"[25] Based on information received by Richard Owen, the zoologist, in 1847 from a church missionary in western Africa, Anne's picture of the great ape anticipates King Kong. The enormous beast that she describes is a fearsome creature that reaches down from the lower branches of a tree with his horrible, thumbed foot, snatches a hapless native by the throat, "draws him up into the boughs, and, as soon as his struggles have ceased, drops him down, a strangled corpse." What is significant about this essay is that it was published in the same year that Darwin's *Origin of Species* created the greatest crisis of the Victorian era and intensified the war between science and religion—a war in which lingering skirmishes are still being fought. A major confrontation took place at the meeting of the British Association for the Advancement of Science in 1860, when Bishop Wilberforce and T. H. Huxley, the biologist, had at each other like two armored jousters in the lists. Both had backers in the audience, including a crowd of women, whose presence has never been explained, who waved their handkerchiefs in support of the bishop.[26]

The title of Anne's essay on the gorilla makes it plain that she would not have been a handkerchief waver. In the biography, Herbert erroneously reports the title as "Our Poor Relation" and repeats the error in his biographical sketch of his mother in the *Dictionary of National Biography*. The actual title of the essay, as it appeared in *All the Year Round*, was "Our Nearest Relation." With this title Anne puts herself unequivocally on the side of science—and in opposition to the ministerial majority of the Anglican Church and its tenets, which she had been unable to accept even as a schoolgirl, when she declared that she would "never be confirmed with my own consent." In the essay she gives a detailed tabulation of the ways in which the gorilla differs from the previously known manlike apes—the gibbon, the orangutan, the chimpanzee—and is higher in a demonstrable scale of organization than they, and therefore more like man. In addition to having a larger and more complex brain than the others, Anne notes that there are other points of proof of the gorilla's superior position in an ascending order of development:

> He [the gorilla] has other claims to precedence, besides this cogent one of more brain and a more convoluted brain. The distinctive characteristic of the order, that which supplies it the name, quadrumanna, is, as we all know, the having hands instead of feet—four hands. And in the comparative anatomist's eyes, the most characteristic peculiarity of man's structure is the great toe; it is mainly this which enables him to walk erect, which constitutes the great difference between a foot and a hand, and entitles him, sole genus of his order, sole species of his genus, to his zoological appellation bimana, or two-handed. In the gorilla, the thumb of the hind hand is more like a great toe than it is, either in the orang-outang or chimpanzee; it is thicker and stronger. The heel also, makes a more decided backward projection, and in the fore-hand, that important member, the thumb, is better developed. A disproportionate length of arm gives, as we notice in the deformed, a singularly awkward and ungainly aspect to the figure. This is a familiar attribute of all monkey-kind, and one which, in its gradual diminution, marks the gradual rise in the scale of organization. In the gibbons, or long-armed apes, these members hang down to the feet, so that the whole palm can be applied to the ground without the trunk being bent. In the orang, they reach the ankle; in the chimpanzee, below the knee; in the gorilla, a little short of the knee; while in man, below the middle of the thigh. There are other advances of structure interesting to the anatomist, and all tending to support the gorilla's claims to the topmost place. Now and then we come across a human face in which the

bony framework of the eye is almost circular, with a repulsive, cunning, monkey-like look. This, though universal, is one of the ugliest characteristics of the monkey. The gorilla, however, is exempt from this particular detail of ugliness; the bony setting of the eye is squarish, as in most men.[27]

Perhaps to make possible the publication in a popular periodical of an article on so controversial a subject, Anne concludes her essay on the gorilla by conceding that "the honey-making, architectural bee, low down in the scale of life" more nearly displays man's type of industry and skill. In contrast, "this apex in the pyramid of the brute creation, this near approach to the human form, what can it do? The great hands have no skill but to clutch and strangle; the complex brain is kindled by no divine spark; there, amid the unwholesome luxuriance of a tropical forest, the creature can do nothing but pass its life in fierce sullen isolation—eat, drink, and die?"

In the nineteenth century, the branch of science that created the greatest excitement was the new science of electricity. The invention of powerful batteries in the preceding century led in the nineteenth century to new concepts of the universe and the elements of life, as well as to new inventions. The construction of the first dynamo made possible the development of electrical machinery for industry; the telegraph was invented; and a successsful transatlantic cable was laid. Electricity was hailed by the medical profession as an effective means of curing numerous disorders. It was used as a dramatic device by writers of fiction. It captured the imaginations of theologians and philosophers—including Emerson, who, in "Circles," described the center of each man's universe, with its infinitely expanding circumference of concentric circles, as an electric generator.[28] And, although Anne Gilchrist was not yet aware of it, at midcentury Walt Whitman was exuberantly announcing, "I sing the body electric."

In a climate so charged with interest in and excitement about electricity, it would seem an almost foregone conclusion that one of Anne's scientific essays would be on so popular a subject. "What is Electricity?" was published in *Once a Week* on 2 February, 1861. It is a knowledgeable and clearly documented history of the science of electricity and a comprehensible explanation for the general reader of the nature, manifestations, and potential uses of electric energy. Beginning with the invention of the Leyden jar in 1746, Anne traces the history of electrical scientific progress, with emphasis on the experiments of Franklin, Beccaria and Priestly, Sir Humphrey Davy, De la Rive, and Silliman in developing electric light from wires that had been made incandescent. In simple terms she defines static and dynamic electricity, conductors, insulators, electrodes and the voltaic arc. She explains that "Electro-Chemistry" has exploded the old notion that electricity is a fluid, or two fluids, and "led to its being universally regarded as a force." And she gives in detail De la Rive's theory that every atom has two electric poles of contrary but equal force; and that atoms attract one another and unite either by cohesion or by chemical affinity according to the strength of their polarity. Anne ends the essay with an eloquent defense of scientists and science—a profession and field bitterly denounced by many Victorians—addressed, one suspects, to clerical as well as unordained antagonists:

> It is to be bourne in mind these are not the fanciful speculations of men eager for the goal yet impatient of labour, who suffer a lively imagination to outrun knowledge. Neither do they pretend to claim acceptance as established truth, but simply as an hypothesis which, in the judgment of some of those standing foremost in the ranks of discovery, seems best to harmonise and bind together a great body of anomalous facts: an hypothesis that will stand or fall according as increased knowledge shall strengthen or undermine its foundations; but by no means to be rejected on the ground that it contradicts the evidence of the senses, or handles a subject beyond our reach. Unless a man is prepared to say, "The earth stands still, the sun moves, because *I see them to do so*," he has no right to regard the evidence of his senses as impregnable ground. It was a singular lesson Astronomy taught us on this head, though we are now so familiar with it as to have ceased to perceive its meaning. Think what a slumberous stillness rests upon the face of Nature; how endlessly broad and deep seem to spread out the foundations of the earth. Then think again what is the truth: a little rounded star in rapid, ceaseless, threefold motion; not slumbering on its broad foundations, but hung baseless mid infinity, it "taketh no rest." Perhaps we have been equally deceived at the opposite end of the scale: perhaps the fundamental idea we have of solid matter—that its particles are relatively at rest, may be overthrown, and ceaseless motion proved the condition of existence for atoms as for worlds. What then? We cannot afford to despise our senses, since through them alone comes our report of the world without. Science deals with them as an able lawyer deals with a pack of stupid or roguish witnesses: cross-questions them, sets one against the other, sifts and balances the conflicting evidence, marshals it, puts sense into it,—and in the end triumphantly draws truth out of it. It is but shallow philosophy to sneer at the senses, for without them man's reason would be a king without a kingdom. Dwell rather on the ingenuity with which—when once he has got a hint of new fields to be explored—man provides himself with supplementary senses, as it were: with the telescope, makes his eyes as the eyes of a giant; with the microscope, sees into the mysteries of the smallest flower, like King Oberon himself; with electroscope, galvanometer, and other dainty devices, achieves a delicacy of perception which can detect the feeblest trace or lightest movement of Nature's stealthiest agent.[29]

Five months earlier, on 22 September, 1860, another of Anne's essays was published in *Once a Week*. Like "What is Electricity?" "The Parentage of a Sunbeam" is an explanation for the general reader of a field of science. In this case Anne's subject is the sun and the light transmitted by it to the earth. Without sacrificing either scholarship to simplicity, or a light and readable style to sound and comprehensive knowledge, she explains the sun's size, structure, and distance from the earth, and how these have been determined by the observations of astronomers over many centuries—from the Chinese, possibly the Peruvians, Fabricius, and Galileo to a recent expedition to Chili sent by Americans to verify these calculations by a series of observations of

Venus. She discusses sunspots at length: what they are, their periodic variations, and the validity of the theory that there is a connection between these spots and the magnetic state of the earth. She reminds the reader that light is of two kinds, natural and polarized, and describes the polariscope and how it is used to determine which kind of light is imaged in it. Her list of sources is impressive: General Sabine, a leader in the field of terrestrial magnetism; a Mr. Carpenter of Reigate, who was also currently conducting experiments in magnetism; M. Maedler, the Prussian astronomer; Sir William Herschel, the English astronomer; and Arago, a scientist who, like Herschel, believed that the sun could be inhabited by beings not wholly unlike man. To please her nonscientific Victorian readers, Anne closes the essay with a semisentimental ending—like an antimacassar draped on an otherwise uneasy chair:

> Herschel has told us that they [the sun's rays] are the primary source of all motion of the earth. Like the Prince whose kiss awoke the Sleeping Beauty, their touch rouses the germ of every green thing to put forth the life that is in it. They are the presiding genii in nature's grand chemical laboratory. They set the winds in motion; draw up out of the earth mere watery vapour, which shaped by those winds into a canopy of cloud, they paint with varying hues.[30]

Although Anne's last scientific essay was published after she left Chelsea, it would seem reasonable to suppose that the extensive research that was necessary, and possibly even the writing of a first draft, were done while she was still living at 6 Cheyne Row, rather than in the turbulent and emotionally devastating months after Alex's death. "The Indestructibility of Force," published in *Macmillan's Magazine* in August 1862, is Anne's longest and most scholarly scientific article. Her detailed description of the indestructibility that underlies what appears to be universal destruction is a brilliantly organized and presented dissertation, intended for the enjoyment of the reader with considerable knowledge of science as well as for the general reader. She explains that this indestructibility is due to the fact that the atoms with which seemingly ever-changing forms are built are themselves changeless. She lists the qualities of matter that resolve themselves into forces: weight, cohesion, chemical affinity, heat force, visibility, and electricity, "sublest, most Protean of all the forces of Nature." She mentions briefly the principle of the conservation of force, which had been called "the grandest generalization of modern science," and then discusses at length the second half of this principle, the indestructibility of force, which had been securely grasped only within the past twenty years. She names those most prominently involved in this study and the contributions made by each: M. Meyer of Heilbronn; Faraday, Grove, Carpenter, Scoresby, Joule, Owens, and Tyndall of England; and Helmholtz, Mossotti, Boscovich, and Mateucci. She devotes four double-columned pages to an analysis of heat, its nature and manifestations. And she presents the evidence that the indestructibility of force operates in the organic as well as the inorganic world, although under new conditions, "under the control of that higher agency which we call Vital Force." According to Carpenter, vital force is in essence a directive power. This Anne sees as "a gain worth all the toil to recognize vividly that there *is* a deep mystery not only in that which lives and grows, but in the very stocks and stones. No longer mistaking our own shallow conceptions for complete and absolute truth, our minds may become as a clear unclouded mirror, where in dim and shadowed grandeur some suggestions of this far-off absolute truth will perhaps be reflected." Anne ends the essay with her most spirited defense of science and her most gloves-off attack on its critics and belittlers, both religious and literary—including Wordsworth:

> ... in the expression "the vital force is directive power," we stretch out our hands towards a truth that for ever eludes us, and find ourselves grasping an empty garment of words. Though it be good to recognise this, it is not good to be daunted or discouraged. If God have set a limit to the conquering power of man's intellect, He has left it for man himself to discover where that limit lies; left it to be discovered by the gifted and laborious, aided by "the long results of time," not to be predicted by the timid and indolent. It is not piety, but self-satisfied ignorance and cowardice, which makes a man shrink from pressing on into the dim unknown, and decry, as presumptuous and irreverent, those whose heaven-sent impulse it is to do so.
> These remarks might seem uncalled for at the present day, when science confessedly occupies so honourable a position. But there still lingers in the minds of the religious a tendency to view with distrust and suspicion its bolder flights. Why should this be? How can harm come of the faithful and earnest study of God's works, seeing that He has implanted both the faculty and aspiration to gain understanding of them? Perhaps there is even a touch of what has, with just severity, been called "that worst kind of infidelity, the fear lest the truth be bad," in this shrinking from face-to-face encounter with some of the facts of nature, and the inevitable deductions from them. Conflicting opinions among the wisest there may be, conflicting truths there cannot. If, therefore, science bring to light facts which seem to militate against that which we hold as high and sacred truth, we may rest calmly assured that a fuller knowledge of such facts, a deeper insight into their true bearings, will dispel the appearance of antagonism. But then we must go boldly on to reach this higher stage, not turn back and basely seek the dark shelter of ignorance. Or rather, the man of science goes boldly on for us. How ungenerous to reproach him for his boldness!
> It cannot be denied that there is also in our highest literature a tone, not of open hostility, but of covert contempt for science. It is looked down upon as tending to materialism; and its devotees as men whose eyes, long scrutinizingly fixed upon the outward aspects of things, grow dim to all beyond; and who, in Wordsworth's memorably unjust words, "would peep and botanize upon their mother's grave." Does, then, a too curious searching into nature's works strip them of their beauty, their mystery? Does it tend to debase the heart and dull the imagination? Impossible. The beauty, the mystery, are not of such flimsy, shallow kind, as to vanish beneath an earnest questioning gaze. What it was worth God's while to make, it is surely worth man's while to understand. As to the charge of materialism, of course the business of physical science is with the material world. But if it have one decided tendency at the present day, it is to exalt and spiritualize our idea of matter, and, far from destroying, to enhance the sense of mystery. Why should literature treat

science as men treat one another—each expecting in his neighbour all his own virtues added to all theirs, with the faults of both left out? Why, because it does not comprise all man seeks for of truth and knowledge, should he slight what it does? Rather should we honour the humblest labourer in the fields of science, and prize the fruits of his labour. What man is so rich in intellectual possessions that he can afford to despise the smallest fragment of truth? Nature has not denied legs to those creatures whom she has endowed with wings; neither can the soaring imagination wisely leave unvisited the solid ground of fact, whereon science is so notably extending her possessions. Like the birds, she must come down to feed if she would be strong on the wing.[31]

Anne's seventh work written in the Chelsea years is so different from her essays that it is hard to believe that it was written by the same hand. The essays reveal the author, Anne Gilchrist, as a learned woman of science, years ahead of her time. "Lost in the Wood," published in *The Magnet Stories: For Summer Days and Winter Nights* in 1861, reveals the author, Mrs. Alex. Gilchrist, as a model Victorian mother and a typical Victorian writer of stories for children. "Lost in the Wood" is an account, slightly fictionalized, of the six weeks that Anne, Johnny, and their mother spent with Mrs. Burrows's brother and his family in Tolleshunt Knights in Essex, when Anne was nine or ten years old. The format of this narrative, in four chapters with five illustrations, is that of a mother recounting events of her own childhood to her small son and daughter. And that might well have been the genesis of this minibook—Anne relating to nine- and seven-year-old Percy and Beatrice, not once but many times, the events of that memorable visit. Like all Victorian literature for children, "Lost in the Wood" contains a generous supply of "little lessons" interspersed in the text—lessons in deportment, moral responsibility, natural history, and the meanings of unfamiliar words. And in "Lost in the Wood," as in all Victorian juvenile literature, a disobedient child always gets into trouble, causing great anxiety and potential peril; but the remorseful miscreant is always rescued by a stern but forgiving adult. However, in spite of its dated conventionality, "Lost in the Wood" is a charming reminiscence, warm in tone and filled with colorful details. Its episodes of suspense may not be cliff-hangers by modern standards, but they are so skillfully managed that they still hold a reader's interest. Why did Anne, the specialist in advanced science, write a ginger-cookie comfit like "Lost in the Wood"? One reason may have been for a profitable variety of prestige; each monthly issue of the popular *Magnet Stories* contained only one story and each issue sold for threepence, which could indicate that the price paid for a manuscript might have been above average.[32] However, another reason must have been that Anne, always the devoted mother as well as a woman of letters, wrote it for the pleasure of her children.

After her marriage, Anne spent a month or so every year, in summer or early autumn, at Earls Colne with her mother. She took her children with her, as Mrs. Burrows had taken little Annie and Johnny back to the family ancestral home for frequent visits. In an unpublished memoir of her mother written in the 1920s, Grace Gilchrist Frend wrote: "Much I loved our annual visit to Earls Colne, though the social element was not ... congenial to my mother. ... At Earls Colne, the squire and the parson reigned supreme. ... But there were beautiful interludes when local society and squirearchy had gone home to dinner, then we were happy."[33] A society in which the parson was a supreme ruler would have been decidedly uncongenial to Anne Gilchrist. When he came to tea, were her essays mentioned? On Sundays, with a reluctant Anne in the family pew, did he fulminate from the pulpit against the heretical new theories of science? In the records of the beautiful gray-stone Saint Andrew's Church at Earls Colne, which dates back to Norman times, there is evidence of Anne's continuing rebellion against Anglican ritual—and evidence that once again, as was probably the case in her refusal to be confirmed, it was necessary for her to give in to pressure in order to spare the feelings of those she loved. Anne's children were apparently not baptized shortly after birth according to the established custom of the church, which must have been deeply distressing for Mrs. Burrows, and possibly for Henry Carwardine as well. However, on Sunday, 20 July, 1859—when Percy was nearly nine, Beatrice almost five, Herbert two and a half, and Grace six months old—all of the Gilchrist children were baptized at Saint Andrew's.[34] The only possible explanation of this singular event is that it was done to keep peace in the family. As Julia Newton observed, even as a schoolgirl Anne's love of freedom in theology for herself "was combined with an anxiety not to unnecessarily shock those who thought orthodoxy essential."

During Anne's visits to Colne, Alex missed her terribly. Some of his letters written to her during these absences have been preserved. Addressed most often to "Dear Little Bird," they contain accounts of what he had been doing, fond inquiries about the children, and some domestic trivia: a bad piece of cheese at luncheon had made him ill; he had given Susan, the servant girl, "of my own offering on Sunday, an evening with her sister: a new loaf, tea & sugar to take with her. She was very grateful." But they are primarily letters from a man very much in love. "Sitting lonely and loving," he wrote from Guildford on 23 September, 1853, "there is one thing I think of, *our reunion*, I can perhaps manage to speak to Thee on. Let me try—Well!—I think, I feel, I *know* that were we by any chance separated I should again seek Thee, dear, the whole world over to make Thee mine, seek Thee with passion, and pine in thy absence." On 22 May, 1856 he wrote to "Dear Lassie": "Thou must be sure and come home at the [promised?] time: for I cannot get on at all, at all, without Thee." A letter from 6 Cheyne Row on 13 May, 1857, written on mourning paper by a grieving Alex not long after the death of his elder brother, begins: "Sweet Friend & Dearest, only Friend I've ever had—dearer to me than I have ever been to Thee." After six years of marriage, Alex is conceding that his love is still the greater. But he seems never to have doubted that the sexual aspect of their marriage was everything that it should be, since for him, the husband, it seems to have been totally blissful. Another letter, undated—and written in crosshatch, that eye-crossing device used by frugal Victorians—is signed "Thine most loving, longing, yearning, struggling—Alex." And below this is written as a postscript line: "My Dear Little Birdie: My Mate: My Mistress."[35]

The most tenderly passionate letter that Alex wrote to Anne during these periods of separation is also the most revelatory. It discloses that after their marriage Anne's mother provided them with some financial support; and that as she grew older Henrietta Burrows became difficult, cold, and ill-natured. It shows Anne as a young wife chiding her young husband for his love of good food. But, most important of all, this fragment of a letter, written from Guildford on Wednesday evening, 28 September, 1853 at nine o'clock, reveals Alex's loving and supportive understanding of his wife's unusual nature—her dual nature, as he astutely calls it.

> Dear Little Bird: Well! here I am, pining and longing for the dear girl, as if I had ne'er untied her virgin zone in Guildford town. So it is: a week's absence places us (Alick) where we were. The years that have passed are as not. Does this satisfy Annie? Does she prefer the longing and the misery to the tranquillity and the felicity? We are poor children—are for having the joys of two different states in one. Sometimes I can hardly bear myself, restless as a squirrel in its cage in banishment. I cannot spare Thee again for longer than a fortnight, dear. How I would count out the golden sovereigns from my Etty money for but one evening of little Birdie in our sweet room; for one evening that thy full form might fill the crimson chair. I look and look, but how sternly it continues vacant. Yes! Thou art to me as Thou wast, with the added association of our mutual life since, the habit that has grown up of daily confidences, daily interchange of thought & feeling. Were it all to be lived o'er, I should live it all the same—all save accept thy Mother's money. We did not know, did not then understand her ill disposition's continued nature. If Thou remember, every fresh evidence of this was a fresh surprise to us. . . .
> No! with none but Thee, none I have ever seen or dreamed could I have been happy, or in the slightest degree mated. Thou art one of a million as I am concerned. Now it may seem egotistic but I have ever felt that even if I could not make Thee happy, none other could—thy nature is so unique. Thou wouldst have been unhappy as *Thou* canst not realize, choosing, for daily companion, one as *distant* as thy Mother, and as *mean* as [?]'s father. They wouldn't have understood Thee, thy higher self—would have been impatient with Thee, with thy difficulties—the frictions of thy dual nature.
> In two little ways is Annie wrong. For one, to lay such daily, hourly stress on Alick's faults. Is his self-indulgence at the table such a great matter, it must weigh down everything else? Must be momently in his eyes? And he can so little help it . . . Thou'rt unjust too in supposing him incapable of self-restraint. He can put on his suit of armour now and then.[36]

Brave Alex! Even though he was in love with his nagger, he was no Milquetoast.

A few months after the Gilchrists took possession of 6 Cheyne Row, Alex's beloved elder brother died by drowning. It was necessary for Alex to devote the two following years to winding up his brother's extensive business affairs, left in chaos by his sudden death. This done, Alex joyfully returned to literary work, contributing weekly columns of art criticism and reviews of books on art, first to the *Literary Gazette* and then the *Critic*.[37] Most of his time and energy, however, were spent on the *Life of Blake*. On 29 November, 1859, Alex submitted a partially completed manuscript to Alexander Macmillan, who accepted it on the "very fair and liberal" terms, according to Alex, of £150 for a first edition of 2,000 copies, with an advance of £20 for research expenses.[38] In the months that followed, the two men were in constant communication to discuss the details of publication, meeting sometimes at 6 Cheyne Row, sometimes at Macmillan's house in Henrietta Street, and exchanging frequent letters. In spite of the necessity of making innumerable revisions, insertions, deletions, and rearrangements; in spite of problems with Linton, the engraver, whom Alex considered irresponsible and an inferior artisan; in spite of frustrations and disappointments encountered in the search for "historical vestiges"; and in spite of Alex having to tell Macmillan, courteously but firmly, that it is the artist and not his publisher who must decide how he is to work and whether certain passages in a biography should be left out because they might not be "family reading"—in spite of all these difficulties, in the autumn of 1861 the *Life of Blake* was nearing completion.[39] A well-earned sense of achievement was not Alex's only reward. In working on the biography, he had met some of the most brilliant men of the time in arts and letters, including Swinburne, Meredith, Palmer, and most of the "Pre-Raphs." He and Gabriel Rossetti, to whom he had written in the spring of 1861 for information for the *Life of Blake*, had taken an instant liking to each other and had become great friends. They met at the Cheshire Cheese in Wine Office Court, unquestionably at 6 Cheyne Row, and once Alex was invited by Rossetti to join him and two or three friends for an evening of "nothing but oysters, and of course the seediest of clothes."[40] In September 1861, it must have seemed to Alex that he had truly gained the heights "his heritage to seize." And then disaster struck the Gilchrist family.

Scarlet fever was the scourge of the nineteenth century, raging through worldwide populations and, for those who survived, often leaving tragic aftereffects like elephantiasis. In an epidemic in 1863, thirty thousand people died in England alone.[41] In October 1861, Beatrice came down with this dread disease. For six weeks she was seriously, then dangerously ill. Anne remained in the sickroom night and day, isolating herself from the other members of the family. On 23 October, Alex reported to Macmillan that "one of our children is lying ill with scarlatina; & my wife is confined to the sickroom nursing her." In a letter to Macmillan on 20 November, Alex explained that he had been unable to send "a big mass of copy" to the printers because "domestic troubles have during the last month stood in the way." He continues his explanation:

> Our eldest little girl Beatrice (age seven) has during the whole of that time been suffering from a very severe & dangerous attack of scarlatina; & we have been in great misery at times, aggravated by our having had a doctor in whom we had not implicit confidence. On Monday I called in a physician (Dr. C. [?] West) who cheered us by giving a favourable opinion. Yesterday too Dr. Seth K. Norton gave us a call and sympathizing advice. And we have reason to suppose that our little one is in a fair way towards recovery. My wife has during all this time been confined to the sick room, without help!—& has kept up a rigid quarantine towards the rest of the household; who have as yet escaped—but who of course require some attention on my part in the absence of their natural protector. Of hired nurses we have a horror; our friends have mostly children and others regard for whom makes them dread crossing the threshold of a scarlatina infected house.
>
>   Excuse this closing matter;
>   and believe me my dear Sir,
>   Yours most faithfully
>   Alex Gilchrist[42]

This was one of the last letters Alex ever wrote. Just as Beatrice was beginning to recover, Percy had contracted the fever, although fortunately in a milder form. Then, in the last days of November, an exhausted Alex came down with it and immediately became critically ill.

In this crisis, the Gilchrists' friends rallied. Emma Brown offered to come and help, but since she had children of her own, Anne refused this generosity. Another friend, Isabella Ireland, made the same offer. Gabriel Rossetti sent a note offering his own and his brother's help with any literary business that might need transacting until Alex was well again. And Jane Carlyle, who was ill herself, had been supportive throughout the anxious weeks, sending frequent notes next door. On 25 October, she wrote to Anne: "My Dear: I am very sorry for your anxiety—but, it is the price one has to pay for the joy of having such nice children!" In another note, she wrote: "I am most sincerely sorry for you in this long solitary confinement. I am sure both your health and spirits must be suffering from it. . . . When lying awake in the dark nights I think of you and your troubles on the other side of the wall! . . . Give poor little Beatrice a kiss for me." When the seriousness of Alex's illness became apparent, Jane wrote: "Oh God help you, poor afflicted soul!—What can any human being say to comfort you? Nothing—nothing!—But is there anything I can do? or Mr. Carlyle do? Can I write any letters for you?—you would only need to give me the addresses. Can I send anywhere? Get anything?—Have you money at hand? Oh do use me in some way!"[43]

As Alex's condition worsened, the two youngest children were sent to Earls Colne. Unfortunately Alex, still dissatisfied with Beatrice's progress, had recently again dismissed his medical man, one who had at least been conscientious and, as Carlyle said, had "stood at many a death bed." On one of the five nights that Alex lay critically ill, Carlyle brought a new doctor, a fashionable physician, who looked at the patient from the sickroom door, remarked that there was enough "fever at number six to stock the parish," and hastily departed.[44] Worn out from six weeks of previous night-and-day watching, Anne, whose servant girl was ill in the hospital, was left alone in the house, except for a drunken nurse, to struggle as best she could against "spectral Death," no longer stalking from "you horizon dim," but clearly close at hand.

In her memoir of Alex, Anne describes those terrible final days and hours: "The brain was tired with stress of work; the fever burned and devastated like a flaming fire: to four days of delirium succeeded one of exhaustion, of stupor; and then the end; without a word, but not without a look of loving recognition. It was on a wild and stormy night, November 30, 1861, that his spirit took flight."[45]

Ten years after Alex's death, Anne would write to Whitman in her first letter to him, on 3 September, 1871:

> In 1861 my children took scarlet fever badly: I thought I should have lost my dear oldest girl. Then my husband took it—and in five days it carried him from me. I think, dear friend, my sorrow was far more bitter, though not so deep, as that of a loving tender wife. As I stood by him in the coffin I felt such remorse I had not, could not have, been more tender to him—such a conviction that if I had loved him as he deserved to be loved he would not have been taken from us.[46]

Without in any way contradicting this private confidence, nearly twenty years after Alex's death, Anne would close her memoir with a lovely and tenderly appreciative public tribute:

> If life be measured not by years, but by what it contains, this life of thirty-three summers was not short. With a sweetness of disposition, a tenderness of heart that gave and took the utmost of happiness in domestic life; a sturdy enjoyment of work; fair, though not strong health; a fineness of perception and an ardent love for all that is genuine or great in literature, in art, in nature, in humanity, and a silent faith in immortality, I think he knew no moments of tedium or ennui, though of sorrow, toil, pain, and privation he had his share. To such a nature the cup of life is full of fine flavours.[47]

Alex's funeral was held on 4 December, 1861. He was buried in Kensal Green Cemetery, only a few feet from the common grave of John Parker Burrows, Anne's father, and her brother, Johnny.[48]

7
BROOKBANK

The untold want by life and land ne'er granted,
Now voyager sail thou forth to seek and find.
                                        Walt Whitman

In the days following Alex's death, messages of sympathy poured in—from Madox Brown, Alexander Macmillan, Julia Newton, and a host of others. "Even for me," Gabriel Rossetti wrote to Anne the day after the funeral, "no greater shock has ever occurred in my life than this. I truly valued and loved your husband, more I think than I had ever felt towards anyone on the same length of acquaintance or, I should say friendship, for such I believe it was on both sides." "Thank God the children are saved!" wrote Samuel Palmer, whose young son had died only a few months before. "That house in Cheyne Row, and that family, so happily and so lovingly compacted within it, will not flit in and out of memory. . . . I see it as it *was* and as it *is*,—I see too, my own once happy and hopeful home before the destroying angel poured forth upon it calamity. . . . We are both of us in the thick darkness." And Jane Carlyle, still bedridden, sent an imploring note next door:

> My Dear Friend: Will you be brave and good, and come to *me*? You might wait till *after dark*, when you would only have to throw a shawl over your head—and I would send you the latch-key, and you could let yourself in, and come straight up to my bedroom without having to see or speak to anybody. I have been on the drawing-room sofa most part of the last two days. I am *much* better—and please God I shall soon be able to go to *you*.[1]

Anne's most supportive friend during those first dreadful days and weeks seems to have been warm-hearted, generous, thoughtful Isabella Erskine Ireland,[2] who had heard of Alex's illness too late for her immediate offer of help to be accepted. Many years later in a letter to Grace, who had asked her for reminiscences about her mother that Herbert might use in his biography, Isabella pictured a distraught and exhausted Anne a few days after the funeral:

> I hurried to Cheyne Row as soon as the first shock of the disastrous news had subsided, and called there every day till, able to suppress for some moments the

outburst of her terrible grief, she was able to see me. Your dear father's illness and death happened, as you know, within the limit of a week; and in spite of every precaution on her part to keep him outside the range of infection. He persisted, however, in visiting every night the upper bedroom in which she was nursing your dear sister Beatrice, and in making up the fire; while she kept far away from him near the windows: he satisfied with the look at them: she with the hope no harm had been done.

But, as she told me bewailing, the medical men after his death assured her your father ought not to have continued in the infected house. His literary labours carried on far into the night and early mornings had no doubt prepared the way, with the super-added anxiety on her account and yours, for making him, alas, too easy a victim to the fever.

Never can I forget that interview with her, bearable but for a few moments, such at least they seemed, yet full of a lifetime of sorrow and unavailing regret. Leaving her children in one room with the nurse, she came to me where I stood in an other, and standing we remained opposite each other. I see her now in her widow's weeds, as, all but maddened with grief, she uttered short outbursts reproachful of the sort of darkness, she conceived, she had been kept in of the true nature of the peril to which your father had been exposed. Everything, now, appeared to her had been sacrificed to the rescue of the children from danger and death, and *he* had fallen the victim. Only with short hurried exclamations could she revert for an instant to the sudden seizure—to the swiftness of his doom. Little comfort had she from me save gestures of pity and eyes raining incessant tears. This was a few days after your father's funeral. By a verbal message brought me by the nurse, she had asked me to be in the room where the mourners assembled, and where for the first time I met and conversed with Mr. Carlyle; his theme your father's rare and admirable qualities, and his own regret at the swift loss of a young friend, whose fine blossom promised rich fruit.[3]

Within hours after this meeting, the news reached Chelsea from Earls Colne that Herbert and Grace had come down with the fever, and Anne rushed off to Essex to nurse them, leaving Percy and Beatrice, now convalescing, in the care of a nurse and a doctor. Isabella visited the children daily, and Jane Carlyle sent regular reports to Colne. "Things seem to go on very well in your house," Jane wrote to Anne on 7 December. "That nurse, from all my girls say of her, seems to be a most anxious painstaking woman. I have good accounts of the children every day."[4] Since Herby was extremely ill and then suffered a relapse, it was several weeks before Anne could bring him and little Grace back to London, wrapped in blankets for the journey.[5] Jane seems to have seen to it that the two children alone at 6 Cheyne Row—still not entirely recovered and certainly badly frightened—were not neglected at Christmas. In the Gilchrist Collection, on one of Jane's cards that must have accompanied a gift, is written: "Miss Beatrice Gilchrist / with kind regards and best wishes / Xmas day, '61." The card that must have accompanied a gift for Percy has not been preserved. Isabella Ireland had a household of her own, but while Anne was away, in addition to daily visits to the two little convalescents, she superintended the thorough disinfecting and cleaning of 6 Cheyne Row.[6]

Jane Carlyle's card that accompanied a gift to Beatrice Gilchrist, Christmas 1861. Private collection.

When she returned to Chelsea, all of her children with her for the first time in many weeks, Anne made a bold decision. In the nineteenth century, widowhood was regarded as a catastrophe that destroyed the foundation on which a woman's financial, social, and emotional security depended. A widow was seen as a helpless and pitiful creature. It would have been expected, as the only logical course, that Anne, as a young widow, would return to the protective haven of her family ties at Earls Colne. But Anne had no desire to return on a permanent basis either to the bondage of being "the daughter at home" or to the restrictions of a society that she found intensely uncongenial. On the other hand, remaining at 6 Cheyne Row, with its bitter memories, would be unbearably painful. As the second major decision of her life—and her first strike for true independence—newly widowed Anne Gilchrist decided to make a home for herself and her children in totally new surroundings.

The Carlyles begged her to stay on at No. 6, even suggesting that she join forces with another woman to save expenses.[7] And Isabella Ireland heard Anne's resolve to live elsewhere "with a disappointment proportional to my hopes." But Anne was not to be dissuaded. In many consultations with the Carlyles and in Anne's daily walks with Isabella, various places that might be suitable were discussed. There was the enormous task of completing Alex's *Life of Blake* to be considered, a task that Anne had already committed herself to undertake. And the children's health, as well as their education, had to be thought of. A place in the country, not too far from London, seemed the ideal solution, and Anne began house hunting. All alone, on a cold, rainy night in February 1862, she found Brookbank Cottage in the village of Shottermill, a mile from the town of Haslemere in Surrey.

"Since you *are* to go," Jane wrote to Anne later that month, "I wish to Heaven you were out of all this! I know how dreadful the details must be! how little chance of calm there is for you, till you have gathered yourself together in a new scene."[8] Before the move to Shottermill, Jane and Isabella helped Anne collect, sort, and return to the owners the pictures and books that had been lent to Alex for the *Life of Blake*. Anne's own collection of Blake's watercolor drawings was left in London with Isabella, and Alex's library—which Isabella took down from the shelves, dusted, and packed— was sent to William Haines.[9] When the day of departure came, Thursday, 3 April,[10] Isabella watched from the Carlyles' windows "the vans for Brookbank driving off loaded with the beautiful old carved furniture which had been your father's delight. Mrs. Carlyle shrugging her shoulders avouching her belief, that your mother would 'skin and bury herself alive for the benefit of you children.'"[11]

It would be difficult to imagine a setting in England in 1862 in greater contrast to Cheyne Row, with its shoulder-to-shoulder houses close to the splendor and bustle of London, than the village of Shottermill in southwest Surrey. A crayon-and-wash drawing of the village in 1857 shows a few houses, wide spaces between them, situated on gentle slopes and banks on either side of two unpaved roads leading down to a pond and a mill. Many of the houses of this period are still standing, although their interiors have been divided into two or more modern residences and their large gardens split up into building lots for new houses. In the mid–nineteenth century, although some of the local residents made their living by spinning, weaving, and brick making, the principal industry was the making of brooms from heather and birch. These brooms were used at Hampton Court and Windsor, and their makers—"the broom squires"—were famous in their day.[12] A mile from Shottermill, in the town of Haslemere, once a coaching town between Portsmouth and London, there was a general store managed by Clarke, the barber, where Herbert recalls, one "might have bought most commodities ranging from a watering-pot to a ham," and on market days farmers set up their stalls around the town hall. In 1862, trains to and from London stopped at Haslemere. This convenience undoubtedly influenced Anne in choosing Shottermill as the place to make a new home for herself and the children. But the paramount reason for her choice was the glorious countryside that surrounded the village: the fields and ponds and woods and hills on every side, where children could run and play and explore; the pure, invigorating air; the breathtaking views from the village and from commanding heights within easy walking distance. Another reason was the charm of Brookbank Cottage itself.

When Anne discovered it, the tile-hung cottage stood on the summit of a steep bank with a brook flowing at its base. In her unpublished memoir of

Brookbank Cottage, drawn by Herbert Gilchrist, 1884. Author's collection.

her mother, Grace recalls it fondly as "our pretty cottage home among the Surrey hills, where the pink and crimson china roses climbed to the low casement windows opening on the sloping lawn, bounded at one end by a large gilly-flower apple tree, and at the other end by a dusky gnarled yew."[13] Anne closed her first letter to William Rossetti from Brookbank, written on 28 April, 1862, with a postscript paragraph:

> This place is a bona fide Cottage, and would stand in your drawing-room at Tudor House. I found myself on first arrival in a dense wilderness of furniture. But having stowed a good deal in the attic we are now tolerably comfortable and as there is plenty of scope for the children out of doors, I think it will do well enough. The scenery round is of surpassing loveliness.[14]

In the summer of 1864, Anne finding no other suitable house in the neighborhood, had the cottage enlarged. The furniture was moved down from the attic, a profusion of fine pictures was hung, and, as a result, visitors found the interior of the cottage as charming as its spectacular exterior setting.

The best description of the interior of Brookbank can be found not, as one would suppose, in a family chronicle or reminiscence, but in a famous novel. In 1871, during her annual visit to Earls Colne, Anne leased Brookbank to George Henry Lewes and George Eliot. "Ever since the 1st of May we have been living in this queer cottage which belongs to Mrs. Gilchrist," George Eliot wrote in a letter. "We have old prints for our dumb companions . . . charming children of Sir Joshua's and large hatted ladies of his and Romney's."[15] Brookbank's long and irregularly shaped drawing room would be the model for the Meyricks' drawing room in *Daniel Deronda*:[16]

> Mrs. Meyrick had borne much stint of other matters that she might be able to keep some engravings specially cherished by her husband; and the narrow spaces of wall held a world-history in scenes and heads which the children had early learned by heart. The chairs and tables were also old friends preferred to new. . . . [T]here was space and apparatus for a wide-glancing, nicely-select life, open to the highest things in music, painting, and poetry. . . . The small front parlour was as good as a temple that morning . . . soft air came in through the open window; the wall showed a glorious silent cloud of witnesses—the Virgin soaring amid her cherubic escort; grand Melancholia with her solemn universe; the Prophets and Sibyls; the School of Athens; the Last Supper; mystic groups where far-off ages made one moment; grave Holbein and Rembrandt heads; the Tragic Muse; last century children at their musings or their play; Italian poets,—all were there through the medium of black and white.[17]

In an earlier chapter of *Deronda*, the sight of a picture suddenly disclosed by the accidental opening of a panel terrifies Gwendolen, who has a morbid horror of death. The picture is a Blake engraving, *The Soul Leaving the Body*, one of the pictures that hung on the walls at Brookbank.[18]

The countryside that surrounded Anne's new home had been well-known to Alex. Hind Head, the majestic hill with its panoramic view that was so often the goal of his long walks from Guildford, which lies fifteen miles north and east of Shottermill, is two miles from Brookbank Cottage. Anne often walked there. Those who have been skeptical about Anne's claim in her first letter directly to the poet that she had never been in love with her husband— that "To the last my soul dwelt apart & unmated & his soul dwelt apart unmated"—have pointed out a letter that Anne wrote to Alex's sister in the summer following his death. Speaking of her cottage in "the dear Surrey hills," Anne wrote: "There Alec's spirit is with me ever—presides in my home, speaks to me in every sweet scene; broods over the peaceful valleys; haunts the grand wild hill tops; shines gloriously forth in setting sun, and moon and stars."[19] Like Anne's letter to Julia Newton with its almost-postscript announcement of her engagement and perfunctory assurance that "your friend is very happy"—which skeptics have quoted as proof that time and her passion for Whitman had distorted Anne's memory—these few lines taken from a long letter to Mrs. Burnie[20] seem flimsy evidence. In its conventional sentimentality, isn't this exactly what a widow in the mid–nineteenth century would be expected to say to a grieving sister? And isn't it possible that Anne was describing not her actual emotions but the sense of loss and desolation that she wished she could have felt?

On the other hand, Anne never denied to anyone that she missed Alex after his death—his intellectual companionship, his encouragement of her ambitions, the shared responsibility for the children's welfare. And she never denied that she was haunted by memories of a past that, although it may not have been totally idyllic, had been happy in many respects. "I am glad Christmas is over," she wrote to William Haines in 1864. "It is a trying time—a time that cannot but bring up vividly what was and what might have been." And in a letter to Alex's sister Milly Thomas, speaking of the countryside around Shottermill that Alex had talked about so enthusiastically that it "was as familiar to me at Guildford ten years ago as it is now," Anne wrote: "I prize inexpressibly these fine subtle links of association that, subtle as they are, seem tangibly to link my present here with that happy past.[21]

Immediately after Alex's death Anne threw herself into the completion of the *Life of Blake*. She had not been able to love its author as she felt that he had deserved to be loved, but she was determined that his book would be presented to the public as it deserved. On 6 December, two days after the funeral, she wrote a letter to Macmillan on mourning paper with many words crossed out:

My Dear Sir
   I try to fix my thoughts on the one thing that remains for me to do for my dear Husband. I do not think that any one but myself can do what has to be done to the Book. I was his amanuensis. It was also his own intention that I should make the Index. Many things were to have been inserted—anecdotes, etc. collected during the last year, which he used to say "would be the best things in the book." Whether I shall be able to rightly use the rough notes of these and insert them in the fittest places I cannot yet tell. He altered chapter by chapter as he sent it to the Printers. I fear—I know it will never be as he would have had it but in fact I cannot write coherently. I only wanted to say that I do not need rest. Rest is very terrible to me.
. . .
   Is there not some small book to be had containing instructions how to correct for the press? What little I ever needed in that way my dear Husband did for me. Also I do not know the printer's address. I have had kindest offers of assistance from Mr. Linton and the Mr. Rossettis. In the "Selections" I shall stand greatly in need of this help.
                                                          I am Dear Sir
                                                          Yours very truly
                                                          Anne Gilchrist

It was a kind thought to send me the little book. But no "rays of comfort" penetrate the black darkness that envelopes me. My two eldest children are better. The two youngest I trust well in the country.[22]

Three months later, in a letter to Macmillan on 20 March, Anne reported that she had sorted and arranged all of Alex's material relevant to the *Life of Blake*, and, this done, it seemed to her that the book could be finished sooner than expected. She assured the publisher that once the move to Shottermill had been made, "You shall not find me dilatory or unreliable; least of all in this sacred trust, and toward yourself, who have shown me a generous kindness, consideration, forbearance which I have recognized with deep though silent gratitude."[23]

Anne was as good and even better than her word. In spite of the difficulties of moving out of one house and into another, caring for her children, and making the adjustments necessary to living in new surroundings, for nearly two years she devoted all the time and energy that she could command to the *Life of Blake*. Like Alex, she was a perfectionist. No detail was too trivial for her to go to any length to make certain that it was presented correctly. She copied great quantities of material that had been lent to Alex and had to be returned to insistent owners; in hasty trips from Shottermill, she spent days in the British Museum checking and rechecking information there; she followed leads about new material, most of which turned out to be "mares' nests"; she rejected forgeries that dishonest dealers sought to press on her; she diplomatically rejected the offer of the painter John Linnell, who had known Blake, to "edit" the proofs, suspecting rightly that his motive was to delete anything derogatory to himself;[24] she compiled the index and wrote a brief preface; she dealt firmly with careless and foot-dragging printers; and she wrote letters, letters, letters, letters. She became, by necessity, an authority on Blake herself.[25] And, perhaps inheriting the talent from her "webster" forbears, she became an excellent businesswoman.[26]

In the completion of the *Life of Blake*, Anne had the assistance of some distinguished helpers. William Michael Rossetti, with whom she worked closely—exchanging many letters and meeting to confer both in London and Shottermill—compiled the Annotated Catalogue of Blake's Paintings, Drawings, and Engravings. "Well might your Brother call it 'a herculean labour'!" she wrote to him on 29 January, 1863, when she received the completed version. "Even I, who have seen it in previous states of growth and order, am astounded. How would my husband rejoice in so exhaustive and harmonious a complement to the biography." Gabriel Rossetti edited the selections from Blake's poetry, with an introductory note to each section, and rewrote the final chapter, the only chapter that Alex had left in an unfinished state. In response to Anne's letter of thanks, Gabriel wrote: "I, on my side, hardly know how to thank you for so many kind expressions about the little I could do for the book, or rather the arrangement of it. However, such as it is, I would have done it gladly for Blake's or gladly for your husband's or gladly for your sake."[27] Kindly Samuel Palmer gave advice and contributed a memorial note on Frances Oliver Finch, one of Blake's young disciples.

Anne's most loyal and continuously supportive helper was William Haines, whom she described to Macmillan as "my dear Husband's oldest & most valued friend, [who] is with me, who is both able and willing to render me all the assistance I could need or desire.[28] Haines had been almost a brother to Alex, and he continued to be like a brother to Anne.[29] He had purchased Alex's collection of books—"a more extensive collection than you would suppose—one middle-sized room entirely filled from floor to ceiling."[30]—which would otherwise have had to be sold at auction. Haines, who had copied the entire contents of at least one Blake manuscript for Alex, helped with proofreading, delivered corrected copy to the printer in London, and shared tedious copying chores. "After much letter writing, I got Mr. Monckton Milnes to lend me down at Shottermill, his magnificent copies of some of these [Blake's mystic writings]," Anne wrote to Mrs. Burnie, "but they were to be fetched and returned by hand, and only to be lent for a week; so, as they are far too difficult to understand or to give any intelligible account of in a hurry, William Haines and I copied them all out."[31]

A warm bond of friendship seems to have developed between Anne and Alexander Macmillan with whom she carried on a steady correspondence between meetings in his London office and at Brookbank. Several of her letters to him are signed "Annie" Gilchrist—a diminutive that she used only with those with whom she felt on very intimate terms.[32] Nevertheless, they had their differences. The publisher, with an eye on expenses, suggested omissions and deletions; Anne vigorously protested any deviation from Alex's intent, backing up her pleas with valid arguments. In an apparently heated exchange, since Anne felt that "the tone of your letter is somewhat unwarranted," Macmillan had criticized Alex's style in one section as being "Carlylese," and Anne snapped back that "nothing had more vexed my Husband than to be accused of imitating Carlyle's manner." She added that where she and Haines, "the only friend my Husband ever took into his confidence in literary matters and on whose judgment in the higher parts and refined taste & acuteness in minor ones he placed entire confidence," had found superficial stylistic flaws that had escaped Alex, due to spectacles "from which he suffered especially in the correction of proofs,"[33] they had made judicious changes. The principal bone of contention between them, as it had been between Alex and the publisher, was Macmillan's adamant stand that the *Life of Blake* should be "family reading." "I was afraid to adopt entirely that most vigorous and admirable little bit apropos of the 'Daughters of Albion,' " Anne wrote to William Rossetti. "But it was of no use to put in what I was perfectly certain Macmillan (who reads all the Proofs) would take out again. . . . Mr. Macmillan is far more inexorable against any shade of heterodoxy in morals than in religion . . . in fact, poor 'flustered propriety' [has] to be most tenderly and indulgently dealt with."[34] When it was necessary to surrender to Macmillan's squeamish sensibilities, she did so graciously. "I have erased the four lines according to your request," she wrote to him on 29 August, 1862. "I know that my dear Husband considered it fully due to you that the pecuniary interests of the book should not be sacrificed or injured by any selections or extracts."[35] But once she could not resist a gentle attempt to mellow his point of view. On 1 December, 1862, she wrote: "I believe that much that is calculated to shock devout minds might be shown to be the unfamiliar side of old truths which have the knack like the moon of turning always the same face towards us so that only very soaring, daring adventurers get a peep round behind and the tidings they bring back are sometimes calculated to scare the uninitiated."[36]

Although the *Life of Blake* was finished in the summer of 1863, Macmillian waited until October to release two thousand copies of the handsome, lavishly illustrated, two-volume book. "It is but *very little* I have done after all," Anne had written to the publisher. "But what would have cost my dear husband weeks has taken me months. If only I have succeeded in doing it as he would approve! I feel no doubt but that the Book will succeed for I know it is a very remarkable one."[37] Her judgment proved to be correct. Letters of congratulation poured in. "I have been upon the book these three evenings, with all the leisure I could amass for it," Carlyle wrote, "and find everywhere that it is right well done—minute knowledge well arranged, lively utterance, brevity, cheerful lucidity. . . . Your own little Preface is all that is proper;— could but the Queen of these realms have been as *Queen*-like in her widowhood!" Samuel Palmer proclaimed it "the richest Book of all illustrated ones that I have ever seen. It is not a pearl thrown to the swinish many, but a tiara of jewels."[38] Although the critics could not resist some minor nit-picking, and although they were clearly impressed by the editorial participation of the Rossettis, their response was also overwhelmingly favorable. In a seventeen-page article on the *Life of Blake* one reviewer wrote:

> The readers of the two volumes which contain the Life of William Blake, selections from his writings, and illustrations of his art, have reason to thank the biographer and his editors, the brothers Rossetti, for the faithfulness with which they have collected and arranged such material as exists for representing a man who had long waited, and must still perhaps long wait, for due recognition by the world. . . .
> This account has been drawn up after a painstaking examination of all the sources of information: it is thorough as respects the external features of Blake's life, and does not offend by the officious analytic exhibition of that which lay behind; while the biographer has furnished to the critical reader most excellent material for discovering the more remote current of the artist's life. We can easily forgive certain affectations of style, bungling English, and what we think an occasional ill-mannered air for the affectionate interest which the biographer feels in his subject, and for the confident belief in Blake's genius and sanity which makes him willing to tell all that he can learn about the man: a more timid biographer might have hesitated about making so open an exhibition of his hero's singularities.[39]

The years that followed the completion of the *Life of Blake* were difficult for Anne. Without the pressures of the monumental task that had occupied her since Alex's death and without the stimulation of almost daily communication with those who were working with her, suddenly life seemed bleak, foreshortened, circumscribed. "That beloved task (the Blake) kept my head above water in the deep sea of affliction and now that it is ended I sometimes feel like to sink—to sink, that is, into pining discontent—and a relaxing of the hold upon all high aims," Anne wrote in a letter from Brookbank on 12 November, 1863. "I find it so *hard* to get on at anything beyond the inevitable daily routine."[40] But, in spite of despondency and the treacherous quicksand of household drudgery, she fought the temptation to give up her old ambitions and made a brave attempt to resume her writing. "It seems odd and unreasonable perhaps to you that in the teeth of all my difficulties and limitations within and without, of time and opportunity and ability, I should still persevere in trying to write," Anne wrote to Haines from Colne on 24 July, 1864, "but I feel that I must do it, for this reason: that else I should slowly gravitate downwards into entire absorption in busy, bustling, contriving working-day material life—weakly and basely giving up all attempts to fulfill dear Alec's hopes of me. For after all, when youth and growing time are left behind and *ripening* time comes—if there be anything to ripen—reading is not enough. Prose reading becomes either oppressive or useless unless the mind rouses itself to take a more active part than that of being a bucket pumped into."[41]

In her determination not to become merely an intellectual bucket for the ideas of others, in the period after Alex's death Anne managed to write two articles, which were published in *Macmillan's Magazine*. One was her long and scholarly "The Indestructibility of Force," published in August 1862 and, because of its length and depth of research, undoubtedly written for the most part before scarlet fever struck the Gilchrist family. Herbert proudly mentions this in his biography, although he gives 1865 as the date of publication.[42] The second article, which appeared in October 1865, he does not mention at all. One wonders why. He could hardly have been unaware that his mother had written it. Is it possible that Herbert—who in many ways was an ultraconventional Victorian—found the subject matter embarrassing? "A Neglected Art," totally different from Anne's scientific essays and from the cozy semifiction of "Lost in the Wood," is about cooking—and recommends, in terms bound to offend the fashionable world, that ladies should learn to do their own.[43]

In a letter written on 24 March, 1859, which begins "Hearken, oh, incredulous lady," Walter White, Alex's old friend and walking companion, gave Anne some literary advice that he said "ought to be as good to you as a cheque for ten guineas." It was not as blunt as Southey's advice to Charlotte Brontë that literature could not be a serious undertaking for a woman, but it was in the same vein. White seems to have felt that scientific themes like "A Glance at the Vegetable Kingdom," Anne's only published work at the

time, were not appropriate for a woman. "Don't lose too much time pumping from too deep a spring," he wrote, affectionately but patronizingly, "but toss off your literary omelettes soufflées. For subjects you may take—
On the foolishness of Women as compared with that of Men
On the passive domination of Men
Breakfast Table Talk
Hospitality not necessarily an expensive Virtue."[44]
White would have approved of an article on cooking as eminently suitable subject matter for a woman. But Anne was no British Fanny Farmer. And "A Neglected Art" is no literary omelette soufflée.

In her scientific articles, Anne offers her own views only in the closing paragraphs, briefly and timidly in the early essays, more boldly and at greater length in "What is Electricity?" and "Force." In "A Neglected Art," for the first time, the voice of Anne Gilchrist—the strong, clear voice that would one day defend Whitman so eloquently in "Estimate"—is heard all the way. Heedless of social repercussions, she expresses her own observations, convictions, recommendations. And she fires some well-aimed shots. For although the art that she consideres neglected is cooking, "A Neglected Art" is not a culinary treatise laced with recipes. Far from it. It is trenchant social commentray. It reveals to the public for the first time the salient characteristics of the author herself—her intelligence, her energy, her independence, her willingness to sweep tradition into the dustbin with the vigorously applied broom of common sense. It reveals, obliquely but still clearly, her estimate of the majority of English women of her own class. But, most important of all, "A Neglected Art" is a statement of Anne Gilchrist's position in the campaign for equal rights for women. That the equality of women should eventually be achieved is her passionate hope. However, equality of rights should mean equality of responsibility as well. Equality, she believes, should not be one more gratuitous offering to those who, in her opinion, are already overpampered; it is something that must be earned.

As a starter, Anne suggests that if young women want young husbands, rather than doddering old men who can afford to support them in what genteel convention considers appropriate style, they would do well to learn firsthand how to manage a household efficiently. They would do well—and this is what Herbert must have found embarrassing—to descend into their own kitchens, roll up their sleeves, and find out for themselves what skillful cooking and prudent purchasing of food are all about. For, she points out, a young husband, in his struggle to keep a family going in the manner that is expected of him, often breaks down in health and solvency and becomes an object of mingled pity and scorn to his affluent bachelor friends. However, his ascent up a very "steep hill" need not be so arduous, Anne contends, and would not be if his wife would forget social customs and taboos and share his burden more actively.

With admirable fairness, she compares the gentlewoman of the past with her present-day counterpart:

> Speaking generally, our excellent but illiterate grandmothers (all but a very small professedly intellectual and literary class, or rather clique) absorbed their whole time and thoughts in domestic affairs. Great in the culinary art, achieving miracles of patient labour with the needle, lynx-eyed in supervision of her servants, the lady of the old school thoroughly understood and thoroughly carried out the business of providing for the material wants of her husband. . . . [But] certainly her want of education and of its resultant widening of sympathies and interests must have made her, when the vivacity and charm of youth and beauty were gone, but a tedious companion of his leisure hours. . . . The woman of the present day seeks a larger life, and would fain be not only the best of wives but also the dearest of friends to her husband. She cannot return to mental stagnation. Having lifted up her head and opened her eyes upon a wider, fairer horizon, she can never again be content to keep them bent down and fixed exclusively upon the narrow field of domestic economies.[45]

But in spite of the present-day woman's widened vision and higher goals, there are certain inexorable facts, Anne cautions, that make it impossible for "human creatures to shape our lives wholly according to our own theory of what is best and most beautiful."

One of these inexorable facts, Anne continues, is that only "an insignificant fraction of mankind is born with a golden, or even a silver, spoon in its mouth"—the great remainder must "fulfil with toil and struggle" the task of bread earning. And then she speaks directly to the women of her generation—supposedly "enlightened" but still imprisoned in their role as symbols of their husbands' financial success in the same way that they were imprisoned in their constrictive clothing, still imprisoned by the insidious concept of "fine-ladyism":

> Hence it is but right and fair that those who are the sharers of these earnings should, whatever else they have to achieve in fulfilment of the higher demands of their nature, at least not fail to master the art of how to make the best and the most of these toil-won earnings. This, surely, is bare justice; and it is mainly because women have quite lost the secret of this indispensable art that we witness, at the present day, the singular and unhappy phenomenon of a sort of snarling antagonism between those who were created for mutual help and comfort, the one sex tacitly saying, "A wife is too costly an incumbrance; I can get on better without her:" the other, bridling up in pardonable pride and resentment, and rejoicing, "Marriage is not the sole, or necessarily the highest lot for a woman; we have faculties like yours, and can provide for ourselves, and live a life worth living alone, if you do not unjustly shut us out from the business of the world." True it is, this independence on the one side, this resentment on the other, quickly vanish under the beams of Love. But then, too often, the sequel is such as almost justifies the croakers and sneerers, and the pair have to wade for long years through the mire of pecuniary difficulties. Yet a little sense, a little effort on the wife's part would triumphantly refute the

prophets of evil, and enable her husband to reap the just fruits of his labours in a tranquil, well-ordered home.

But this is just the point at issue. Can sense and effort accomplish this important end? I suppose none in their senses would advocate or imagine possible a return to that engrossment in household duties which preceded the present complacent and entire ignoring of them. We might as well be asked to return to the habits and costume of the ancient British women at once. But whether, education having got us into the difficulty, it might not get us out of it again; whether, with the advantage of being able to see round and over these duties, we might not, instead of altogether overlooking, deal with them in a lighter and more masterly way, subordinating them within due limits; whether, finally, helplessness is inseparable from refinement, bodily indolence from mental culture;—these are questions which to answer truly and convincingly would be a thing worth doing.[46]

Taking for granted the upstairs-downstairs domestic social structure of Victorian England, Anne notes that in any occupation the basis of success is that the employer should have accurate knowledge of the work to be done, what it consists of, how it should be done, and how long it should take. And she warns that "the mistress of a household who neither understands what a servant's duties are, . . . still less how and when they may be best fulfilled, will certainly not get them fulfilled in the best manner, or by the smallest number of hands, and hence will manage, or rather mismanage, her income in a wasteful, ineffectual manner."[47] According to the prevailing system, the entire control of domestic expenditure—even the number of servants to be kept—is in the hands of servants who are too often neither capable nor conscientious. This situation has come to pass, Anne believes, because "the word Mistress no longer means one who governs, but merely one who pays"; because "we have invented the theory that our horse goes best with the reins upon his neck." By what dexterous feat might the reins be snatched again? She replies that of the only two ways of governing—by superior knowledge or by superior strength—happily only the former is possible for women. And how is this superior knowledge that is needed to regain control to be attained? "Not," Anne says emphatically, "by sitting with folded hands meditating about it."[48]

The most important part of domestic management for a mistress to acquaint herself with is cooking, for it is there that the worst and most uncontrollable leakage in expenditure takes place. Anne understands both sides in this problem. On the one hand, good cookery is so essential, and yet so little understood generally, that a cook who is only moderately competent must be paid whatever price she demands—not only in wages, but in self-indulgence, petty thievery, and dishonest understandings with tradesmen. On the other, it is unfair to blame servants for moral shortcomings under circumstances of such temptation, since most have been brought up "in the lap of grim Poverty"—and "the first requisite for learning to manage money well is that one should have some to manage." However, in spite of her compassionate understanding of the "genus Cook," Anne believes that good cooking is truly an art and, as such, should not be entrusted entirely to the uneducated female mind. It is an art, she notes pointedly, that is "far more difficult to achieve than bad pianoforte playing, or even than school-girl drawing, or the most elaborate embroidery."[49]

Anne feels a storm of indignation gathering in the breasts of her "fair readers" who have read thus far. " 'What! to cook our own dinners!' " she hears them say. " 'To spend half our time in the kitchen getting red faces, coarse hands and sour tempers? To run about after our servants like an old-fashioned farmer's wife; and all to screw down expenditure a hundred or two a year? Existence itself, much less marriage, were it with an archangel, is not worth having on such terms' "[50] Anne agrees that it would not be. But, from experience, she can attest that the price to be paid for a practical insight into cooking is not heavy, and neither time nor complexion need be sacrificed. For it is the preparation of food for cooking that chiefly demands skill and clever management, not the tedious standing over the fire. The best rule is to teach a servant of even ordinary capacity to do the latter satisfactorily, while her mistress performs the lighter, though more difficult, preliminary task—a task, Anne assures her readers, that is not extraordinarily fatiguing. "Happily, too," the list-run-on-calico alumna of the Misses Cahusacs' school adds, "it is the very reverse of needlework in this important respect: that, whereas the needle consumes an enormous amount of time in proportion to the result and demands as good as no brains, these culinary achievements, on the other hand, take only a moderate portion of time, but *do* require head."[51]

Dethroning a reigning cook may not be easy, Anne warns. If, instead of a ceremonial visit for a few minutes at a stated hour, a young mistress "should make her appearance for the first time in the kitchen, prepared for business in real earnest (with white apron and tucked-up sleeves—not by any means an unbecoming costume, by the way), [she] would be greeted by her cook, as soon as indignation and astonishment subsided to the point of recovering voice, with the request to 'suit herself by that day month.' "[52] But the abdication would be no permanent loss. What must be done is to take in hand raw material—a young girl who has little to *un*learn. Working together, mistress and servant girl, after a few failures and arduous experiences, can eventually achieve success. For, says Anne, obviously speaking from firsthand knowledge, "there is no better apprenticeship for an inexperienced mistress, than that of having a thoroughly incompetent servant."[53]

Economy will not be the only benefit of this arrangement. Providing a husband with a well-cooked and appetizing dinner when he returns home exhausted from his day's work will not only make him a happy man, but can add years to his life. And, in addition, "it is no small satisfaction to be able, if hospitably inclined, to insure your friends a dinner which, if modest in its pretensions, is thoroughly excellent; not a specious display, such as a second or third rate 'professed' cook, or the neighbouring confectioner, would set before them; everything looking like what it isn't and tasting of nothing in particular."⁵⁴

And Anne lists another benefit of a mistress-servant working partnership in the kitchen. In Victorian England, with its rigid class distinctions, this benefit may have been no more appealing to many readers of "A Neglected Art" than the suggestion that they take an active part in the cooking of their own dinners.

> It is not without its compensations as well as its drawbacks, this having to train young servants. . . . For the specific set of circumstances which form the servant class into what it is, which give to it its distinctive and most unadmirable peculiarities, are—to our shame be it spoken, who have had the chief shaping of these circumstances—unwholesome and deteriorating. Servants are what their employers have made them. We take them from dense ignorance and poverty to place them in the midst of comparative luxury, without guidance and control, asking, in return for high pay and unlimited means of self-indulgence, to be spared all trouble ourselves, all consciousness of the life below stairs, save so far as it ministers to our comfort. . . . We do but reap the natural and inevitable fruit when we find ourselves groaning under the tyranny of a race who dwell in our homes like a hostile tribe. . . . But once let a mistress enter actively within their sphere; let there be, so to speak, a human relation established between them, and she will find it quite possible, by the sole magic of her influence and example, to subdue the hostile into a faithful, loyal, serviceable race. . . . You may be a sublime instance of perfection in the drawing-room, and they [your servants] not so much as discover the fact, far less be operated upon by it, if you are always over their heads, morally and intellectually as well as physically.⁵⁵

These lines are among the most significant in the essay. Here Anne is expressing not only her impatience with the majority of women of her own class, but protesting the inequities of the English socioeconomic system and the chasms of misunderstanding and antagonism between classes that it creates. This is the first indication in print of Anne Gilchrist's sympathy with socialism—her sympathy, that is, with a modified form of socialism, for she is too Victorian, too English, too practical to suggest so radical a solution as abolishing class distinctions altogether.⁵⁶ But she does believe that by working together, rather than in isolated spheres, mutual respect, understanding, and even affection between classes can be achieved. And this belief must have been responsible, to at least some degree, for her wholehearted response to the poet who, in the majestically rolling lines of his great catalogues, extols the joy, the beauty, the dignity of every kind of labor.

The question Anne urges on her readers is: What would be the cost for a woman to take the management of her kitchen into her own hands? At the cost of nothing at all, Anne answers; and in doing so paints a revealing picture of herself—her selfdefined and tested values, her zest for living, her true gentility:

> Not of her habits and claims as a gentlewoman; for these must be of a superficial, weakly kind indeed, if an hour or two daily of practical usefulness can prove detrimental to them. . . . Not of her intellectual tastes and accomplishments; for a better prelude to exercising these with vigour and enjoyment could not be conceived than the bodily activity and the development of common sense involved in an efficient discharge of domestic duties. . . . As to the time consumed, it will in the end be found a gain rather than a loss. For one hour with zest is worth half-a-dozen burthened with the consciousness of an affluence of leisure. Those who are not compelled to *make* time for their favorite pursuits, end by using them to *kill* time. . . . To a woman who has no special pursuits or mental activities, here is at least one occupation which will redeem her life from the charge of entire triviality and uselessness.[57]

Anne ends "A Neglected Art" on a note of admonition. If women wish to have equal status with men, they must begin by learning to manage with expertise the one area that is already indisputably theirs. In short, they must get off their genteel derrières and prove their right to equality, rather than merely clamoring for it.

> *"He who would be more than others must do more."* There is the whole secret of success. Fortune cannot baffle ambition that has so sound a foothold. And in these days, when there is much eagerness to obtain as wide a scope as possible for the energies and talents of women, there certainly could not be a better starting-point than to begin by carrying a masculine efficiency and thoroughness into the regulation of this their special and inalienable domain.[58]

After *Macmillan's Magazine* accepted "A Neglected Art," Anne wrote to her sister-in-law from Brookbank on 21 January, 1865: "Masson[59] has accepted the article I wrote last spring. And that will be the last thing I shall attempt for many a long day, as I have fully made up my mind to give myself up wholly to educating the children: I find it such a harassing strain to attempt *two* things—bad for me—because to be hard at work from the time you step out of bed in the morning till you step into it at night is not good for any one—it leaves no time either for general culture—for drinking at the refreshing fountain of standard literature and of music. Bad for the children because it made me grudge them my time of an evening, when so much indirect good may be done to them by reading aloud and showing them prints. And after all they will not always be children; and if I have it in me to do anything worth doing with my pen, why, I can do it ten years hence, if I live—when I shall have completed my task so far as direct instruction of the children goes—I shall only be forty-six, then—not in my dotage. Do you think I am right?"[60] When she read Whitman's lines from "A Song of Joys" a few years later, they must have seemed to Anne a mirror image of herself during this period of her life:

O the mother's joys!
The watching, the endurance, the precious love, the anguish, the
    patiently yielded life.[61]

The following years, which Anne devoted entirely to her children, left happy memories for them. "In a marvelously happy way she made her children the companions of her simple studious days, young though we were, in our pretty cottage home among the Surrey hills. . . . Here [on the sloping lawn] she often read aloud to us, Blake's beautiful 'Songs of Innocence.' Much of our education being conducted in the open air," Grace writes in her unpublished memoir of her mother. At Saint Stephen's Church in Shottermill there is no record of Anne and her children being parishioners or attending services. "Our Sunday evenings (to many children in the sixties and seventies of the last century a period of unmitigated dreariness) were filled with beauty," Grace continues. "These she devoted to showing us Blake's designs to the 'Job,' or rare prints of Reynolds and Hogarth."[62] Under their mother's tutelage, the three oldest children developed the interests that would shape their lives. For Percy it was metallurgy. For Beatrice it was medicine. For Herbert it was art. Sturdy little Grace happily absorbed her mother's teaching, but she developed no strong, early inclinations. Walter White, a frequent visitor at Brookbank, also had poignant memories of Anne as a devoted young mother. On 8 April, 1887, in a letter written in a shaky hand to "Dear Herby," congratulating him on the publication of his mother's biography, he wrote: "Reading the name Wagoners' Wells [a site not far from Brookbank] reminded me of a Sunday when your mother sat there, the children were playing about, your mother spoke, I looked at her: a transfiguration ensued, and for half a minute she had the face of an angel."[63]

Much as she loved her children, and even though she willingly gave up her own interests to devote herself to them during their formative years, this period was hardly idyllic for Anne. Teaching, she told William Rossetti, was "real hard work and I spend five hours a day at it, and then the amount of industry that goes to making two hundred a year do the work of four or five is not small." There were times when, like all mothers of young children, she felt very much like a treed cat. Then she would escape for a little while and walk alone to Hind Head. "My prime rest, pleasure, society all in one—what keeps me going in a tolerably unflagging way,—are the glorious walks," she wrote to Rossetti. "Hind Head is as fresh to me as the day I first set eyes on it. And if I go out feeling ever so jaded, irritable, dispirited, when I find myself up there alone (for unless I have perfect stillness and quietness and my thoughts are free as a bird, the walk does not seem to do me a bit of good) care and fatigue are all shaken off and life seems as grand and sweet and noble a thing as the scene my bodily eyes rest on—and if sad thoughts come they have hope and sweetness so blended with them that I hardly know them to be sad—and I return to my little chicks quite bright and rested, and fully alive to the fact that they are the sweetest, loveliest chicks in the whole world—and Giddy says, 'Mamma has shut up her box of sighs.' "[64] One can picture Anne walking resolutely up the steep path, wearing sturdy shoes and a country skirt. Like Whitman she could say:

> I tramp a perpetual journey, (come listen all!)
> My signs are a rain-proof coat, good shoes, and a staff cut from the woods.[65]

Anne had frequent visitors at Brookbank. "Heartiness that made you at once feel at home was the prevailing characteristic of her hospitality, especially when illuminated by a crackling wood fire," Walter White reminisced to Herbert years later. "And she never seemed better pleased than when a visitor took her by surprise."[66] White and William Haines, who seems to have lived nearby, came often. Emma and Madox Brown came, with William Rossetti, for Saturday to Monday visits. Samuel Palmer occupied the spare room in "your sweet home on the 'L'Allegro' upland." And shortly after the publication of the *Life of Blake*, Rossetti brought his famous sister for a visit of several days. Anne was charmed with Christina. "There is a sweetness, an unaffected simplicity and gentleness, with all her gifts that is very winning," Anne wrote to Mrs. Burnie. "She was so kind to the children and so easy to please and make comfortable that though a stranger to me, she was not at all a formidable guest."[67] Anne and Christina became great friends, exchanging long newsy letters, books, and photographs, although meeting infrequently. Christina was fond of Anne's children. In her letters one catches glimpses of them as individuals. "Funny little Grace: I daresay various of your correspondents don't omit 'love' to her," Christina wrote in the summer of 1865. "Please present mine with all due gravity, and to Herbert, and to Beatrice." "Beatrice must be coming into bloom now, though rather like a lily than like a rose as I recollect her," she wrote in 1869. "But can Grace be as funny as she used to be?"[68]

When she was a schoolgirl, Carlyle was one of Anne's intellectual heroes. On 15 September, 1866, she met another. She was sitting under the yew tree on the lawn when her maidservant brought her a card—the card of "Mr. Alfred Tennyson." The Tennysons, who were looking for a summer home where the poet could work without interference from his admirers, wanted to see some property at the "Devil's Jumps," near Haslemere, that was for sale and had called on Anne, probably at the Carlyles' suggestion, to ask if she could give their driver directions. This was the beginning of an association that would be a stimulating diversion for Anne in her isolated existence with her children. The poet looked older than Anne had expected, but "every inch a king; features

Beatrice Gilchrist, ca. 1864, artist unknown. Private collection.

massive, eyes very grave and penetrating, hair long, still very dark and, though getting thin, falls in such a way as to give a peculiar beauty to the mystic head." Mrs. Tennyson she found to be a sweet and gentle woman with winning manners, but "painfully fragile and wan." Giddy, then seven, came into the room. Tennyson set her on his knee, stroked her sturdy legs, made Mrs. Tennyson feel them, and told Anne afterward, "I admire that little girl of yours. It isn't everyone that admires that kind of very solid development of flesh and blood." He asked Anne how many children she had, and when she told him four, he replied quickly, "Quite enough! Quite enough!"[69]

The property near the "Jumps" did not suit, but the Tennysons were impressed by the surrounding scenery and returned in a month to stay ten days—two days with Anne and a week in lodgings. This time they leased Greyshott Farm, a handsome country house with spacious grounds near Shottermill, for short stays during the following summer to test the effect of the climate while they continued to look for a permanent summer home.[70] Anne volunteered to see to the repairs and furnishing of the house, and all through the winter made the long walk back and forth to Greyshott, adding the anxiety involved in the undertaking to her own strenuous domestic routine. "I have put my hero worship into very practical shape this winter," she wrote to Haines in March 1867, "and done some real hard work for Tennyson."[71] The Tennysons took possession in May and were well pleased, although Mrs. Tennyson complained in her journal that "the cellar at Grayshott alas! proves rather a receptacle of drains than a cellar."[72]

Tennyson delighted in long walks in the countryside and Anne often shared them with him. They found one another congenial company.[73] As always, Anne found communication with a keen, creative, masculine mind exhilarating; and it must have been refreshing to the husband of a porcelainlike, perennial invalid to have a vivacious young woman, whose conversation was both sparkling and knowledgeable, walking briskly beside him. Once, after a luncheon party at Greyshott, while the rest of the guests drove home, the poet accompanied Anne part of the way to Brookbank and, as she put it, "talked gloriously." They discussed Spencer's *Nebular Hypothesis*, materialism, and the futility of argument about matters like immortality that are unprovable. On one occasion that she never forgot, Anne pointed out during one of their walks some springs bubbling up through sand. Tennyson was nearsighted, and, in order to see them, he lay down at the edge of the brook with his face almost touching the water.[74]

Herbert and Grace also had lifelong memories of the laureate. In his biography, Herbert writes: "We remember Tennyson staying at Brookbank, indeed can see him now (wearing a dark cloak, big hat in hand) as he shuffled across the long unequally shaped drawing-room, to stand before a glorious water colour by Blake of 'Elijah mounted in the Fiery Chariot.' . . . We recollect being impressed by the Poet's tall, gaunt figure, and felt vaguely conscious of the propriety in the fact of Tennyson's confronting such a poet's picture."[75] Grace remembers that Tennyson "would stroke my elder sister's long, thick yellow hair and say:—'Hearts, little maid, will lie in those golden locks one day.' And at another time . . . coming up to me, as I played on the lawn and sitting down beside me on the grass beneath the apple tree, he tried to make me talk, but I was somewhat shy and frightened at this tall, dark stranger, and he laughed and said:—'You are as grave as a mustard-pot.' "[76]

Eventually, in July 1867, the Tennysons bought thirty-six acres near the top of Blackdown that commanded a splendid view of Surrey, Sussex, Hampshire, and the South Downs. Anne and a neighbor, Mr. Simmons, were instrumental in getting it for them at a moderate price. "Tennyson was so pleased," Anne reported to William Haines, "[He showed] a sort of childlike glee that is beautiful; contrasting curiously enough with his saturnine moods."[77] On 23 April, 1868, in an elaborate ceremony that Anne attended, the foundation stone of Aldworth, the Tennysons' magnificent new house designed by James Thomas Knowles, was laid. Fragile Emily Tennyson, whom Ellen Terry remembered as "a slender-stalked tea rose," who supervised everything in the Tennyson household while lying on a crimson sofa in the drawing-room—and whom Carlyle observed seemed constantly "sick without a disorder"—was not well enough to attend the festivity.[78] But Anne seized a few minutes after the stone was laid and before post time to write her a full account of the day.[79]

There seems to have been some tension between Anne and Emily Sellwood Tennyson. In 1871, Anne, fearing that she had spoken depreciatingly of Emily to William Rossetti, would write him a contrite letter the following morning to correct that impression. In reply, he assured her that "I do not think you said viva voce anything beyond what still appears to be the fact—that she attaches to position and appearances a certain value beyond what you do."[80] In the frequent mention of Anne in her journal, Emily always expresses appreciation of Anne's many kindnesses—including a donkey and chair that Anne procured for her from Guildford so that the invalid could join her family in outings. However, in the entry for 9 November, 1866, after expressing her admiration for Anne—"One ought to be the better for knowing Mrs. Gilchrist & seeing her so beautifully contented under her great sorrow"—she adds: "I never before saw any one so really convinced apparently of the good of poverty."[81] Was Emily Tennyson, also the daughter of a solicitor, a little condescending to Anne because of her limited means? And was Anne, who made no secret of her need to make a small income go a long way, but who hardly thought of her circumstances as poverty, aware of it? And understandably both irritated and hurt?

During the family's annual summer visit to Colne, Brookbank was seldom unoccupied. As soon as the *Life of Blake* was finished, Anne offered it to the

Carlyles to use during her absence, but Jane declined since "Mr. Carlyle is getting on very peaceably with his work, suffering nothing from heat as yet— and it would be most imprudent, *while that is the case*, not to let well enough alone."[82] Isabella Ireland and her family were Anne's guests at Shottermill for two summers while the Gilchrists were away. Brookbank, covered with a profusion of white clematis and situated in quiet but spectacular surroundings, was an ideal summer retreat, and, when she needed to augment her income, Anne had no difficulty in renting it. In 1869, Gabriel Rossetti, whose health was rapidly deteriorating from drugs and alcohol, and whose doctor had prescribed a country life with no regular work for six months, asked to rent the cottage, but Anne had let it to someone else only a few hours before his letter arrived.[83] Her most famous tenants were, of course, George Eliot and George Henry Lewes, to whom she leased it for an extended period of time in 1871. George Eliot wrote part of *Middlemarch* there. The novelist, unaccustomed to country tempo and country ways, was something of a complainer. "The butcher does not bring the meat," she wrote to Anne, "everybody grudges selling new milk, eggs are scarce, and an expedition we made yesterday in search of fowls showed us nothing more hopeful than some chickens six weeks old which the good woman observed were sometimes 'eaten by the gentry with asparagus.' Those eccentric people, the gentry!" And Lewes added a note on Mrs. Garland, the cook: "Kind, attentive, honest, she is, but *on n'est pas aussi bête*!" On the whole, however, the couple were delighted with Brookbank: the wealth of books in Anne's library; her pictures—"If I ever steal anything in my life, I think it will be the two little Sir Joshuas over the drawing-room mantel-piece," George Eliot wrote; and the quiet that enabled them both to work hard and successfully.[84] Anne and the Lewes-Evans duo never met. When they left Brookbank, they urged her to attend their Sunday afternoons at The Priory whenever she might be in London, but she never accepted the invitation. The prospect of attending a crowded reception, at which sixty or more people might be present, appalled her. "Friendly intercourse in my own home," Herbert tells us, was what his mother most enjoyed.

The years at Brookbank followed one another in monotonous procession. The annual visit to Colne, where her mother was becoming more and more disabled, occasional visits from friends, occasional hasty trips to London, now and then a summer outing with her Shottermill neighbors,[85] and long walks were Anne's only diversions. In 1862, Percy, who had progressed beyond the limits of home education, was enrolled in the Felsted Grammar School, a boarding school for boys.[86] Anne was left with the three younger children, a rugged daily routine of household chores, staggering amounts of sewing for herself and the children, since employing a seamstress was costly—"I do not fail daily to bless the inventor of the sewing machine," she would write to William Rossetti in 1870[87]—and teaching the multiplication tables. She continued her independent studies as best she could—reading Herbert Spencer and Hugo, among others—and she made a valiant attempt to resume her writing. But the results were disheartening. "In such chance moments as I could snatch 'as from a conflagration' I have not failed to try and carry forward an inch or two my literary scheme," she wrote to Haines in 1867, "but have not much to show for it—the separate bricks have such a sorry aspect one's faith in anything of an architectural result sometimes fails."[88] As she stood on Hind Head in her solitary walks, she must have felt trapped in a stagnant backwater of existence. Still a young and vibrantly healthy woman, she was a nun within invisible but still cloistering walls.

And then a momentous event occurred. In June 1869, Madox Brown lent Anne *Poems of Walt Whitman*, a book of selections that William Rossetti had recently edited.[89] And her life was changed forever.

8
GODIVA

> Through me forbidden voices,
> Voices of sexes and lusts, voices veil'd and I remove the veil,
> Voices indecent by me clarified and transfigur'd.
>
> Walt Whitman

On 22 June, 1869, Anne Gilchrist wrote the first of a series of extraordinary letters to William Rossetti, letters that more than a century after they were written are still charged with excitement. "I was calling on Madox Brown a fortnight ago, and he put into my hands your edition of Walt Whitman's Poems," she wrote. "I shall not cease to thank him for that. Since I have had it, I can read no other book; it holds me entirely spell-bound, and I go through it again and again with deepening delight and wonder."[1]

Rossetti, whose purpose in editing selections from Whitman's poems was to gain support in England for the American poet beleaguered in his own land,[2] was delighted also and replied by return post:

> Your letter has given me keen pleasure this morning. That glorious man Whitman will one day be known as one of the greatest sons of Earth, a few steps below Shakspeare on the throne of immortality. What a tearing-away of the obscuring veil of use and wont from the visage of man and of life!
>
> I am doing myself the pleasure of at once ordering a copy of the Selection to you, which you will be so kind as to accept. Genuine—i.e. *enthusiastic*—appreciations are not so common, and must be cultivated when they appear. . . .
>
> Anybody who values Whitman as you do ought to read the whole of him. If I have the pleasure of seeing you before you leave for Colne, I will proffer you his book. My own complete copy is already lent out; but I have the unbound copy which Whitman himself sent over for possible English republication, with his own last corrections, also the separate original editions.

Rossetti's letter also included a warning: "The sort of thing that people object to in Whitman's writings is not so easily surmised until one sees them. It might be expressed thus—that he puts into print physical matters with the same bluntness and directness almost as that with which they present themselves to the eye and mind, or are half worded in the thought. From one point of view this is even blameless; but from another, the modern reader's point of view, it is quite intolerable."³

Undaunted, Anne immediately sent a note—on the same day, 23 June—eagerly accepting the offer. She wrote:

> This gift of yours I have not any words to tell you how priceless it will be to me. ... I am very sure you are right in your estimate of Walt Whitman. There is nothing in him that I shall ever let go my hold of. For me the reading of his poems is truly a new birth of the soul.
>
> I shall quite fearlessly accept your kind offer of a complete edition certain that great and divinely beautiful nature has not, could not infuse any poison into the wine he has poured out for us. As for what you specially allude to, who so well able to bear it—I will say, to judge wisely of it—as one who, having been a happy wife and mother, has learned to accept all things with tenderness, to feel a sacredness in all?

Then, with what sounds surprisingly like a touch of Victorian prudery—or was it a momentary reticence, the genteel tradition that was her background asserting itself in spite of her claim of being fearless?—she added cautiously: "Perhaps Walt Whitman has forgotten—or, through some theory in his head overridden—the truth that our instincts are beautiful facts of nature, as well as our bodies; and that we have a strong instinct of silence about some things."⁴

Anne received the copy of Rossetti's selections and Walt's own copy of the complete fourth edition of his work and took them with her to Earls Colne. In her unpublished memoir, Grace describes her mother reading Walt's book in "a little wooded summer house, the shelter perched on the banks of the slow running river Colne," which was "a favorite spot for this labour of love." Grace was only ten in the summer of 1869, but the scene left a lasting impression. "She read and absorbed it. She read and re-read and dreamed over the book, making notes with a broad blue pencil, as the water lapped against the base of the shelter, and the bell in the grey stone tower of the Norman Church on the hill chimed the hours. Only these and birds' notes broke the summer morning's silence."⁵ Grace's style in the memoir tends to be as overloaded with sentimental imagery as a Victorian valentine, and this recollection of her mother in the summerhouse, reading Walt's work in its entirety for the first time, may be slightly embellished— with birds and chimes and lapping water. But even so it must be a drawn-from-life picture of Anne in some of the most rapturous hours that she ever experienced. On 11 July, she wrote again to Rossetti. "Mrs. Gilchrist writes me another (3rd) incredibly enthusiastic letter about Whitman," he wrote in his diary on 13 July.⁶ Suddenly words, which only a short time before had seemed to Anne like bricks with such a sorry aspect that there seemed no hope of assembling them into any architectural result, were flowing swiftly and easily from her pen. Suddenly they were assembling themselves, almost without effort on her part, into lucid and inspired prose. For the first time in her life Anne Gilchrist was deeply, truly, joyously in love.

But how could that be, skeptical critics have asked again and again. How could a woman fall passionately in love—truly in love—with a man whom she knew only in words printed on paper? Few women could. But the fact remains that Anne Gilchrist did. And the scenario—as well as the logic behind it—is not hard to follow.

It begins, of course, with Rossetti's carefully culled selections. No poet has ever been on such intimate terms with his readers as Whitman. No poet has ever given them such specific directions for reading his work. His readers must meet him halfway, share the creative process, exert all their skills and powers. "The process of reading is not a half-sleep, but, in highest sense, an exercise, a gymnast's struggle," Walt wrote in *Democratic Vistas*, "The reader is to do something for himself, must be on the alert, must himself or herself construct indeed the poem."[7] If understanding does not come immediately, he urges his reader to persevere:

> Failing to fetch me at first keep encouraged,
> Missing me one place search another,
> I stop somewhere waiting for you.[8]

"Not the book needs so much to be the complete thing," Whitman wrote, "but the reader of the book does." [9] And in Anne Gilchrist Walt found such a reader. Like other early admirers of the poet—John Burroughs, William O'Connor, Swinburne, Edward Carpenter, Rossetti himself—she was willing, and qualified, to make the "gymnast's struggle." Since in his selections Rossetti had scrupulously included only "the whole poems, wherever a necessity arose of missing out so much as a word,"[10] this sampling of Whitman's work, fragmentary as it was, was authentic enough to introduce her to a style that was totally new, totally unfettered, and to a scope of content that was literally boundless.

Anne, a woman of science, had never been deeply interested in poetry. It was Blake the artist, rather than Blake the poet, who captured and held her admiration. One can imagine that she found traditional poetry, even Tennyson's and Christina Rossetti's, too confining and artificial, both in form and subject matter, for her freewheeling mind. But everywhere in Whitman's poetry she found—her excitement increasing with each new discovery—echoes of her own interests and convictions. In the bold, inventive, uninhibited style she recognized her own impatience with stale tradition; in the orchestral beauty of the flowing lines, her own love of music; in the rejection of orthodox religion, her own rebellion against it; and in the appreciation and knowledge of science in poem after poem, her own dedication to it. For her the reading of the poems "was truly a new birth of the soul." Most exhilarating of all was a new communion with a strong, creative, masculine mind, always the most powerful intellectual stimulus for Anne. As she wrote to Rossetti after first reading the selections, "There is nothing in him that I shall ever let go my hold of." Ardent though these words may seem, her response to Walt's poems at that time was primarily intellectual.

Then she read the complete edition and a whole new experience enveloped her—the experience, and the acknowledgment of it to herself, of a powerful physical attraction. Although Rossetti prided himself on printing the poems used in the selections without any omissions or changes, nevertheless he had fussed over the volume like a pursed-lipped English nanny in order to make the work acceptable to the British public—changing titles, altering Walt's arrangement of the poems, leaving words like *womb* and *prostitute* out of the 1855 preface. The result of this tinkering was, Rossetti's pious denials to the contrary, an expurgated version of the book,[11] with its author presented as "a properly dressed up Whitman invited to a proper afternoon tea," to quote Paul Ferlazzo.[12] Reading the complete edition, for the first time Anne encountered the real Walt Whitman—the poet with the magnificent physique wearing his shirt open at the throat, the poet exulting in every phase of life, the poet with the "hospitable vocabulary,"[13] the poet with the hands-on approach to his reader, the poet who like no poet since Ovid exuberantly and unabashedly sang the joy of sex. The emotional impact was almost more than she could bear. The "Calamus" poems, "Children of Adam," and parts of "Song of Myself" that Rossetti had omitted—with their rapturous sexuality, explicit sexual imagery, and subtle rhythms—were especially overpowering. "Strong as I am," she wrote to Rossetti, "I feel sometimes as if I had not bodily strength to read many of these poems."[14]

Anne frequently felt "obliged to lay the book down for a while." "There is such a weight of emotion," she explained to Rossetti, "such a tension of the heart that mine refuses to bear under it,—stands quite still."[15] Reading these poems, she had made a wonderful discovery. In Whitman's insistence that sex should be a glorious experience for both male and female, Anne had found confirmation at last of the instincts of her own healthy body and confirmation of the belief she had always held that something vital had been missing in her marriage to Alex. Experiencing the one-to-oneness, the intense intimacy that is the essence of Whitman's rapport with his reader—"Whoever you are, now I place my hand upon you, that you may be my poem, / I whisper with my lips close to your ear"[16]—Anne felt, perhaps for the first time without guilt, the impulse to reach out her hand and touch in turn. The measure of her sexual frustration during all of her adult life—the torment of instincts denied and dreams that compounded bewilderment—can be seen in her response to the whole of Walt's poetry. This time Anne Gilchrist responded to the Poet of the Body totally, honestly, logically—with her own body. And with a passionate love that she had never known before.

Anne was not the only woman who responded orgasmically to the eroticism of Whitman's poetry. In 1860, Susan Garnet Smith, a total stranger, had written a steamy letter to the poet. On the envelope Walt wrote in pencil: "? insane asylum." Years later, in 1889, he fished the letter out of the piles of papers that littered his room in the house on Mickle Street and asked Traubel to read it to him.

> Hartford, July 11th, 1860
> Know Walt Whitman that I am a woman! I am not beautiful, but I love you! I am thirty-two years old. I am one of the workers of the world. A friend carelessly lends me Leaves of Grass for a day. Stealing an hour from labor I take it out for a walk. I do not know *what* I carry in my arms pressed close to my side and bosom! I feel a strange new sympathy! a mysterious delicious thrill! . . .
> Know Walt Whitman that thou hast a child for me! A noble beautiful perfect manchild. I charge you my love not to give it to another woman. The world demands it! It is not for you and me, *is our child*, but for the world. My womb is clean and pure. It is ready for thy child my love. Angels guard the vestibule until thou comest to deposit our and the world's precious treasure. Then Oh! how tenderly, oh! how lovingly will I cherish and guard it, our child my love. Thine the pleasure my love. Mine the sweet burden and pain. Mine the sacrifice. Mine to have the stinging rebuke, the shame. I am willing. My motives are pure and holy. Our boy my love! do you not already love him? He must be begotten on a mountain top, in the open air. Not in *lust*, not in mere gratification of sensual passion, but in holy ennobling pure strong deep glorious passionate broad universal love. I charge you to prepare my love.
> I love you, I love you, come, come. Write.
> Susan Garnet Smith
> Hartford, Connecticut[17]

When the reading was over, Traubel said; "Why did you write '? insane asylum' there?" "Isn't it crazy?" Walt asked. "No: its Leaves of Grass," Traubel replied. Then, in one of his few recorded differences of opinion with the poet, he hotly defended Susan's letter on the grounds that Walt had asked for it.

> "It sounds like somebody who's taking you at your word. . . . You should have been the last man in the world to write 'insane' on that envelope. . . . You might as well write 'insane' across Children of Adam and the Song of Myself." He said: "Many people do." "Yes," I replied: "They do—but you don't. . . . I don't know who she was, good or bad, wise or foolish: her letter itself is extraordinary in what it offers, in what it imposes. . . . the Hartford woman honored herself and honored you."[18]

Who or what Susan was, although the mystery piques the imagination, is still unknown.[19] But there is a basic difference between her response to Whitman's poetry and Anne's. What Susan from Hartford seems to have had in mind was a melodramatic but brief encounter. Anne's response was love with many dimensions.

Skeptical critics, insisting that Anne was not really in love, have offered a variety of theories to prove their case. She was hallucinating. Of course she was. Isn't hallucinating, to at least some extent, a basic—and delightful—aspect of being in love? She was a victim of self-hypnosis. Of course she was. Isn't every lover under the enchantment of a self-administered spell? She was a little daft. Of course she was. Katherine Anthony, sympathetically labeling Anne's passion "A Normal Madness," points out that Freud describes the state of being in love as "remarkable psychologically, and the normal prototype of the psychoses."[20] She was in love with a myth that she had created. Of course she was. But don't we all mythologize the one with whom we are in love? And didn't everyone mythologize Whitman? His friends saw him as a god, as Christ, as the Good Gray Poet. His future biographers would make up legends about him. And no one so mythologized Whitman as Whitman himself. In the poems he is a loafer, a rough, a seer, a savant, the American bard, the tenderest lover, the chanter of Personality, the wound dresser, the vagabond poet, the poet of democracy, the caresser of life, and the great literatus of the modern, to name only a few of his changes of garment. To a composite of all of these, Anne added a myth of her own—the solitary singer searching for a perfect mate. And it was her instant and unshakable belief that she was the mate he was seeking.

Anne's belief was not illogical. She did not have Margaret Fuller's abrasive egotism; to paraphrase Margaret, she would never have said, "I now know all the people worth knowing in England, and I find no intellect comparable to my own."[21] On the other hand, like Whitman, Anne Gilchrist never underestimated herself. She was aware that in both intellectual achievement and potential she was far ahead of the majority of women of her time, who had only the most shallow of educations and were seldom given the opportunity to use the little they had learned. It would be false modesty to deny that few women had either the preparation or the capacity to read Whitman's poetry creatively, as she had, or to grasp the magnificence of the work as a whole and in its separate parts. Intellectually she knew that she could meet the poet more than halfway. Sexually she knew that she could meet the virility that his poetry celebrated more than halfway too. In the "fleshy" poems, so offensive to others, she had found assurance that the inhibitions, taboos, and medical misinformation that had smothered her natural feelings and instincts were absurdities, and, with a heady new sense of freedom, she knew that she could respond to the poet with her body as ecstatically as she had with her mind. In describing to Whitman, in her first letter to him, what happened to her when she read his books, she would write: "I never before dreamed what love meant: not what life meant. Never was alive before—no words but those of 'new birth' can hint the meaning of what then happened to me."[22] If one is inclined to play the game of ifs—an extensive game of ifs—Anne Gilchrist's belief that she was uniquely qualified to be Whitman's perfect mate may not have been too wide of the mark.

Anne's reception of Walt's poetry had astounded Rossetti. He would describe her to William O'Connor as "a lady of earlyish middle age, & more than common literary cultivation. She is a person of remarkably strong sense, firm perception, solidity of judgment, with a rather strong scientific turn. My impression is that hitherto she has cared very little for *poetry*. . . . If I had been asked how this lady would receive Whitman's poems, I should have replied—'She will glance into them, set them aside in her own mind as eccentric unavailable sort of work, & never touch the book again.' And see how utterly I should have been mistaken. The result fairly astonishes me."[23] As he read Anne's "incredibly enthusiastic" letters about Whitman, Rossetti found himself faced with a dilemma. These were no ordinary letters. Here, he immediately recognized, was brilliant, perceptive criticism of Walt's poetry based on total acceptance, with no reservations whatsoever. It was exactly the kind of criticism that, in 1869, was desperately needed by the poet upon whose work every unfavorable phrase and expletive in the vocabulary of criticism had been leveled. Anne's criticism, because it came from a woman, especially a woman of culture and refinement, was doubly valuable as a testimonial to poetry that was considered unfit for a woman to read. Publication in some form, Rossetti realized with growing excitement, would be a bonanza for the poet whom he sincerely admired. On the other hand, he felt equally strongly that he must protect a woman whom he regarded as almost a sister. He knew only too well that her open championship of poetry that had been labeled "an outrage upon decency, and not fit to be seen in any respectable house"[24]—that even he himself, in his introduction to *Poems of Walt Whitman*, had conceded was sometimes "gross" and "crude"—would be not only damaging to her reputation but embarrassing to her family. Knowing her as well as he did, Rossetti must have sensed that Anne's letters, written "in a truly fervent and exalted strain,"[25] were inspired by something more than literary enthusiasm and must have felt an additional need to protect her. His solution of the dilemma was a masterful piece of diplomacy.

There was a rapid-fire exchange of letters and crossing of letters. On 13 July, Rossetti wrote to Anne: "I wish you cd. find it practicable to print something about Whitman. The very words of your letters wd. be the best you or any one cd. find to express what claims to be said."[26] Anne answered by return post that it would rejoice her heart "to be able to write anything that should help to clear away the clouds of mis-apprehension that now hide

Walt Whitman from men's eyes."[27] On 19 July, Rossetti replied with a confession:

> As you favour the idea of turning your letters to some general use, I am emboldened to make a clean breast of it, & confess that, on receipt of your letter of 11 July, I thought it wd. be a sin not to give Whitman a chance of knowing what cd. not fail to be a real pleasure & internal triumph to him—the immense enthusiasm his book had succeeded in inspiring in a thoroughly cultivated Englishwoman. I therefore wrote out with my own hand the passages wh. I have (now) marked in red-ink brackets in your 3 enclosed letters, & sent the copy—not direct to Whitman, as I thought there mt. be some suspicion of intrusiveness in that, but to his prostrate admirer O'Connor, with authority (wh. no doubt amounts to the certainty of its ensuing) to show the transcript to Whitman. Of course I *did not give your name*, nor the *least hint* of it; I even said that I wd. not wish any questions to be asked of me on the subject—& added (in all sincerity) that, tho' I did not consult you before hand as to sending the extracts, not being very confident of your response I thought you wd. not resent my doing the thing under conditions wh. in no way involved yourself. However, I must apologize to you for using this freedom, & do so, & hope to be forgiven.

If any public use should be made of the extracts from Anne's letters, with the "communication to Mr. O'Connor a convenient starting-point for *American* publication," Rossetti added some earnest advice:

> In your place I wd. most certainly suppress my name. I *dislike* both deliberate suppression & mere anonymity: but there are cases where one has to consult one's own private comfort, & I most decidedly think this is one. I am sure it is brave enough in you to accept the book with such fervency, & to say so with such strength and conviction & feeling, & you are by no means called upon to be (wh. you wd. undoubtedly become) the object of much foolish & disgusting clamour.[28]

At first Anne objected to what seemed to her the cowardice of hiding behind anonymous publication. But Rossetti repeated his strong recommendation in a letter on 23 July:

> We have to remember that the Leaves of Grass is so anathematized a book in America (& the same is the case in England, so far as its fame extends) that the hero of 100,000 sick men ministered to during the war was summarily dismissed from his government clerkship previously: & it is too certain that a woman who mt. say—tho' with the conscience & tongue of an angel—that the book is a good one, wd. not be treated with *more* chivalry & rectitude than a man, but with less.
> I am sure you will not think that my cautious limitations in this matter arise from any *indifference* to what you might express on the entire subject. No literary matter that I cd. well name has given me deeper or more unmixed delight than your resplendent enthusiasm for Whitman consequent (originally) on the Selection I was concerned in—&, as I say expressly in that Selection, I long to see the complete book diffused & appreciated here. But I must & do make it a matter of conscience—as you so kindly consult with me on the point—not to represent as free from noble

peril any course of action wh. mt., to the best of my judgment, involve you at some time or other in great tho' unmerited anxiety & discomfort. Nor do I even think that the publishing *anonymously* in England wd. be a decisive safeguard, tho' it wd. make the thing less unfeasible: secrets do ooze out in an astonishing way.[29]

On 28 August, O'Connor, with unconcealed excitement, wrote to Rossetti from Washington apologizing for his delay—which had been due to his "engrossing occupation in official (Light-house) business"[30]—in answering Rossetti's letter with "its precious enclosure." Rossetti sent the letter, which "gratifies me extremely," to Anne with the comment that its phrasing "is rather magniloquent: but quite in harmony with what one finds in his pamphlet 'The Good Grey Poet'—& I regard it as entirely genuine, & by no means wanting in effective eloquence."[31] And eloquent it was:

         Washington
         28 August 1869

My dear Mr. Rossetti,— . . . your kind and welcome letter of July 13th, . . . with its precious enclosure, duly reached me, as also did your note of the 8th instant.

I will not ask the dear lady's name, since you prefer not to be questioned about it; but, if I knew it, I would treasure it in my heart of hearts. . . . I would not seem high-flown or extravagant in my avowals, but it is only the simplest truth to say that I read these extracts with the deepest emotion. . . . Doubtless, they affected me as they could not you. For I am a daily and intimate witness of the multiform varieties of insult and outrage showered upon our poet—all that can show the littleness and baseness, the indescribable stupidity and malignity, of human beings, from the petty affronts of titmen and mannikins on the pavement to the sweltered venom of Lowell in the dull Review. Living in the midst of all this, judge of my indignation and dejection; and judge then of the re-assurance, the comfort, and the exaltation, such words as your friend's must afford me. . . . I felt, after reading them, as one who, surrounded by a vast and crowded amphitheatre, tiers upon tiers of faces wrinkled with derision or puckered with hostility, sees, lonely amidst the multitude, a countenance radiant with the soul.

It would be idle to attempt to say what comes to me, in the brief space of a letter; but, among the many precious things in your friend's MS., I must treasure her perception of the organic character of *Leaves of Grass*—its mutuality of relations, sense and form corresponsive, like body and spirit, and her apprehension of its electrical and ample grandeur. . . . There are, besides, many sentences which have a divine eloquence. "Our instincts are beautiful facts of Nature, as well as our bodies." . . . "Who so well able to judge wisely of the book as one who, having been a happy wife and mother, has learned to accept with tenderness, to feel a sacredness in, all the facts of nature?" . . . These lines are themselves poems. . . . I confess to brooding upon them with as much amazement as thankfulness.

I could not see Mr. Whitman immediately, so sent the packet to him, and did not meet him till the succeeding day. He said little, but his tone and manner were of deep import. He read the extracts several times, and wished to keep them. I think he was profoundly moved, and for days afterwards it seemed to me that his Olympian front was surcharged with a tender pensiveness. One day he said, referring to the packet, that he "often felt that his book was mainly written for great wives and mothers, and its purport would be best apprehended by them." This is the most memorable or reportable thing I heard from him.

I gave him your messages, and he bade me return you his kindest remembrances.

Receive my cordial thanks for your letter and the ever-prized enclosure. You could not have given me a gift more beautiful. I am as one endowed with a branch of stars.[32]

"You see he starts no faint suggestion even of *publishing* what I sent him of yours," Rossetti noted in his letter to Anne that accompanied his enclosure of O'Connor's. "Still one can't be much mistaken as to what he wd. like to do in the matter—or at least to receive authority for doing."[33]

O'Connor's letter was clearly a green light. A month later Anne sent Rossetti the manuscript of the reworking of her letters about Whitman. Rossetti reread it, penciling in a few suggestions as she had requested, and offered to recopy it so that "your handwriting should not appear—for things do get traced out in a surprising way, if any clue is permitted."[34] On 18 October, he wrote in his diary: "Called on Mrs. Gilchrist. She authorizes me to send to America what she has written on W, to be published in such form as he O'C may approve, but without any public or private avowal of her name."[35] In his entry on 19 November, Rossetti noted that he had finished copying Anne's essay, composed a few prefatory words to it—which he had told her would be "a pride & delight to me to add"[36]— written a letter to O'Connor, and sent it all on to Anne for final approval.[37] On receiving the essay from Rossetti, O'Connor wrote: "Your letter of the 20th November, enclosing the precious manuscript, is to hand, and we are of course immensely gratified and thankful. The lady's contribution is simply superb, which is all that *can* be said, and we shall use every effort to have it fitly given to the world, and as soon as possible. . . . Unquestionably, it is the finest and fullest appreciation yet uttered."[38]

In spite of O'Connor's jubilant enthusiasm, it was several months before it seems to have dawned on Whitman that, as Gay Wilson Allen puts it, a prize had been dropped in his lap.[39] During the summer O'Connor had shown him the extracts from Anne's letters that Rossetti had sent in July. Whitman had been "profoundly moved." But then he apparently forgot about his unknown English admirer. It was not until early December, when he reread copies of the extracts made for him by O'Connor, that he wrote his gracious and often-quoted letter of thanks to Rossetti, and through him to "the lady."

Washington, December 9, 1869

Dear Mr. Rossetti,

Your letter of last summer to William O'Connor with the passages transcribed from a lady's correspondence have been shown me by him, and a copy lately furnished me, which I have just been re-reading. I am deeply touched by these sympathies & convictions coming from a woman, & from England, & am sure that if the lady

Walt Whitman, 1863. This is the photograph that Walt sent to William Rossetti in 1869 to give to Anne. Feinberg Collection, Library of Congress.

knew how much comfort it has been to me to get them, she would not only pardon you for transmitting them to Mr. O'Connor, but approve that action. I realize indeed of such an emphatic & smiling *Well done* from the heart & conscience of a true wife & mother, & one too whose sense of the poetic, as I glean from your letter, after flowing through the heart & conscience, also comes through & must satisfy Science, as much as the esthetic, that I had hitherto received no eulogium so magnificent.

I send by same mail with this, same address as this letter, two photographs, taken within a few months. One is intended for the lady (if I may be permitted to send it her)—and will you please accept the other with my respects & love? The picture is by some criticized very severely indeed, but I hope you will not dislike it, for I confess myself to a (perhaps capricious) fondness for it as my own portrait over some scores that have been made or taken at one time or another.

. . . If the pictures don't reach you, or if they get injured on the way, I will try again by express. I wish you to read or loan this letter to the lady—or, if she wishes it, give it to her to keep.

Walt Whitman[40]

On 24 December, Rossetti sent Anne Whitman's letter, which he knew would be "a great pleasure to you & no doubt you will choose (as he suggests at the end) to confiscate it. . . . The photograph is a really fine version of his face, but with a hat on, wh. somewhat reduces its value as portraiture. It is a big affair, wh. I must bring round to you personally."[41] The letter and photograph were thrilling Christmas gifts for Anne. When Rossetti answered Whitman's letter, he included Anne's thanks as well as his own: "I gave your letter, and the second copy of your portrait, to the lady you refer to, and need scarcely say how truly delighted she was. She asked me to say that you could not have devised for her a more welcome pleasure, and that she feels grateful to me for having sent to America the extracts from what she had written, since they have been a satisfaction to you."[42]

O'Connor submitted Anne's essay to the *Galaxy*, but the editors, W. C. and F. P. Church, returned it with the explanation that they doubted that it would be of interest to their readers. The actual reason for the rejection, Jerome Loving believes—and believes that O'Connor strongly suspected—was that the *Galaxy*, a journal that was lukewarm on the subject of women's rights, did not want to become involved in "the woman question" for fear of jeopardizing its circulation.[43] O'Connor submitted the essay a second time, this time to the *Radical*, a monthly published in Boston, where it was promptly accepted.

"A Woman's Estimate of Walt Whitman (From late letters by an English lady to W. M. Rossetti)" was published in the *Radical* in the spring of 1870.[44] It was the lead article in the May issue of the gray-paper-covered periodical, about the size and shape of today's *National Geographic*. The table of contents on the cover of this issue lists, in addition to "Estimate," an impressive roster of articles on serious subjects, such as "The Character and Powers of Judaism" by Mary N. Adams. In spite of its title, the tone of the periodical is dignified, conservative. On the back cover, Fields, Osgood & Co. advertises its new books: Bret Harte, *The Luck of Roaring Camp* (1 vol., $1.50); Lowell, *Among My Books* (1 vol., $2.00); Emerson, *Society and Solitude* (1 vol., $2.00); and the novels of George Eliot (complete in 2 vols., cloth, $3.50). The commercial advertisements, in addition to many for insurance companies, include one for the American Button-Hole, Over-Seaming, and Sewing Machine; one for the Landscape Lawn Mower, which its makers claim "a boy of fourteen can use with greatest ease: instead of being tiresome will afford him pleasant amusement"; and a notice that a dentist, who fills medium-sized cavities with gold for $2.00, is moving his office to 15 Beacon Street. One advertisement leaps from a page of this decorous publication. It is for the fifth edition of a "new and thrilling work" by Paschal B. Randolph, entitled *Love and its Hidden History: and the Master Passions* (two volumes in one, $2.50, postage 28 cents). Offered by Randolph & Co., 89 Court Street, its description reads:

> The statements contained in this book are indeed startling. Its exposure of simulated and morbid love and the monster crime of this age are withering, and will go far toward changing the current of the thought of the century upon matters affectional, social, and domestic, for a FIRM, VIGOROUS HEALTH pervades every page....
> ON THE GREAT SOCIAL QUESTION which is beginning to be appreciated as one of paramount importance, its position is sound and healthful, and if its advice is studied and obeyed, it will introduce happiness into thousands of unhappy households.[45]

Was straitlaced Boston privately reading a fifth edition of this "new and thrilling work" while it publicly held up its hands in horror at *Leaves of Grass*? It must have been at least secretly gratifying to Whitman that "Estimate," an "emphatic & smiling *Well done* from the heart & conscience of a true wife & mother," was published in Boston, the bastion of the prestigious Saturday Club, whose members—Longfellow, Lowell, Emerson, Whittier, Holmes & Company—included some of his most vituperative critics.

Anne Gilchrist was not the first woman to defend Whitman's poetry in print. Sara Payson Willis Eldridge Farrington Parton, whose pen name was Fanny Fern, reviewed *Leaves of Grass* in her column, "Peeps from Under a Parasol," in the *New York Ledger* on 10 May, 1856. "'Leaves of Grass' thou art unspeakably delicious," she wrote in her frothy style, and declared that the poems are not sensual because Whitman frankly reveals the whole naked body rather than individual parts exposed in a way to arouse prurience.[46] Acceptance of Whitman by an enormously popular female journalist—Gay Wilson Allen calls her "the highest paid purveyor of sentimental pap" of the time[47]—should have had a favourable effect on public opinion, but it did not. As Paul Ferlazzo points out, Fanny dodged the question of *why* Whitman wrote about the body, and, as a result, her review was shallow and unsatisfying. Whitman had reason to be less than enthusiastic about her effusive defense.

To begin with, he disliked admirers "of the gushing kind."[48] And in addition he held Fanny, not her husband, responsible for the highly publicized lawsuit that the Partons brought against him in 1857 because of a misunderstanding about the repayment of two hundred dollars that they had lent the poet. "One genuine woman is worth a dozen Fanny Ferns," Walt commented bitterly in the *Brooklyn Times* on 9 July, 1857.[49] Long after the affair was settled, supposedly to everyone's satisfaction, new variations of the story kept cropping up to persecute him; and there is little doubt about who, in Walt's opinion, kept fueling the fire. "Venom, jealousies, opacities: they played a big part," Walt told Traubel, "and if I may say it, women: a woman certainly—maybe women: they kept alive what I felt James Parton would have let die, left dead."[50] It has been suggested that rather than anger over an alleged unpaid debt, Fanny's was the wrath of a woman scorned.[51]

After the publication of the 1860 edition, more women came to Whitman's defense. In June 1860 Juliette Hayward Beach, a writer from Albion, New York where she and her husband published a newspaper, wrote to Henry Clapp, editor of the *New York Saturday Press*, protesting the publication under her name of an article that described Whitman as a sexual pillager of women, vaunting "his prowess as a stock-breeder might that of the pick of his herd," and advising the poet to kill himself, but by no usual means so that no one would have to bear the shame of "going to death as did Walt Whitman."[52] The piece had been written and initialed by her husband. The following week, in a "correction," the *Saturday Press* explained that a review of the new edition of *Leaves of Grass* had been requested from Mrs. Beach, and when a manuscript arrived it had been sent to the printers without careful inspection. Two weeks later Clapp published a warmly appreciative review of *Leaves*, undoubtedly Mrs. Beach's, but signed simply "A Woman"—probably to avoid further airing of a marital quarrel that Walt described as "quite a stew."[53] The article proclaimed Whitman the new "National Genius," predicted that his "bold and truthful pages will inevitably form the standard book of poems in the future of America," and ended, "God bless him. I know that through 'Leaves of Grass' Walt Whitman on earth is immortal as well as beyond it."[54] According to Ellen O'Connor, Juliette Beach was the "certain lady" for whom Walt wrote the tender and hauntingly beautiful "Out of the Rolling Ocean," the lady whose jealous husband forbade her further correspondence with the poet.[55] On 3 June 1860, the *New York Sunday Mercury* printed another laudatory reivew of *Leaves* written by a woman. This time the author was Adah Isaacs Menken, a poet and a flamboyant actress, famous for her exit in the melodrama *Mazeppa*, where she was lashed to the back of horse, wearing a G-string over pink tights. "The most perfectly developed woman in the world," known also as "the naked lady"—who lost a ten-pound wager with Gabriel Rossetti that she could seduce Swinburne—wrote in her review that Whitman, "centuries ahead of his contemporaries," was like Poe "swimming against the current," but would one day have "marble statues erected in his honor."[56]

Fanny, Juliette, Adah—colorful women, intelligent, independent. But sincere and brave as their defenses of Whitman were, Anne Gilchrist's differed from and went beyond theirs.[57] In addition to defending Whitman's work against the charges most commonly leveled against it—sensuality, indecency, the lack of "poetic" diction and form—"Estimate" is a thoughtful and penetrating consideration not only of what he wrote, but how and why. It explores and defines his philosophy and analyzes in depth the close relationship between Walt's poetry and science. And it contains an eloquent plea for new understanding of the physical nature and needs of women. In its structure, in the management of its varying tensions, in the sure touch that creates crescendo after crescendo without loss of control, in the logical progression of points that are made, and in its persuasive skill, Anne's essay is a flawless piece of expository writing. Thanks, no doubt, to her years of apprenticeship as Alex's amanuensis, she presents her defense as if she were pleading a case in court.

"Estimate" has been called "a love letter masquerading as criticism."[58] And it is a love letter—offered, rather than disguised, as a literary critique. That was what Anne intended it to be, and what she later, in her first letter to Whitman, acknowledged that it was. But even though its inspiration may have been amorous, the strong emotional undertone of the essay is the excitement of intellectual discovery—of a brilliant and receptive mind suddenly aware of an exhilarating new world of ideas and concepts and ways of expressing them—and "Estimate" is superb criticism. O'Connor was quite right when he recognized it as unquestionably "the finest and fullest appreciation yet uttered." In his splendid essay "Anne Gilchrist, Critic of Walt Whitman," Paul Ferlazzo agrees.

Ferlazzo points out that before 1870—in addition to the reviews by Fanny, Juliette, and Adah—there had been a number of appreciative American criticisms of *Leaves of Grass*. The first was Emerson's famous letter on 21 July, 1855. Another was a review in the *New York Tribune* on 23 July, probably written by Charles A. Dana, a good friend of Whitman, who did his best to comment favorably by using stock phrases like "bold, stirring thoughts" and "passages of effective description," but had to admit that he found his friend's language "too frequently reckless and indecent."[59] Edward Everett Hale, reviewing *Leaves* in the *North American Review* in 1856, praised its poetic quality and reflection of Whitman's love of life, but ended with the usual charge of indecency. O'Connor himself was, of course, Whitman's most outspoken supporter. In a long article in the *New York Times* in December 1866—printed under a stern notice by the editor that O'Connor's opinion of *Leaves of Grass* "in no way reflects the opinions of this establishment"— O'Connor pushed aside Walt's treatment of bodily matters and concentrated on the poem itself, noting that its size and structure correspond to those of its great subject, America; and explaining that Whitman's seemingly egotistical "I" represents not the poet himself but nineteenth-century American man. O'Connor's pamphlet *The Good Gray Poet: A Vindication*, an impassioned defense of Whitman after the poet was dismissed from the Indian Bureau of the Department of Interior on the charge that he was the author of an obscene book, was also published in 1866. In his *Vindication*, O'Connor defended Whitman's "frank mention of forbidden subjects" because these same subjects described with the "freest use of language, the plainest terms" can be found in the Bible, Shakespeare, Homer, Dante, and a long list of other illustrious sources.[60] However, Ferlazzo believes that this argument only reveals the limitation of O'Connor's understanding of the body in Whitman's poetry: "He is able to appreciate Whitman only insofar as Whitman is like other writers and fits into the tradition. O'Connor sees the flesh as an historically acceptable form for expressing ideas poetically, and fails to see that perhaps it is itself the subject of the poetry. He is able to vindicate Whitman but not to explain him"[61] In England, defenders of *Leaves of Grass* before 1870 followed the same pattern as their American counterparts; they found much to admire in the poetry, but the "indecency" distressed them. Like Rossetti, they felt that a laundered *Leaves of Grass* was improved. Anne's "Estimate," appearing in 1870, was, in Ferlazzo's opinion, "refreshing and original in comparison to what had been written before her about the poet." Unlike her predecessors, in "Estimate" Anne neither apologizes for nor shies away from any aspect of Whitman's poetry; she simply accepts, understands, and loves it. In Ferlazzo's view, "Mrs. Gilchrist stands as the first great critic of *Leaves of Grass*."[62]

In "Estimate" Anne's critical stance is never detached. From the very beginning she moves bodily into the poem, sharing its moods, participating in its events. She finds the vast expanses of space and time that the poem encompasses, the variety and number of scenes that flash by, its multitudes of people almost overpowering. "I had not dreamed that words could cease to be words, and become electric streams like these. . . . I am as one hurried through stormy seas, over high mountains, dazed with sunlight, stunned with a crowd and tumult of faces and voices, till I am breathless , bewildered, half-dead." The contrasting serenity of other passages also draws her into the poem with irresistible force. "Then come parts and whole poems in which there is such calm wisdom and strength of thought, such a cheerful breadth of sunshine, that the soul bathes in them renewed and strengthened. Living impulses flow out of these that make me exult in life, yet look longingly towards 'the superb vistas of Death.' "[63] As it is for all devotees of Whitman, even reluctant devotees like Pound, her sense of communion with the poet goes beyond imagination to the reality of experience.

Early in the essay, Anne makes a ringing pronunciamento about Whitman's genius: "I know that poetry must do one of two things,—either own this man as equal with her highest, completest manifestors, or stand aside, and admit that there is something come into the world nobler, diviner than herself, one that is free of the universe, and can tell its secrets as none before."[64] Then, using the barrister-at-law technique, with which Alex had defended Etty and Blake so eloquently, she proceeds to defend *Leaves*, point by point, against the charges that had been made against it.

She begins by answering those "who admire this poem and do not care for that, and talk of formlessness, absence of metre, and so forth," and who "are quite as far from any genuine recognition of Walt Whitman as his bitter detractors." She points out that, although of course all the pieces are not equal in power and beauty, "all are vital; they grew—they were not made." Whitman's poems are organic in nature, she explains, and this accounts for their intense and enduring vitality. She illustrates her point in a passage that may be the finest analysis of *Leaves of Grass* in capsule that has ever been written.

> We criticise a palace or a cathedral; but what is the good of criticising a forest? Are not the hitherto-accepted master pieces of literature akin rather to noble architecture; built up of material rendered precious by elaboration; planned with subtile art that makes beauty go hand in hand with rule and measure, and knows where the last stone will come, before the first is laid; the result stately, fixed, yet such as might, in every particular, have been different from what it is (therefore inviting criticism), contrasting proudly with the careless freedom of nature, opposing its own rigid adherence to symmetry to her wilful dallying with it? But not such is this book. Seeds brought by the winds from north, south, east, and west, lying long in the earth, not resting on it like the stately building, but hid in and assimilating it, shooting upwards to be nourished by the air and the sunshine and the rain which beat idly against that,—each bough and twig and leaf growing in strength and beauty in its own way, yet, with all this freedom of spontaneous growth, the result inevitable, unalterable (therefore setting criticism at naught), above all things vital,—that is, a source of ever-generating vitality: such are these poems.[65]

Anne, the music lover and accomplished pianist, has only sympathy for those who deplore the absence of the rocking-chair rhythms of traditional poetry. "And the music takes good care of itself too," she replies to the frequent charge of dissonance in Walt's lines:

> As if it *could* be otherwise! As if those 'large, melodious thoughts,' those emotions, now so stormy and wild, now of unfathomed tenderness and gentleness, could fail to vibrate through the words in strong, sweeping, long-sustained chords, with lovely melodies winding in and out fitfully amongst them! . . . I see that no counting of syllables will reveal the mechanism of the music; and that this rushing spontaneity could not stay to bind itself with the fetters of metre. But I know that the music is there, and that I would not for something change ears with those that cannot hear it.[66]

One great source of the vitalizing power in Whitman's poems, Anne points out, "is the grasp laid upon the present, the fearless and comprehensive dealing with reality." Anne, the woman of science, the rebel against dead tradition, the believer in the excitement of the present and the promise of the future, warms to her subject.

> Hitherto the leaders of thought have (except in science) been men with their faces resolutely turned backwards; men who have made of the past a tyrant that beggars and scorns the present, hardly seeing any greatness but what is shrouded away in the twilight, underground past . . . bidding me warm myself at fires that went out to mortal eyes centuries ago; insisting, in religion above all, that I must either "look through dead men's eyes," or shut my own in helpless darkness. Poets fancying themselves so happy over the chill and faded beauty of the past, but not making me happy at all,—rebellious always at being dragged down out of the free air and sunshine of today.
> But this poet, this "athlete, full of rich words, full of joy," takes you by the hand, and turns you with your face straight forwards. The present is great enough for him, because he is great enough for it. . . . Here is one come at last . . . whose songs are the breath of a glad, strong, beautiful life, nourished sufficingly, kindled to unsurpassed intensity and greatness by the gifts of the present.[67]

One feels that Alex would have applauded.

A curious paragraph follows, a paragraph that seems almost out of context. It is intensely personal. Here, for a brief moment, Anne seems to be stepping out of her role as a nameless critic and speaking directly to Walt, believing that he will understand this half-rueful, half-joyous confession.

> I used to think it was great to disregard happiness, to press on to a high goal, careless, disdainful of it. But now I see that there is nothing so great as to be capable of happiness; to pluck it out of "each moment and whatever happens;" to find that one can ride as gay and buoyant on the angry, menacing, tumultuous waves of life as on those that glide and glitter under a clear sky; that it is not defeat and wretchedness which come out of the storm of adversity, but strength and calmness.[68]

The "Calamus" poems Anne sees as teaching what it means to love one's fellow man. "These 'evangel-poems of comrades and of love' speak, with the abiding, penetrating power of prophecy, of a 'new and superb friendship,'" she explains, "speak not as beautiful dreams, unrealizable aspirations to be laid aside in sober moods, because they breathe out what now glows within the poet's own breast, and flows out in action toward the men around him." To illustrate this point, she cites Walt's loving service to the wounded during the war. "Had ever any land before her poet," she asks, "to go and with his own hands dress the wounds, with his powerful presence soothe and sustain and nourish her suffering soldiers,—by day and by night, for weeks, months, years?" And she quotes these lines from "Drum-Taps":

> I sit by the restless all the dark night, some are so young,
> Some suffer so much, I recall the experience sweet and sad,
> (Many a soldier's loving arms about this neck have cross'd and
>   rested,
> Many a soldier's kiss dwells on these bearded lips.)

Walt's kisses, Anne declares, "touched with the fire of a strange, new undying eloquence the lips that received them." "The most transcendent genius,' she continues, with unconcealed emotion, "could not, untaught by that 'experience sweet and sad,' have breathed out hymns for her dead soldiers of such ineffably tender, sorrowful, yet triumphant beauty."[69]

The present offers many things that we must deal with besides those in which it is easy to see greatness and beauty. "A poet would be unfaithful to his calling," Anne argues, "as interpreter of man to himself and of the scheme of things in relation to him, if he did not accept all—if he did not teach 'the great lesson of reception, neither preference nor denial.'" In a powerful passage, she defends Walt's fearless, and often denigrated, declaration of love for all levels and conditions of mankind.

> If he feared to stretch out the hand, not of condescending pity, but of fellowship, to the degraded, criminal, foolish, despised, knowing that they are only laggards in "the great procession winding along the roads of the universe," . . . how could he roll the stone of contempt off the heart as he does, and cut the strangling knot of the problem of inherited viciousness and degradation? And, if he were not bold and true to the utmost, and did not own in himself the threads of darkness mixed in with the threads of light, and own it with the same strength and directness that he tells of the light, and not in those vague generalities that everybody uses, and nobody means, . . . the *brotherhood* of the human race would be a mere flourish of rhetoric. And brotherhood is naught if it does not bring brother's love along with it. If the poet's heart were not "a measureless ocean of love" that seeks the lips and would quench the thirst of all, he were not the one we have waited for so long. . . . All occupations, however homely, all developments of the activities of man, need the poet's recognition, because every man needs the assurance that for him also the materials out of which to build up a great and satisfying life lie to hand, the sole magic in the use of them.[70]

Anne admits that she, like so many readers, had difficulty at first with Walt's long catalogues. "I murmured not a little, to say the truth, under these enumerations, at first. But now I think that not only is their purpose a justification, but that the musical ear and vividness of perception of the poet have enabled him to perform this task also with strength and grace, and that they are harmonious as well as necessary parts of the great whole."[71]

Anne does not even blink at the words that many of Walt's staunchest male admirers found distressing. She has no sympathy "with those who grumble at the unexpected words that turn up now and then." Here she is clearly speaking to Rossetti, chiding him gently but firmly for his fussy objections to some of Walt's not-fit-for-the-parlor words:

A quarrel with words is always, more or less, a quarrel with meanings; and here we are to be as genial and as wide as nature, and quarrel with nothing. If the thing a word stands for exists by divine appointment (and what does not so exist?), the word need never be ashamed of itself; the shorter and more direct, the better. It is a gain to make friends with it, and see it in good company. Here, at all events, "poetic diction" would not serve,—not pretty, soft, colourless words, laid by in lavender for the special uses of poetry, that have none of the wear and tear of daily life; but such as have stood most, as tell of human heart-beats, as fit closest to the sense, and have taken deep hues of association from the varied experiences of life— those are the words wanted here. . . . It is not mere delight they give us,—*that* the "sweet singers," with their subtly wrought gifts, their mellifluous speech, can give too in their degree; it is such life and health as enable us to pluck delights for ourselves out of every hour of the day, and taste the sunshine that ripened the corn in the crust we eat—I often seem to myself to do that.[72]

Anne vigorously defends Walt's self-appointed—and relentlessly criticized— status as poet of the body. Here the woman of science speaks. Novalis, she notes, said that we touch heaven when we lay our hand on the human body, "which, if it mean anything, must mean an ample justification of the poet who has dared to be the poet of the body as well as of the soul." But Novalis, she points out—"who gazed at the truth a long way off up in the air, in a safe, comfortable German fashion"—is respected by the highest authorities, while "the great American who has dared to rise up and wrestle with it, and bring it alive and full of power in the midst of us, has been greeted with a very different kind of reception." However, Anne is deeply persuaded—and here there are unmistakable echoes of Alex's impassioned defense of Etty's "nymphs with unbound zones"—that "a perfectly fearless, candid, ennobling treatment of the life of the body (so inextricably intertwined with, so potent in its influence on the life of the soul)" will be welcomed by those who are tired of the belief that it is the greatness of the spirit that has taught it to despise the body and its influences. She declares that the opposite is true; that the spirit does not have strength enough to infuse itself into the body and make it holy by its own intensity. Instead, "the spirit must lovingly embrace the body, as the roots of the tree embrace the ground, drawing thence rich nourishment, warmth, impulse."[73]

She supports Walt's philosophy of sex unflinchingly. A truthful recognition of what life comprises is needed, she insists, and especially of that which is the basis of humanity's most fundamental ties—"the love of husband and wife, fatherhood, motherhood." Religion, most of all, needs this recognition, Anne maintains, in order to learn "that the basis of all true worship is comprised in 'the great lesson of reception, neither preference nor denial,' interpreting, loving, rejoicing in all that is created, fearing and despising nothing." And she supports Whitman's philosophy of death. What religion, the dignity of men and women, and the intellect need, she believes is the ability to say with Walt, the celebrant of death as well as life, "I accept reality, and dare not question it." In addition to acceptance of physicality as a healthy and ennobling aspect of life, Anne contends, what all three need is recognition that death is also a scientifically demonstrable aspect of life. In proof of this, she gives her view of the interrelationship between science and poetry, a relationship that is an inseparable partnership between two intellectual giants—the man of science and the poet.

> For science has opened up such elevating views of the mystery of material existence that, if poetry had not bestirred herself to handle this theme in her own way, she would have been left far behind by her plodding sister. Science knows that matter is not, as we fancied, certain solid atoms which the forces of nature vibrate through and push and pull about; but that the forces and atoms are one mysterious, imperishable identity, neither conceivable without the other. She knows, as well as the poet, that destructibility is not one of nature's words; that it is only the relationship of things—tangibility, visibility—that are transitory. She knows that body and soul are one, and proclaims it undauntedly, regardless, and rightly regardless, of interferences. Timid onlookers, aghast, think it means that soul is body,—means death for the soul. But the poet knows it means body is soul,—the great whole imperishable; in life and death continually changing substance, always retaining identity. . . . Science knows that whenever a thing passes from a solid to a subtle air, power is set free to a wider scope of action. The poet knows it too, and is dazzled as he turns his eyes toward "the superb vistas of death. . . ." The man of science, with unwearied, self-denying toil, finds the letters and joins them into words. But the poet alone can make complete sentences.[74]

Anne sums up her estimate of Whitman with another parallel between science and poetry. The man of science bequeaths the fruits of his toil to the future, but the poet—and Whitman in particular—bequeaths himself to every man and woman.

> For he taught them, in words which breathe out his very heart and soul into theirs, that "love of comrades" which, like the "soft-born measureless light," makes wholesome and fertile every spot it penetrates to, lighting up dark social and political problems, and kindling into a genial glow that great heart of justice which is the life-source of Democracy. He, the beloved friend of all, initiated for them a "new and superb friendship;" whispered that secret of god-like pride in a man's self, and a perfect trust in woman.[75]

And she ends her essay with this: "Happy America, that he should be her son! One sees, indeed, that only a young giant of a nation could produce this kind of greatness, so full of the ardour, the elasticity, the inexhaustible vigour and freshness, the joyousness, the audacity of youth."

This was Anne's assessment of Whitman's techniques, philosophy, and genius. But there is something else in "Estimate," something that was apparently missed in the general brouhaha about Whitman at the time the essay was written, and by later critics in their preoccupation with finding only heavy-breathing passion in Anne's exuberant praise. Surprisingly, it has also been missed by the feminist scholars. Inspired by the "Children of Adam" poems and embedded unobtrusively in a few passages near the end of the essay, there is a poignant plea for the sexual liberation of women—for the acknowledgment of the reality of their sexuality. It is a clarion protest against the nineteenth-century belief that women were asexual; a protest against the suffering caused by false concepts of modesty and by equating ignorance with innocence; a Victorian cry—a hundred years too soon—for the wisdom and support of Masters and Johnson.

Speaking of the charge that Whitman's poems are unfit for a woman to read, Anne writes, "None of them troubled me even for a moment; because I saw at a glance that it was not, as men had supposed, the heights brought down to the depths, but the depths lifted up level with the sunlit heights, that they might become clear and sunlit too." Then, speaking for all women of her generation with a sense of sisterhood that is missing in "A Neglected Art" (where she seems to distance herself from the majority of women of her time), speaking out for all women who like herself had found only frustration and "dark and gloomy" times in marriage, she continues with unconcealed bitterness.

> Always, for a woman, a veil woven out of her own soul—never touched upon even, with a rough hand, by this poet. But, for a man, a daring, fearless pride in himself, not a mock-modesty woven out of delusions—a very poor imitation of a woman's. Do they not see that this fearless pride, this complete acceptance of themselves, is needful for her pride, her justification? What! is it all so ignoble, so base, that it will not bear the honest light of speech from lips so gifted with "the divine power to use words?" Then what hateful, bitter humiliation for her, to have to give herself up to the reality! Do you think there is ever a bride who does not taste more or less bitterness in her cup? But who put it there? It must surely be man's fault, not God's, that she has to say to herself, "Soul, look another way—you have no part in this. Motherhood is beautiful, fatherhood is beautiful, but the dawn of fatherhood and motherhood is not beautiful." Do they really think that God is ashamed of what He has made and appointed? And, if not, surely it is somewhat superfluous that they should undertake to be so for Him.[76]

Whitman stated that "the full-spread pride of man is calming and excellent to the soul." Pride in herself, rather than the feelings of shame about her femaleness that have been imposed on her, would be calming and excellent to a woman's soul above all, Anne vehemently contends:

> It is true that instinct of silence I spoke of is a beautiful, imperishable part of nature too. But it is not beautiful when it means an ignominious shame brooding darkly. Shame is like a very flexible veil, that follows faithfully the shape of what it covers,—beautiful when it hides a beautiful thing, ugly when it hides an ugly one. It has not covered what was beautiful here; it has covered a mean distrust of man's self and of his Creator.[77]

This sort of silence, this evil spell, has needed to be broken, she insists. And this is what the "Children of Adam" poems do. Now, for those who accept their message, "silence may brood again; but lovingly, happily, as protecting what is beautiful, not as hiding what is unbeautiful."

Her pent-up indignation still spilling over, Anne has still more to say about the outrage that has been committed against women in the past and the new freedom that awaits them in enlightenment about the true nature and dignity of femininity.

> Now none need turn away their thoughts with pain and shame; though only lovers and poets may say what they will,—the lover to his own, the poet to all, because all are in a sense his own. None need fear that this will be harmful to the woman. How should there be such a flaw in the scheme of creation that, for the two with whom there is no complete life, save in closest sympathy, perfect union, what is natural and happy for the one should be baneful to the other? The utmost faithful freedom of speech, such as there is in these poems, creates in her no thought or feeling that shuns the light of heaven, none that are not as innocent and serenely fair as the flowers that grow; would lead, not to harm, but to such deep and tender affection as makes harm or the thought of harm simply impossible. Far more beautiful care than man is aware of has been taken in the making of her, to fit her to be his mate. God has taken such care that *he* need take none; none, that is, which consists in disguisement, insincerity, painful hushing-up of his true, grand, initiating nature.[78]

Brushing aside the commandment to suffer and be still—the eleventh commandment for her generation of women—Anne continues her assault. What of the charge that reading Whitman's poetry would be harmful to a young girl? Nonsense, Anne replies. "I believe that even here fear is needless. For her innocence is folded round with such thick folds of ignorance, till the right way and time for it to accept knowledge, that what is unsuitable is also unintelligible to her; and, if no dark shadow from without be cast on the white page by misconstruction or by foolish mystery and hiding away of it, no hurt will ensue from its passing freely through her hands." Giving a young girl access to great literature, no matter what its content, is never dangerous, Anne declares—no doubt remembering herself at sixteen reading Rousseau's *Confessions* in Highgate Cemetery—even though it is little understood or realized by men that this is so. And she closes her case with an impassioned recommendation that Whitman's poetry, with its confirmation and glorification of feminine sexuality, be made available to all women.

> Wives and mothers will learn through the poet that there is rejoicing grandeur and beauty there wherein their hearts have so longed to find it; where foolish men, traitors to themselves, poorly comprehending the grandeur of their own or the beauty of a woman's nature have taken such pains to make her believe there was none,— nothing but miserable discrepancy.[79]

A courageous act for a woman in 1869? It was indeed. And Anne knew that it was. When she sent her completed essay to Rossetti, she wrote: "I often feel as if my enterprise were very like Lady Godiva's—as if hers indeed were typical of mine. For she stripped the veil from a woman's body for a good cause and I from a woman's soul for a great cause. And no man has ever dared to find any fault with her."[80]

No one can say with certainty what effect, if any, the publication of "Estimate" had on Whitman's career. It certainly did not bring about the miracle of acceptance of the poet by the Boston literary establishment. On the other hand, it may have contributed to a gradual, grudging tolerance by that august body, acknowledgment that "that awful Whitman"[81] was an authentic poetic force. But if the publication of "Estimate" was not a turning point in Whitman's career, it was at least a milestone. Walt was both elated and deeply grateful to "the lady." "I do not even know her name," he confessed to Helen Price.[82] Years later, he told Traubel: "You can imagine what such a thing as her Estimate meant to me at that time. Almost everybody was against me—the papers, the preachers, the literary gentlemen—nearly everybody with only here and there a dissenting voice—when it looked on the surface as if my enterprise was bound to fail—bound to fail. Then this letter—these letters: this wonderful woman. Such things stagger a man—leave him without words to say,"[83] Louisa Van Velsor Whitman, Walt's mother, read the article and commented shrewdly to her son in her semiliterate way: "that Lady seems to understand your writing better than ever any one did before as if she could see right through you.she must be a highly educated woman."[84]

On 9 June, Rossetti received half a dozen copies of the *Radical* and immediately sent one to Anne at Earls Colne.[85] Even though one paragraph had been cut,[86] she was overjoyed and eagerly awaited the quick response from Whitman, this time directly to her, that she was certain would come. Surely, she believed, in reading her essay in which every line breathed love and understanding, he would recognize the voice of his perfect mate—as in reading his poetry she had heard the voice of hers.

She waited, and waited, and waited. But no word came from Walt. Neither to Rossetti nor to her. Reversing his original intention, Rossetti decided not to show his copies of the magazine to anyone. It was clear that the incident was closed.

Anne's disappointment was devastating. After months of pining, she was prostrated by a mysterious illness that her alarmed friends attributed to nerves and that Herbert in his biography, for want of a better explanation, blamed on overwork in behalf of the Tennysons. Late in 1870, strong energetic Anne, her Victorianness surfacing, took to her bed where she "lay dying as it seemed."[87] And for a moment an odor of smelling salts and rose water applied to the wrists seems to hang in the air.

9
MY DEAREST FRIEND

Thou, thou, the Ideal Man,
Fair, able, beautiful, content, and loving,
Complete in body and dilate in spirit,
Be thou my God.

Walt Whitman

Months went by. To the mystification of her physician, as well as her family and friends, Anne's prostrating illness continued. But its source was no mystery to her. Later, describing her illness to Whitman, Anne would write: "The doctor called it nervous exhaustion falling with tremendous violence on the heart which seemed to have been strained: & was much puzzled how that could have come to pass. I left him in his puzzle—but it was none to me. How could such a dazzling radiance of light flooding the soul, suddenly kindling it to such intense life, but put a tremendous strain on the vital organs? how could the muscles of the heart suddenly grow adequate to such new work?"[1] Then, after months when she truly believed that she was dying, the ebb ceased and she felt life begin to flow back again. On 8 January, 1871, William Rossetti, who had been deeply concerned, wrote to her: "It was a pleasure to see your handwriting again the other day—especially so firm a specimen."[2]

Then Anne suffered another blow. In August 1871, Walt sent Rossetti a copy of his new edition of *Leaves of Grass*, a copy of *Democratic Vistas*, and a packet for "the Lady" containing one of each. Again no letter, not even a note, directly to Anne was enclosed, and again she was bitterly disappointed—so disappointed that "when the Book came but with it no word for me alone, there was such a storm in [my] heart I could not for weeks read in it." Because she believed that it is a woman's instinct to wait to be sought rather than to seek, she had waited for some word from Whitman before speaking. Now she could wait no longer, no longer "shut down in stern silence the love, the yearning, the thoughts that seem to strain & crush my heart."[3] After asking Rossetti if something intended for her had somehow not been enclosed in the packet, Anne asked if in his opinion she might now, with propriety, write directly to the poet. He replied on 3 September:

I dispatched to you Whitman's packet exactly as it stood, save for the addition of your address, written by me. . . . I think you would be quite right now in addressing Whitman: the letters seem to have made their way in the right quarters without stirring up any noisy outcry—& the time for the latter may be supposed mainly gone by now. . . .

"Walt Whitman, Washington, D.C." (i.e. District of Columbia, for there are I believe several other Washingtons in the U. States) is all that is needed by way of address. He never gives—& I infer does not want to receive—either Mr. or Esq.[4]

Anne lost no time. The same day, 3 September, she went out into the fields near Colne[5] and wrote her first letter to Whitman.

It is a very long letter—pages and pages written in Anne's firm, free-flowing hand.[6] Edwin Haviland Miller has called it "one of the most pathetic love letters ever written."[7] But to other critics—Clara Barrus, Katherine Anthony, Kate Buss, Edith Wyatt—her letter is a courageous declaration of incredibly generous love that needs no apologists. In it, releasing more than two years of pent-up emotion, Anne pours out her heart to the poet—freely, fervently, intimately. More than a hundred years later one cannot read her ardent letter, intended for Whitman's eyes alone, without a guilty sense of having steamed open and read someone else's very private correspondence.

Anne begins her first letter to Whitman, addressed to "Dear Friend," by thanking him for "the beloved books," although her heart "is so rent with anguish, my eyes so blinded, I cannot read in them." She will struggle, she tells the poet, to tell him her story.

She begins with an account of her marriage: Alex's persistent courtship; her refusals; her decision to marry him even though she "felt no faintest gleam of true, tender, wifely love," since Alex said he would rather have her on those terms than not at all. "Ah, Annie, it is not you who are so loved that is rich; it is I who so love," he told her many times. And she knew that this was true, felt that her nature "was poor & barren beside his." But after reading *Leaves of Grass*, she tells Walt, she knew that this was not so; she knew that her nature had been "only slumbering —undeveloped." In her intimate confession with its moving plea for understanding that follows, Anne is speaking out, as she had in "Estimate," not only for herself but for all women for whom marriage had meant only the bitterness of frustration.

> For, dear Friend, my soul was so passionately aspiring—it so thirsted & pined for light, it had not power to reach alone and he could not help me on my way. And a woman is so made that she cannot give the tender passionate devotion of her whole nature save to the great conquering soul, stronger in its powers, though not in its aspirations, than her own, that can lead her forever & forever up and on. It is for her soul exactly as it is for her body. The strong divine soul of the man embracing hers with passionate love—so alone the precious germs within her soul can be quickened into life. And the time will come when man will understand that a woman's soul is as dear and needful to his and as different from his as her body to his body.

> This is what happened to me when I had read for a few days, nay, hours, in your books. It was the divine soul embracing mine. I never before dreamed what love meant: not what life meant. Never was alive before—no words but those of "new birth" can hint the meaning of what then happened to me.

She continues her story. She tells Walt about the "dark and gloomy" first months of her marriage, when she sometimes "had misgivings whether I had judged aright"; the compensating joy of having children; the good and happy life that she and Alex, both working hard to make ends meet, led together for ten years, "he ever tender and affectionate to me—and loving his children so." She describes Alex's tragic death and her own terrible remorse as she stood beside him in his coffin because she "had not, could not have been more tender to him—such a conviction that if I had loved him as he deserved to be loved he would not have been taken from us." For, as she explains, "to the last my soul dwelt apart & unmated & his soul dwelt apart unmated." Her youngest child was then still a baby. Left alone, she tells the poet, "I have had much sweet tranquil happiness, much strenuous work and endeavour raising my darlings."

Then, her résumé of introduction concluded, Anne makes the declaration of love that she had hoped Walt would recognize between the lines of "Estimate." And it is more than a declaration of love. It is a modestly oblique, but nonetheless clear, proposal of marriage.

> In May, 1869, came the voice over the Atlantic to me—o, the voice of my Mate: it must be so—my love rises up out of the very depths of the grief & tramples upon despair. I can wait—any time, a lifetime, many lifetimes—I can suffer, I can dare, I can learn, grow, toil, but nothing in life or death can tear out of my heart the passionate belief that one day I shall hear that voice say to me, "My Mate. The one I so much want. Bride, Wife, indissoluble eternal!" It is not happiness I plead with God for—it is the very life of my Soul, my love is its life. Dear Walt. It is a sweet & precious thing, this love; it clings so close, so close to the Soul and Body, all so tenderly dear, so beautiful, so sacred; it yearns with such passion to soothe and comfort & fill thee with sweet tender joy; it aspires as grandly as gloriously as thy own soul. Strong to soar—soft & tender to nestle and caress. If God were to say to me, "See—he that you love you shall not be given to in this life—he is going to set sail on the unknown sea—will you go with him?" never yet has bride sprung into her husband's arms with the joy with which I would take thy hand & spring from the shore.

Why has she kept silent so long? Anne explains that she was obeying the voice of conscience. She had felt that she must wait for the right opening, and Rossetti's request that she allow her thoughts about Whitman to be put into print provided this. She had consented to his advice that she withhold her name from her essay because she was not certain how her "dear Boy"— Percy, who was eighteen when "Estimate" was published—might accept it, since she thought "perhaps he was not old enough to judge and understand me aright; nor young enough to let it altogether alone." But not standing openly and proudly as the author of the essay had been hateful to her, she tells Walt, because her nature is as proud and defiant as his own. She adds: "And, my darling, above all I love thee so tenderly that if hateful words had been spoken against me I could have taken joy in it for thy dear sake."

Still speaking of "Estimate," Anne asks reproachfully, "O dear Walt, did you not feel in every word the breath of a woman's love? did you not see as through a transparent veil a soul all radiant and trembling with love stretching out its arms towards you? I was so sure you would speak , would send me some sign: that I was to wait—wait. So I fed my heart with sweet hopes: strengthened it with looking into the eyes of thy picture." She adds hopefully, "O surely in the ineffable tenderness of thy look speaks the yearning of thy man-soul towards my woman-soul?" And she makes one more impassioned appeal: "O come. Come, my darling: look into these eyes and see the loving ardent aspiring soul in them. Easily, easily will you learn to love all the rest of me for the sake of that and take me to your breast forever."

In a few lines near the end of the letter there is a startling revelation. Apparently, from the time that she was first aware that she was in love with Whitman, Anne had planned to go to America with her children as soon as she was free to do so. A year ago, she tells Walt, when she was so ill that she feared that she was dying, she told her children about her love for him—"told them all they could rightly understand." And she instructed them, if she died, and after the death of her own mother, to "go fearlessly" to America, since, if she had lived, she would "have planted them down there—Land of Promise, My Canaan."

Anne closed the letter "Good-bye, dear Walt" and signed it "Anne Gilchrist." Before mailing it, she added a postscript, dated three days later:

> How I have brooded & brooded with thankfulness on that one word in thy letter [to Rossetti] "the comfort it has been to me to get her words," for always day & night these two years has hovered on my lips & in my heart the one prayer: "Dear God, let me comfort him!" Let me comfort thee with my whole being, dear love.[8]

Walt did not answer her letter. He was understandably taken aback by "the Lady," about whom he knew nothing except that she was an Englishwoman and a widow, suddenly materializing and not only professing passionate love but proposing marriage. But he did not write "? insane asylum" on the envelope of her letter and relegate it to his collection of curios, as he had with Susan Garnet Smith's fevered proposal. Anne's letter could not be summarily dismissed. To begin with, he was indebted to her. In addition, he recognized at once that the love that she offered was totally sincere and an even greater tribute to himself than her "Estimate"; that it sprang not only from exalted idealism but from a touching naïveté. How could he answer her? Walt put Anne's letter aside very carefully—and stalled for time.

Six weeks passed. Tormented by fear that her long letter had fallen into the wrong hands, on 15 October Anne wrote again to Walt—a short note this time—asking if he has received it.[9] Still there was no answer. On 23 October, unable to bear her anxiety any longer, she wrote another long and impassioned letter, begging Walt to spare her the needless suffering of uncertainty and let her have "one line, one word, of assurance that I am no longer hidden from you by a thick cloud—I from thee—not thou from me." She tells him again of her soul's passionate yearning toward his, "every hour, every deed and thought—my love for my children, my hopes, aspirations for them, all taking new shape, new height through this great love." "Do not say I am forward," she pleads, "or that I lack pride because I tell this love to thee who have never sought or made sign of desiring to seek me. . . . Besides, it is not true thou hast not sought or loved me. For when I read the divine poems I feel all folded round in thy love: I feel so often as if thou wast pleading so passionately for the love of the woman that can understand thee—that I know not how to bear the yearning answering tenderness that fills my breast." "Try me for this life, my darling," she entreats the poet, "see if I cannot so live, so grow, so learn, so love, that when I die you will say, 'This woman has grown to be a very part of me.'" And she adds: "I am yet young enough to bear thee children, my darling, if God should so bless me. And would yield my life for this cause with serene joy if it were so appointed, if that were the price for thy having a 'perfect child.'"[10]

Walt could no longer remain silent. He wrote to Anne on 3 November. His wonderfully tactful letter was carefully composed. It was very kind, very cautious, very brief.

> Washington City, U.S.—November 3, 1871
>
> Dear friend,
>
> I have been waiting quite a long while for time & the right mood to answer your letter in a spirit as serious as its own, & in the same unmitigated trust & affection. But more daily work than ever has fallen upon me to do the current season, & though I am well & contented, my best moods seem to shun me. I wished to give to it a day, a sort of Sabbath or holy day apart to itself, under serene & propitious influences—confident that I could then write you a letter which would do you good, & me too. But I must at least show, without further delay, that I am not insensible to your love. I too send you my love. And do you feel no disappointment because I now write but briefly. My book is my best letter, my response, my truest explanation of all. In it I have put my body & spirit. You understand this better & fuller & clearer than any one else. And I too fully & clearly understand the loving & womanly letter it has evoked. Enough that there surely exists between us so beautiful & delicate a relation, accepted by both of us with joy.
>
> Walt Whitman[11]

Anne replied by return packet. His long-awaited letter, she told the poet on 27 November, had brought her both joy and pain. The word *enough* was like a blow in the breast to her, for she truly believed that the tie between them "would not grow less but more beautiful, dear friend, if you knew me *better*: if I could stand as real & near to you as you do to me. But I cannot, like you, clothe my nature in divine poems & so make it visible to you. Ah, foolish me! I thought you would catch a glimpse of it in those words I wrote." But she was not disappointed by the shortness of his letter. "I do not ask nor even wish you to write save when you are inwardly impelled & desirous of doing so," she tells the poet humbly. "I only want leave and security to write freely to you."[12]

And in the years that followed Anne did write freely to Walt. Legend has it that she bombarded the poet with letters that for the most part went unanswered. This was not the case. Over a period of four-and-a-half years Anne wrote twenty-nine letters to Whitman—some long, some little more than extended notes—which hardly constitutes a bombardment. And Whitman did respond, in one way or another, and with more or less regularity. At Anne's suggestion, he sent her an American newspaper—"any one you have done with"—on the day that he received a letter from her as a token that it had reached him, and other American newspapers from places that he visited so that she might know that he was well and where he was. After Walt suffered a stroke in 1873, he put a small dash under the London in her address to signify that he was better, again at Anne's suggestion. And he wrote a number of letters.

With one letter he enclosed a "ring I have just taken from my finger, & send to you, with my love."[13] In another he came close to paraphrasing one of the poems in the "Calamus" cluster in which he wrote:

> Are you the new person drawn toward me?
> To begin with take warning, I am surely far different from what
>   you suppose;
> Do you suppose you will find in me your ideal?
> Do you think it so easy to have me become your lover?
> Do you think the friendship of me would be unalloy'd satisfaction?
> Do you think I am trusty and faithful?
> Do you see no further than this facade, this smooth and tolerant
>   manner of me?
> Do you suppose yourself advancing on real ground toward a real
>   heroic man?
> Have you no thought O dreamer that it may be all maya, illusion?[14]

Concerned about the romantic image of himself that Anne was creating in her imagination, Walt added some words of caution to a letter to her that he wrote in March 1872: "Dear friend, let me warn you somewhat about myself—& yourself also. You must not construct such an unauthorized & imaginary ideal Figure, & call it W.W. and so devotedly invest your loving nature in it. The actual W.W. is a very plain personage, & entirely unworthy such devotion."[15] But Anne put her fingers in her ears. "Please, dear friend, do not 'warn' me any more," she pleaded in her next letter, "—it hurts so, as seeming to distrust my love. Time only can show how needlessly."[16] And Walt let it go at that.

Anne continued to express her love for the poet, but with more restraint than in her first three letters. In a letter in April 1872, she could not resist pointing out to Walt that if he finds something strange in a love that has grown up entirely without personal contact, it is because he does not realize his own power or understand the full meaning of his own words—"whoso touches this, touches a man," for example. "Real effects imply real causes," she tells him. "Do you suppose that an ideal figure conjured up by her own fancy could, in a perfectly sound, healthy woman of my age, so happy in her children, so busy & content, practical, earnest, produce such real & tremendous effect—saturating her whole life, colouring every waking moment—filling her with such joys, such pains that the strain of them has been well nigh too much even for a strong frame, coming as it does, after twenty years of hard work?[17] But she assures him that she will never again take anything he says to mean anything it does not mean and promises to write no more letters like the first few that she wrote; or if she does, "because my heart is so full it cannot bear it," they will not find their way to the post. "But do not, because I give you more than friendship, think that it would not be a very dear & happy thing to me to have friendship only from you," she tells the poet with winning humility. "I do not want you to write what it is any effort to write—do not ask for deep thoughts, deep feelings . . . but for the simplest current details."[18]

Although they were less effusively ardent, as the years went by Anne's letters to Walt—most of them to "My Dearest Friend"—became even more intimate, but in a different way. They were chatty, newsy, filled with "the simplest current details." Walt wrote that he had had letters from Tennyson and an invitation to visit him; Anne replied with the story of her friendship with the laureate. Walt described his elderly mother; Anne described hers. Anne sent pictures of her children; he sent them his remembrance and best love. Walt sent copies of new poems; Anne responded with "tears of joy & I know not what other deep emotion." Anne sent greetings on his birthday and celebrated her own—a day when her children made her promise to "do nothing but what I like all day"—by writing to him. She took a lively interest in events reported in the newspapers that Walt mailed—from New York, Philadelphia, Springfield, Burlington. And she sent him news of their increasing number of mutual friends: of Rossetti's marriage to Madox Brown's daughter;[19] of frequent visits with Moncure Conway and his family; of two callers sent by Walt with letters of introduction—Joseph B. Marvin, "a valued friend of mine,"[20] and Kate Hillard, a talented young woman from Brooklyn.[21] When Walt suffered a stroke in 1873, Anne longed to be at his side to comfort and care for him. His beloved mother died in the same year, and she shared his grief. The Atlantic was still between them. But Anne's warm and charming letters—which were more and more frequently signed "Annie Gilchrist," or "Your loving Annie," or "Your own Annie"—achieved what she had dreamed of. After four years, if he had been questioned, Walt would have had to admit what Anne had hoped he would say when she died: "This woman has grown to be a very part of me."

Anne's letters to Walt from 1871 until 1876 have a second dimension: they are also her autobiography for this period. In November 1871 Anne told the poet that she and her children were planning to go to London to live because Haslemere—"one of the wildest, sweetest spots in England"—offered no educational advantages. In January she wrote that after a long search she had found "a comfortable, dear, little home—small, indeed, but not so small as to interfere with health or comfort," and at a rent within her means. This was important, Anne explained, because her husband had died too young to provide for his family, and she had had to depend on her mother, who had generously spared her half of her own income. Now her mother, eighty-six and failing, needed "an easier scale of expenditure," and so Anne needed to "manage a little more cleverly to make a less sum serve for us." "But I succeed capitally, dear friend," she told Walt cheerfully, "never get behind & find it no hardship." In 1871 Percy had finished his education and was employed in South Wales. This made it possible for Anne to give her girls a turn in education, and she chose the little house at 50 Marquis Road, Camden Square, because it was near an excellent day school for them.

After the move to London, it was necessary for Anne to spend a great deal of time in "domestic management," but she found it happy and invigorating work and, with Walt's books beside her, even the needlework that she detested no longer seemed tedious. Her recreation, as always, was reading, writing letters, taking long walks—although making her way through the busy streets of London must have contrasted sadly with the solitary climb to Hind Head that she had loved.[22] In the winter she skated with her children and occasionally she went to concerts. Her social life was confined almost entirely to entertaining in her own home. "I am a home bird," she confessed to Walt, "don't like staying out—wanted at home and happiest there."[23] But she did attend a party at the Madox Brown's before their daughter's marriage to Rossetti; and she was a guest—one of a number of *"good Whitmanites"*[24]— at a dinner party that Rossetti gave for Marvin. During this period, Anne made the acquaintance, transatlantically, with another of Walt's friends—John Burroughs. In 1875 she wrote to Burroughs offering her help in raising funds to aid Whitman, who was still ill and had lost his government post. She closed her gracious letter with a tribute to the naturalist's *Wake-Robin*, that "brings the fresh, moist atmosphere of the woods, the ways of its denizens, the delightful sense of outdoor life, very enjoyably home to me."[25]

In the 1871 to 1876 years, Anne's daily life revolved around her children, and in her letters to Walt their talents, ambitions, problems and personalities are lovingly and vividly portrayed.

Percy was a brilliant student. After finishing the curriculum at the Felsted Grammar School, he enrolled at the Royal School of Mines, where he was a Murchison Medalist.[26] His first employment—he was not quite twenty—was at a large copper and iron mining and smelting works in South Wales, where he lodged at a farmhouse not far from the sea. He was able to come home only at Christmas, but more than once Herby spent his summer holiday with his brother, and the two had happy times together, swimming every day and both "looking brown as a nut."[27] In November 1873, Anne reported to Walt that Percy was working zealously to master the process of making the quality of copper used in telegraph wires, which so far his company had been unable to produce;[28] adding, with motherly concern, that his looks "do not quite satisfy me—it is partly rather too long hours of work—but still more not getting a good meal till the end of it. It is so hard to make the young believe that the stomach shares the fatigue of the rest of the body." Music was Percy's greatest pleasure; he preferred it to literature, Anne told Walt, and was "acquiring some practical skill."[29]

Percy and his mother were close friends. In 1875, Anne left the other children in London and went to Wales to be with him. Percy was extremely unhappy. He had fallen in love with a young girl, Norah Fitzmaurice,[30] whose parents had welcomed him at first, but when he declared his feelings to her father, forbade the two to see each other again. The Fitzmaurices had no objection to Percy, but they believed it wrong for a man to engage a girl's affections until he could afford to marry her. The separation was very painful, especially since Percy and Norah lived within sight of each other. Anne called on the Fitzmaurices, who were very courteous and friendly, she told Walt, and she believed that she had won the mother over into allowing Percy and Norah to spend a reasonable amount of time together, but the father remained obdurate. Percy, he said, might marry his daughter on £300 a year. But poor Percy had only £175—and, to make matters worse, even though he was well qualified for a higher paying berth, it was difficult for him to get one because he looked so young, "not having yet any beard or moustache to speak of." Anne left him with the promise that Beatrice and Grace would spend their holiday with him to cheer him up, and feeling "on the whole happier than not about him." She had liked Norah, she told Walt, and felt that "there is a true & deep love between them—also, she took to me very much, & I feel will be quite another child to me." And she added: "It is besides no little joy to me to find how Percy has confided in me in this & chooses me as the friend to whom he tells all—far from being any separation, as sometimes happens, this love of his seems to draw us closer together."[31]

Herbert followed Percy at the Felsted Grammar School. However, he was very different in temperament and aptitudes from his scientifically gifted, business-minded brother. Herby was an artist. His ultimate dream, of course, was to be elected a member of the Royal Academy, to be able to write the distinguished letters R.A. after his name. In 1871, at the age of fourteen, his more immediate hope was to be admitted to the Academy as a student. After the move to 50 Marquis Road, Herby attended the best drawing school in London, Anne told Walt, adding that "his bent is unmistakably strong." "My little artist Herby is still chiefly working from the antique," Anne reported in November 1873, "but tries his hand at home occasionally with oils & to life & has made an oil sketch of me which, though imperfect in drawing &c., gives far more the real character & expression of my face than the photographs." In February 1874, she told Walt that she had had two great pleasures since she last wrote to him. One was that Herby "has read with a large measure of responsive delight 'Leaves of Grass' quite through, so that he now sees you with his own eyes & has in his heart the living, growing germs of a loving admiration that will grow with his growth & strengthen every fibre of good in him." The other was that Herby also "read & took much pride in my 'letters,' now shown him for the first time."[32] In May of the same year Herby, now seventeen, was still drawing from the antique in the British Museum and hoping to get into the Academy that summer; in September his mother sent Walt the happy news that he had indeed been accepted by the Academy "& will begin work there Oct. 1st!" After that, in keeping Walt abreast of her family's news, Anne noted that her "artist boy is working away cheerily at the R. Academy, his heart in his work."[33]

"Grace is blooming," was the comment on her youngest child that Anne sent to Walt most frequently. Only twelve when the family moved London, Grace—or Giddy—was a pretty, happy, healthy girl. Unlike her brothers and sister, she had no strong early inclinations or unmistakable talents. "Grace means to study the best system of kindergarten teaching," Anne told Walt in 1874, but made no further mention of the plan. "Grace is less developed in intellect but not less in character than the others," her mother explained to Walt in 1875, when Grace was sixteen. "I can't describe her but send you her photograph. There is a freshness & independence of character about her— yet withal a certain waywardness & reserve. She is a good, instinctive judge of character—more influenced by it than by books—yet with a growing taste for them too."[34]

And then there was Beatrice, "sweet Beatrice" her father had called her.[35] Anne loved all of her children tenderly and devotedly, but Bee was especially dear. "I think that her daughter Beatrice was to my mother more like a sister, such close companions were they," Grace recalled in her memoir of her mother.[36] The two were much alike. Bee had her mother's keen mind, love of learning, deep interest in science, independence, and unswerving singleness of purpose. Her goal was a medical career. In spite of the obstacles that such a course presented for a woman in England in the mid–nineteenth century,

Bee was determined to study medicine—and her mother wholeheartedly supported her ambition. In November 1872, Anne told Walt that "Beatrice is working hard to get through the requisite amount of Latin, &c. that is required in the preliminary examination—before entering on medical studies." A year later she sent the poet a more extended report on Bee's progress—a report that also shows how confidently Anne was planning to go to America.

> My children all continue well in the main, I am thankful to say, though Beatrice (the eldest girl) looks paler than I could wish and is working her brains too much and the rest of her too little just at present, with the hope of getting through the Apothecaries Hall exam. in Arts next Sept., which involves a good bit of Latin and mathematics. This is all women can do in England toward getting into the medical profession & as the Apoth. Hall certificate is accepted for the preliminary studies at Paris & Zurich, I make no doubt it is also at Philadelphia & New York; so that she would be able to enter on medical studies, the virtual preliminary work, when we come. For she continues steadfastly desirous to win her way into that field of usefulness, & I believe is well fitted to work there, with her grave, earnest, thoughtful, feeling nature & strong bodily frame. She is able to enjoy your Poems & the vistas; broods over them a great deal.[37]

In July 1874 Anne sent Walt the good news that Bee had just got through one of the government examinations in mathematics, and six months later the even better news that she had passed the dreaded examination at Apothecaries Hall.

For nearly a year, beginning late in 1874, Bee took time from her medical studies to care for her increasingly failing grandmother. "Beatrice is at Colne," Anne reported to Whitman in December, "and is a very great comfort to my Mother—as I well knew she would be; for a more affectionate, devoted, caretaking nature does not breathe." On 21 February, 1875, Anne wrote to Walt from Colne:

> I have run down to Colne for a glimpse of my dear Bee, whom I have not seen for five months, and of my Mother; & now I am alone with the latter, Beatrice taking my place at home with her brother & sister for a week or two. A wonderful evergreen my Mother continues; still able to face the keen winds & frost daily in her Bath chair—well swathed, of course in eiderdown & flannels. Beatrice takes beautiful care of her & is happy & content with her life here, loving the country as dearly as I do & having time enough for study & reading, as well as for domestic activities, to keep her mind as busy as her body.[38]

Henrietta Carwardine Burrows died, at the age of eighty-nine, in August of that year.[39] On 26 November, Anne told Whitman proudly that "Beatrice has begun to work at anatomy at the School of Medicine for Women lately founded, & seems to delight in her work. She will not enter on the full course all at once—I am for taking things gently. Women have plenty of strength but it is of a different kind from men's & must work by gentler & slower means—Above all I do not like what pushes violently aside domestic duties & pleasures."[40]

These were her children in 1875—but what of Anne herself? She was in her forties. A photograph taken at the time shows that the round-faced young girl who had stared into the daguerreotypist's lens for her wedding picture had matured into a lovely woman. Each generation of women has its own look, a look that is a reflection of the ideal of womanhood that happens to be in fashion at the time and of the way the women of the period view themselves. In nineteenth-century England and America, the Ideal Woman, judging by the illustrations in books and periodicals, was a creature with large, doelike eyes (usually raised to heaven), a low brow, a small oval face with a slightly receding chin, a long swanlike neck, steeply sloping shoulders, a minuscule waist, and tiny, helpless-looking hands. This was the look that photographers of the period tried to capture to please their subjects, and the results were the stilted "likenesses" now fading in family albums. But in the striking photograph of Anne Gilchrist taken in 1874 there is no trace of the posed, the pallid, the too-pure-for-this-world look that was prized by her generation of women.[41] She is dressed, simply but elegantly, in the fashion of the time: a black silk dress, a white fichu edged with lace, white lace at her wrists, her dark hair parted in the center and combed smoothly into two large puffs. She is looking intently into the camera, as if she were about to speak, and her hands—capable-looking hands—are folded gracefully in her lap. There is an unmistakable vitality about her. But it is her face that arrests and holds one's attention: a beautifully molded face, with wide cheekbones, a generous mouth, and dark, direct, expressive eyes. After her death, William Rossetti would write a tender reminiscence of Anne's face:

> She had an eminently *speaking* face: not merely in the ordinary sense that the countenance was genuinely expressive of the mind and character, but it seemed besides to be full-charged with some message to which the mouth would give word: it was at once a mirror and a prelude. The eyes were the marked feature—full, dark, liquid, and extremely vivacious. There was a humorous glance in them, free from causticity. Falsehood or pretence stood little chance with that pair of eyes: they would look through and through all ambiguity and all flimsiness, but the scrutiny was not barbed with the malicious pleasure of exposure.[42]

Anne's most memorable feature, to those who knew her, could not be captured in a photograph—her lovely voice. Walt would say that "with its varied modulations and blended tones" it was "the tenderest, most musical voice" ever to bless his ears.[43] And another of her most winning attributes could not be recorded by a camera—her charm and skill as a conversationalist. Walt was to consider her even more gifted as a conversationalist than as a writer. Rossetti too would remember her as "a good and rather copious talker—serious, and amusing as well," adding that if "she talked well, she

Anne Gilchrist, 1874. Collection of Justin Kaplan.

listened well also."[44] Herbert closes his biography with one of his few intimate descriptions of his mother, a description of Anne talking: "whilst conversing her face became radiant as with an experience of golden years: humour was present in her conversation—flecks of sunshine, such as sometimes play about the minds of deeply religious natures. Her animated manner seldom flagged, and charmed the taciturn to speaking in his or her best humour.[45]

As the years passed, even though her passion for the poet was only one of many topics in her letters, Anne's ardor—and firm belief that Whitman would return her love with equal fervor once they met—never waned. On 18 May, 1875, Anne sent Walt a birthday "greeting of love" from her "patiently waiting heart, with the fibres of love and boundless trust & joy & hope which bind me to you bedded deep." "Let me sit close beside you, my Darling," she wrote five months later on 16 November, "& feel your presence & take comfort & strength & serenity from it." "O I passionately believe there are years in store for us, years of tranquil, tender happiness," she wrote the following February, "—me making your outward life serene & sweet—you making my inward life so rich." When Walt sent her a copy of *Two Rivulets* in April 1876, she responded with sexual imagery as explicit as Walt's own:

> Ever the deep inward assent, rising up strong, exultant my immortal self recognizing, responding to your immortal self. . . . O I cannot put into any words what I perceive nor what answering emotion pervades me, flows out towards you—sweetest, deepest, greatest experience of my life—what I was made for—surely I was made as the soil in which the precious seed of your thoughts & emotions should be planted—try to fulfil themselves in me, that I might by & bye blossom into beauty & bring forth rich fruits.[46]

And in letter after letter to Walt, Anne spoke ecstatically of her plan to go to America to be near him. She pictured her children clustered round him, "shone upon, vivified, strengthened by your presence"; she pictured herself working while he sat beside her, doing his needlework, playing and singing for him in the evening; and when she heard that he was seriously ill again, she pleaded, "O cling to life with a resolute hold, my beloved, to bless us with your presence, unspeakably dear, beneficent presence—me to taste of it before so very long now—thirsting, pining, loving me."[47]

Walt probably never believed for a moment that this English gentlewoman—independent though she might be and passionate in nature as she certainly was—would actually uproot her family and cross the ocean. In November 1875, three months after her mother's death, Anne's plans became more specific. She and her children wanted to transplant their home bodily as far as possible, "bring as much as we can of our own furniture because we have beautiful old things precious in Herby's eyes & that we are all fond of"; and they believed that this could be done by going straight to Philadelphia and taking a house somewhere on its outskirts. Walt still did not take her seriously. However, when Anne wrote early in 1876 that she had taken tickets and would sail for Philadelphia on 30 August, the poet panicked. Having his "own loving Annie" breathing "deathless, ever young, ever growing, ever learning, aspiring love, tender, cherishing, domestic love"[48] on the other side of the Atlantic was one thing; having her on the other side of the river from Camden, where he was living with his brother George and his family, was quite another. With undisguised alarm, he dispatched an urgent letter, tactfully attempting to put her off by suggesting the possibility that he might be going to England—but leaving no doubt about how he felt about her exuberant plan to come to America. After some preliminary chitchat about his new edition and an assurance that his health was perhaps a shade better, Walt wrote:

> I even already vaguely contemplate plans (they may never be fulfilled, but yet again they may) of changes, journeys—even of coming to London & seeing you, visiting my friends, &c. My dearest friend, *I do not approve of your American transsettlement. I see so many things here you have no idea of—the social, and almost every other kind of crudeness, meagreness, here (at least in appearance).*
> Don't do anything towards it nor resolve in it nor make any move at all in it without further advice from me. If I should get well enough to voyage, we will talk about it yet in London.[49]

But Anne was not to be dissuaded. She was neither discouraged nor surprised by what he had said of American "crudeness," she told Walt, and she had not shut her eyes to the trials and difficulties that transsettlement would involve; but, through his poems, she was strongly drawn to America for her children's sake as well as her own, and she was certain that "we shall light on our feet & do very well." Besides, she went on to explain, things were falling into place in England in such a way that now it was not only possible but the best thing for everyone concerned that she make the move that she had been planning and dreaming of for seven years. Since Percy was now employed by the Blaenavon Iron Company, with an excellent opportunity for advancement and a good salary, the Fitzmaurices had relented, and he and Norah were engaged. Anne had stored away her mother's furniture for the young couple, and she felt certain that they would be able to marry sometime in 1876. This meant, of course, that Percy would not be coming to America with her, but "leaving him so happy with his young wife will make it easier for us to part."[50] When Kate Hillard called, Anne had "felt a little cross with her" because she had given Herby "a dismal account of his chances as an artist in America." But, Anne told Walt, she and Herby refused to be discouraged, for they firmly believed that "if you can only paint the really good pictures the rest will take care of itself, somehow or other," and Herby was "looking towards America full of cheerful hopes."[51] Grace, now seventeen, was coming to America "with a gay and buoyant curiosity, declining to make up her mind about anything till she gets there.[52] But it was Beatrice who, in Anne's opinion,

Anne's cousin, Major John Carwardine, who fought with the Army of the Potomac in the Civil War. Private collection.

would benefit most from the move, and even if she could be of help to Percy by staying in England, Anne told Walt, the balance would "go down on Beatrice's side." The past year had been both a loss of time and waste of money for Bee. "In England women have at present no means of obtaining a complete medical education. They cannot get admission to any Hospital for the clinical part of the course," her mother explained to Walt. Bee had had a very satisfactory account of the Woman's Medical College in Philadelphia and had introductions to its head. For this reason, Anne continued, "she is exceedingly anxious to come where it is possible for her to follow out her aims effectually. Then, I am confident she will find America congenial to her—that she is in her essential nature democratic—& that she has the intelligence, the sympathies, earnestness, affectionateness, unconventionality needed to pierce through appearance's surface crudeness & see & love the great reality unfolding below."[53]

Anne's last letter to Whitman before leaving England was dated 18 May, 1876. One can imagine the weeks of sorting, disposing, and packing that followed. Rossetti, who seems to have had reservations about the wisdom of Anne's venture,[54] brought letters of introduction for her to take to America. Anne's cousin John Carwardine, who had fought with the Army of the Potomac, may have had some words of advice.[55] Hosts of friends called to say good-bye. There were last-minute financial arrangements to be made and domestic details to be attended to. A sense of high adventure must have hung in the air in the dismantled house,[56] with its furniture tagged for shipment, its empty rooms piled with packing crates, trunks, hatboxes, shawls, and an assortment of luggage.

The great day came at last. On Wednesday, 30 August, Anne, Beatrice, Herby, and Grace sailed from Liverpool directly to Philadelphia. Their ship, the *Ohio*, and her sister ships were advertised prominently in the *Philadelphia Public Ledger:*

AMERICAN LINES
Weekly Mail steamship service between
Philadelphia and Liverpool
Every Thursday from Philadelphia and
Wednesday from Liverpool
The only Trans-Atlantic line sailing under
THE AMERICAN FLAG
The only steamships carrying LIFE RAFTS
The following steamships are appointed to
sail from Philadelphia:

Illinois	Sept. 7	*Pennsylvania*	Sept. 28
Lord Olive	Sept. 14	*City of New York*	Oct. 5
Ohio	Sept. 21	*Indiana*	Oct. 12

Rates of passage in currency, Saloon $75 to $100
Round trip tickets on very favorable terms
Intermediate passage $40, Steerage $28
For other information apply to
Peter Wright & Sons, General Agents
307 Walnut Street, Philadelphia.[57]

10
MRS. G

O living always, always dying!
O the burials of me past and present,
O me while I stride ahead, material, visible, imperious as ever;
O me, what I was for years, now dead, (I lament not, I am content;)
O to disengage myself from those corpses of me, which I turn and
    look at where I cast them,
To pass on, (O living! always living!) and leave the corpses behind.
                                                    Walt Whitman

In the summer of 1876, Philadelphia was America's gala city. The great Centennial Exposition opened in Fairmount Park on 10 May, with the bell at Independence Hall signaling the event, and President Grant and Emperor Dom Pedro of Brazil starting up the immense Corliss Engine in Machinery Hall. The opening day crowd, reported as the "largest ever assembled on the North American continent," was officially 186,272, with about 110,000 more entering on free passes. Afterward the Japanese commissioner observed: "The first day crowds come like sheep, run here, run there, run everywhere. One man start, one thousand follow. Nobody can see anything, nobody can do anything. All rush, push, tear, shout, make plenty noise, say damn great many times, get very tired, go home."[1] After the first day, attendance dropped off drastically due to a heat wave that lasted through July. However, in August it picked up, and by September soared to a daily average of 94,000. Word had spread that the Exposition was not only exciting but educational, and visitors poured in from all over the world, taking advantage of the railroads' Centennial excursion fares, the huge, temporary, wood hotels built near the fairgrounds, and excellent public transportation from the city out to the park. Food, music, and entertainment were offered in abundance. Memorial Hall housed miles of art exhibits—although Eakins's *The Gross Clinic*, painted especially for the Exposition, was relegated to the medical section among displays of trusses and artificial limbs."[2] Fifty nations had exhibits. But it was machinery and new inventions that drew the crowds. Although the Corliss Engine was the stellar attraction, Thomas Alva Edison exhibited the Quadruplex Telegraph, George Westinghouse his air brakes, and George

Pullman the Pullman Palace Car. Almost as sensational as the Corliss Engine was a much smaller device—Alexander Graham Bell's telephone. "My God, it talks!" Emperor Dom Pedro is reported to have said.[3] In the fall of 1876, when Anne Gilchrist and her children arrived, Philadelphia had become America's first great tourist attraction, and its celebration-cum-carnival-cum-spectacle atmosphere introduced them to Anne's "Land of Promise, My Canaan."[4]

The voyage to America had to be a momentous event in the lives of all four Gilchrists. Not one of them had ever been outside of England; not one of them had ever set foot on a ship; and Anne had never seen the Atlantic until she visited Percy in Wales in 1875. But neither Herbert in his biography, nor Grace in her memoir of her mother, nor Anne in her letters that still exist described their days at sea. Was it a rough crossing? Was one, or were all, of them ill? Were cabinmates uncongenial? The only record is a postcard that Anne sent to William Rossetti two days after they landed, telling him that they had arrived after "a fairly good voyage."[5]

The *Ohio* docked at the port of Philadelphia on Sunday, 10 September. In January, Anne had written to Whitman that all she needed was the name of a comfortable lodging or boarding house, avoiding hotels if possible, where she and her children could stay while they hunted for a house and waited for their furniture, which was to sail a week after they did. Walt furnished no information. On the advice of someone who knew Philadelphia—could it have been Moncure Conway?—Anne booked rooms at the Montgomery House.[6] John Burroughs had come to Philadelphia to see the Centennial and was staying at the same hotel. He was the first American friend whom the Gilchrists met after their arrival.

"Much we liked him," Anne later wrote to Rossetti. And much the naturalist liked the Gilchrists. "Mrs. Gilchrist is a rosy woman without a gray hair in her head. I like her much," he wrote to his wife. "The daughters are fresh and comely, like soft light-skinned peaches. I went house-hunting with them."[7]

Whitman seems to have been uncertain about the exact date of Anne's arrival. In a letter to Rossetti from Camden on 1 September, he wrote: "I expected to have heard of Mrs. Gilchrist's arrival in the U.S. & to have had perhaps the great happiness of meeting her—but have heard nothing to date." On 10 September, the day the Gilchrists landed in Philadelphia, he ended another long letter to Rossetti with *"I want to hear about Mrs. Gilchrist."*[8] Burroughs undoubtedly sent word to the poet that she had arrived, and on Wednesday, 13 September, Walt took the ferry to Philadelphia and called on the Gilchrists at the Montgomery House.[9]

In the history of letters, few meetings have been the subject of so much conjecture and speculation—and of so many conflicting opinions about what happened—as the first meeting of Anne Gilchrist and Walt Whitman. Each had a preconceived image of the other. For each it was meeting both a total stranger and a singularly intimate friend. For each it was an intensely dramatic moment. And what did happen?

On one point there seems to be no disagreement. Like Burroughs, Walt was instantly taken with the Gilchrists. If he had been uneasy about the possibility that, when they met, the woman who had wooed him so passionately for six years would fling herself into his arms uttering ardent entreaties, his fears vanished when he met Anne Gilchrist, with her gracious manners and gentle dignity. From the first moment he was charmed with the lovely Englishwoman and her attractive children, and from the first moment he felt wonderfully comfortable with them. As a family there was no doubt about their admiration of him as a poet or their affection for him as a man. And the warmth of family love and respect and the exhilaration of being the center of attention that was as essential to living as oxygen for Walt Whitman were something that the poet needed desperately. He had become more and more unhappy living with his brother George and his wife in Camden. Not that George and Louisa were unkind to him—far from it.[10] But George had little interest in his brother's literary life; freedom-loving Walt had to adjust his daily habits to family routine; and in Camden, where he had no friends, the still-ailing poet felt neglected, isolated, "lonesome utterly." Sometimes he escaped to his friends the Staffords in Kirkwood, New Jersey, where in the simple farm family he found a replica of his own home life when he was a boy. Now, in the Gilchrist family, he recognized another refuge, closer at hand, intellectually stimulating, and emotionally fulfilling. "Walt came over every evening from Camden and took supper with us, and we had much talk," Burroughs wrote to his wife from the hotel. "He likes Mrs. Gilchrist and her family, and they like him. They are going to housekeeping and expect to spend several years in this country. It will be a god-send to Walt."[11]

So much for the joyous outcome of the meeting for Walt. What about Anne? What was the outcome for her of the meeting that she had dreamed of and longed for for seven years? What happened when she came face to face with "the real I myself" that was Walt Whitman: the poet whose words had roused her sexually as she had never been roused before; the poet she had ecstatically pictured as the Ideal Lover seeking his Ideal Mate, who, she believed, she was uniquely qualified to be? She had been convinced that he was speaking directly to her when he wrote lines like these:

> Among the men and women the multitude,
> I perceive one picking me out by secret and divine signs,
> Acknowledging none else, not parent, wife, husband, brother,
>   child, any nearer than I am,
> Some are baffled, but that one is not—that one knows me.
>
> Ah lover and perfect equal,
> I meant that you should discover me so by faint indirections,
> And I when I meet you mean to discover you by the like in you.[12]

And lines like these:

> Whoever you are holding me now in hand,
> Without one thing all will be useless,
> I give you fair warning before you attempt me further,
> I am not what you supposed, but far different.
>
> Who is he that would become my follower?
> Who would sign himself a candidate for my affections?
>
> The way is suspicious, the result uncertain, perhaps destructive,
> You would have to give up all else, I alone would expect to be
>   your sole and exclusive standard,
> Your novitiate would even then be long and exhausting,
> The whole past theory of your life and all conformity to the lives
>   around you would have to be abandon'd,
> Therefore release me now before troubling yourself any further, let
>   go your hand from my shoulders,
> Put me down and depart on your way.
>
> Or else by stealth in some wood for trial,
> Or back of a rock in the open air,
> (For in any roof'd room of a house I emerge not, nor in company,
> And in libraries I lie as one dumb, a gawk, or unborn, or dead,)
> But just possibly with you on a high hill, first watching lest any
>   person for miles around approach unawares,
> Or possibly with you sailing at sea, or on the beach of the sea or
>   some quiet island,
> Here to put your lips upon mine I permit you,
> With the comrade's long-dwelling kiss or the new husband's kiss,
> For I am the new husband and I am the comrade.[13]

Anne had accepted Walt's challenge. She had not put him down and departed on her way; she had abandoned the whole past theory of her life, and her novitiate had been long and exhausting; she had surrendered joyfully to the secret seduction the poet describes; and with his ring on her finger she had indeed thought of him as a "new husband." By faint indirections, eagerly followed, Anne had discovered a lover who was a perfect equal—and she had hoped and prayed that in the same way the poet would discover the like in her. What was the outcome of the encounter for Anne when she met the Tenderest Lover, whose voice she had heard calling across the Atlantic? Here there is disagreement.

Whitman critics and scholars, with few exceptions, have claimed that Anne Gilchrist never abandoned her one-sided courtship of the poet. They have pictured her returning forlornly to England "disappointed" and "disillusioned" or, more often, "defeated." They have said that she continued to write love letters to Walt as long as she lived. And they have taken it for granted that, while she was in America, Anne was languishing with love for the poet and persistently pressing her suit. Edward Carpenter, describing a visit with the Gilchrists in 1877 at their house in Philadelphia, where Whitman was also a guest—describing it in 1924, more than forty years after the event—wrote that it was clear to him "that Anne Gilchrist was suffering."[14] One critic, speaking of the poet's frequent visits to the Staffords, has even suggested—the most astonishing suggestion of all—that Walt had to retreat to Kirkwood to escape the "importunities" of his admirer.[15] And by admirer he meant Anne Gilchrist. There is no evidence anywhere to support these myths.

The scenario that evidence does support is that when she and Whitman met, Anne Gilchrist knew immediately that she had made a mistake. A wild error. A mistake of heroic proportions. Walt was an impressive figure. His admirers often recalled that on meeting the poet for the first time they were overwhelmed by the majesty of his appearance: his imposing height; his splendid features; his white hair cascading down to his shoulders; his long, full, snow-white beard; and the dramatic impact of all of these accentuated by the clothes that he always wore—a gray suit and a white shirt, with its wide, lace-edged collar open at the throat. But in spite of the poet's magnificent appearance, when they met Anne must have realized almost at once that, although "W.W." was clearly not "a very plain personage," on the other hand he was not the "unauthorized & totally imaginary figure" in whom he had advised her not to invest her loving nature. She must have known within a very few minutes that the man who stood before her was not the great Adamic lover she had dreamed of. Broken in health, dragging a paralyzed left foot, looking older by twenty years than his age of fifty-seven, in 1876 by his own description Walt was "a batter'd, wreck'd old man." Edith Wyatt has suggested that Anne had envisioned the object of her devotion as Jove, but she found him much more like another immortal creature—Santa Claus.[16] But it would not have been Walt's infirmities that made it clear to Anne that she had made an error; she had been prepared for his infirmities.[17] Something was missing. Something she had counted on and believed with all her heart for seven years. It was the instant recognition on his part—which she had been certain would happen when they came face to face—that she was the ideal mate she believed he was seeking; it was instant recognition, followed by a rush of chemistry, on his part—as it had been on hers when she first read *Leaves of Grass*. It is likely that from their first handclasp Anne knew that, although the poet was genuinely happy to see her, neither the recognition nor the chemistry that she had hoped for were there—and, for some reason that she sensed rather than understood, never would be.

What was Anne's reaction? It had to have been split second, unblinking, incredibly valiant. Quite simply, in a matter of moments, Anne Gilchrist's long and consuming passion for the imagined gave way to loving compassion for the actual. And what is the evidence for this? It could not be clearer. If Anne had continued her romantic pursuit of the poet as critics have claimed that she did; if Walt had really been pressured by "importunities"; if he had believed that Anne was secretly suffering; if he had had to be cautious about every word and glance and gesture when he was in her presence, he would not have been comfortable with Anne Gilchrist and her family—and heaven knows Walt Whitman was comfortable with the Gilchrists during the nearly two years that they lived in Philadelphia!

This was Anne's emotional metamorphosis in public in the parlor of the Montgomery House. In the privacy of her hotel room, one guesses that it took her longer to say "Good-bye My Fancy" with composure, and to accept reality. There had to have been, temporarily at least, a terrible sense of loss. She must have suffered the humiliation of fearing that she had made a fool of herself and questioned the wisdom of having come to America. But after the initial pain had lessened, Anne's common sense unquestionably told her that coming to America was the most fortunate thing that could have happened. For if she had remained in England, if she had never met the poet, she could have continued to be, perhaps for the rest of her life, the prisoner of an erotic fantasy that fed on itself, distorting her thoughts and emotions. It was clear that the union with the American Bard that she had dreamed of was unthinkable— and Anne accepted this without rancor, without face-saving demeaning of the unattainable. But it was also clear that there was another womanly role that she could play in the life of the poet, whom she had loved intellectually before she had loved him romantically, and whose infirmity touched her heart. Walt was to call her his noblest woman friend. A measure of Anne Gilchrist's nobility lies in the warm and nurturing, almost maternal, love that she gave so generously to the aging poet, not only while she was in America but as long as she lived.

The Gilchrists found a house at 1929 North Twenty-second Street.[18] Their household goods—the beautiful carved furniture that Alex and Anne had collected, the blue-and-white china, Anne's piano, Sir Joshua's children and other rare prints, Blake's *Elijah in the Fiery Chariot,* Anne's silver—must have arrived promptly from England. For Walt called on 25 September and made the first of his extended visits. He stayed until 9 October.[19] On 11 October, he wrote an affectionate note to Anne from the Staffords' farm:

Oct 11 p m

Dearest friend
    I am spending a few days down at the old farm, "White Horse"—wandering most all day (well clad & shod, for it is cool weather here) about the banks, trees, grass &c. by the very secluded beautiful druidic creek—have just picked up a few leaves that seem'd to offer themselves to send specially to you, which I enclose.
    I am feeling middling well, for me. Shall send you word—or rather shall send *myself*—soon as I come back to town—Meanwhile love to you all—
Walt Whitman[20]

Nineteen twenty-nine North Twenty-second Street was within walking distance of the Woman's Medical College of Pennsylvania, which Beatrice was planning to attend.[21] Although its location was ideal, 1929 was not without its drawbacks. "Since we saw you we have been slowly settling in our new home and in the main satisfactorily; not, however, without verifying a few of Mr. Marvin's predictions as to the misfortunes that would befall us if we took a perfectly new house," Herbert wrote to John Burroughs in December. "A furnace that wouldn't heat, range that wouldn't burn, pipes that would leak, etc. etc., but we have such a jolly lot of room, and so pleasant a situation, that we do not repent our choice."[22] A letter from Anne to Burroughs at the same time gives an even clearer picture of the Gilchrists' "settling-in":

> If business does not bring you this way ere long, then I hope friendship will—for we long very much for the society of a friend or two in this new home. However, we must not definitely say, "Will you come on such a day?" till our landlord has fulfilled his promise of giving us a good brick furnace to warm our rooms—for I believe an American would be fairly perished here—the iron ones we now have are just a mere gulf for coals to disappear in without sending out any equivalent heat in return—and as we are on high ground, facing northwest, no houses opposite, and doors and windows and floors, for that matter, so ill-fitted that you see daylight through, you may judge if it has not been pretty Arctic here of late. Still we are not the worse in health, I am glad to say, and not having yet been able to hear of a trustworthy servant, we have an amount of indoor activity which is very healthful and cheerful under the circumstances.
>
> As soon as we can get the thermometer up to a reasonable point in our rooms, say 65 degrees, I will write again.[23]

A chilly house seems not to have deterred Whitman; throughout the fall he alternated visits to 1929 with visits to the Staffords. He visited "Mrs. G" on the evening of 31 October, and spent 18, 19 and 20 November—"dark & rainy three days"—as well as 24 November with the Gilchrists in Philadelphia.[24] In December Walt wrote Anne the following suggestion: "As (though better this winter) decidedly sensitive to the cold—how would it do for me to have a little sheet-iron stove, & some wood sawed & cut, & carried up in the south room, immediately adjoining the one I before occupied? Could it be done? Is there a hole in the chimney in that room—or place for a stove pipe?"[25] He followed this with a plaintive letter to Herbert:

> 431 Stevens Street Camden
> My dear Herbert
>   Though I am pretty well physically it is very lonesome & dreary to me here, & I have been thinking all day how much I would like to come over & see you all, & stay awhile with you. Herbert, see about the stove & have put up as soon as convenient—& have some *dry oak wood* sawed the right length, split, & carried up there, & piled in the room. Send me word before the end of the week. I wish much to come—Love to all—
>
>   Walt Whitman[26]

The stove was installed, the wood supplied, and on 16 January Walt wrote to Burroughs: "I have been over here with the Gilchrists for a week—go back to Camden this afternoon or tomorrow—I have a nice room here with a stove and oak wood—everything very comfortable and sunny—most of all *the spirit* (which is so *entirely lacking* over there in Camden, and has been for more than three years)—"[27]

The Gilchrists found Philadelphia very different from smoky London, with its labyrinth of winding streets, and mews, and squares. In a long letter to Rossetti in December, Anne wrote:

> As to definite impressions of this vast complex contradictory phenomenon America, I am further from arriving at any such than I was in England. You can see a mountain as a whole—its complete outlines and relative proportions when you are at a distance, but when you are on it these merge into the few square yards around you and the distant prospect beyond.
>
> As to the bit immediately round us, this city of Philadelphia, it is more picturesque and more foreign-looking than I expected; long straight streets at right angles to each other, long enough and broad enough to present that always-pleasing effect of vista—converging lines that stretch out indefinitely and look as if they must certainly lead somewhere very pleasant, and being tolerably well planted with trees deserve their names—Girard Avenue, Columbia Avenue, and so forth. Also the clear bright atmosphere, the immunity from soot and smoke (owing to the use of hard coal), and the prevalence of cloudless skies, enable the sunshine to have fair play and bring out in their utmost strength and intensity all colours and forms.

She added a little wistfully: "One may have too much of a good thing, however, and sometimes this is a little wearying and monotonous; a film of smoke and a cloudy, fitful sky are not unmitigated evils." But she continued on a cheerful note: "It is not a distressingly new-looking city however, for the Queen Anne style in vogue when its prosperity began, has been in the main adhered to with Quaker-like precision; good red brick, numerous rather narrow windows with white outside shutters, a block cornice along the top of the facade, and the added American feature of marble steps and entry, have a solid, cheerful and indeed, when the trees were in leaf and the abundant flags hung out, a very gay aspect.[28]"

Did the Gilchrists visit the Exposition? There is no record of it. But one cannot imagine that a family adventurous enough to cross the Atlantic on their own would not have gone out to the Exposition at least once—by train from Market Street or by local streetcar—before it closed in November.[29] However, even without the fair, in the mid-1870s Philadelphia was a lively city. There was excellent theater, including a resident company under the direction of Mrs. John Drew. Music, with a strong Germanic flavor, was provided by a Germania Orchestra, a Männerchor, a Beethoven Society, and the Philadelphia Philharmonic Society; and concerts by the black Jubilee Singers were so enthusiastically received that the audience overflowed onto the stage. Sports were available in abundance: boating on the Schuylkill;

swimming at the Natatorium on Broad Street or in the river; sleighing in Fairmount Park and skating to music on the lake at the zoo; croquet; the new sport of roller-skating; and amateur and professional baseball games. Social dancing was extremely popular, with the elite dancing at Assemblies at the Academy of Music, the not-so-elite at advertised balls.[30] On the first page of the *Philadelphia Public Ledger* for Monday, 11 September 1876—probably the first newspaper that the Gilchrists read after their arrival, since there seems to have been no paper on Sunday, 10 September—eight dancing schools advertised dancing and etiquette classes for "Misses and Masters," with the Boston and the Glide taught correctly.[31] In 1876, Philadelphia was a medical center, a publishing center, and an intellectual center. There was much for the Gilchrists to see and explore (including John Wanamaker's Grand Depot, his palatial new store in the remodeled Philadelphia Railroad's freight depot) while they were getting settled at 1929—and striving to raise its temperature to 65 degrees.

Immediately after the Gilchrists arrived in Philadelphia, Beatrice enrolled in the twenty-seventh Annual Session of the Woman's Medical College of Pennsylvania which began on 5 October. Fifty-two students registered for the session, with one withdrawing "at the expiration of two weeks on acc't of bitter opposition in her home." Beatrice applied for "tickets" for chemistry, *materia medica*, physiology, and the practice of surgery.[32] In the minutes of the monthly meeting of the faculty on 25 November, Dean Rachel L. Bodley, professor of chemistry and toxicology, wrote:

> The case of Miss Gilchrist presented by Dean. This young lady, now in attendance at the College, had attended lectures in the London (England) School of Medicine for Women. She asked whether her tickets would be accepted by our faculty. On motion the *London School of Medicine for Women* was placed on our ab enundum [sic] list, and the tickets therefore were accepted.[33]

The fee for a matriculation ticket (paid but once) was $5.00; professors' tickets were $15.00 each; a practical anatomy ticket was $10.00; and the graduation fee $30.00. Board could be obtained "at a convenient distance from the College, for prices varying from $5.00 to $7.00 per week." In order to graduate, a candidate must have reached the age of twenty-one, studied medicine for three calendar years, and attended at least two full courses of lectures on chemistry and toxicology, anatomy, physiology and hygiene, *materia medica* and general therapeutics, principles and practice of medicine, principles and practices of surgery, and obstetrics and diseases of women and children— with attendance of at least one course at the Woman's Medical College. In addition, a candidate must have taken two courses in practical anatomy, with "at least one creditable dissertation of each of the usual divisions of the subject; one course in the Chemical and one in the Pharmaceutical Laboratory, and one in Microscopy." The faculty reserved the right "to refuse examination to any applicant on the ground of what they may deem moral or mental unfitness for the profession."[34]

In the mid-1870s, the medical profession in America still adamantly closed many doors to women. An impressive list of facilities was available to students at the Woman's Medical College. However, most were available only under certain conditions, which meant to classes or groups of women only. At the nearby Woman's Hospital, daily dispensary service "under proper restrictions," daily bedside instruction "to a limited number," and weekly clinics in the various departments "by private arrangement" were open to Medical College students. Under special conditions, they could attend clinics and lectures at the Pennsylvania Hospital, the Philadelphia Hospital (Blockley), the Wills' Hospital for Diseases of the Eye, the Eye and Ear Department of the Philadelphia Dispensary, and the Orthopaedic Hospital and Infirmary for Nervous Diseases.[35] Women students attended the separate clinics provided for them, but it was frustrating to know that lecturers brought their most interesting cases to the much larger male classes.

Even these privileges had not been won easily. From the time that the Medical College—the first college in the world regularly organized for the education of women for the medical profession—was incorporated on 11 March 1850, it had been an uphill fight to acquire recognition, equipment, a competent faculty, and admittance to clinical instruction in other institutions. On 6 November 1869, about thirty students of the college appeared at a clinical lecture at the Pennsylvania Hospital by permission of the managers. When they entered the amphitheater, they were "greeted by yells, hisses, catcalls, mock applause, and offensive personal remarks; during the lecture wads of paper, tinfoil, and tobacco-quids were thrown at them, and tobacco juice spat on their dresses; and when they left several hundred male students followed them into the street shouting insults."[36] As a result of the uproar, even though the faculty of the Medical College tried valiantly to stand its ground, on 15 November the faculties of the University of Pennsylvania and Jefferson Medical College, the medical staffs of Philadelphia's various hospitals, and the members of the medical profession at large voted unanimously—in the name of decency—to prohibit the joint participation of male and female students in clinical instruction and demonstrations.[37]

Like her fellow students, Bee must have found this professional discrimination and segregation galling. Nevertheless, she enjoyed her two years at the Medical College. "It was a happy time with her," her mother would write. "How zealously and successfully she worked, with what cordial warmth of friendship she regarded those of her teachers and fellow-students with whom she was brought into close relation."[38] One of Bee's classmates, and a close friend, was Caroline Virginia Still Wiley of Philadelphia, one of America's first black women physicians. Born in 1848, she was the daughter of William and Letitia Still, two of the founders of the Underground Railroad. When she was only fifteen, Caroline had entered Oberlin College and received her degree four years later, the only black and the youngest member of a class of forty-five. She taught school for a year and then married E. A. Wiley, an Oberlin student. He died in 1874. After her husband's death, she studied medicine at Howard University for one year, at the same time teaching elocution and freehand drawing. In October 1876 she matriculated at the Woman's Medical College with Bee.[39] Caroline Wiley was frequently a guest at 1929 and met Whitman there.

Professionally, things seem not to have gone as well for Herbert. Kate Hillard's warning that Philadelphia had little to offer an aspiring young artist was well-founded. To most upper-class Philadelphians, as well as to most Americans, medicine and science were accepted professions, but a career in the arts was viewed quite differently. "The truth of the matter is that the accomplished portion of our native population manifest a very slight regard for American art," one journalist wrote, "and consequently not much encouragement is extended in that direction."[40] Philadelphia's taste in art was rigidly "genteel." The sensation of the art exhibit at the Centennial was Randolph Rogers's sentimental sculpture *Nydia, the Blind Girl of Pompeii,* and in Philadelphia, as in the rest of America, John Rogers's "democratic" sculpture, made available to the public by inexpensive plaster replicas— *Checkers Up At The Farm* was one example—was enormously popular.[41] Nevertheless, in 1876 the Pennsylvania Academy of Fine Arts moved to a handsome, if ornate, new building on the corner of Broad and Cherry Streets, with display galleries on the second floor, and rooms on the first floor set up for life models and classes offering lectures on "artistic anatomy," perspective, and architectural styles. Instruction was offered at no cost to a student presenting a drawing that indicated suitable talent.[42] In the same year, Thomas Eakins, who had studied anatomy at Jefferson Medical College, began teaching at the Academy and revolutionized its curriculum: working from live models was substituted for working from antique casts; oil painting took precedence over line drawing; and students learned anatomy by doing dissections and by elaborate electric devices used to demonstrate the actions of the body. There were times, one student recalled, "when a skeleton, a stiff, a model and the Negro janitor Henry all jerked and jumped when the battery was turned on."[43] The concept of respectability in art was appalling to Eakins, but when he removed a male model's loincloth to demonstrate the action of the pelvis, respectable Philadelphians, as well as some of his lady pupils, were also appalled, and he was forced to choose between restraint and resignation. He resigned in 1886. Although Herbert would return to Philadelphia and teach at the Academy for a short time in 1888, there is no record of his having studied there while he and his family were living at 1929. Were Eakins's methods too iconoclastic for the young Englishman?[44] Did the other instructors' classes fall short of those he had attended in London? Whatever the reason, Herby began to spend more and more time at the Staffords' farm painting—for the most part, painting Walt.

Whitman at Timber Creek, sketch by Herbert Gilchrist. Department of Special Collections, Van Pelt Library, University of Pennsylvania.

In 1876, pretty seventeen-year-old Grace had abandoned her plan to teach kindergarten. While she was in Philadelphia, she took singing lessons, hoping for a career on the concert stage or in opera.[45] These lessons seem not to have begun immediately, and Giddy's main occupation for several months after the Gilchrists' arrival must have been helping her mother, not only with unpacking and arranging the family's belongings, but with the daily housework at 1929. Rossetti wrote to Anne in early January that he was alarmed by her report that she was "servantless."[46] In a country where there was no servant class in the British sense, Anne seems to have had difficulty in finding household help, even an inexperienced girl whom she could train in English ways. On 21 November, after returning to Camden from the Gilchrists', Walt wrote: "Upon talking more fully with my sister about the colored woman Rosy, I am convinced she *would not do.*"[47] One hopes that Anne found someone to at least carry firewood and empty ashes when Herby was away, and to take over the boiling-rubbing-sadiron ordeal of a nineteenth-century washday. But with Bee fully occupied at the Medical College, no matter what helping hands Anne was able to hire, Grace must have been her mother's mainstay during the Philadelphia years.[48]

And what about Anne herself during the first months in America—aside from servant problems, a cold house, a cranky range, and coping with foreign currency, unfamiliar accents, and strange terms like *stoop*?[49] There is a clear picture of an emergence. She may not have been immediately aware of it, but release from her passion for an imagined Whitman was another "new birth of the soul" for Anne Gilchrist. For seven years her total preoccupation with a fantasy that had become a pivotal reality in her life had drained her emotionally and limited her relationships with others. With release from the bondage that her imagination had imposed and from the suffering that the intensity of her love had inflicted, the capacity for enjoyment that had been so much a part of Anne's former self came back—enjoyment of new friends, new challenges, the pleasures of daily life. And on her own in a new country, where she had expected to establish her identity in the supporting role of a wife, a new self began to emerge. It was Anne Gilchrist, the mature woman, whose dignified and respected independence was the sort of freedom that nineteenth-century feminists were clamoring for; Anne Gilchrist, whose warmth and intelligence and gracious manners captivated those who met her; Anne Gilchrist, about whom Horace Scudder, the Boston author and editor, would write that no one "who knew her even slightly, [is] ever likely to forget that fine presence, the dignity which could bear the added title of quaintness without offence, the equipoise of manner which told of an equanimity of life."[50]

As a first step in the emergence of this new self, the "home bird"—perhaps remembering Jane Carlyle's example—began to stretch her social wings. Heretofore, had shyness, one wonders, been partly responsible for a "home bird's" protective coloring? Moncure Conway had given Anne letters of introduction to two distinguished Philadelphians: William Henry Furness, theologian, early antislavery champion, lifelong freind of Emerson, and father of Horace Howard Furness, the Shakespearean scholar; and Professor J. Peter Lesley, state geologist of Pennsylvania and secretary of the American Philosophical Society. Shortly after her arrival, Anne presented the letters, and the Gilchrists were warmly received. Although Herbert commented to Burroughs, in a letter on 18 December, that "Philadelphians, as far as we have an opportunity of judging, do not impress us as a very genial or hospitable race," he gave a glowing report of the Gilchrists' visit to Furness père: "We presented our introductions to Dr. Furness: his son Horace is a Shakespearean scholar and possesses a pair of theatrical gloves said to have belonged to Shakespeare; they were given to Mr. Horace Furness by Fanny Kemble, who had them from Garrick, which in itself makes them sufficiently interesting."[51] Three days earlier, Anne wrote to Rossetti that "of society here we have at present seen very little," but "there is one delightful family circle to which the Conways gave us an introduction—that of Prof. Lesley (the geologist), Director of the State Survey, with wife and daughter of the very best type of American women."[52] While she was living in Philadelphia, Anne became a member of the New Century Club. The first women's club founded in Philadelphia (1877), it was organized to provide women with "a forum for discussion of their interests."[53]

Anne's absorption in her passion for an imaginary Whitman had had another stultifying effect on her life. It had paralyzed her own creative powers. For seven years, with the exception of "Estimate," she had written nothing for publication. As another sign of the return of her former self and the emergence of a new and more eclectic self, not long after her arrival in America, Anne began to write again. A new field this time. She began a prose translation of Hugo's *La Légende des Siècles*. Why she chose to do this is a mystery. Perhaps in translation she found a diversion from household chores that was less demanding than original composition. Walt would say of her translation: "The best renderings of Hugo were Mrs. Gilchrist's. She put the Legende des Siecles into English: copied it for me—showed it to me—while she was here. It was nobly done. Do you know it?—the Pan and Deity business? Oh! how superb it was—how it opened up the great mines!—rich with ore: finer even than the French to English renderings of my French friend in Washington years ago."[54]

As Burroughs had predicted, the Gilchrists and 1929 were a godsend to Walt. "We have good meals, & take our time over them—I have the best room in the house, breezy & cool (& the water in it)," he wrote to Jack Johnston, a young Philadelphia friend.[55] And a day earlier, 19 June, 1877, he described life at 1929 to the Staffords' son Harry:

> ...it is all very pleasant here, every thing is so gentle & smooth, & yet they are all so jolly & much laughing & talking & fun—we have first rate times, over our meals, we take our time over them, & always something new to talk about....I dont suppose it would be so much fun for you here—but it suits an old man like me, (& then it pleases one's vanity to be made so much of)....At present it is about 11 ½ o'clock—Herbert is down stairs painting—the girls are sewing—Mrs. G is out shopping & at the groceries ... & I am sitting here in my front room in the great bay window at a big table writing this—a nice cool breeze blowing in—Why there it goes, the bell for 12 o'clock—right opposite us, the masons &c building a big house, all knock off work, & there are groups sitting down in shady places & opening their dinner kettles—I too will knock off for this time.[56]

With such a comfortable room always kept ready for him and such a cordial atmosphere always waiting, Walt's visits to 1929 became more frequent and more prolonged. "At Mrs. G's," "with the G's," "visit at Mrs G's," "dinner each day at 1929 22^d st," appeared more and more often on the pages of his daybooks.

Speaking of Anne and his time spent with her and her children, Walt would later say to Traubel: "Rossetti mentions Mrs. Gilchrist. Well, he had a right to—almost as much right as I had: a sort of brother's right: she was his friend, she was more than my friend. I feel like Hamlet when he said that forty thousand brothers could not feel what he felt for Ophelia. After all, Horace, we were a family—a happy family."[57] This sense of being a family, and the warmth and affection with which the Gilchrists shared it, is captured in *The Tea Party*, which Herbert painted from memory in 1884. In this totally-terrible-as-a-work-of-art, absolutely-charming-as-a-picture canvas, Anne and Walt and Grace are seated at a tea table, its intricately carved legs just visible under the white cloth. There are four blue-and-white china cups in front of Anne and a handsome silver teapot and cream pitcher beside her. A plate, shaped like a pie plate, holds something shiny—a tart of some kind? something jellied? Seated on Anne's right, Walt, dressed in gray and looking very old, is leaning forward to smell a flower. Grace, a pink flower in her dark hair—and a cat beside her chair, rubbing affectionately against her—is seated on her mother's left. The strange thing about the picture is that Walt is looking down, Anne is looking over his head, and Grace, her napkin in her hand, is looking off and up, as if she were listening for something. No one is looking at anyone else, not even at the artist. But in spite of its curious composition, or perhaps because of it, Herbert's picture conveys a wonderful sense of suspended motion—as if the principals, like children playing "statue," would come to life again at any moment, and continue their tea drinking and conversation.[58]

Walt was very fond of Anne's children. Although Grace would later write two magazine articles about him, in 1898 and 1927,[59] and close her memoir of her mother with an imagined picture of the poet's deathbed that pulls out all the stops of sentimentality, there seems to have been less rapport between the two while the Gilchrists were in America than between Walt and her brother

The Tea Party, **painted by Herbert Gilchrist, 1884. Department of Special Collections, Van Pelt Library, University of Pennsylvania.**

and sister. Since young Grace had little interest in literature, conversation with the poet would have held no special fascination; and to an eighteen-year-old he must have seemed incredibly ancient, Father Time himself. Walt was unquestionably aware of a lack of enthusiasm toward himself on her part. On 19 June, when Anne was out for the evening, Walt wrote from 1929 to Harry Stafford: "The girls & I had our supper together, & had a jolly time—the younger daughter came out finely, & she showed that she could make herself very agreeable & interesting when she has a mind to."[60] In describing Walt's farewell to the Gilchrists when they left for England, Grace wrote the following revealing passage in her memoir of her mother:

> On the eve of our departure, Walt called to take leave. We were all gathered in the parlour of our boarding house, in Madison Avenue, Walt kissed each in turn, my mother, brother and sister. When it came to my turn, I drew back, I hardly know what youthful caprice actuated me, or whether it was caprice. In some part it was constitutional dislike to being kissed by "bearded lips" but the larger part lay in a jealous concern for my family. Subconsciously I felt they had invested so large a capital of love and devotion in the wayward poet, that by a certain rough, youthful justice, I was constrained to give no more.
> "Not a kiss for Walt?" argued the "good grey poet." I shook my head, and remained silent. Carlyle has described his hero Teafelsdrockh [sic] as made "immortal by a kiss." I fear being young and callow I remained indifferent to any chance of immortality.[61]

Did she feel that "the wayward poet" had imposed not only on her family's love and devotion but on their hospitality? One can hardly blame her. And what did she mean by *wayward*?

Walt was devoted to Bee and she returned his affection. "The elder one is the noble one," he wrote to Harry. "The more I see of her the better I like her."[62] And to Jack Johnston, in describing the Gilchrists, Walt wrote: "There are two grown daughters—the eldest is a *first class trump*, she is my favorite every way."[63] Walt was deeply interested in Bee's medical studies. In the early 1860s, he had regularly visited sick stage drivers at the New York Hospital on Broadway, where he became friends with the members of the medical staff and watched surgery. This experience, in addition to his devoted service to wounded soldiers in field hospitals and in the army hospitals in Washington, gave him a very clear idea of what Beatrice was required to accomplish and endure. He admired her ambition, understood the emotional stress that was involved, and worried about the effect that the hard work might have on her health. On 13 December, 1877, he wrote to her from Camden:

> Bee, I have been thinking much the few hours past of what Mr Eldridge told me of a young Mrs Needham (an intimate friend of my Washington friends, & two years ago a fine healthy woman of 26) who too overwhelmingly swamped herself as a student at your Phila: medical school, a year & a half since, (crowding too much & too intense

study into too short a time) resulting in terrible brain troubles & a general caving in, & now (as Mr E told me last night on our journey down) of *death lately in a lunatic asylum*—just from sheer overwork, & too intense concentration, ardor, & continued strain—

My own trouble is an illustration of the same danger & I feel peculiarly sensible of it in others near to me.[64]

Herby and Walt were especially close.[65] Following the example of his father with Carlyle, during his first months in America Herby took copious notes of conversations with the poet. Walt enjoyed having the young artist with him in Camden or at the Staffords' and posed for numerous sketches and a portrait at Timber Creek, his favorite haunt near the farm. Walt often gave him orders in an affectionately paternal tone. "I have invited Mr. Eldridge, a Washington friend, to come up to your house & spend a couple of hours this evening," he wrote to Herby from Camden on 12 December, 1877. "Please have a fire made ready in the stove up in the room."[66] How Herby felt about "Dear Darling Walt"[67] is made dramatically clear in the portrait of him that he painted in 1887.

Unfortunately for Herbert, Eakins painted his famous portrait of Whitman in the same year. Eakins's portrait was generally considered the finer (although some of the poet's friends said it made him look like an old Dutch toper), and Walt openly preferred it. He felt that Herbert's portrait lacked "guts"; that it "prettified" him by giving him "Italianate curls" in his beard; that the picture needed "to be sent to a barber."[68] But in spite of disparaging comments made about it in comparing it with Eakins's *Whitman*—comments that Traubel seemed to delight in recording[69]—Herbert's is a magnificent portrait. Now in the Van Pelt Library at the University of Pennsylvania, it dominates the reading room of the Rare Books Department. A large canvas, it is awesomely majestic, breathtakingly beautiful—and obviously done with love. The details of the armchair in which Walt is seated, his gray suit, his white shirt with lace at the cuffs and on the collar are exquisite, the soft colors blending together in perfect harmony. The beard *is* curly. But rather than "prettifying" the poet, as Walt claimed that it did, it adds an almost upside-down-halo effect to the gentle dignity of the august face. Eakins emphasized the jovial side of Whitman's nature; Herbert emphasized his impressive size. Walt fits so tightly into Herbert's portrait that he fills the picture, dwarfing everything else; the top of his head touches the top of the canvas, and his arms press against its sides. Herbert's Whitman is unmistakably a powerful father image. And there is an equally unmistakable godlike quality about the massive figure and Olympian face. Herby saw Walt as God the Father.

Whitman could be a trying guest. He was not known for punctuality. In 1865, when John and Ursula Burroughs were living in Washington, Walt had Sunday breakfasts with them that he remembered ecstatically all his life. Burroughs would recall:

Walt Whitman, painted by Herbert Gilchrist, 1887. Department of Special Collections, Van Pelt Library, University of Pennsylvania.

Walt was usually late for breakfast, and Ursula, who was as punctual as the clock, would get in a pucker. The coffee would boil, the griddle would smoke, and car after car would go jingling by, but no Walt. The situation at times verged on the tragic. But at last a car would stop, and Walt would roll off it and saunter up to the door—so cheery, and so unaware of the annoyance he had caused, that we soon forgot our ill-humor. He always said Ursula's pancakes and coffee couldn't be beat.[70]

Walt was also notoriously untidy. He liked to have the floor, as well as every other flat surface in his room, heaped with litter—a turmoil of letters, books, manuscripts, notes, clippings, newspapers. "Now, Alma! Now Alma!" he would protest if Mrs. Johnston appeared with basket and broom, intent on "clarin' up" his room, when he was visiting his friends the John H. Johnstons in their house on Fifth Avenue.[71]

If these traits annoyed Anne, she never mentioned it. "I need not tell you our greatest pleasure is the society of Mr. Whitman, who fully realizes the ideal I had formed from his poems, and brings such an atmosphere of cordiality and geniality with him as is indescribable," she wrote to Rossetti.[72] And there is no question that Walt's society was a delight to Anne. Here again, after a long hiatus, was close communication with a strong and cultivated masculine mind, always exhilarating for Anne Gilchrist. With her father, her brother, her uncle Thomas Probert, and with Alex, the communication had been direct; with Emerson, Rousseau, and her study of Carlyle when she was a girl, it had been indirect. Here, once more, the communication was direct, personal, and on an almost daily basis. Anne enjoyed it to the utmost—and so did Walt.

Walt was not always taken with intellectual women. He detested Louise Chandler Moulton, a poet and one of this admirers, who was "of the gushing kind." "I can't endure her effusiveness," Walt told Traubel, "her dear this and dear that and dear the other thing make me shudder!"[73] He could not abide the "smart woman" or "the repartee woman—the woman who would prefer the false to the dull."[74] And solemnly intellectual women bored him beyond endurance. In a letter to Peter Doyle from Providence in 1868, he wrote:

> It is quite a change here from my associations either in Washington or New York. Evenings & meal times I find myself thrown amidst a mild, pleasant society, really intellectual, composed largely of educated women, some young, some not so young, every thing refined & polite, *not* disposed to small talk, conversing in earnest on profound subjects, but with a moderate rather slow tone, & in a kind & conciliatory manner—delighting in this sort of conversation, & spending their evenings till late in it. I take a hand in, for a change. I find it entertaining, as I say, for novelty's sake, for a week or two—but I know very well that would be enough for me. It is all first-rate, good & smart, but too constrained & bookish for a free old hawk like me.[75]

But conversation with brilliant, unaffected, serious but fun-loving Anne Gilchrist was a continuing source of wonder to Walt. With her, he told William Sloane Kennedy, "you did not have to abate the wing of your thought downward at all, in deference to any feminine narrowness of mind."[76] It was a pity, in his opinion, that her wonderful talk, like O'Connors', had not been somehow preserved. Writing was not the best of her, he would tell Traubel in 1888:

> The best of her was her talk—to hear her perfectly say these things which she has only imperfectly written. I shall never forget—never forget: she is over there now, where you are—eyeing me, overflowing with utterance. She was marvellous above other women in traits in which women are marvellous as a rule—immediate perception, emotion, deep inevitable insight. She had such superb judgment—it welled up and out and I only sat off and wondered: welled up from a reservoir of riches, spontaneously, unpremeditatedly. Women are ahead of us in that anyhow—way ahead of us. It was because she was that kind of a woman that I always trusted Mrs. Gilchrist's picture of Carlyle—of the Carlyles. She was not a blind dreamer—a chaser of fancies: she was concrete—spiritually concrete, I might say: not in the sordid sense of it but the big, the high. She was practical enough to know just how to ask that dangerous question, will it pay? and to answer it with high meanings. I know nothing more miserable, sickening, than Will it pay? as it is usually asked.[77]

The indissoluble bond that developed between Walt and Anne in the Philadelphia years was a genuine comradeship. The two had much in common. Both were, to a great extent, self-educated. They held the same view of conventional theology, and both were deeply interested in science. They both loved flowers, and children, and music. "By the bye, I feel a little sulky at your always taking a fling at the poor piano," Anne had written to Walt from London. "I see I have got to try & show you it too is capable of waking deep chords in the human soul when it is a vehicle of a great master's thought & emotions—if only my poor fingers prove equal to the task."[78] However, she seems not to have persuaded Walt that her instrument could compete with grand opera, his passion—"Ah this is indeed music—this suits me." Traubel would report that years later, when someone spoke of a "pee-a-nist," Walt "laughed and asked: 'Do you mean a pianner player?' W. objected to the piano anyway. 'It seems to be so unequal to the big things.' "[79] At 1929, Walt and Anne discussed art, science, literature, philosophy, politics, and personalities—always with spirit, if not always in agreement.

To illustrate the tenor and content of conversation when Whitman was with the Gilchrists, Herbert included a hodgepodge of extracts from his notebook in his biography of his mother: the poet's opinions of writers ranging from George Eliot to Plutarch; his reminiscences of Count Gurowski; and anecdotes that Walt related about a variety of celebrities—among them an English ambassador to Washington, Fredrika Bremer, Jenny Lind.[80] Giving the impression that conversation was primarily between himself and the poet, Anne is neither quoted nor mentioned. Walt must have chuckled when he read this. It was talking with Herby's mother that had delighted him at 1929 and that lingered vividly in his memory. The sparkle and depth not only of her conversation but of Anne herself were captured in the aged poet's tender recollections of her that Traubel recorded.

"Mrs. Gilchrist, with all her supreme cultivation, was gifted in a rare degree with a necessary don't-care-a-damn-ativeness," Walt told Traubel admiringly. "In fact, this was so marked in her that it was often thought she was inviting destruction."[81] Was he thinking of her gossip-defying trip to America? She was a woman, he was fond of saying, who "goes the whole distance of justifying woman—of proving her power, her equality, her consummate possibilites." Herbert, in the poet's words, was not strong—"puts no resisting front to the conventionalities of the time—but *she*—oh! she was *all* courage, bravery, power—yet all *womanly*, too—not a jot of the womanly abated for all the force. She was never conventional, unless she chose to be—unless she thought it as well to be conventional as not."[82]

Walt, who idolized "great mothers," was disturbed by Anne's intense dislike of Queen Victoria. "Even Mrs. Gilchrist, splended as she was—fair, discriminating—could never speak of the Queen but with contempt—the heartiest disdain." Traubel asked if these negations weren't rather for the queen than for the woman. Walt hesitated, then replied: "You may be right but they didn't sound as impersonal as that: as negations of the queen I would have assented to them."[83] Anne may have had no kind words for Victoria, but she was incensed by published gossip about the Carlyles' domestic problems. Walt applauded her angry defense of her friends. "I feel that I know all about that story and on good authority, too: from no less a person than Mrs. Gilchrist, who associated with both the Carlyles intimately and was in no sense a woman to be fooled," he told Traubel. "I attach oh! so great an importance to all she said to me on that subject: facts, pertinent facts, weighty; things she saw, again and again—goings on—enough to turn topsy-turvy all the alleged truths of newspaper gossip, the indecent generalizations of scribblers."[84]

It was as a scientist that Walt found Anne especially fascinating: "She was always abreast of the times: as to science she would be classified with the extreme radicals if anywhere: indeed, I imagine she'd take the logic of science and follow it out to the full, even beyond the adventurous limits of the savant himself."[85] Anne often told Walt that she firmly believed, indeed it was the core of her philosophy, that, in spite of turbulent and revolutionary tendencies of the time, humanity was "going somewhere." "It was Mrs. Gilchrist's favorite expression—when she looked out on this surging seething man— that we were all going somewhere—not only that, but somewhere good," the poet recalled. He added: "And I believe it."[86]

The Good Gray Poet flourished at 1929. "Never saw Walt look so handsome—so new and fresh," Burroughs wrote in his journal after spending a night with Walt at the Gilchrists'.[87] Grace would remember the poet singing about the house or in his room before breakfast—opening bars and snatches from operas, street songs, even "The Star-Spangled Banner"—as "an outburst of pure emotional and physical *abandon* to the delight of living."[88] And she would remember that, when the family was together, Walt always insisted that the younger members be drawn into the conversation no matter what the subject might be; when a discussion was at its height, he would turn to a young listener and ask, "And what does G[iddy] say to this?" Sometimes in the evening there was music for entertainment, and sometimes Walt recited poetry: seldom his own—with the exception of "The Mystic Trumpeter," which he loved to declaim—but often Tennyson's. And on summer evenings the poet introduced the Gilchrists to the American custom of socializing around the "stoop." Walt would sit in a large rattan rocking chair that was carried out to the pavement for him, and the others sat beside him on the white marble steps. Even when he was not actually in residence at 1929—and when he was not with the Staffords at Kirkwood—Walt would come over by the afternoon ferry from Camden every evening except Sunday for six o'clock "tea-supper," riding the red cars of the Market Street line out to North twenty-second. Walt loved food and he enjoyed Anne's "tea-suppers" enormously. In a letter from Camden to Herby, who was at the Staffords' painting, he wrote: "I went over to your mother's yesterday afternoon about 5½ & staid till after 8.... We had a good tea—I punished a fearful quantity of good oatmeal mush & stewed blackberries."[89] Walt invited his friends to 1929 and entertained them there as freely as if it had been his own home.

Many of the guests at 1929 were Walt's as well as Anne's. Burroughs came down from Esophus-on-Hudson; "Come on to Mrs. Gilchrist's 16th or 17th—I will prepare them—I will be there," Walt wrote to him before one visit.[90] George and Louisa Whitman came over from Camden to dinner. Charles Eldridge spent an evening at 1929 at Walt's invitation, and Joseph Marvin came to see him there. Hattie and Jessie Whitman, Walt's nieces from Saint Louis, spent five days with Anne when they were visiting in Camden.[91] Joaquin Miller, one of Walt's old friends and a loyal admirer, came to tea. And in May 1877, at Walt's suggestion, Edward Carpenter came to spend a week.

Like Anne, Carpenter had first read *Leaves of Grass* in 1869, when he was a student at Cambridge; and, like Anne, reading it had changed his life. Deeply moved, especially by the "Calamus" poems, he had corresponded with the poet for several years and came to America specifically to see him. Walt had not been expecting him, and, shortly after the young Englishman's sudden appearance at the Whitmans' house in Camden, the poet invited him to join him at 1929. The Gilchrists, particularly Grace, were immediately taken with the handsome young poet, who "slid into friendly intimacy in no time."[92]

Carpenter had arrived, bag in hand, at 1929—where, in his words, "a kind of prophet's chamber" was always ready for Walt—to find the whole family sitting out on the doorstep, with Whitman seated in his armchair, the moonlight shining on his beard and hair. "After this for a week of evenings I made one of the party. How pleasant it was!" he would recall warmly. Writing in 1906, still dazzled by the poet, he would picture his hostess only as a figure in the background, describing her briefly as "a capable and large-minded woman," the first Englishwoman to recognize Whitman's genius publicly.[93] However, writing in 1924, more than forty years after his trip to Philadelphia—and six years after the publication of Anne's letters to Walt had created a sensation on both sides of the Atlantic— he would make her a focal point of his stay at 1929. "The general situation was evident enough—it could hardly be concealed," he would write knowingly, as if suddenly endowed with CAT scan hindsight. "I saw that Anne Gilchrist was suffering."[94] And he was undoubtedly right. Much as she enjoyed having guests, after a week of extra bed making, bread making, shopping for groceries, breakfasts, dinners, and "tea-suppers," it is very likely that Anne Gilchrist was suffering acutely— from fatigue.

And, in addition, Anne was not feeling well. A few months later—in September 1877—she had what she described in a letter to Mrs. Simmons, her neighbor at Brookbank, as "a somewhat severe operation (under ether) to cure an injury received at the birth of one of my children which has always troubled me." "Its success," Anne continued, "depended largely on skilful nursing afterward and this Bee accomplished as only medical training could have enabled her to accomplish it. The surgeon too was very skilful—indeed I believe there are some of the ablest in the world here. I was laid by [?] for about a month—am now quite well again, & very glad I went through with it, for the benefit I received is great."[95] The surgery probably was performed at the Woman's Hospital, near the Medical College. Bee sent Walt regular reports on her mother's condition, and he wrote affectionate notes to Anne before the operation and during her convalescence, "abstaining from coming over for fear of being in the way."[96] On 5 October, Walt noted in his day-books: "After three weeks absence visited Mrs. G's—Mrs. G temporarily sitting up." On 22 October, he resumed having supper at 1929.[97]

Anne was on the friendliest terms with George and Louisa Whitman. Several times she went over to New Jersey to have dinner with them in Camden—a "somewhat dreary and ugly suburb," in Grace's opinion[98]—and to enjoy a drive in the country afterward. Once she ventured even farther into Jersey. On Walt's birthday, she and Giddy and Bee went down to Kirkwood and paid him a surprise visit at the Staffords' farm. "Thursday was Mr. Whitman's birthday and as he was down at Kirkwood we kept it by all going down there for the day, taking our dinner with us and eating it by the stream, Timber

Creek," Anne wrote to a friend. "It was tremendously hot, but in the buoyant stimulating air, you can stand the heat and we all enjoyed the day."[99]

Anne had understood "Children of Adam" immediately, but she never seems to have grasped the full meaning of the "Calamus" poems. Although she must have become aware that there was a great energizing force in Walt's life that she could not share, she never seems to have recognized his homosexuality. Like Emerson—who objected to the explicit heterosexuality throughout *Leaves of Grass*, but did not seem to object to the equally explicit homosexuality in "Calamus"—Anne may have believed that the masculine nouns and pronouns and the erotic imagery in the "Calamus" cluster were used symbolically or metaphorically. One wonders what she thought of Walt's intense attachment to nineteen-year-old Harry Stafford. Burroughs seems to have been equally naive—or affectionately tolerant. "A great event! Walt came home with me from New York Friday night, the 16th, and stayed till 4 this afternoon. Harry Stafford came with him," he wrote in his journal on 21 March, 1877. "They cut up like two boys and annoyed me sometimes. Great tribulations in the kitchen this morning. Can't get them up to breakfast in time."[100]

With other friends, Walt was more cautious. When he took Harry with him to visit the Johnstons in New York, he told them in one letter that his "(adopted) son" would be with him, and in another: "My nephew & I when traveling always share the same room together & the same bed."[101] Like Peter Doyle, who had previously given Whitman "perturbations," Harry was semiliterate. He was also moody, jealous, insecure, and quick-tempered. He and Walt frequently quarreled, said good-bye, then reconciled. Speaking of his temper, a penitent Harry wrote to Walt: "I will have to *controol* it or it will send me to states prison or some other bad place."[102] Like Anne, Harry wore a ring on his finger that the poet had given him. His parents were extremely fond of Herby, but Harry detested the young Englishman. In a letter from Kirkwood to Walt, who was in Camden, Harry wrote:

> Herbret cut me pretty hard last night at the supper table, you must not let on if I tell you; he called me a "dam fool," I wasn't talking to him any way! we was all talking of telegraphing, and father said he was reading of a man who was trying to overdo it and I said that I did not think he could do it and the[n] Herbret stuck in that, it did not sit very well, and if I had been near enough to smacked him in the "Jaw" I would of done it. you must not say anything about it to him or any one, he thinks he can do as he wants to with me but he will find out sometime [t]hat he is fooling with the wrong one.[103]

Walt replied in a more severe tone than he usually used with Harry: "Harry, I don't know the particulars about the Herbert scrape, but you must let up on him—I suspect you said something pretty tantalizing before he call'd you that—Let it go—Of course I shan't say any thing about it to any one."[104]

At the same time that he was involved with Harry, Walt carried on intense, although briefer, relationships with three other young men: Jack Johnston, son of a Philadelphia artist;[105] Albert Johnston, the son of his friend, the New York jeweler; and Edward Cattell, a twenty-five-year-old farmhand and friend of the Staffords. In the draft of a letter to Ed on 24 January, 1877—telling him to stay away from the Staffords—Walt invited him to come over "to 1929 north 22d street Philadelphia & see me," thought better of it, and left out the passage.[106]

Walt spent the 1877 Christmas season—10-30 December—at 1929. It was a festive time. "Out every day—evenings at Mrs G's," Walt wrote in his daybook. "—walks at 1 & 2 o'clock along Chestnut st—the crowds of promenaders, purchasers, visiters from the country &—the toy-sellers along the curbstones—the shows of goods & really rich, wonderful, ingenious things in the shop windows."[107] On 23 December, Anne wrote to Mrs. Simmons: "We shall have an American Poet & a Russian singer to dinner with us on Christmas day. The latter and her children cannot speak a word of English, but we get on in French. Grace is taking singing lessons of her. She is a true artist."[108] These guests would have been an additional pleasure to Walt, although he spoke no French. Speaking of Walt's taste in music, Grace would write in her memoir: "The music that could be given in a drawing-room with only a piano, left him somewhat unresponsive. But singing almost always appealed to him. A Russian prima donna came often to our house and he would listen to her with keen enjoyment. She had a fine contralto voice. She sang songs from 'Faust' and from Glinka's 'A Life for the Czar.' "[109]

The prima donna and her children were not the Gilchrists' only Russian guests while they were living at 1929. "The integuments of national character are always markedly interesting—to me full of attractions. It must have been ten years ago, I met Russians—a number of them—at Mrs. Gilchrist's," Walt told Traubel in 1889. "She lived here at that time—on 22^d street, north—far up—it must have been near where you went to the opera. There was a Russian vessel came up into the harbor about then—several of her crew got into the habit of stopping at Mrs. Gilchrist's—so of course I met them, benefited, enjoyed. One was young—fell in love with one of her daughters—even proposed marriage, which was declined."[110] Did Grace's teacher introduce the Russian crew to the Gilchrists? And was it Giddy with whom the young sailor fell in love?

On Christmas Eve, Walt went with Joaquin Miller to the opening of Miller's new play, *The Danites*. And on 27 December, the poet took the Gilchrists to see it.[111] Walt sat in a recess of the box, now and then nodding approval with the reserve of a seasoned playgoer who has seen all the best.[112] But Anne enjoyed every minute of her night at the theater. The play gave a lively picture of the California miner and his ways, she reported to Rossetti, and she hoped that it would be produced in England with the same cast.[113]

In her long, woman-to-woman letter to Mrs. Simmons on 23 December, Anne gave her friend some delightfully candid observations on America. "Christmas is kept pretty much as it is in England. The streets are quite green with the display of sapling fir trees for the children—and the giving of presents even more universal than with us," Anne wrote. She found the custom of decorating graves in a cemetery "a distinctive American trait" and marveled at the "people continually wending past our house to a large cemetery close by with garlands & crosses of flowers." American markets were "a pretty sight" and American cranberries a wonderment: "Cranberries not like those poor little things we see in casks in England from Sweden, but round & red and about as large as a cherry are made into a jelly or jam & eaten with every kind of meat & poultry here." "Perhaps you will take a house-wifely interest in prices—my turkey was 7½ cents [?] per lb., my beef was 8½ cents [?]" thrifty Anne told her former neighbor. She would bring back an American cookery book, she thought, for Americans "are great at all kinds of light delicate cakes, rolls, biscuits." And she was sure that she would bring some rocking chairs, for "they are the most comfortable chairs in the world—not hot & enervating like a great stuffed armchair, but equally good for leaning back or sitting up in."[114]

In addition to the letter's descriptions of new scenes and new experiences, and Anne's patent enjoyment of them, it also contains a confession of homesickness. "If all went well Percy was married yesterday....He has a pleasant cottage in Blaenavon and my mother's furniture all nicely done up makes it look thoroughly comfortable, he wrote me now, and I need not say he is very happy. I think he has chosen a woman well fitted to make home happy and to give him real companionship. How I long to go to see them! and indeed when I get thinking about it, and about dear friends and family scenes, I feel as if I must start off at once on our return." On "our return"—Anne has clearly abandoned her original plan to settle permanently in America. "What a splendid country it is," she writes, "and what a future it has before it! with its boundless productiveness, its beauty, its brilliant climate, its keen-witted, energetic, high spirited people. I rejoice that we came—to see it all with our own eyes." Then she adds: "But I also rejoice very much that I do not feel as if I ought to stay—as I should have done if it had offered manifestly better advantages and opportunities for Herby and Bee than England." She also seems to have seen enough of Philadelphia. She and her children would "hold on" in the States for another year and a half because, after her graduation, Bee was anxious to spend a year at the Boston Hospital— "and we to see something more of America."[115] Fond as she was of Walt, had Anne seen enough of him too on a daily basis? Had she discovered that the American Bard had a second calling—a professional guest?[116]

After completing the two-year course at the Woman's Medical College, Bee received her degree of Doctor of Medicine at the twenty-sixth annual commencement, held in Association Hall, Philadelphia, on Thursday, 14 March, 1878, at 12:00 M. In the faculty balloting on the candidates, she had received sixty-seven white balls and three black—one of the highest scores in her class. Bee's thesis was "Lacerations of the Perineum"; Caroline Wiley's was "Fibromata." Degrees were conferred on seventeen graduates by the president, T. Morris Perot Esq., and the valedictory address was delivered by Benjamin B. Wilson, M. D., professor of the principles and practice of surgery.[117] After graduation, Bee was accepted as an intern at the New England Hospital for Women and Children in Boston. Caroline Wiley also applied for an internship at the New England Hospital, but was refused because of her color by the Board of Physicians. She was afterward admitted by unanimous decision by the Board of Management.[118]

The Gilchrists left Philadelphia in late April. Walt wrote to Burroughs from Camden on 29 March: "Beatrice Gilchrist is over here with us this evening—the G's break camp here in three or four weeks—spend the ensuing year excursively in America."[119] On 7 April, Bee and Herbert went down to Kirkwood, presumably to say good-bye to the Staffords, stopping in Camden to see the Whitmans on the way back. And on 23 April, Walt spent his last evening at 1929. A few days later, Herby went to Brooklyn to begin studying art in New York, Bee may have gone directly to the New England Hospital in Boston, and Anne and Giddy went to the Round Hill Hotel in Northampton, Massachusetts, recommended by the Lesleys, to spend the summer.

"I think I told you that when we had accomplished our purpose in Philadelphia, when, that is Bee had graduated, I should store my furniture and see a little of other parts of America," Anne wrote to Mrs. Simmons from Northampton. "[We left] the 'City of Homes' as they call Philadelphia, after a pleasant year and a half, not without regrets and leaving behind some friends whom we cordially like, and shall not, I hope quite lose sight of."[120] However, dismantling 1929 had proved to be more of an undertaking than Anne had anticipated. She lent her pictures and prints to the New Century Club, "a ladies club of which I am a member, to hang on the walls of their beautiful drawing-room, which not only gives them the opportunity of enjoying them, but was much better for my treasures."[121] Her "jolly antique furniture" was lent to the loan exhibition of the Pennsylvania Museum in Memorial Hall, "where they will store it for me as long as I please for nothing, and glad to have it." Inexpensive bedroom furniture that Anne had bought when she came to Philadelphia was sold, and china, glass, blankets, carpets— "all that would pack in moderate compass"—were packed and stored.[122] John and Ursula Burroughs had invited the Gilchrists to stop at Esophus for a visit on their way to Massachusetts, but this proved to be impossible, and, on 1 May, Anne wrote to Burroughs from Round Hill:

You have my post-card long ere this, I trust, but still feel quite guilty for having put off writing it as long as I did. The truth is, I could not see my way or tell, to a day or two, when we should get off, we had planted our tent so firmly and spread our possessions around us so, at 1929.... We were so dead tired after completing all this and rushing about to say good-bye to many kind friends, etc., that we should have been the stupidest and dullest of guests—so it was best to come straight on here, and have the pleasure of seeing you in your beautiful home as something in store for the future.

She added a brief note about Walt: "He is fairly well again—not so strong as before yet, but in a way to be so soon, now he can get out and be so constantly in the open air."[123]

Nineteen twenty-nine "stands empty and forlorn now," Anne told Burroughs. And so ended what three years later, looking back with wonderment, she would call: "Strange episode in my life!"[124]

11
A BRITISH LIONESS

> Upward again on slow-firm pinions slanting, their separate diverse flight,
> She hers, he his, pursuing.
>
> Walt Whitman

Samuel Palmer had spoken of Brookbank as "your sweet house on the 'L'Allegro' upland among the green hills." At the Round Hill Hotel in Northampton, Anne felt that she was again a dweller on L'Allegro upland. "First let me describe our hotel which is a large rambling old-fashioned, picturesque house built mostly of wood, as are all the houses in New England, and I believe in America generally except in the cities. It would hold at a pinch 200 guests," she wrote to Mrs. Simmons. "All along the garden front is that delightful appendage of American houses, a broad piazza (ours is 150 feet long) where you can have shade and enjoy the air and view at all times. Of course it is well supplied with rocking-chairs. At your feet is a terraced garden and lawn with a border of old-fashioned flowers, below that a large orchard hanging on the slope of the hill, when we came it was in full bloom. And below that the village or small town of Northampton entirely nestled in trees, beyond that again, the valley of the Connecticut, meadows with a river which is about ¼ mile broad winding through them. And still further on ranges of hills encircling the whole, much as Blackdown, Iron Hill, Hind Head, and the South Downs, jut out and encircle the weald of Sussex."[1]

Round Hill was a welcome change for Anne and Grace after their twenty memorable but arduous months in Philadelphia. Giddy reveled in respite from housework and in croquet on the lawn after dinner.[2] Anne completed her Hugo translation,[3] took long country walks—her first since she had left England—and explored Northampton, the subject of a long essay, "Three Glimpses of a New England Village," that she wrote during the summer. Although "Three Glimpses" was not published until 1884, several years after her return to England, in this charming study the voice of the author of the scientific essays and "A Neglected Art" is heard for the first time after a long silence.

Anne had a keen and appreciative eye for local color. Everything about Northampton delighted her: its magnificent elms, "from the branches of one of which Jonathan Edwards preached to the Indians"; its "excellent free library, with spacious airy reading-room," where she researched the town's early history; the unusual-to-an-English-eye sights in the surrounding countryside—tobacco barns, apples "half as large and quite as red as full-blown peonies," rattlesnakes, "chipmucks," the tall, slim, mild American robin, so unlike his saucy English cousin.[4] However, "Three Glimpses" is not the usual enthusiastic travel piece so popular in the nineteenth century. Like Anne's scientific essays, it is based on scholarly research, and, like "A Neglected Art," it offers some perceptive social commentary.

Socially, Anne saw Northampton as another Cranford: "There is the same preponderance of maiden ladies and widows—for what should the men do there? New England farming is a very slow and unprofitable affair compared with farming in the West, and there are no manufactures of any importance. There are the same tea-parties, with a solitary beau in the centre, like the one white flower in the middle of a nosegay; the same modest goodness, kindliness, refinement, making the best of limited means and of restricted interests." However, although it shared the circumstances of its English counterpart, in Anne's view Northampton was a Cranford with a difference. In the single women of the American Cranford, she found a public spirit and a spirit of enterprise that "strikes out boldly in some direction or other:

> What would Miss Jenkyns have said to the notion of a college which should embody the most advanced ideas for giving young women precisely the same educational opportunities as young men? She would justly have felt that it was enough to make Dr. Johnson turn in his grave. Yet such a scheme has been realized by one of the maiden ladies of Northampton or its immediate neighbourhood, in Smith College—a really noble institution; where, also, the experiment is being tried of housing the students, not in one large building, but in a cluster of pretty-looking, moderate-sized homes, standing amid lawn and garden, where they are allowed under certain restrictions, to enter into and receive the society of the village, so that their lives may not be a too monotonous routine and "grind."[5]

And she cited another Northampton maiden lady, who, without any funds of her own, had achieved an even more remarkable success. Miss Harriet Rogers had perfected and introduced on a large scale the system of "visible speech" or lipreading, which enabled the deaf and those who cannot speak to hear and speak. Her success with a few private pupils had led to the founding of the Deaf and Dumb Institution in Northampton.[6] Anne concluded this segment of "Three Glimpses" with her first public defense of the single woman; her first public declaration of the right of the woman who is widowed or has never married to a respected place in society and to an active, productive, rewarding life. In the same tone that she used to urge Englishwomen to take over the management of their own kitchens, she urged the single women of England to follow the example of their American sisters:

Our actual Cranford over the sea, then, has a considerable advantage over the Cranford of romance, in that her heroines do not wait for the (in fiction) inevitable, faithful, long-absent, mysteriously-returning-at-the-right-moment lover to redeem their lives from triviality, and renew their faded bloom. And, in the present state of the world's affairs, what is more needed than the single woman who succeeds in making her life worth living, honourably independent, and of value to others? Through such will certainly be given new scope and impetus to the development of women generally, and in the long-run, therefore, good results for all.[7]

Before long, Herby was a dweller on a L'Allegro upland of his own. Shortly after his arrival in Brooklyn, he wrote an enthusiastic letter to Walt. He found Brooklyn and New York tremendously exciting, he told the poet, and he had already met a number of publishers and artists, among them Wyatt Eaton, the painter. "I don't wonder you like, & are exhilarated by, New York & Brooklyn—They are the places to *live*," Walt replied on 10 May. "Pleas'd to hear you go around with the New York artists, designers, young fellows, & folk in the picture trade, publishing, &c—I think with the superb *foundation* you have it will be just the thing for you."[8] However, Herby did not stay long in "mast-hemm'd Manhattan" and "Brooklyn of ample hills." Perhaps there were no classes at the Art Students League of New York during the summer months. Perhaps, after the novelty had worn off, he found the cities hot and lonely and living in a boarding house in Brooklyn not conducive to painting on his own. Whatever the reason, he joined Anne and Grace at Round Hill for a short time, and by mid-July he was boarding at a farm belonging to George Rogers near the village of Chesterfield. "You see at length I moved into a farm some 15 miles from Northampton on the top of a mountain," he wrote to Bee on 22 July. "I feel very much more comfortable & at home here & am able to concentrate my energies entirely on painting."[9]

During the months that she lived in Philadelphia, Anne Gilchrist is visible to the modern reader almost entirely through the eyes of others: in Walt's letters and his notations in his daybooks; in the aged poet's memories of her that Traubel recorded; in the observations of Burroughs and Carpenter. What she was thinking and feeling during those months, the modern reader, who knows her so intimately in her letters to Whitman before her trip to America, can only guess. The few letters to friends in England that Anne had time to write, and that still exist, were primarily descriptive; her letters to Percy and Norah were undoubtedly more personal, but none of these has survived. However, after the family broke camp at 1929, Anne's voice can be heard again speaking intimately in miraculously preserved letters to Herby and Bee—chatty, confiding, sometimes rebuking, but always loving letters, which describe Anne's new experiences and also reveal her concerns. In a letter to Herby from Round Hill on 9 May, there is the first evidence that, even with the income inherited from her mother, Anne found living in America required sailing very close to the wind financially. "I enclose a P.O. order for $10.00 as you decidedly wish to stay on. But please observe that $30.00 for three weeks besides travelling expenses is pretty stiff under present circumstances," she wrote, and added an urgent postscript: "Don't get boots if you can possibly help it in N.Y. As you can buy a really good pr. here fit for country wear for $4."[10] With so many guests and extra tea suppers at 1929, did Anne have to manage her funds very carefully there too? Did she have no servant because she could not afford a competent one?

Her mother's loving and supportive letters must have been especially welcome to Beatrice. By no stretch of the imagination could Bee have been considered a dweller on a L'Allegro upland. The New England Hospital for Women and Children in Boston, one of the nineteenth century's outstanding medical institutions for women, was under the demanding direction of its founder, German-born Dr. Marie Zakrzewska.[11] Dr. Zak, as she was called, one of the first doctors in America to use sanitary and sterilizing methods,[12] was determined that her hospital would achieve the same standard of excellence as male-dominated institutions. And it did. In one area it even surpassed them. After a new and larger hospital, designed by Dr. Zak, was built in 1873 with a separate "maternity cottage," the incidence of puerperal sepsis at the New England Hospital was six times less than at the prestigious, male-directed Boston Lying-In.[13] Dr. Zak was not interested in all women in medicine, only in the best—and she was determined that her hospital would produce them. It did. Augusta and Emily Pope, Mary Putnam Jacobi, Emma Call, Lucy Sewall, and Fanny Berlin were only a few of the distinguished early women physicians in America who were interns or resident physicians at the New England Hospital. When Bee began her internship in May 1878, interns were appointed for a training period of twelve months, serving three months each in the medical, obstetrical, and surgical wards and three months in the outpatient dispensary. Fifteen "Rules for Students" governed every aspect of their lives. In April 1876, the interns had presented a list of grievances to Dr. Zak, complaining that they were treated harshly, "ruled with an iron rod, so as to feel like guilty children." The only concession that Dr. Zak made was that, although interns would still be called "Miss" or "Mrs." in the hospital (a regulation that they felt was intended to "lower them in their position"), they would be addressed as "Doctor" in the outpatient dispensary.[14]

In a letter to Walt, Bee described an intern's day at the turreted New England Hospital on Codman Avenue, Boston Highlands.

> Hospital life is beginning to seem a long-accustomed life. I enjoy all the duties involved & all the human relations. Even getting up at night is compensated for by yielding a sense of importance & independence. I sleep in a large room with three windows, & three beds in a row. Breakfast at 7, & we are supposed to have seen all our patients before breakfast, but do not keep to that rule.

After breakfast, round to count pulses & respirations, note condition, dress any wound, in charge, etc. At ½ past 8 o'clock go the rounds with the resident physician (Dr. Berlin), all the students, & superintendent of nurses. Then put up medicine, each for her own patients (about 8 in no.), give electricity, etc. If one's patient has an ache or pain, the nurse whistles for the student (my whistle is 2). She sees the patient, orders what is necessary, or if serious reports to Dr. Berlin. Then there is some microscopic work, & copying out the history & daily record of the case & making out the temperature charts more than fills in the day. . . . In the evening we go round again & count pulses & respirations & note temperatures.[15]

Bee was devoted to the resident physician, Fanny Berlin, who would be an attending physician at the hospital for many years. She described her to Walt as "a learned, charming woman of 28 . . . perfectly unaffected, very intelligent, & has been thoroughly trained. She is a Russian." Bee did not mention Dr. Zak in her letter to Walt. But she had told her mother about the stern directress, and Anne sent some words of comfort to the daughter whom she always addressed as "my darling." The father of a former intern had told her that his daughter "couldn't bear Dr. Zakshefska [Anne was spelling phonetically]—says she reserves all her kindness for the poor, and is unfeeling & disagreeable to the rest."[16]

During the three months that she was required to spend at the hospital's outpatient dispensary on Warrenton Street, Bee had some respite from Dr. Zak's daily surveillance. She and Caroline Wiley served together. "Down at this Dispensary we work just as hard as at the Hospital, but our spare minutes are our own (no records to write out); our work is under our own control; we are out in fresh air half the day, sometimes half the night, making intimate acquaintance with all sorts of people & places & with far distant parts of Boston," Bee wrote to Walt in February. "Only two students live at the Dispensary—Dr. Wiley (the coloured Philadelphia student you saw) & myself. In tastes we have much in common & on the whole I prefer to live with her rather than with any of the other students." She added proudly, "Last Tuesday I had twins all by myself."[17] Through Caroline, Bee had a wide circle of black friends in Boston. "Bee is seeing a great deal of the educated coloured people at Boston," Anne wrote to Walt, "was at the meeting of a literary club—the only white among 20 or 30 coloured ladies—likes them much."[18]

Anne's voice can be heard again in the letters that she wrote to Whitman after she left Philadelphia, and which, like her earlier letters to the poet, were published in 1918. If any proof is needed of what happened when Walt and Anne met, it is patent in these letters. They reflect a warm, affectionate, comfortable friendship between two persons who find each other consummately stimulating and congenial. They are *not* love letters. There is no faintest trace of the ardor, the impassioned declarations, the fervent phrasing of Anne's pre-Philadelphia letters to the poet. To "My Dearest Friend" she sends news of herself and her children, inquires solicitously about his health, sends remembrances to the Staffords and Whitmans, and ends with "love from us all." Reading these letters, it couldn't be clearer that after meeting the real WW, Anne abandoned forever her fantasy of the poet as her destined lover; and out of the anticlimax of their meeting—which would have sent a lesser woman flouncing home in disappointment—built a friendship that gave a new dimension to both their lives.

Anne's post-Philadelphia letters to Whitman reveal something else. She was not in love with Walt, but she missed him. Writing to him from Massachusetts and New York, she hoped that he would join her and her children; later, writing from England, she wished that he could come for a visit. "Please write soon; I am longing for a letter," she would add as a postscript from London. Whitman had a mesmerizing charm. In spite of his idiosyncrasies and monumental absorption in himself—and even when he was a very old man preoccupied primarily with his bowels—this charm held his admirers spellbound. The list of genuflectors, who allowed him to impose on them as if he were granting a privilege, is a long one, and, in all fairness, the name of Anne Gilchrist must be added to the list. In her memoir of her mother written after the publication of Anne's letters to the poet, Grace, who seems to have been immune to Walt's charisma, would comment caustically on "the Poet on the other side of the Atlantic, the inspirer of ideal affection and devotion." She would ask: "Was he not in reality a strange blend of personalities? the Walt Whitman Super-man, creator of 'Leaves of Grass' and the man Whitman of many moods, good and bad. Wayward, colossal, in egoism with an almost child-like vanity and love of applause and notoriety."[19] Surely Anne, a woman known for her astuteness, was not blind to the duality of Walt's personality, which was so apparent to her daughter. Surely, as she trudged to the market for extra groceries and cheerfully took in Walt's guests, she was aware that she was being imposed upon. But, like her coadmirers of Walt—like Burroughs, Harned, Traubel, and the rest—she was a willing victim of his powerful charm.

However, it was not only Walt's charm that Anne found irresistible. As Grace shrewdly observed, there was something childlike about the poet. Others have pointed out that Whitman accepted what was offered to him by his friends—money, hospitality, gifts—as a child unquestioningly accepts what is offered. Anne Gilchrist's mothering instincts were as strong as her sexuality, and the childlike was irresistibly appealing. For as long as she lived, her devotion to the poet was loving, loyal, serving, and also tenderly maternal.

In midsummer Anne found the hot weather in Northampton enervating. "Mamma is not at all well at Northampton. I think this clean dry air would suit her wonderfully well," Herby wrote to Bee from Chesterfield.[20] Anne and Giddy joined him at the Rogers's farm on 25 July, and in the higher altitude Anne's energy returned. She enjoyed the country life and her rural neighbors, and she and Giddy stayed until mid-September. To his mother's disappointment, Herby left them in August and returned to the Staffords'—to paint a landscape of Timber Creek and a portrait of Walt. "Must tell you about Herb's picture, he calls *September Days*—(name not very good, but will do)," Walt wrote to Anne. "Picture itself, in my opinion, *very good*, the best he has painted."[21] "What you say of Herby's picture delights me, dear Friend. I have been grieving he was not with us, sharing the pleasant times we have had and enlarging his circle of friends," Anne replied. "I wonder if you are as satisfied with his portrait of you as with the landscape."[22] The disappointment of Herby's return to New Jersey was offset by joyful news from England: Percy and Norah's son, Alexander Fitzmaurice Gilchrist, was born on 10 September. "I can't settle to anything or think of anything since I received Percy's letter but the baby & Norah," an ecstatic Anne wrote to Walt.[23]

From Chesterfield, Anne and Grace went to Concord. They boarded with the wife of Lidian Emerson's brother, Dr. Charles Jackson—"a frank sensible unpretentious kind of woman—not literary or intellectual herself, but accustomed to live among those who are."[24] Anne was enchanted with "dear little Concord," where she found the townspeople "as friendly as they are intellectual." "We are rowed on the beautiful river every day that is warm enough," she wrote to Walt in October. "Never in my life have I enjoyed outdoor pleasures more—I hardly think so much—enhanced as they are by the companionship of very lovable men and women. They lead an easy-going life here—seem to spend half their time floating about on the river—or meeting in the evening to talk & read aloud.[25]

Concord seems to have been equally enchanted with the charming friend of the Carlyles, the Rossettis, and Tennyson.[26] Miss Ellen Emerson came to tea—"she is tall, large-featured, pleasing," Anne told Herby—and George Bradford, Emerson's classmate at Harvard and a close friend of Hawthorne, came with her.[27] Anne met Bronson Alcott (no mention of Louisa); she met Judge Rockwood Hoar, brother of Elizabeth Hoar, faithful fiancée of Emerson's brother Charles, who died on the eve of their wedding; she met Franklin Sanborn ("the most magnificent looking man I ever saw in my life," she told Bee),[28] founder of a progressive coeducational school that Sophia Hawthorne would not allow her daughters to attend because she did not approve of "this commingling of youths and maidens at the electric age in school";[29] and she met Frederick May Holland, author of *The Reign of the Stoics*, and his wife, who became her lifelong friends.

Anne's most memorable meeting in Concord was with Emerson, her girlhood idol. "He looked very beautiful—and talked in a friendly, pleasant manner," she reported to Walt.[30] And to Rossetti she wrote: "Emerson is of course the central figure, and is personally beloved and honoured by his townsmen in a way that is pleasant to see; as well he may be. . . . We spent two evenings with him. His conversation reverted continually to Carlyle and their early intercourse. His memory fails somewhat as to recent names and topics, but as is usual in such cases, all the mental impressions that were made when he was in full vigour remain clear and strong."[31] However, she gave Burroughs a more candid account. Burroughs wrote to a friend:

> Mrs. Gilchrist told me she visited Emerson last fall in Concord, twice. He is very serene and cheerful, remembers earlier things and events, but is fast losing his hold on later. He saw Walt Whitman's photograph in her album, and on being told who it was asked her if he was one of her English friends.
> "What was the name of my best friend?" he will inquire of his wife.
> "Henry Thoreau," she will answer.
> "Oh, yes, Henry Thoreau."[32]

Since Concord was not far from Boston, Anne had looked forward to seeing Bee frequently. "Surely, my darling, you can come and spend each Sunday here. I am sure your fellow students would not mind that little extra amount just while I am here," she wrote, adding, "I hope you are not looking as tired as when I last saw you." Anne went to the station the following Sunday morning, but Bee did not come. "Now make up your mind you will come next Sunday," her mother entreated. "The babies will go on coming into the world all right by somebody else's help and you will be working there all day long and every day for the whole year, you surely need not scruple."[33] Bee was able to spend one Sunday with Anne and Grace. She and her mother walked to Hawthorne's old house in the morning, "& in the afternoon to the 'Old Manse' and to Sleepy Hollow, most beautiful of last resting places."[34]

While Anne and Grace were in Concord, Herby stayed on at the Staffords'—still painting Timber Creek, still painting Walt. Although it would mean a long separation from Bee, who would not finish her internship until May, it seemed to Anne that it would be best if she and Grace spent the winter in New York with Herby so that he could have professional instruction without having to live alone in the great city. Wyatt Eaton had seen the sketches from life that Herby had made at the Royal Academy. In Eaton's opinion, Anne confided to Bee, if Herby had gone to study in a Paris atelier instead of coming to America, "he would be painting fine pictures now." "I see now that it was a delusion to suppose he could teach himself from the point he had got to," Anne continued sorrowfully. "Last winter in Philadelphia was almost wholly lost for him, don't you think?"[35]

Was there a sexual attachment of some sort between Herby and Walt? There are indications that cannot be ignored that this was so and that it was more intense on Herby's part than Walt's. Small things fit together like the pieces of a jigsaw puzzle to form a picture that must be recognized: Herby's frequent visits to Camden; his lengthy stays at Kirkwood; his ingratiation of himself with the elder Staffords; the antagonism between himself and Harry Stafford that may have been mutual jealousy; his obsession with sketching and painting the poet; his letters to "Dear Darling Walt," composed to play up his own importance. In Edwin Haviland Miller's opinion, Herby was unquestionably one of the poet's young lovers. Miller's evidence is that between 1876 and 1885 Whitman wrote twenty-nine letters to the young man.[36] Walt did write to Herby several times a year during this period, mostly brief notes, never the long, passionate letters that he wrote to Peter Doyle or the long, less fervent but still intimate, letters that he wrote to Harry Stafford. Herby may have been one of the young men, like Edward Cattell, Albert Johnston, and John R. Johnston, Jr., with whom Walt had brief affairs during these years.[37] But for Herby the attraction of the older man was clearly more powerful, more obsessive, and of longer duration than a passing fancy would suggest. In February 1874, when Herby was seventeen, Anne wrote to Walt that "Herby has read with a large measure of responsive delight 'Leaves of Grass' quite through, so that he now sees you with his own eyes & has in his heart the living, growing germs of a loving admiration that will grow with his growth & strengthen every fibre of good in him." A year later she told Walt that Herbert was "deeply influenced by your Poems."[38] Understanding the "Calamus" poems completely, had Herby secretly responded to *Leaves of Grass* erotically with a passion much like his mother's? Anne, of course, would not have been aware of this. If she had been told, she would have been incredulous—shocked, disillusioned, self-recriminating.

Before going to New York, Anne and Giddy spent November in Boston with Bee. Anne met Bee's fellow interns and Fanny Berlin—and thereafter her letters to Bee always included "love to the students and to Dr. Berlin." She may even have met the dragon Zak. "It seems to me I have made more acquaintances in the last two months than in the whole of my life before," she wrote to William Rossetti, "and many, nay, most of them people of such intelligence, culture, and geniality that I found it tantalizing to have but brief intercourse with them." Rossetti had given her several letters of introduction. One was to Eliot Norton, professor of the history of art at Harvard, who called immediately, "and a very interesting conversation we had." Another was to Horace Scudder, editor of the Riverside Literature Series and later of the *Atlantic Monthly*, who would recall with admiration Anne's "fine presence" and "dignity which could bear the added title of quaintness without offence." He and "his pretty, graceful wife," Anne told Rossetti, "invited a large and interesting circle of friends to meet me."[39]

One of the Scudders' guests was Colonel Thomas Wentworth Higginson, Emily Dickinson's friend and editor. In a lecture at the Chestnut Street Club that Anne attended, Higginson said that, in his view, England was doomed as a world power because of a trade treaty that Disraeli had negotiated. Anne apparently spoke out at the lecture, and a few days later, still seething, sent a letter to the *Boston Daily Advertiser* indignantly defending her country:

To the Editors of the Boston Daily Advertiser.

I have not the making of a speaker in me, for I left out on Monday the very thing I would best like to have said in answer to Colonel Higginson's remarks on the present and probable future status of England among the nations. He was, I know, only quoting what has been said before, and in England, too, when he observed that England's commercial supremacy was already doomed, and when that was gone she would sink to the rank of a third or fourth-rate power, like Holland. Is then England's commercial supremacy the cause of her greatness? Or is it only one effect, one manifestation and phase of it? What figure did she make among the nations of Europe when her coal was still unworked and her manufactures and export trade non-extant? Certainly not a third or fourth-rate one.

If we are not degenerating in quality, nor dwindling in numbers; if in moral weight and fibre, in intellectual power, indomitable energy, and last but not least, in physical vigour, we are what we were, surely we need not fear the future, need not fear but that we shall find good and ample scope for these qualities and keep the proud position we have now. And if I am told this is a vague, unpractical way of looking at things, I will make bold to answer that not more plastic is clay to the will and imagination of the sculptor than are practical affairs to the national strength, will, and insight underlying them. And that to be great in character and little in destiny does not happen to nations—nor to individuals either, in the long run, spite of transient appearances. History repeats herself, says everyone. Nations must decay as soon as they have culminated. History repeats herself; but not in such a way as to make prophesying a safe trade.[40]

At the Hollands' house in Cambridge, Anne met Longfellow and President Eliot of Harvard. Afterward, Anne called on Longfellow and found him "the most kindly, good-natured, unaffected man possible, quite unspoiled by his great popularity: and lives in the jolliest old house."[41] However, the Gilchrists' social life was not confined entirely to Boston's literati. "Two or three fine young men" were boarding at 39 Somerset Street, where she and Grace were staying, Anne told Walt, "& Giddy & I enjoy their society not a little."[42] When their visit to Boston was over, Anne could not resist spending another day or two in Concord at the urgent invitation of her friends there before finally leaving Massachusetts.

New York was a disappointment. Anne liked it less than anywhere she had been in America. "What with its piled up human habitations, its dirty, noisy streets, its icy winds, it seems to me behind Boston in everything but size and noise," she wrote to Mrs. Holland.[43] Finding a pleasant place to live that she could afford proved to be an arduous and disheartening experience. "It seems to me more difficult to get anything of a medium kind in New York than anywhere else I have been," she told Walt. "If it isn't the best, it is very uninviting indeed."[44] She and Grace went first to a boarding house in Brooklyn, where Herby, who had arrived earlier—after insistent prodding by his mother to get him to leave Kirkwood[45]—joined his mother and sister.[46] Anne knew at once that the Brooklyn boarding house would not do. After much traveling back and forth to New York, she found reasonably pleasant rooms on West 19th Street, with the privilege of using the kitchen, and the Gilchrists spent Christmas there. This arrangement was economical—and Grace, her mother told Bee, was "content to have the work to do for the sake of there being a little more margin of dollars for other things."[47] But the kitchen was dirty, and before a week was out Anne was searching for another boarding house. This was a real hardship. Anne was beginning to suffer from the asthma that would plague her increasingly, and, after a quarter of an hour in the cold, she would begin to wheeze and would have "to creep slowly." "When the icy wind that so often prevails sweeps these streets I find I must either stop in or hold a muff or something of that sort to my mouth all the way," she told her physician daughter.[48] At last she found a suitable boarding house. On 29 December, Anne wrote to Bee from 112 Madison Avenue, where she and Grace and Herby would live for the rest of their stay in New York:

> Well, my darling, I am in hopes we have succeeded and are going to be comfortable at last. Mad[ison] Ave. is next to 5th Ave. the best situation in New York. We are close to Union Square—the most central part. We have a very pleasant room up two flights as in Somerset St. It looks like a pretty sitting room; our bed doubling up by day into a gorgeous piece of furniture like a book case, all carved walnut & plate glass & our sofa & chairs being covered with blue repoc [?]. Out of this opens a large closet one side of which is fitted up as a wardrobe with drawers—the other with washing apparatus, hot and cold water &c. So it really is as good as having a private sitting room—front sunny aspect. A pleasant Scotch lady keeps the house—fellow boarders lady like, highly respectable—certainly no tendency to be fast—rather to the Gorgon type—very safe for Giddy.[49]

There were compensations for the difficulties of living in New York. Herby had the good fortune to study under William Merritt Chase at the Art Students League.[50] "Herby is making great progress," Anne wrote to Walt. "I wish you could see the head of an old woman he has just painted—and I wish he had had as much power when he had such splendid chances of painting you."[51] She sent Bee the happy news that, although his instruction was expensive, Herby's work was improving so rapidly that as soon as he could exhibit a picture that attracted attention, she was confident that commissions and pupils would follow. Both she and Herby were hopeful that a sketch that he had made at Round Hill of ladies bowling on the lawn, worked out on a larger scale, would prove to be that picture.[52] In his letter to "Dear Darling Walt" on 2 February, Herby proudly reported his progress:

> I know that it will please you to hear that I have gained tenfold facility with my brush since the autumn. It has agreed uncommonly well with me having enlisted under such an experienced & able painter as Chase; as a manipulator of the brush he is agreed by the experts (Eaton) to have no rival. I may yet be able to paint a

head of you in *one* sitting that will do justice to you. Three of my pictures are nicely hung at the Water Colour Exhibition Academy of Design, the first time that I have exhibited in New York.[53]

Anne's joy in one son's progress was offset by news that things were not going well with the other. Percy wrote that the Blaenavon Company had gone into liquidation, and, with employment hard to find in England's depressed iron industry, he and his family might soon be left without an income. Deeply distressed, Anne was faced with a dilemma. She must help him, but she could not afford to support two households. There seemed to be only two solutions, she told Bee: she and Giddy could return to England and share their home with Percy and Norah, leaving Herby and Bee in America until Bee had finished her internship; or Percy and his family could join them in America on the chance of his finding employment in the States. Either way, Anne feared that this turn of events would mean that Bee would have to postpone her plan to study in Europe before going into practice, and Herby his plan to study in Paris.[54] In late January, she received a letter from Percy telling her that the crisis was at least temporarily over, and, after weeks of anxiety, Anne began to enjoy being in New York.

New York's literary world, like Boston's, quickly discovered Anne Gilchrist, and by January she had "more gaieties on hand than I know how to get through."[55] The "home bird," who had never accepted George Eliot and George Lewes's invitation to their Sunday afternoons in London, thoroughly enjoyed the receptions, sometimes two and three in one evening, that she and her children were invited to in New York.[56] At these nineteenth-century versions of the cocktail party, in addition to a crowd of guests, there was usually entertainment—music or recitations—and sometimes, to Herby's delight, "ice creams were handed round."[57] "Don't you wonder how I can go out so much?" Anne wrote to Bee. "Well, I make a sort of business of it, just now, because it is quite a new kind of opportunity for me to make the acquaintance of a large number of Americans, and though you may say such intercourse does not amount to much, I have acquired a sort of knack of speedily entering into pleasant relations and having a little really frank and earnest conversation and so I really learn a great deal and enjoy a great deal."[58] The Gilchrists went regularly on Saturday to Miss Booth's, editor of *Harper's Bazaar*; on Wednesdays to Mrs. Bigelow's, one of America's foremost literary hostesses; on Sundays to Mrs. Croly's—the former Jennie June, well-known journalist and founder of the Sorosis Club; on Fridays to the Gilders'—Richard Watson Gilder, poet and editor of *Scribner's Monthly*, and his talented sister Jeanette.[59] Anne met Emma Lazarus and Louise Chandler Moulton, Walt's gushy admirer; several times she encountered Joaquin Miller, who, when he was in an amiable mood, talked with her about Whitman; and Kate Hillard took her to call on the distinguished physician Mary Putnam Jacobi.[60] She was invited to tea, to lunch, and to spend evenings at home with many new friends. In her own way, Anne Gilchrist recaptured New York for the British. Herby wrote to Bee that one of their hostesses told him "that she had fallen in love with mother & said how nice it would be if all women could be like her."[61]

However, in spite of all the "gaieties," Anne missed Walt's companionship. "I shan't really begin to like New York," she wrote, "till you come and we have some chats together."[62]

Many things in New York reminded Anne of Walt; she went over to see friends in Brooklyn, "& it was more lovely than I can tell you on the Ferry—in fact, it was just your poem 'Crossing Brooklyn Ferry.'"[63] All winter she hoped that he would come to New York to visit the Johnstons, but weeks then months, went by and no Walt. "Are you never coming? I do long & long to see you," she wrote. Bee's internship would soon be over, and, when it was, the Gilchrists planned to return to England, for a time at least. Anne was looking forward eagerly to having a home of her own again—somewhere. "Whichever side the Atlantic it is, you will come surely? for you belong to one country as much as to the other," she wrote to Walt in late March. "And I shall always feel that I do too."[64] In the midst of New York's gaieties, Anne was remembering 1929 nostalgically. The New York receptions were delightful, she told Walt, "but they are not half so jolly as our evenings at Philadelphia." The memory of one evening was especially poignant. In the only deeply personal line in any of her post-Philadelphia letters to the poet, Anne wrote: "O how wistfully do I think of one evening in Philadelphia last winter."[65] Close friends by then, had she and Walt talked freely to each other? Had they discussed her passion for an imaginary WW? Might he have told her about his own early loves: the mysterious woman in New Orleans (if she ever existed); the woman for whom he wrote "Out of the Rolling Ocean the Crowd"?

Walt was also thinking nostalgically of 1929. He missed the happy times there, and the thought of the Gilchrists leaving America distressed him. "Herb," he wrote from Camden in February, "why don't you all get a big cheap house in Brooklyn by the month or quarter, with the privilege of keeping it for two or three years?—room enough for all hands—Percy & his if he chooses to come on—a room for me—I would come on & stay & pay a moderate board—Can't we make it pay?"[66]

If Walt did not come to New York, the Gilchrists were planning to spend a few weeks near him in Philadelphia before returning to England. However, on 9 April, the poet arrived at the Johnstons' handsome house on Fifth Avenue near 86th Street. The purpose of his visit was his first Lincoln lecture, "The Death of Abraham Lincoln," which his New York friends had arranged to be given on 14 April at Steck Hall on Fourteenth Street. From the beginning, Anne was apprehensive about its chances of success. "I fear it is being very badly managed," she confided to Bee on the twelfth. "I have just been writing a line to Dr. Addler to ask him to announce it from his pulpit tomorrow."[67]

Anne Gilchrist asking a clergyman for aid! A desperate measure indeed. But her instincts had been accurate. Although she assured Bee that the lecture had gone well—"good in itself, brief and strong, tranquilly delivered"—the general opinion was that it had not been a great successs. Even his friends admitted that Whitman, who had remained seated throughout the lecture and read his manuscript, was not naturally a good public speaker. When Walt began to speak or read in public, Ellen O'Connor would recall, his delivery would become artificial and stagey, and he had "a habit of using his voice as if his throat were stiffened, instead of the clear, flexible voice that he used in conversation." She would note that in the Washington years, when Whitman and the O'Connors lived in the same house, she and her husband "did not flatter him much on his recitations."[68]

If the Lincoln lecture was not a triumph, Whitman seems not to have been aware of it. "Walt is quite in spirits about it," Anne reported to Bee.[69] He stayed on at the Johnstons' until mid-June—and had a glorious time in his "own Manhattan." He walked in Central Park, mingled with the crowds downtown, talked with policemen, marveled at "the beauty animation & individuality of the north river" as he crossed from Jersey City to Desbrosses Street, found the new steam elevated trains "a great nuisance-convenience,"[70] took a three-hour bay trip "accompanying the *City of Brussels* down as far as the Narrows in behoof of some Europe-bound friends, to give them a good send off,"[71] watched other famous ships leave for Europe, went aboard the United States warship the *Minnesota*—rowed "to & from the ship, man-of-war fashion"—and had dinner with the crew,[72] sailed up the Hudson to visit Burroughs, went to literary receptions, and hobnobbed with old Broadway-omnibus-driver friends—attracting attention wherever he went, reveling in it. Offstage the poet had a flawless sense of theater. And he played the role of Walt Whitman superbly.

During the two months that he spent in New York, Walt filled several pages in his daybooks with memoranda about the visit. For some reason, there is no mention of "Mrs. G" in these extensive notes. Yet there can be no question that he saw Anne many times. "Walt came to New York Wednesday, and yesterday (Friday), came here and spent a couple of hours very cosily up stairs with us," Anne wrote to "My darling Bee" on 12 April.[73] Walt must have spent numerous cozy hours at 112 Madison Avenue—an address that was "quite handy" to the Johnstons'[74]—where he and Anne resumed their spirited talks in the Gilchrists' upstairs sitting room with its gorgeous, bed-into-bookcase piece of furniture. Sometimes they attended the same receptions;[75] once they saw each other at the theater;[76] and the Gilchrists were entertained by the hospitable Johnstons. Perhaps Anne joined Walt in his walks in Central Park, and they continued their absorbing conversation as they strolled along the winding paths, stopping to admire the gray rocks cropping out everywhere and the statues of Shakespeare and *Youth and Falcon* that Walt loved.[77]

Certainly, as in the past, the two had much to talk about, much to tell each other.

And yet for Anne, this long-anticipated reunion, like her first, long-anticipated meeting with the poet, must have been anticlimactic. Living in a boarding house, she could not offer him the domesticity that had created so warm a bond between them in Philadelphia. In New York—where he was center stage, where his days were filled with exhilarating events and renewal of ties with a past that she could never share—there was nothing she could offer Walt that he truly needed. Anne seems to have had a lingering hope that someday she might make a home, re-create 1929, for the poet. Not as a wife, but in the brother-and-sister relationship that for Victorians was the ideal bond between the sexes, and which she would celebrate in her biography of Mary Lamb. In New York, the possibility of a permanent re-creation of the homey atmosphere of tea suppers and summer evenings by the stoop must have vanished quickly. Seeing Walt so vibrantly alive in the great, noisy city that he loved—where he was "untranslatable," "not a bit tamed," and his "barbaric yawp" sounded audibly over the roofs—it must have been very clear that, much as he might enjoy it temporarily, genteel domesticity was not Walt Whitman's natural habitat. Once again, with love and understanding, Anne must have revised the role she had hoped to play in the poet's life—for she never again mentioned the possibility of living permanently in America. Less than a month before Walt came to New York, she had written to him that when she returned to England "I shall leave my furniture here, and the question of where our future is to be, open." However, in late May she made a quick trip alone to Philadelphia, undoubtedly to arrange the shipment to England of things that had been left there.[78] The Gilchrists booked passage on the *Circassia*, which would sail from New York for Glasgow on 7 June.

They would leave their American friends regretfully, but, once the decision had been made, the Gilchrists were eager to go. Anne was longing to see her grandson. Bee had finished her internship at the New England Hospital and joyfully joined her family in New York—no longer under the tyranny of Dr. Zak, no longer being whistled for, no longer walking the streets of Boston at all hours, medical bag in hand, sometimes with a policeman as escort, sometimes alone. She was looking forward to further study in Switzerland, especially to advanced work in the use of the microscope. "Although America had been to us a land of promise, England claimed us most," Grace would recall, adding that the Gilchrists were homesick for "the sound of English voices."[79] Herbert seems to have been the most reluctant to leave. He spent the month of May at Kirkwood with the Staffords and returned to New York only a few days before the date of departure.[80]

There are two versions of Anne and Walt's farewell. Both are undoubtedly authentic. In 1912, J. H. Johnston told Clara Barrus that, on the Gilchrists' last day in New York, Anne and Walt said good-bye at his home, where both were guests. Anne and her children were probably midday dinner guests. The two friends had a long private conference in the parlor, Johnston told Dr. Barrus, and both were obviously deeply moved when they rejoined the family. Neither ever revealed what passed between them.[81] In her memoir of her mother, Grace's recollection was that Walt came to 112 Madison Avenue on the eve of their departure to say a last good-bye. The Gilchrists were all gathered in the parlor of their boarding house, and Walt kissed each in turn, Anne, Herbert, and Beatrice—all except obstinate Grace. "Walt turned and walked slowly to the door and we followed him to the front entrance as he descended the flight of steps. He turned when half way down and said sadly, 'It seems kind of tragic-like your all going back to England.'"[82]

The poet loved to watch famous ships leave for Europe, but he did not see the Gilchrists off. If a group of friends was on the pier waving good-bye when the *Circassia* sailed, Walt was not among them. Anne Gilchrist has been pictured leaving America defeated and disconsolate. However, as she watched New York's skyline disappear, Anne was certainly not a pathetic figure. True, she had brought with her a consuming passion that could never be realized. But she was returning to England with an indissoluble bond of love, esteem, and happy memories with the man she had crossed the Atlantic to see; with hosts of new friends; and with the discovery of a new self—a poised, even more independent, astonishingly adaptable self, with a social expertise that the "home bird" would never have believed possible. Leaving America, Anne was looking back with affection, and forward with confidence to the future. If there was something "tragic-like" about her departure, the tragedy was Whitman's. In June 1879, he sensed it. Years later, reminiscing more and more tenderly about Anne to Traubel, he knew it.

For Anne the great tragedy of her life, the blow from which there could be no recovery, was still to come.

12
DARK MOTHER

Dark mother always gliding near with soft feet,
Have none chanted for thee a chant of fullest welcome?
Then I chant it for thee, I glorify thee above all,
I bring thee a song that when thou must indeed come, come
    unfalteringly.

                                                      Walt Whitman

The Gilchrists' second Alantic crossing was memorable. Anne wrote to Walt from Glasgow that, after a few queasy days, they thoroughly enjoyed the sea and sky and invigorating breezes, as well as the companionship—"very pleasant (& learned withal)"—of a professor of Greek and philosophy from Harvard and a young student from Concord. In the last three days of the crossing, there was the added enjoyment of glorious scenery. The *Circassia* sailed in close to the Giant's Causeway on the north coast of Ireland and into Lough Fozle to land a group of Irish folk at Moville, "some of them old people who had not seen Ireland for forty years, and who were so happy they did not know what to do with themselves." From Moville, the ship sailed down the North Channel to the Firth of Clyde, then up the firth among the islands. "This was during the night—we did not go to bed at all it was so beautiful—& then came a gorgeous sunrise," Anne wrote. "I kept thinking of you on the voyage, dear friend, & wondering how you would like it—& whether you could stand being stowed away in a little box-like berth at night."[1]

    The Gilchrists spent a few days in Glasgow, "rushing about shopping," probably for Scottish woolens and other materials for clothes that Bee would need in Switzerland. Then a week in Edinburgh—for more shopping? Percy, whose career was moving ahead again, was living in the village of Lower Shincliffe near Durham, where he was supervising the construction of kilns needed for the dephosphorization process that he and his cousin Sidney Gilchrist Thomas had invented.[2] From Edinburgh, the Gilchrists went to Lower Shincliffe for a long visit with Percy and Norah and little Archie, Anne's beloved grandson, not quite two years old. "I am sitting in my room with my dear litle grandson, the sweetest little fellow you ever saw, asleep beside me," she wrote happily to Walt.[3]

Beatrice Gilchrist, ca. 1881. Private collection.

The first weeks of the visit were spent chiefly with needlework, getting Bee ready to go to Berne. When Anne wrote to Walt on 2 August, Bee was in London on her way to Switzerland. "I miss her sadly—had quite hoped we should have all been together at Paris this winter—but it seems the course is much longer & more arduous [there]."[4] The parting must have been very difficult for both. Of the two, so much alike in so many ways—brilliant, independent, courageous—which was the braver: the young woman setting out alone for a strange country at a time when a respectable young woman did not set out alone to go anywhere, a country where she knew no one and could not speak the language; or her mother, staunchly supporting her daughter's determination to succeed in a traditionally male profession in spite of what may have been excruciating inner misgivings and anxiety?

In the Gilchrist Collection, there is a photograph of Bee taken at about this time.[5] As Christina Rossetti had predicted when Bee was still a child, she is "rather like a lily than like a rose." She is wearing a dark dress with a stand-up, ruffled collar of white organdy or lace that fills in the deep V neckline and ends in a large white bow. The long, thick, blond hair that Tennyson admired is parted in the center and drawn severely back. Bee's features are like her father's as a young man, but she has her mother's clear, hazel eyes, and there is a trace of a smile at the corners of the soft, full lips. It is a lovely, gentle young face that is also strong, self-confident. It is an unmistakably feminine face. And, studying the small, faded photograph carefully, one is struck with something else in this face that, like her mother's, could be described as "eminently *speaking*"—innocence that is not to be confused with ignorance, the capacity for passion, vulnerability.

With Bee off to Europe, Giddy became the center of her mother's attention and concern. Giddy was in love. She was in raptures; Anne was sympathetic—as she had been when Percy fell in love with Norah—but cautious about consenting to a formal agreement based on a shipboard romance and prospects for the future still to be proved. The name of the young student from Concord who had been one of the Gilchrists' companions on the *Circassia* and who was, Anne told Walt, "a very nice fellow," was Frank Bigelow. On 11 September, 1879, Grace wrote a breathless letter to Bee from Shottermill, where she and her mother and Herby were staying for a few weeks in a cottage on Lion Green, not far from Brookbank.

> My dear Beatrice
> You will be interested to hear (for I know you're burning with curiosity) that F.B. has come & gone! He would have stayed four to five months in England. But mama was adverse to our engaging ourselves in any way & you know how constraining English customs are, how without an engagement young people can see but little of each other. So we decided, under the peculiar circumstances, it would be better for him to return at once to America. He has only one more year to finish his studies, & then you know, he will have a living, & can see how he gets on. Of course he would give up the Church *now*, if I *wished* it: but indeed I would be sorry, I would

not undertake such a *responsibility*. No: let him *try* the Church, it is not the hard & fast thing in America it is [in] England. Anyhow, at the end of a year he will see his way more clearly, but for the present he does not wish to make any change.

So three years is the time fixed, & then if at the end of that time we are both of the same mind, & he is in a position to marry, mama won't offer an opposition. Mama, at first, didn't like the idea at all, nor him, but she has rather come round now. Of course you must not breathe a word of this to a soul. Mama has not written about it of course, as she does not look upon it as certain, or as an engagement. After all, I shall have to live in America—mama regrets it on that account as she thinks it would be a great privation for me.

He stopped from Thursday to Wednesday. How constraining & aggrevating [sic] English customs are! We got very few opportunities for conversations alone. It so happened, rather unfortunately, that Carpenter & his Ceylon friend came down the day after he arrived. No doubt Carpenter was disappointed not to find us alone, but though he came down expressly to see us, we saw very little of him. He seemed, & is, so Miss Beke [?] told me, most devoted to his Ceylon friend, a nephew of Lady Cosmra's [?] husband. Still so many strangers was rather untoward, but walking, of course, I had to devote myself as far as possible to F.B. while Carpenter made the effort to talk to me on the other side—but eventually gave me up. I am afraid he must have "smelt a rat." If we had him alone, I should have rather regretted the presence of his Ceylon friend, but as it was I was rather glad. For as he had an inseparable friend he really could not complain of the constant presents [sic] of F.B. Still, it is aggrevating [sic] to have all of one's friends at once in that way, & it was the means of spoiling my talks with F.B.

Sept. 12. Just received a letter from F.B., he sails for America next Tuesday—by the German Line. He has also sent me "[The Impressions of] Theophrastus Such" [1879], is it not good of him, I have always so longed to possess a book of George Eliot's. . . . with best love

Affectionately your sister
Grace Gilchrist[6]

It is a tribute to Anne's powers of gentle and reasonable persuasion, as well as an indication of her daughter's love and trust, that although Giddy resented "how constraining English customs are," she did not resent her mother's authority. But alas for young love! FB is never mentioned again: in family letters, in Anne's letters to Whitman, in Herbert's biography, in Grace's diaries that still exist.[7]

Although she felt that living permanently in the States would be "a privation" for her daughter, after her return to England Anne missed America. "I hardly realized till I left it how dearly I love America—great sunny land of hope and progress—or how my whole life has been enriched with the human intercourse I had there. Give my love to those of our friends whom you know & tell them not to forget us," she wrote to Walt, England was cold, damp, foggy, and Anne confessed that "we sigh for the warmth of an American house indoors often & for American sunshine out of doors." Memories of 1929 were especially poignant. "I wish one of those old red Market Ferry cars were going to land you at our door once more!" she wrote. "What teas and what evenings we would have—you would certainly have to say 'there is a point beyond which'—& would have some pretty late trips back by moonlight. Strange episode in my life! so unlike what went before & what comes after—those evenings in Philadelphia—yet so natural, familiar, dear!" She hoped and dreamed that the poet would come and stay with them for a while when she and her children had a home of their own. "Dear Friend," she wrote. "I think of you continually & know that somewhere & somehow we are to meet again, & that there is a tie of love between us that time & change & death itself cannot touch."[8]

For Anne, one of the highlights of the six or seven weeks that the Gilchrists spent at Shottermill was the renewal of her friendship with Tennyson. The laureate called at the little cottage on Lion Green, and Anne and her children had lunch with him at Aldworth. She sent a leaf of Irish ivy from the poet's garden to Emma Holland, "in case you have any fancy for such relics."[9] From Shottermill, the Gilchrists went to London to establish their permanent home there. In London Anne was reunited with other old friends: William Rossetti and "his beautiful little group of children growing up around him"; Gabriel Rossetti, painting brilliantly and continuing to ruin his health; the Madox Browns; the Moncure Conways. At the Conways, Anne met Henry James one Sunday "& found him one of the pleasantest of talkers."[10] Anne's friends told her that she looked ten years younger when she came back from America than when she went.[11]

Meanwhile Bee was at Berne, "working away merrily, rejoicing in the really splendid advantages for medical study there open to her." Before going to Berne, she had attended a school in Wiesbaden and in two months had mastered German enough to be able to speak it and to understand lectures. In Berne, she had found a comfortable home "with some excellent, intelligent ladies who are fond of her & see to her bodily welfare in every possible way."[12] As the autumn of 1879 ended and the winter of 1880 began, Anne reported to Walt that Bee's letters continued to be "as cheery as ever—she is heartily enjoying work & life, and accomplishing the purpose she has set her heart upon, & the people she is with are so good and kindly, it is quite a home. She is working a good deal with the microscope. Her outdoor recreation is skating."[13]

After extensive house hunting, the Gilchrists concluded that Hampstead suited them best. Although it was not readily accessible to London since trains ran infrequently, and this would cut them off from their friends to some extent, to Anne Hampstead was "the pleasantest & prettiest of all our suburbs." It was the only suburb of London that was not suburban, she told Horace Scudder: "It is really still a picturesque old village, with beautiful views and walks—the steep hill it stands on and the heaths have saved it."[14] Anne bought a charming red-brick row house at 12 Well Road, Keats Corner.[15] Its small, paved courtyard is enclosed by a low wall and must have been filled with flowers and ivy when Anne lived there. In the small garden in the rear, Anne planted fruit trees—plum, greengage, pear, cherry, apple—and trained them up against the fence and house to save room and to take advantage of "our English modicum of sunshine."[16] Since the house would not be available until late summer, the Gilchrists rented houses in Hampstead, first on Heath Street and then at 5 Mount Vernon, from November until the following August. Percy and Norah were leaving Lower Shincliffe for Redcar, and, during their move and resettlement, Anne had an especially happy interlude. "I have my dear little grandson with me here—as engaging a little toddler as the sun ever shone on," Anne wrote to Walt from Heath Street in December. And in January she wrote from 5 Mount Vernon: "That dear little grandson stayed with me two months till I really didn't know how to part with him, & grew more & more engaging & pretty in his ways every day—rapid indeed is the opening of the little bud at that age."[17]

At Hampstead, waiting to take possession of their own house, the three Gilchrists were fully occupied. Giddy was taking singing lessons again. And Herby had had a wonderful piece of good fortune. He had a commission to make designs for a new kind of painted tapestry, and his figures "Audrey & Touchstone," Anne told Walt, were "very much admired & have been bought by a rich American, & he has a commission for more."[18] Anne herself began work on a second edition of the *Life of Blake*, which Macmillan was willing to publish. Again she had the enthusiastic assistance of Gabriel and William Rossetti. Although bringing out the second edition was not the herculean undertaking that editing, completing, and compiling the first edition had been, there was much to do. A few minor corrections were needed; some new Blake letters had come to light and needed to be included. In order to use them, Anne had to recast the text for, as Herbert explained in his biography, "it was a tradition in the family to avoid notes." Anne began work on the new edition in early March 1880.[19]

And then the totally unexpected happened. In mid-March, Bee suddenly came home from Switzerland. She had decided to give up medicine.

The shock waves of this announcement reached across the Atlantic. Herbert sent the news to Whitman, who replied that he was "surprised about Beatrice"; and Whitman wrote to Burroughs that "Beatrice has suddenly abandoned her medical pursuits and intentions."[20] Why, after so many years of study and hard work, after enduring the despotism of Dr. Zak, after earning a professional status that few women achieved in 1880 and at a time when she was apparently enjoying the advanced work in Switzerland that had been her dream—why did Bee suddenly decide to give it all up? On 28 March, her mother sent Walt an explanation—a loving, guarded, protective explanation, but hardly a convincing one. While Bee was in Switzerland, Anne told the poet, she had decided that she was intellectually incapable of being an ideal physician, and therefore she preferred to abandon the profession. And she added, speaking in confidence to her "dearest friend," that medicine had become "like a great man that swallowed her up from me."[21] This observation has been seen as evidence of Anne's possessiveness as a mother. But it can also be seen as evidence of the extent and depth of the inner sacrifice—the loss of cherished companionship, the pain of long separations—that Anne's steadfast support of her daughter's dedication to a profession had cost her. What really happened to Bee in Switzerland? Perhaps the pressure of concentrated work had proved to be too much—even for one so young, so physically strong. Perhaps it was something else.

Whatever had occurred at Berne, in a few months Bee changed her mind again. "Bee, you will be glad to hear, has decided to continue her medical studies," Anne wrote to Walt in August, "& is going to be assistant to a lady doctor at Edinburgh, who is to pay her sufficient salary to cover all remaining expenses."[22] Whatever it was that had happened at Berne, Anne seems to have been deeply disturbed by it. When she wrote to Walt on 22 August, she had left her children in Hampstead and was visiting friends who lived in an isolated house on a heath-covered hill near Haslemere and was wandering by the hour along a winding wood path that led into the coppices below. "I am not quite re-acclimatized," she explained to Walt, "and what with missing the sunshine & working a little too hard, was feeling quite knocked up: so Bee insisted on my coming down, or rather up, here to stay with some very kind & dear friends."[23]

In early autumn, the household belongings that had been left in Philadelphia—the carved furniture, the pianoforte, the silver, the blue-and-white china, *Elijah Mounted in the Fiery Chariot*, and the other pictures and prints—arrived in London, and the Gilchrists took possession of their new house. Bee stayed long enough to help with the move. After she left for Edinburgh—"a sad pinch" it was to part with her again, her mother confided to Walt—Anne turned her attention again to the second edition of the *Life of Blake*. This time there were no problems with Macmillan's concern for "poor flustered Propriety." She and the two Rossettis exchanged letters about small discrepancies in dates and the altered concept of the relationship between Blake and Hayley that the recently discovered letters provided.[24] Anne wrote a new preface and a long biographical memoir of her husband; and several new illustrations were added, including two drawings by Herbert H. Gilchrist—*Blake's Cottage at Felpham* and *Blake's Work-Room and Death-Room: at 3, Fountain Court, Strand*. The handsome, two-volume edition was through the press in late November 1880. Herby described it to Walt as "a richly illustrated 'edition de luxe' . . . the most perfectly gotten up book that I have ever seen."[25] Walt commented to Susan Stafford: "I suppose you & the rest are reading Herbert's books from time to time—though they are very queer in the story of Blake's life and works, there is a deal that is interesting & good to chew on—then they are such beautiful specimens of paper &

printing, it is a pleasure to read them."[26] Years later, speaking of the *Life of Blake* to Traubel, the poet was more appreciative in his appraisal:

> "The Blake book"—he tapped it with his hand—"is charming for the same reason that we find Froude's Carlyle fascinating—it is minute, it presents the man as he was, it gathers together little things ordinarily forgotten: portrays the man as he walked, talked, worked, in his simple capacity as a human being. It is just in such touches—such significant details—that the profounder, conclusive, art of biographical narrative lies."[27]

On New Year's Day 1881, Walt wrote that he had received a "good, long, fine letter" from Bee. He was sorry, he told Anne, to hear from Herbert that she had not been well. "I may say it is a year since I have really felt well, for I was slowly running down all last spring & summer," she replied on 16 February, in her first letter to the poet since the previous August. "But now the sun shines for me & I am picking up very fast. . . . Bee has written to you about herself. It was very hard to be sundered during my illness, but was the right thing to do, she was so much wanted where she was & learning so much too."[28] In April, Anne was well again except for the chronic asthma that still troubled her: "My breath is so short I cannot walk, which is a privation." In June she would be going to Edinburgh to stay with Bee, she told Walt, "as she will not have any holiday or be able to come & see us this year, & much am I longing to see her."[29]

Anne wrote a contrite letter to Walt from Edinburgh on 17 June. Busy with preparations to go north, she had forgotten his birthday, "had not written one word—not just put my hand in yours as I would fain always do on that day." She had stopped at Redcar for a visit with Percy and his family, who were living in a cottage close to the sea, and spent some happy days on the beach watching her grandson playing in the sand. "And now I am with Beatrice & needn't tell you what a pleasure that is. She looks rather pale, but seems otherwise strong & hearty, & to have her heart in her work as much as ever. Gaining more confidence in herself too, which was what she most needed. Much liked by her patients."[30]

From Edinburgh, Anne sent Herby Bee's instructions for the care of a soft corn and her own comment on linoleum—"hideous stuff"—which he and Giddy had suggested installing at 12 Well Road. "Bee is doctoring me up with an inhaler and medicines of various sorts," she wrote. "She says it is not what is called asthma but emphysemia [*sic*], the air tubes having lost their expansive power which causes my difficult breathing. It can't be cured. I joggle around in cars & omnibuses—read a good deal—enjoy much being with Bee."[31] Sometimes Anne went sightseeing alone, and sometimes Bee had time to go with her. On 30 June, Anne wrote from Edinburgh to her old friend Walter White that Bee was seeing something of practice and also carrying on her studies in preparation for further examinations at Berne and Dublin. "It is good to see how much her patients think of her and like her," Anne told him. "We took afternoon tea—or rather strawberries & cream—with a lady whom she attended in the winter through a severe attack of erysipelas in the head who didn't seem to know how to make enough of her."[32] It was a happy visit for the mother and daughter, who, Grace would recall, were like sisters.[33]

Anne returned to Hampstead in July, refreshed and feeling stronger than she had in months. Then, shortly after her return, possibly only a few days, there was alarming news from Edinburgh. Beatrice was missing. Anne and Percy rushed to Scotland. Bee had not been seen since the twentieth of July. An agonizing search began—and continued on, and on, and on.

On 15 August, Bee's body, badly decomposed, was found in a farmer's field on the outskirts of Edinburgh. She had taken hydrocyanic acid.[34]

"My dear dear Children," Anne wrote to Herby and Grace in an unsigned and undated letter from Edinburgh, "you would not want me to live if you knew how I suffered. Not grief alone—that I could learn to bear, to be resigned—but *remorse* that I should have left her; that is like an envenomed wound poisoning all my life. 'Weighed & found wanting' am I. And there where I thought myself surest. O the love for her shut up in my heart!"[35]

Why did Bee take her own life? Was it because of physical or emotional breakdown due to overwork? Was it, implausible as her mother's explanation of her sudden departure from Berne may seem, because Bee believed that she could not be an ideal physician and could not bear to be less? Was it, as has been suggested, because of the unrelenting animosity of male physicians as a whole that had broken the spirits of many women physicians in the nineteenth century? It may have been one or a combination of these. But, reviewing the life of this healthy, attractive, high-spirited young woman, one cannot help speculating about another possibility. Had Bee fallen in love in Berne in some way that was unfortunate? With someone who did not, or could not, love her in return? If Bee had suddenly come home because her health had broken down or because she felt a need to rest, her mother would have acknowledged this freely to friends. However, if a grief-stricken Bee had returned because she had fallen in love either hopelessly or unwisely—in her unhappiness impulsively declaring that she was giving up her career—a sympathetic and deeply distressed Anne would have unquestionably invented a cover-up story to protect her suffering daughter. When Anne left Edinburgh, she seems to have been certain that Bee had recovered from whatever had brought her home so precipitously—"there where I thought myself surest," she wrote to Herby and Grace. But one cannot help believing that there is at least a possibility that, even more than a year later, it was the continuing pain of a traumatic experience in Berne that led Bee to that terrible moment in an isolated field.

The possibility that Bee's death was the result of an unhappy love affair can be supported, it seems to me, by the inscription on her tombstone in Dean Cemetery in Edinburgh. The tender epitaph, unmistakably composed by her mother, is, with the exception of one line, conventionally statistical, unremarkable in tone and comment.

> Beatrice Carwardine Gilchrist
> Student of medicine M.D.
> of the Woman's Medical College
> Pennsylvania U.S.A.
> Beloved daughter of
> Alexander and Anne Gilchrist
> Born at Guildford, Surrey 18 Sep 1854
> Died at Edinburgh 20 July 1881
> FAITHFUL UNTO DEATH

> Many hearts mourn her
> In her short career did she by skill
> tenderness and unwearied devotion to duty
> bring healing and comfort to many
> both here and in America[36]

The line that stands out from the text, that seems to have a special significance, that sounds like an agonized comment by a grieving mother is this:

FAITHFUL UNTO DEATH

Faithful to whom? To someone, surely—since Bee's devotion to her profession is mentioned below. And Anne would have known who that someone was.

Those who scoff at the suggestion that Beatrice, a levelheaded young physician, could have taken her own life because of an unhappy love affair might remember that her mother, a woman known for her common sense, took to her bed and "lay dying as it seemed" for months when Whitman did not send any word directly to her after the publication of "Estimate." And they might remember that her mother, driven by an overpowering passion, had crossed the Atlantic to a strange land without either encouragement or an invitation.

It was not acknowledged publicly that Bee's death was a suicide. In a long, emotional obituary for the Alumnae Association of the Woman's Medical College of Pennsylvania, in March 1882, Anne gave a touchingly protective version of what happened. She wrote that while Bee was working part time in Edinburgh as assistant to Dr. Sophia Jex-Blake, she was preparing for examinations at Berne, where after five months of study she had "suddenly felt the absolute need of rest." Anne explained that the University at Berne required that students' theses be original work of some kind, and, since there was no physiological laboratory open to women in Edinburgh, Bee was obliged to choose a chemical theme: "A thorough investigation of condensed milk as a food for infants was what she proposed to herself, and it was her unboundedly patient carrying out of this extremely difficult and tedious analysis, in dissolving out the fats with ether, that she inhaled an amount which ultimately proved fatal."[37]

And so for a third time Anne Gilchrist picked up her life and, adjusting its focus, went on.

Expressions of sympathy and shock had poured in from England and America. "Indeed all that sympathy and warm & true words of love & sorrow & highest admiration & esteem for my darling could do to comfort me I have had—and most & best from America." Anne would tell Walt.[38] But the "warm & true words of love & sorrow" from America did not include a single word from him until nearly four months after Bee's death.

Herby had sent the dreadful news to Mrs. Stafford, asking her to tell Whitman. Walt wrote in his daybook on 9 September: "some gloomy news—sad, sad,—the death of Beatrice Gilchrist—as accomplish'd and noble a young woman as ever I knew."[39] "I sent your letter to Mrs. Gilchrist," he told his sister-in-law on 18 September. "I have not written yet—it is so sudden and dreadful—I thought I would wait awhile." And he wrote to Burroughs a few days later: "—have you heard of the sudden & dreadful death of our young friend Beatrice Gilchrist in performing some chemical experiment with ether?"[40] In the months that followed, Walt wrote many letters: to publishers and critics, to Louisa Whitman, to the Staffords, to the Johnstons, to Helen Price, to Thomas Nicholson, to Edward Carpenter. Some of the letters that he wrote—one to Louisa Whitman and one to Ruth Stafford in particular—were very long. On 28 November, he wrote to Anne:

My dear friend,
   Have time & its influence at least helped you to calm the terrible loss & shock & dislocation? Have you got so that letters and all outside news are *not* altogether painful intrusions? Hoping so I send just a line. (For a while I thought it must be some false report—I was in Boston at the time—& waited & waited until confirmed.)
   I am as well as any of late years—or perhaps better. My brother & sister are well. The Staffords the same. I am writing this in the sunshine up in my old 3d story room—Best love to you & Herby & Grace.
                                                           Walt Whitman[41]

"I have longed for a word from you—could not write myself—was stricken dumb," Anne replied. "Herby wrote to Mrs. Stafford first, thinking that so the shock would come less abruptly to you. I heard of you at Concord in a kind long letter from Frederick Holland."[42]

Late in 1881, Anne discovered that she was gravely and incurably ill. Perhaps she had suspected it earlier; perhaps the suspicion had been one of the things on her mind in August 1880, when she wandered alone by the hour on a wood path while she was visiting the Pratts in Shottermill; perhaps it had been one reason why she had forgotten Walt's birthday in May. However, in November she knew for certain that what she had feared was true.

She told no one, not even her immediate family. But on 7 November she wrote a long memorandum to her children that she put away among her private papers. One cannot know Anne Gilchrist without knowing her children too. For, more than is ordinarily the case, they were extensions and expressions of their mother's self; in more than the usual sense, since their rearing had been her responsibility, they were her creations. And how well she knew them—their strengths and weaknesses, their potentials, the frictions between them.

> Hold well together my dear children. Be good & affectionate, forbearing, considerate, indulgent, to each other. You each have your faults but thank God you have sound and good qualities that far outweigh them. See to it that these sound and good qualities say the last word in every dispute, difficulty, emergency. I look to you Grace & Herby to be wise and trusty friends to each other; trying always each to understand the other's point of view, feeling, wishes though so different from your own.
> Memorandum of my wishes in regard to the division of my property & effects. It is provided in my marriage settlement that all the property included in it should at my death be equally divided among my surviving children. It is my wish that any property not included in that settlement whether money, land, house, literary copyright should also be divided equally among them.
> In regard to the plate I think the following division will be best.
> To Percy the coffee-pot, soup ladle, skewer [?] and scoop.
> To Herbert the tea-pot, the mustard pot that was my mother's, the large cream jug and a pr. of sugar tongs.
> To Grace all the spoons and forks, the pepper pot, small cream jug, sugar tongs, salver, nut meg grater & the silver topped small mustard pot.
> As to the pictures. Percy to have the copy of Romney's portrait of my grandmother.
> Grace. Phillip's portrait of my mother and grandfather, and the small portrait of my grandmother.
> To Herbert—all my Blakes—all Drawings, Prints etc. in my portfolio and three photographs from drawings by Rossetti via: Hamlet & Ophelia, Mary Magaline [sic] and the portrait of his wife. All the prints on the walls to hang as they are as long as Herbert & Grace live together. But should they cease to live together I wish Grace to have all the prints now hanging in the front dining room & the photograph from Rossetti "How they met themselves."
> 'The books to be equally divided between Herbert & Grace.
> The little Dutch japanese cabinet to Grace.
> The antique urn to Herby.
> The small round marquettrie table bequeathed me by Uncle Henry & now in the Pennsylvania Museum to Herbert.
> Percy to take back what he wishes of the Colne furniture I gave him before we went to America.
> The rest, including what is now with the Pennsylvania Museum for Herbert & Grace's joint use as long as they live together. When they cease to do so if Herbert is doing sufficiently well to be able to afford to buy furniture he needs I wish Grace

to select & have for her own whatever furniture, China, & glass etc. she requires. But if Herbert is not doing so well then I wish the furniture, China, etc. to be divided as fairly as they can between him & Grace.

To Percy dear Beatrice's microscope.

Anne Gilchrist
Nov 7. 1881

On 15 December, 1881, she added a postscript:

Please let Fraulein Miller, Hirschengraven Haus, Bern, Switzerland and Lottie Offord, 299 New Cross Road, S.E. be told of my death because else as I write to them now & then they will think I have forgotten them.

In regard to American friends it would be enough for all save Walt if when you put the death in the papers you say American papers please copy.[43]

Bee was aware that Anne had emphysema, but did she know about her more serious illness? It seems very, very unlikely that Bee would have deserted her mother if she had known that she had cancer of the breast.

"As I write this I am sitting to Herby for my portrait again," Anne wrote to Walt in January 1882, "—he has never satisfied himself yet: but this one seems to be coming on nicely." Herbert used a photogravure of this portrait as one of the illustrations in his biography of his mother. It shows Anne at her writing table, quill in hand. At fifty-two her hair is still dark, and her face, in half-profile, still beautiful; she is looking down, concentrating intently as she writes to "my dearest friend." In the same letter, Anne told Walt that Herby had another picture in mind to be called *The tea-party*. "It is to be the old group round our table in Philadelphia—you & me and dear Bee & Giddy & himself. He thinks that what with memory & photograph & the studies he made when with you, he will be able to put you & my darling on the canvas."[44] Herby apparently found it impossible to paint Bee satisfactorily from memory and possibly symbolized her with the empty place at the table in the foreground of the finished picture.

At William Rossetti's suggestion, in March 1882, John H. Ingram asked Anne to write a biography of Mary Lamb for the Famous Women Series. In directing Ingram to her, Rossetti told Anne that he felt that he had done Mary Lamb a service by obtaining for her "the best biographer & biography that were likely to be forthcoming."[45] Anne willingly accepted the offer, although she made it clear to Ingram that she had had no personal acquaintance with Mary: "But to my mind's eye, her sweet, sympathetic, finely attuned nature, shrouded as it was in the dark shadow of the tragedy of her youth . . . has always appeared a singularly interesting, pathetic, beautiful figure."[46] On 13 April, Anne enclosed a note to Ingram with the publishing agreement. She was clearly looking forward eagerly to losing herself in the pressures of research, writing, and deadlines:

Anne Gilchrist, painted by Herbert Gilchrist, 1882–84. Department of Special Collections, Van Pelt Library, University of Pennsylvania.

I have received the agreement from David Bogue: and see nothing in it I need object to and endorse with my signature except that being tied so rigidly to a date—and that a comparatively near one. I think that both for the sake of the little book that is to be and for my own it would be well to add some small qualifying words after the "31st Aug." as there is after the number of pages—"as near as possible 200 pp."—as near as possible to Aug. 31st. I shall not avail myself of this to delay or dawdle but only to make sure to do my best.

Where do you think I should be likeliest to pick up a copy of *Mrs. Leicester's School*? I would cheerfully invest in one. Do you haunt old book stalls—or run through many booksellers' catalogues? Has it been reprinted in recent years?

To think that I have had a copy reposing on my shelves ever since I was a child, when it was a great favorite with me—and now, when I would give my ears for it, it is gone![47]

Anne kept her promise—she did not dawdle. On 3 December, she wrote to Burroughs that the little book, "the writing of which has been a great solace to me," was finished at last.[48]

Her biography of Charles Lamb's talented and pathetic sister, who collaborated with him in writing *Tales from Shakespeare* and *Mrs. Leicester's School*, has been Anne's most lasting work. It was published in July 1883 and reprinted again as recently as 1972. "I hope you received my little book safely," Anne wrote to Walt in October. "I should be a hypocrite if I pretended not to care whether you found patience to read it—for I grew to love Mary & Charles Lamb so much during my task that I want you to love them too."[49] And in this painstakingly researched book, with its stellar cast of characters—the Wordsworths, the Coleridges, Hazlitt, Landor, Leigh Hunt, Sara Stoddart—Anne's love for Mary and Charles is everywhere apparent; it is her compassion for their tragic lives of "double singleness" that gives the book its warmth and enduring life. Worn out by eleven years of trying to make her living as a seamstress and at the same time taking care of her invalid mother night and day, in a sudden frenzy Mary had fatally stabbed her mother with a kitchen knife and seriously wounded a young apprentice. During the rest of her life Mary had recurring periods of insanity; when she felt an attack coming on, she and Charles would walk together sorrowfully to the asylum.

Feminist scholars might be interested to note that in this small biography Anne quotes, in its entirety, a long article titled "Needlework," which Mary wrote in angry rebuttal to the notion—based on the time-honored maxim "A penny saved is a penny earned"—that it was praiseworthy for women of means to do their own household sewing instead of paying professional seamstresses to do it. Mary's essay had been published in the April 1815 issue of the *British Lady's Magazine* and is the only known instance in which she was writing for adult readers. "It is sagacious and far-seeing," Anne observes, "for Mary does not treat of needlework as an art, but as a factor in social life."[50]

Throughout the nineteenth century, needlework was the single largest paid occupation in England for women who worked in their homes.[51] As one who has been a seamstress herself, Sempronia—as Mary calls herself in "Needlework"—contends that women of means who do their own sewing not only deprive needy seamstresses of their only means of making a living but spend time that might be used to better advantage both to themselves and to their families. For, she points out, women have been advancing in intellectual achievement, and, if a woman wishes to be a conversational companion to her husband, she must "study and understand the subjects on which he loves to talk"; however, because of "the disadvantage we labor under from an education differing from a manly one," this study takes time—time that a woman will not have if she spends hours with her needle. Mary brushes aside the idea of needlework as a means of amusement. If needlework has become so delightful a pastime that one cannot relinquish it, she suggests that a lady who has no need to save could turn to knitting, knotting, and netting—"the good old contrivances in which our grand-dames were wont to beguile and lose their time"—or, as a matter of conscience, give the money saved to poor needlewomen from whom "she has borrowed these shares of pleasurable labor." And she makes very clear her opinion of the present equality of men and women. "*Real business* and *real leisure* make up the portions of men's time,—two sources of happiness which we partake of in a very inferior degree," she writes. "To the execution of employments in which the faculties of the body and mind are called into busy action there must be a consoling importance attached, which feminine duties (that generic term for all our business) cannot aspire to. In the most meritorious discharge of those duties the highest praise we can aim at is to be accounted the helpmates of *man*." However, Mary's most urgent plea is that women be given wider opportunites to earn money with dignity—that women, like men, be trained from childhood to support themselves, if it should be necessary, in a respected and adequately remunerative way.

> Much has been said and written on the subject of men engrossing to themselves every occupation and calling. . . . If, at the birth of girls, it were possible to foresee in what cases it should be their fortune to pass a single life, we should soon find trades wrested from their present occupiers and transferred to the exclusive possession of our sex. The whole mechanical business of copying writings in the law department, for instance, might very soon be transferred with advantage to the poorer sort of women, who, with very little teaching, would soon beat their rivals of the other sex in facility and neatness. The parents of female children who were known to be destined from birth to maintain themselves through the whole course of their lives, with like certainty as their sons are, would feel it a duty incumbent on themselves to strengthen the minds and even the bodily constitutions of their girls so circumstanced, by an education which, without affronting the preconceived habits of society, might enable them to follow some occupation now considered above the capacity, or too robust for the constitution of our sex.[52]

The fact that this lengthy essay is given so prominent a place in the book—a chapter to itself—tells us as much about Anne's views as it does about Mary's.

In "Three Glimpses of a New England Village," written sixty years after the publication of "Needlework," Anne had deplored the plight of the respectable but impecunious single woman in society; in "A Neglected Art," she had expressed her scorn of "busy idleness" as the proper employment for a lady. Unearthing Mary Lamb's long-forgotten essay in a magazine that had become "so rare a book" that it was unavailable to the general reader, Anne was struck with the validity of Mary's protests and recommendations more than half a century later.[53] Anne does not add a printed "Amen!" at the essay's conclusion, but the word hovers almost audibly over the page.

In the early 1880s, although his position in the world of letters was more secure than it had been a decade earlier, Whitman's work was still not universally accepted.[54] In 1882, John Burroughs visited Anne in Hampstead. After his return to Esophus, he wrote: "I am resting in the hope and expectation that before long you will give yourself up and write the article on Walt Whitman, that we are all looking for. I feel sure that you will cut your way to the heart of this matter as no one has yet done." With *Mary Lamb* completed, Anne replied: "Now I am going to put my heart into an article on Walt; I do not the least know whether or where I shall get it published; but anyhow I must try once more and give a reason for the faith that is in me."[55] She began "A Confession of Faith" in 1883. However, Anne, who in a euphoria of inspiration had written "Estimate" in a few weeks, found writing this second defense uphill work. In May 1884, she told Walt that she was "busy, still hammering away to see if I can help those that 'balk' at 'Leaves of Grass.' Perhaps you will smile at me—at any rate it bears good fruit to me—I seem to be living with you the while."[56] When "Confession" was finished, finding a publisher was not easy. For one thing, unlike "Estimate," it had no borrowed glory from the magic name of Rossetti. For another, an endorsement of Whitman by a woman was no longer as sensational as it had been in 1870. "My poor article has so far been rejected by editors," Anne told the poet in December, "so I have laid it by for a little, to come with a fresh eye & see if I can make it in any way more likely to win a hearing—though I often say to myself 'If they have not ears to hear you, how is it likely one can unstop their ears?' "[57] In February 1885, she reported downheartedly to Walt that she could not get the article into any of the magazines that she most wished, but she believed it would be coming out in *To-Day*, a socialist publication.

Although it had to go begging for a publisher, "A Confession of Faith" is a skillfully presented defense.[58] Anne argues that a great poet is "a challenge and summons," and the question is not whether we like or dislike him, "but whether we are capable of meeting that challenge, of stepping out of our habitual selves to answer that summons." Fifteen years ago, she confesses, she first read Whitman's poems "with feelings partly of indifference, partly of antagonism—for I had heard none but ill words of them." But as she read she became conscious of receiving "the most powerful influence that had ever come to me from any source." And why? Because in Whitman's poems "humanity has, in a sense, found itself; for the first time has dared to accept itself without disparagement, without reservation."[59]

Anne concedes that a poet makes greater demands upon his reader than any other man, and Whitman is no exception. However, she points out—using the barrister-building-his-case technique, which she had learned from Alex—Whitman is like Wordsworth, whose contemporaries were also slow in recognizing his genius:

> So far as the suffrages of his own generation go Walt Whitman may, like Wordsworth, tell of the "love, the admiration, the indifference, the slight, the aversion, and even the contempt" with which his poems have been received; but the love and admiration are from even a smaller number, the aversion, the contempt more vehement, more universal and persistent than Wordsworth ever encountered. For the American is a more daring innovator; he cuts loose from precedent, is a very Columbus who has sailed forth alone on perilous seas to seek new shores, to seek a new world for the soul, a world that shall give scope and elevation and beauty to the changed and changing events, aspirations, conditions of modern life. To new aims, new methods; therefore let not the reader approach these poems as a judge, comparing, testing, measuring by what has gone before, but as a willing learner, an unprejudiced seeker for whatever may delight and nourish and exalt the soul. Neither let him be abashed nor daunted by the weight of adverse opinion, the contempt and denial which have been heaped upon the great American even though it be the contempt and denial of the capable, the cultivated, the recognized authorities; for such is the usual lot of the pioneer in whatever field.[60]

In her second long defense of Whitman, Anne's emphasis is not on the controversial form and content of *Leaves of Grass*, as it was in "Estimate," but on the underlying philosophy in the poet's prose—in *Democratic Vistas* and the preface to the 1885 edition—as well as in his poetry. She points out the compatibility of his philosophy and the tenets of science. And, not surprisingly, the author of "Our Nearest Relation" puts special emphasis on what she sees as correlations with the Darwinian theory of evolution. One suspects that the emotional undertone of "Confession" is, at least in part, her own enthusiasm for this hotly debated philosophy; and at times she seems to be not so much interpreting Walt as speaking for herself—once again rowing upstream against the powerful current of Victorian prejudice against independent thought by a woman. One illustration of her enthusiastic agreement with the views of the author of the *Origin of Species* is the following passage:

> Above all is every thought and feeling in these poems touched by the light of the great revolutionary truth that man, unfolded through vast stretches of time out of lowly antecedents, is a rising, not a fallen creature; emerging slowly from purely animal life; as slowly as the strata are piled and the ocean beds hollowed; whole races still barely emerged, countless individuals in the foremost races barely emerged:

"the wolf, the snake, the hog" yet lingering in the best; but new ideals achieved, and others come in sight, so that what once seemed fit is fit no longer, is adhered to uneasily and with shame; the conflicts and antagonisms between what we call good and evil, at once the sign and the means of emergence, and needing to account for them no supposed primeval disaster.[61]

Another illustration is:

CONTINUITY again is one of Nature's irrevocable words; everything the result and outcome of what went before; no gaps, no jumps; always a connecting principle which carries forward the great scheme of things as a related whole, which subtly links past and present, like and unlike. Nothing breaks with its past.[62]

And yet another:

Going somewhere! And if it is impossible for us to see whither, as in the nature of things it must be, how can we be adequate judges of the way? how can we but often grope and be full of perplexity? But we know that a smooth path, a paradise of a world, could only nurture fools, cowards, sluggards. "Joy is the great unfolder," but pain is the great enlightener. . . . It is the double misfortune of the churches that they do not study God in His works—man and Nature and their relations to each other; and that they do profess to set Him forth; that they worship therefore a God of man's devising, an idol made by men's minds it is true, not by their hands, but none the less an idol.[63]

Although it too is a thoughtful examination of Whitman's work by one whose grasp of it, in the poet's words, "was tremendous—so sure, so all around, so adequate," "Confession" is very different from "Estimate." The exuberance of new discovery is not here, nor is the powerful undercurrent of personal passion. Most of all, the crusading spirit that rose above the brilliant analysis of the music, form, and content of the poems and gave "Estimate" its force and vitality is missing. "Confession" is a sober, although still brilliant, assessment made by a mature mind. In this essay Anne is not speaking out boldly on a great issue, for herself and for all women. In "Confession" Anne is no longer Godiva.

Anne had hoped to write another biography with a celebrated brother-and-sister relationship as its central focus—a biography of Dorothy Wordsworth. In 1884, she wrote to William Wordsworth, the poet's grandson, for permission, enclosing a copy of *Mary Lamb* as a credential. Wordsworth replied from Bombay, courteously but with a minimun of encouragement, on 10 August.

Dear Madam
  I have read with much interest the memoir of Mary Lamb which you kindly sent me. The book will always, I am confident, be a valuable help to an understanding of Charles Lamb's life and character, and the pathetic element which is everywhere mingled with his lightest moods. I am not, however, persuaded that my Aunt

Dorothy's life admits of being handled biographically with the same success. Her life was not an eventful one. She consistently declined all independent aims at literary distinction, and whatever she wrote was written for the delight of her own home circle, and with an almost conscious aversion from publicity. Her life, in short, was so merged in that of her illustrious brother that it can hardly be contemplated apart from his; and I am sure that she could not have foreseen without pain that it ever would be so contemplated. Knowing her I am disinclined to promote an undertaking which would be so little in harmony with her feelings.

The publication of her Scotch journal, for which I am principally responsible, was [unreadable] quite justified, I think, by the merits of that charming book and the light it casts on one part, and that a very important part, of her brother's poetry. . . . I am not aware of the existence of any published letters of hers, and I rather think that she was not a very active correspondent. . . .

I have now expressed pretty fully—as you wished—my personal feeling towards your proposal. It only remains for me to say that I have no claim to be a final judge on this subject, and do not claim for my own feeling that it should outweigh that of more independent judges.

Yrs. truly [?]
W. Wordsworth[64]

Anne apparently decided to postpone her plan, for on 12 November Wordsworth wrote: "I think you have decided wisely to await the publication of Professor Knight's Memoir of Wordsworth before undertaking the task of which you have given so interesting an outline in your last letter. . . . If after the completion of Prof. Knight's labour you are still disposed to continue your own I shall be happy to assist you to the extent of my power. I hope to visit England in the summer of 1886."[65] But the summer of 1886 would be too late for Anne.[66]

On Sunday afternoons the Gilchrists' friends, many of them in the arts or in science, called at 12 Well Road. And, to Anne's delight, many American friends came to visit. Among them were Kate Hillard, the Lesleys, Emma Lazarus, Dalton Dorr (curator of the Pennsylvania Museum), and the Drs. Emily and Augusta Pope, twin sisters who had known Bee in Boston. Edward Dowden, professor of English Literature of Dublin University—playwright, biographer, Shakespearean scholar, and an ardent admirer of Whitman—came to call for the first time in May 1884. In 1871, two months after "Estimate" had been published in the Boston *Radical*, after a year's struggle Dowden had finally succeeded in publishing his article on "The Poetry of Democracy: Walt Whitman" in the July issue of the *Westminster Review*. The editor of *Macmillan's* would have nothing to do with Walt Whitman; other editors said, "God save us from Whitmanism!"; and the *Contemporary Review* accepted the article, set it up in type, then refused to publish it.[67] Small wonder that Dowden and Anne found each other exceptionally congenial. "I know not when I have set eyes on a more beautiful personality," Anne wrote to Walt after Dowden's first visit. "We had a very happy two or three hours together, talking of you."

Herby and Grace were members of the Fabian Society. Anne sympathized with socialist views, and she knew a number of Fabians, but there is no evidence that she was a member. A meeting of the society was held at 12 Well Road on 11 March, 1885, at which a fiery-haired young Irishman named George Bernard Shaw read an abstract from *Das Kapital*. It was the first time that Grace and Shaw met, and their short-lived "affair," frequently mentioned by Shaw's biographers, may have begun at that meeting. Anne was not at home that evening.[68]

Walt continued to be a focal point in Anne's life. Her long letters to the poet were filled with news of mutual friends and news of her children. Percy was prospering; her grandson, "rosy & bright & healthy," was going to school, "which, being an only child, he enjoys mightily for the sake of companionship of other boys"; Herby had been disappointed again by not getting anything into the Royal Academy, but was painting away in his studio at home and at the British Museum; Giddy's voice had developed into a fine contralto, and she was "going to sing at a Soiree of socialists & revolutionary folk in general"—her songs were to be "The Wearing of the Green," "Poland Dirge," and the "Marseillaise."[69] Anne seldom mentioned her own health. "I have never envied anything in this world but a man's strong legs & powers of tramping, tramping over hill & dale as long as he pleases—" she told Walt in 1884. "Legs would content me and a sound breathing apparatus! I am in no hurry for wings."[70]

Only once, and even then only in a single sentence, she sounded a somber note: "I could hardly express to you how welcome is the thought of death to me—not in the sense of any discontent with life—but as life with fresh energies & wider horizon & hand in hand again with those that are gone on first."[71] Was Anne depressed by Bee's death and by the death of Gabriel Rossetti in 1882? Or was she preparing Walt for what she knew was coming?

Anne did not dwell on her own health, but she was deeply concerned with Walt's and with his welfare. In 1884, George and Louisa Whitman built a new house in Burlington, about twelve miles from Camden. Walt could not be persuaded to live where he did not have easy access to the ferries to Philadelphia and refused to go with them. In spite of his brother's angry protest, Walt bought a run-down little house with no furnace, so close to busy railroad tracks that his "shanty" at 328 Mickle Street was filled night and day with smoke, soot, and the clamor of freight trains and switch engines. "I think I like the idea of the shanty, if you have any one to take good care of you, to cook nicely, keep all neat & clean," Anne wrote guardedly in May 1884. Early in 1885, Mary Davis, who would be Walt's much-imposed-upon housekeeper for the rest of the poet's life, moved in with her furniture. In late spring, Anne wrote that she hoped "that home affairs go smoothly & comfortably & that Mrs. Davis is attentive & good & every way adequate as care-taker."[72] But even with the advent of Mary Davis and the kindness of

Walt's many friends, the poet's circumstances were desperate. His royalties, such as they were, were dwindling, and he was becoming more and more crippled. News of his distress reached England, and Anne threw herself into her last crusade for the poet.

In June 1885, William Rossetti received a letter from Charles Aldrich of Webster City, Iowa, an autograph collector who had visited Walt in Camden and found him in great want. Rossetti sent the letter to Anne, who quickly replied: "Mr. Aldrich's letter (which you have kindly sent me to read) does indeed confirm what I was surmising, that Walt Whitman's pecuniary resources are more than ever straitened; and it seems a kind of disgrace to his admirers (let alone his country) that the little needed to make his remaining years more comfortable should not be in some way or other supplied to him."[73] Anne and Rossetti joined forces and, with Herbert acting as secretary, organized a campaign to raise funds in England to assist Walt.[74] They wrote countless letters, including a letter from Rossetti to President Cleveland. Between 24 June and 20 July, Anne wrote seven letters to Edward Pease, one of the founders of the Fabian Society, asking his advice about publicity for the campaign and the possibility of an annuity for Whitman. In her first letter to Pease, she wrote: "Walt Whitman *is* very poor—and I think that if those who admire & love him (& it is hardly possible to do one without the other) were to give tangible expression to their feeling in the shape of a gift of money it would do honour to themselves & give him much comfort both in material respects & even more as a token of sympathy from England & that he could & would accept it with sweetness & dignity."[75] However, although Rossetti and Herby would continue to work—and work successfully—on the fund for Walt, Anne's participation was over. Her last letter to Pease bore the same date—20 July, 1885—as her last letter to Walt, in which she described the "free-will offering" that to his friends was a token of their gratitude for the priceless gifts he had given them, as a joyful response "to that Poem of yours, 'To Rich Givers.' "[76]

Even in late summer, Anne's family and friends were unaware that she had an illness other than the emphysema that she had found such a nuisance for so long. Rossetti would write:

> The last time I saw her was in August 1885, soon after I had come back from my annual holiday at the sea-side. I remember walking up to Hampstead on a Sunday of steady sultry heat, and passing in her house as friendly and agreeable an afternoon as I ever enjoyed. . . . She had then for a long while suffered from an illness, of which the chief obvious symptom was an oppression of breath. It affected her voice to some extent, and prevented her from moving about with much freedom, even in her sitting-room; but her manner, her readiness of conversation, and the vivacity of her mind remained wholly unimpaired. I left the house without the faintest idea that this was to be our last meeting.[77]

Anne Gilchrist, painted by Herbert Gilchrist, June 1885. Department of Special Collections, Van Pelt Library, University of Pennsylvania.

Herby's last, and finest, portrait of his mother was painted at this time. Anne is seated beside a sunny window, its wide sill filled with flowering plants. As usual, she wears a dark dress—it seems to be made of black silk—with a wide, white collar of either organdy or lace. Her hands are folded in her lap. Her expression is pensive, preoccupied. And there is an unmistakable sadness in her face. Herbert, the artist, had captured something that Herbert, the son, did not know.

In September, Anne's secret illness suddenly became apparent and worsened rapidly, although those around her seem not to have recognized its seriousness immediately. On 20 September, Herby reported to Walt only that "Mother is very sickly."[78] But Anne had no illusions about her condition. In October she added a second postscript to her memorandum to her children: "I hope Herby & Grace will now & then go and see that dear Bee's grave is kept in order."[79]

A month later, on 19 November, a distraught Herby sent Whitman dreadful news: "Her condition is critical. Four years ago our dear mother was attacked by cancer with left breast. . . . Her strength seems daily ebbing and her heart is very weak."[80] Walt replied by return mail on 30 November: "What on earth can I say to you in response to the news about your dearest mother in my letter rec'd this morning?—words are such weak things any how in so deep & solemn a case—makes me heavy hearted indeed, & have been so, all the day. As it is, I can only send best love & thoughts dwelling with her all the time. . . . O how I wish I could see your dearest mother—again my best, dearest love to her."[81] And on 8 December Walt wrote directly to Anne: "I think of you very often, & cannot but trust your illness is less gloomy than Herbert states it—I know I have myself felt convinced several times during the last twelve or thirteen years of serious conditions & finales that the endurance has tided over—& O I so hope that you will surmount all—& that we may yet meet each other face to face. . . . God's peace & blessing to you, beloved friend."[82] But his two letters never reached her.

Anne had died on 29 November—twenty-four years, almost to the day, after Alex's death. "The lovely spirit fled on Sunday afternoon at five o'clock," Herby wrote to Whitman on 2 December. "Ten days ago mother asked me if I had written to you. . . . On her tomb I shall find a line from Leaves of Grass. In a little memoranda addressed to us she noted your name down as the one friend in America to whom we were to write to, in announcing darling mother's death. She died in my arms."[83]

Walt could write only a brief reply.

Dec. 15 1885

Dear Herbert

    I have rec'd your letter. Nothing now remains but a sweet & rich memory—none more beautiful, all time, all life, all the earth—

> I cannot write any thing of a letter to-day. I must sit alone & think.
> Walt Whitman[84]

Anne was buried with Alex in the Gilchrist tomb in Kensal Green Cemetery in London, not far from the common grave of her father and brother. By pulling back the tall grass, one can read "Author of Mary Lamb" after her name and dates. But if there is also a line from *Leaves of Grass*, the bronze tomb has sunk too deeply into the earth for it to be seen.

A long obituary notice was printed in *The Academy* on 5 December.

> On Sunday last there died at Hampstead, Mrs. Anne Gilchrist, a lady well known to a small literary circle, both in England and in America. . . . Mrs. Gilchrist had for some years had grave apprehensions that her life was doomed, but showed her characteristic bravery in maintaining an exceptional brightness of spirit and manner, hiding the baneful secret even from her own children. To those who had the privilege of knowing her well, those fated last years will always seem a marvel of quiet heroism, and of noble resolution to be energetically active under the most depressing conditions. Her gifts and attractions in the chosen society that she loved were many and rare. . . . It was a treat, which the more crowded haunts of the literary world can hardly afford, to hear her discourse of men and books, of both of which her knowledge was wide and accurate, and her estimate at once sympathetic and discerning.[85]

Friends added their tributes. "Few men have had such a mother as you," John Burroughs wrote to Herbert. "She was the only woman I have ever seen to whose strength of mind and character I humbly bowed." And Edward Dowden wrote: "I shall always have the memory of her brightness, kindness, wisdom; and of the varied learning and culture which appeared, as it were, under and through a genial humanity that put a spell on one beyond culture or learning."[86] Rossetti's tribute was the prefatory notice that he wrote for Herbert's biography of his mother.

Whitman's public tribute was the poem that he wrote in Anne's memory:

> *"GOING SOMEWHERE."*
>
> My science-friend, my noblest woman-friend,
> (Now buried in an English grave—and this a memory-leaf for
>   her dear sake,)
> Ended our talk—"The sum, concluding all we know of old or
>   modern learning, intuitions deep,
> "Of all Geologies—Histories—of all Astronomy—of Evolution,
>   Metaphysics all,
> "Is, that we are all onward, onward, speeding slowly, surely
>   bettering,
> "Life, life an endless march, an endless army, (no halt, but it is
>   duly over,)
> "The world, the race, the soul—in space and time the universes,
> "All bound as is befitting each—all surely going somewhere."[87]

His private tribute was made years later, speaking again and again to Traubel about Anne. "I think he delights to conjure with that name," the young man observed to himself as he took notes. "Oh! she was strangely different from the average," the poet told him, "entirely herself: as simple as nature: true, honest, beautiful as a tree is tall, leafy, rich, full, free—*is* a tree." "She was a wonderful woman—a sort of human miracle to me," Walt told him on another occasion. "I guess I should not talk about her: not even to you, maybe: my emotion gets the better of me."[88]

There are those who believe that even though the poem was written long before they met, and written for another woman, "Out of the Rolling Ocean the Crowd" describes with uncanny clairvoyance the circumstances that brought Anne Gilchrist and Walt Whitman together and established their enduring love for each other:

OUT OF THE ROLLING OCEAN THE CROWD

Out of the rolling ocean the crowd came a drop gently to me,
Whispering *I love you, before long I die,*
I have travel'd a long way merely to look on you to touch you,
For I could not die till I once look'd on you,
For I fear'd I might afterward lose you.

Now we have met, we have look'd, we are safe,
Return in peace to the ocean my love,
I too am part of that ocean my love, we are not so much separated,
Behold the great rondure, the cohesion of all, how perfect!
But as for me, for you, the irresistible sea is to separate us,
As for an hour carrying us diverse, yet cannot carry us diverse
　　forever;
Be not impatient—a little space—know I salute the air, the ocean
　　and the land,
Every day at sundown for your dear sake my love.[89]

EPILOGUE

What happened to Anne's three children who survived her—Percy, Herbert, and Grace? After a brilliant career as an internationally known metallurgist, Percy died in 1935, at the age of eighty-four. Herbert never became a member of the Royal Academy. His professional success was limited to being "a rather well-known artist." Anne was spared the agony of knowing that Herby too would take his own life. He died in 1914, at the age of the fifty-nine. Grace, the survivor, died in 1947, at the age of eighty-eight. For many years, during the latter part of her life, she lived with a companion, Miss Porter, in Saffron Walden, in a cottage near the gate of Audley End, one of England's stately houses. Canon Gilchrist often visited her there when he was a child. He remembers Grace and Miss Porter ranging the countryside in a two-seater Morris Cowley—Miss Porter driving, Grace blowing the horn. Like Alex and Anne Gilchrist when they were first married, the two would arrive at a great house, announce to whoever opened the door that Grace Gilchrist Frend had come to see the pictures—and nine times out of ten they would be invited in and shown around.

Percy Carlyle Gilchrist, painted by Herbert Gilchrist. Private collection.

Herbert Gilchrist in his studio, 1889. Department of Special Collections, Van Pelt Library, University of Pennsylvania.

NOTES

Abbreviations

Barrus — Clara Barrus, *Whitman and Burroughs: Comrades* (Boston: Houghton Mifflin Co., 1931).

Corr. — *The Correspondence of Walt Whitman*, ed. Edwin Haviland Miller, 6 vols. (New York: New York University Press, 1961–1977).

DBN — *The Collected Writings of Walt Whitman: Daybooks and Notebooks*, ed. William White, 3 vols. (New York: New York University Press, 1978). Vol. 1, *Daybooks, 1876*–1881, cited as *DBN*.

EST — Anne Gilchrist, "A Woman's Estimate of Walt Whitman," *Radical* (Boston), May 1870, 345–59. Reprinted as "An Englishwoman's Estimate of Walt Whitman" in *Anne Gilchrist: Her Life and Writings*, 287–307.

Frend — Typescript of unpublished memoir of her mother by Grace Gilchrist Frend. Feinberg Collection, Library of Congress.

GC — Gilchrist Collection. Collection of family letters, documents, and memorabilia belonging to Canon James Gilchrist.

HHG — *Anne Gilchrist: Her Life and Writings*, ed. Herbert Harlakenden Gilchrist (London: T. Fisher Unwin, 1887).

LG — Walt Whitman, *Leaves of Grass: Comprehensive Reader's Edition*, ed. Harold W. Blodgett and Sculley Bradley (New York: New York University Press, 1965; New York: W. W. Norton, 1973).

Letters — *The Letters of Anne Gilchrist and Walt Whitman*, ed.

Thomas B. Harned (New York: Doubleday, Page; London: T. Fisher Unwin, 1918).

"Memoir"   Anne Gilchrist, "A Memoir of Alexander Gilchrist," in *Life of William Blake*, by Alexander Gilchrist, 2d. ed., 2 vols. (1863; London: Macmillan and Co., 1880), 2:359–76.

Probert   Probert family genealogical chart.

WMR-Letters   *Letters of William Michael Rossetti: Concerning Whitman, Blake, and Shelley; to Anne Gilchrist and her son Herbert Gilchrist*, ed. Clarence Gohdes and Paull Franklin Baum (Durham, N.C.: Duke University Press, 1934).

WMR-Papers   William Michael Rossetti, *Rossetti Papers, 1862–1870* (London: Sands, 1903).

WMR-Rem   William Michael Rossetti, *Some Reminiscences of William Michael Rossetti*, 2 vols. (New York: Charles Scribner's Sons, 1906). Vol. 2 cited as *WMR-Rem*.

WWWC   Horace Traubel, *With Walt Whitman in Camden*. Vol. 1 (28 March–14 July 1888) (Boston: Small, Maynard and Co., 1906); vol. 2 (16 July–31 October 1888 (1908; New York: Rowman and Littlefield, 1961); vol. 3 (1 November 1888–20 January 1889) (1914; New York: Rowman and Littlefield, 1961); vol. 4 (21 January–7 April 1889), ed. Sculley Bradley (Philadelphia: University of Pennsylvania, 1953; Carbondale: Southern Illinois University Press, 1959); vol. 5 (8 April–14 September 1889), ed. Gertrude Traubel (Carbondale: Southern Illinois University Press, 1964); vol. 6 (15 September 1889–6 July 1890), ed. Gertrude Traubel and William White (Carbondale: Southern Illinois University Press, 1982).

Chapter 1. *O Pioneer!*

1. *The Correspondence of Walt Whitman*, ed. Edwin Haviland Miller, 6 vols. (New York: New York University Press, 1961–77), 2:137. Hereafter cited as *Corr.* with volumes indicated.
2. *Anne Gilchrist: Her Life and Writings*, ed. Herbert Harlakenden Gilchrist (London: T. Fisher Unwin, 1887), 284. Hereafter cited as HHG.
3. Edward Carpenter, *Days with Walt Whitman: With Some Notes on His Life and Work* (London: George Allen, Ruskin House, 1906), 16.
4. Letter to Beatrice from Anne Gilchrist, winter 1878–79, 177 Remsen Street, Brooklyn. Feinberg Collection, Library of Congress.

5. *The Letters of Anne Gilchrist and Walt Whitman*, ed. Thomas B. Harned (New York: Doubleday, Page; London: T. Fisher Unwin, 1918), 194. Hereafter cited as *Letters*.

6. Gay Wilson Allen, *The Solitary Singer: A Critical Biography of Walt Whitman* (New York: Macmillan, 1960), 510.

7. Richard Maurice Bucke, *Walt Whitman* (Philadelphia: David McKay, 1883; reprint, New York and London: Johnson Reprint Corporation, 1970), 204–6. Anne was not totally enthusiastic about Dr. Bucke's biography. In the appendixes, in addition to favorable criticisms of WW, Bucke included many of the most abusive attacks on the poet—attacks that, among other epithets, labeled him coarse, indecent, filthy, blasphemous, disgusting, insane, In a letter to Walt on 30 July, 1883, Anne wrote: "There are some things in it [Bucke's *Walt Whitman*] I prize very highly. . . . But why & why did Dr. Bucke set himself to counteract that beneficent law of nature's by which the dust tends to lay itself? And gathering together again all the rubbish stupid or malevolent that has been written of you, toss it up in the air again to choke and blind or disgust as many as it may? What a curious piece of perversity to mistake this for candour & a judicial spirit" (*Letters,* 217).

8. When Thomas Harned and WW met in 1884, Harned lived at 528 Federal Street in Camden. Later the Harneds moved to Germantown.

9. Thomas Corwin Donaldson, *Walt Whitman: The Man* (New York: Francis P. Harper, 1896), 57.

10. Bliss Perry, *Walt Whitman* (Boston: Houghton Mifflin, Cambridge, Mass.: Riverside, 1906), 188–91. Perry had read the first volume of Traubel's *With Walt Whitman in Camden*, also published in 1906 (Perry, vii).

11. Horace Traubel, *With Walt Whitman in Camden*, vol. 4 (21 January–7 April 1889), ed. Sculley Bradley (Philadelphia: University of Pennsylvania, 1953; reprint, Carbondale: Southern Illinois University Press, 1959), 361. Hereafter cited as *WWWC* 4.

12. Ibid., 72.

13. Horace Traubel, *With Walt Whitman in Camden*, vol. 3 (1 November 1888–20 January 1889) (1914; reprint, New York: Rowman and Littlefield, 1961), 395–96. Hereafter cited as *WWWC* 3.

14. *WWWC* 4:73.

15. Elizabeth Porter Gould, *Anne Gilchrist and Walt Whitman* (Philadelphia: David McKay, 1900), 55.

16. *Letters,* 66.

17. Henry Bryan Binns, *A Life of Walt Whitman* (London: Methuen & Co., 1905), 265. The name of George Rice Carpenter should be added to the list of early biographers of Whitman who admired Anne Gilchrist and believed that the publication of "Estimate" was an important milestone in Walt's career. In *Walt Whitman* (New York: Macmillan, 1909), Carpenter wrote that the influence of her essay "in decreasing the attacks on Whitman for indecency of expression is scarcely to be exaggerated. When once a woman of refinement had declared that the wife and mother understood his meaning and was not shocked by it, the ground was, as it were, cut out from under the prudish male critic. At the same time, the limitations which she placed upon her admiration defended her from any imputation of recklessness in opening wide the realm of song for the indiscriminate admission of poems that dealt with love in this fashion" (136–37).

18. HHG, v.

19. On 11 January, 1889, Whitman asked Traubel to read aloud to him the draft of a letter he had written to Anne on 3 November, 1871. WW had been talking to Traubel about Anne and added: "And now that I have said this much to you about Mrs. Gilchrist I don't mind giving you a draft of a note I once wrote to her acknowledging her wonderful recognition and understanding of me." He directed Traubel to a table, where he found the draft "written on two pages of the American Institute poem pasted together. I asked W: 'Do you mean me to read this aloud, too?' He was very still. In a glow, too. 'Yes, if you will' " (*WWWC* 3:512–13). The letter was Walt's wonderfully tactful reply to the passionate declaration of love that Anne had written to him on 3 September, 1871. Traubel records this one instance of being allowed to read a letter from WW to Anne; he records no instance of being allowed to read a letter from Anne to the poet. WW either gave him the draft of his letter or allowed him to make a copy of it, since Traubel includes the entire text.

20. *Letters*, xx–xxi.

21. Three of the "sympathetic friends" who read Anne's letters during the twenty-five years

that Harned had them in his possession were John Burroughs, William Sloane Kennedy, and Clara Barrus. In *Reminiscences of Walt Whitman* (1896; reprint, New York: Haskell House, 1973), William Sloane Kennedy, a close friend and champion of Whitman, noted in his only reference to Anne that WW spoke of her as "one in conversation with whom you did not have to abate the wing of your thought downward at all, in deference to any feminine narrowness of mind. Her articles on Whitman are proof enough of this, which is also strikingly evident from her letters to the poet, which I had the pleasure of reading one July day in John Burroughs' summer-house overlooking the Hudson" (9). Clara Barrus, John Burroughs's friend, personal physician, and biographer, noted in *Whitman and Burroughs: Comrades* (Boston: Houghton Mifflin Company, 1931) (hereafter cited as Barrus) that, in the Harned home in Germantown, "Harned gave me many books, photographs, and mementoes that had been in Whitman's room at the time of his death. Later he accorded me the privilege of reading the original letters of Anne Gilchrist to Whitman, several years before he published them" (369).

22. Grace Gilchrist Frend, letter to the *Nation*, 5 Oct. 1918, 16. *Letters* was published in 1918 by Doubleday, Page & Co. in New York and T. Fisher Unwin in London. However, according to Grace's diary for 1919-20 (Gilchrist Collection), Unwin did not release the book until late 1919, probably because Grace—and possibly Percy—threatened to block publication by legal action. Grace finally agreed not to bring action if Unwin would omit one of her mother's letters; the publisher agreed, but when the book appeared, only one paragraph of the letter had been deleted. On 5 January, 1920, Grace noted that the book had fallen flat in England: there were few sales except to libraries and not a single review.

23. Katherine Anthony, "A Normal Madness," *The Dial*, 11 Jan. 1919, 15.

24. Quoted in an unsigned review of *The Letters of Anne Gilchrist and Walt Whitman*, "Walt Whitman and his 'Noblest Woman-Friend,'" *Current Opinion*, Dec. 1918, 394-95.

25. Barrus, 154.

26. Ibid., 156.

27. Kate Buss, "Anne Gilchrist to Walt Whitman: Some Comments on the Love Letters of a Woman to the Great American Poet, Whose Centenary is now Being Observed," *Boston Evening Transcript*, 31 May 1919, 3, col. 1.

28. Barrus, 155.

29. Edith Franklin Wyatt, "Anne Gilchrist and Walt Whitman," *North American Review*, Sept. 1919, 391, 398.

30. Barrus, 154.

31. Frances Winwar (Grebanier), *Poor Splendid Wings: The Rossettis and Their Circle* (Boston: Little, Brown, and Co., 1933), 309.

32. Frances Winwar (Grebanier), *American Giant: Walt Whitman and His Times* (New York: Harper & Brothers, 1941), 301, 312.

33. Frederik Schyberg, *Walt Whitman* (1933; reprint, trans. Evie Allison Allen, New York: Columbia University Press, 1951), 236.

34. *Corr.* 5:6.

35. *Corr.* 2:2.

36. Paul Zweig, *Walt Whitman: The Making of the Poet* (New York: Basic Books, 1984), 280.

37. HHG, 325. Anne Gilchrist, "Three Glimpses of a New England Village," *Blackwood's Edinburgh Magazine,* Nov. 1884; reprinted in HHG, 309-30.

Chapter 2. Clergy, Gentry, Weavers of Fine Cloath

1. In a letter to Richard Garnett (addressed to the British Museum) dated 8 September, 1886, Herbert told Mr. Garnett; "My Ms is in the publisher's hands and I expect the first proof in a week's time" (Library of the Harry Ransom Humanities Research Center, University of Texas at Austin). Herbert maintained a close relationship with Whitman as long as the poet lived. One reason why he wrote his mother's biography and pushed it through to publication so rapidly was that he was eager to return to America to paint Walt's portrait. He returned to Philadelphia in May 1877.

2. "Anne Gilchrist: Her Life and Writings," *The Athenaeum*, 26 March 1887, 409.

3. *Corr.* 4:370.

4. Robert Innes-Smith, "The Chapel-Barn of St. Stephen, Bures and the de Vere Monuments" and "The Earls of Oxford," reprints from *East Anglia Life*, n.d., n.p. Richard Harlakenden Carwardine Probert—a cousin of Anne Gilchrist collaterally descended—has kindly supplied me with these reprints. Just before World War II, the Priory estate—which had passed by descent to the Probert family—was sold. However, the tombs of the earls of Oxford were excluded from the sale and moved to the lovely little manorial Chapel-Barn of St. Stephen in nearby Bures.

5. HHG, 5.

6. HHG, 6–9 (history of merging of Harlakenden and Carwardine families and details of marriage of Ann and Thomas Carwardine). Date of Ann Holgate's birth from Probert family genealogical chart; hereafter cited as Probert. Richard Harlakenden Carwardine Probert has kindly supplied me with a copy.

7. Probert.

8. HHG, 2.

9. HHG, 11. Sir Thomas Lawrence (1769–1830) was a fashionable English portrait painter who succeeded Reynolds as painter in ordinary to the king (1792) and was knighted in 1815. Among his best-known portraits are *The Calmady Children, Pinkie,* and a portrait of Mrs. Siddons.

10. Gerald Curtis, *The Story of the Sampfords* (Witham, Essex: Mansell Bookbinders, 1981), 94–95. I am indebted to Mr. H. C. Stacey of Saffron Walden, Essex, for making photocopies of pages 94–95 and 108–13 of Mr. Curtis's book. Mr. Stacey was town clerk of the Saffron Walden Borough Council for thirty years and afterward honorary archivist. In a letter to me on 10 August 1985, Mr. Stacey wrote: "In 1981 Gerald Curtis (High Sheriff of Essex & a member of the Essex County Council) who lived at Howes, Great Sampford, a village about 7 miles to the east of Saffron Walden, wrote 'The Story of the Sampfords.' Mr. Curtis came to me for information about the Burrows and I was able to help him from records with the Saffron Walden Borough Council."

11. Curtis, *Story of the Sampfords* 109.

12. Ibid., 110. Richard's wife was Elizabeth Andrewes Burrowes.

13. This information about Richard Burrows and his son Henry was copied for me by Mr. Stacey from the records of "The Treasurers & Chamberlains of the Town Corporate of Walden."

14. Probert. The exact date of birth of John Parker Burrows is not given. However, since he was baptized on 17 June, 1788 and was fifty-one when he died in April 1839, he would have been born in 1788.

15. Probert.

16. In the Probert family chart and in Herbert's biography, the name of Anne's brother is given only as John T. Burrows. In a letter to Herbert on 1 April, 1886, William Haines—an old friend of both Alexander and Anne Gilchrist, who was apparently criticizing Herbert's manuscript of the biography chapter by chapter—indicates that Anne's brother's name was John Thomas Burrows. Haines suggests that "on page 20—'he' [be substituted] for 'John Thomas Burrows,' the full name occurring overleaf in better connexion."

This letter is in the collection of Canon James Gilchrist. Canon Gilchrist is Anne's great-grandson; his grandfather was Percy Carlyle Gilchrist, Anne's oldest child; his father was Percy's son Alexander. Canon Gilchrist has kindly permitted me to use his collection of family letters, manuscripts, documents, and memorabilia, many of which have never been published; hereafter cited as GC.

Chapter 3. A Child Went Forth

1. Janet Horowitz Murray, *Strong-Minded Women & Other Lost Voices from Nineteenth-Century England* (New York: Pantheon, 1982), 82.

2. HHG, 2.

3. Neither Herbert's biography nor the Probert family genealogical chart give John T. Burrows's date of birth. When Johnny died in 1847, Anne was nineteen and he had not quite reached his majority; therefore it would seem that he was about a year older, possibly born late in 1826, a year after his parents' marriage.

4. HHG, 12.

5. Entry in the Probert family genealogical chart: Reverend Charles William Carwardine, rector of Tolleshunt-Knights; born 23 February 1775; M. A. Cambridge University; died 20 April 1857; buried at Tolleshunt-Major. "How I used to admire Uncle on Sunday! He walked along the lanes to church in silk gown and cassock and bands, black silk stockings and knee breeches, looking as one fancied an archbishop must look, and mightily proud was I of taking his hand and trotting along beside him" (Anne Gilchrist, "Lost in the Wood," *The Magnet Stories: For Summer Days and Winter Nights* [London, no. 16, 1861] 85–86).

6. Anne Gilchrist, "Lost in the Wood," 51–52.

7 GC. Letter from Isabelle Erskine Ireland to Grace Gilchrist, no date, but probably early 1886. Apparently in reply to a letter from Grace asking for reminiscences about Anne that Herbert might use in his biography of their mother.

8. Anne Gilchrist, "Lost in the Wood," 54.

9. Ibid., 69–70. Herbert relates this near-tragedy as an outstanding incident in Anne Gilchrist's childhood in the biographical sketch of his mother that he wrote for the *Dictionary of National Biography* ("Anne Gilchrist," in the *Dictionary of National Biography*, ed. Leslie Stephen 26 vols. [London: Smith, Elder & Co., 1890], 21:341).

10. HHG, 19–20.

11. Ibid., 20.

12. Ibid., 21.

13. GC. Three letters to Anne Burrows from John Parker Burrows: 10 August 1836; 6 September 1836; 10 December 1837.

14. HHG, 20.

15. "Highgate Cemetery, clinging to the southern slope of Highgate Hill, looks out across London to the Epsom Downs in the distance. It is one of the great cemeteries of the world (to those who know it, one of the Wonders) but in many ways it is also one of the most secret. A maze of rising terraces, winding paths, tombs, and catacombs, it is a monument to the Victorian age and the Victorian attitude to death. [It contains] some of the most celebrated—and often most eccentric— funerary architecture to be found anywhere" (*Highgate Cemetery: Victorian Valhalla*, ed. John Gay and Felix Barker [Salem, N.H.: Salem House, 1984], title page). It was in Highgate that Dante Gabriel Rossetti buried his wife, Lizzie Siddal, with manuscript poems he had written for her. He later regretted this impulsive act, had the body exhumed, and retrieved the poems by lantern light on a night in October 1869.

16. HHG, 22.

17. Ibid., 29.

18. Walt Whitman, "Song of Myself," *Leaves of Grass: Comprehensive Reader's Edition*, ed. Harold W. Blodgett and Sculley Bradley (New York: New York University Press, 1965; New York: W.W. Norton, 1973), 48. *Leaves of Grass: Comprehensive Reader's Edition* hereafter cited as *LG*.

19. HHG, 21.

20. The "Elsie Dinsmore" books, originally intended to be Sunday-school stories for girls, were written by Martha Farquharson Finley of Chillicothe, Ohio (1828–1909). There were twenty-eight "Elsie" volumes, each with a pansy imprinted on its red or blue cover. The enormously popular series finally went out of print in the middle 1940s. The episode referred to here is from *Elsie Dinsmore* (1868), the first book of the series (Ann Douglas, *The Feminization of American Culture* [New York: Alfred A. Knopf, 1977], 72). The "Kathie" stories were written by Miss Amanda M. Douglas and published in Boston by Lee and Shepard. The episode referred to here is from *Kathie's Aunt Ruth*, the second book in the series. Six of the seven "Kathie" books are in my collection, inherited from my grandmother; these volumes, reprinted by Lee and Shepard in 1890, were entered at the Library of Congress in 1870 and 1871.

21. Ann Douglas, "The Domestication of Death," in *The Feminization of American Culture* (New York: Alfred A. Knopf, 1977), 200–226.

22. Ibid., 200.

23. Ibid., 220.

24. HHG, 23.

25. Ibid., 25–26.

26. Ibid., 26.

27. Ibid., 29–30.

28. *LG*, "Song of Myself," 75.

29. HHG, 23–24.

30. J.H. Murray, *Strong-Minded Women*, 101–2.
31. HHG, 23. Anne may have been paying another visit to her uncle at Tolleshunt-Knights, since an all-day outing by the sea is described in "Lost in the Wood."
32. Henry Burrows, a chemist and druggist (as well as a mayor and alderman) in Saffron Walden, was John Parker Burrows's brother. The "real and personal property" that Henry Burrows was holding for Johnny until he reached his majority may have been an inheritance from his grandfather Richard Burrows, a cabinetmaker (and also a mayor and alderman) in Saffron Walden. See chapter 2.
33. GC. Letter to Anne Burrows from John T. Burrows, 15 January 1847. Annie Probert was Johnny's first cousin. Her mother was Anne Carwardine, Henrietta Burrows's sister, who married Thomas Probert of Newport, Essex (Probert). In the Gilchrist Collection there is one other memento of Johnny—a poem, "Advent," copied laboriously in a childish hand on ruled paper and inscribed: "For dear Mama—January 8th, 1837—John Burrows."
34. HHG, 24–25.
35. An eolophon, sometimes called a seraphine, was played very much like an accordion, except that it rested on a stand or table (*Funk & Wagner's New Standard Dictionary of the English Language*, 1935).
36. GC. Letter to Anne Burrows from Henrietta Burrows, 1847.
37. HHG, 27. Henry Holgate Carwardine, Henrietta Burrows's older brother, was not married. He died on 6 August, 1867 (Probert).

Chapter 4. Alex

1. For some reason, in her letter to Whitman Anne altered the difference in age between Alexander Gilchrist and herself. Alex, born 25 April, 1828, was actually two months younger than Anne.
2. *Letters*, 58.
3. William Michael Rossetti, *Some Reminiscences of William Michael Rossetti*, 2 vols. (New York: Charles Scribner's Sons, 1906), 2:305. Vol. 2 hereafter cited as *WMR-Rem*.
4. Anne Gilchrist, "A Memoir of Alexander Gilchrist," in *Life of William Blake: With Selections from his Poems and Other Writings*, by Alexander Gilchrist, 2d ed., 2 vols. (1863; London: Macmillan and Co., 1880), 2:359–76. Hereafter cited as "Memoir."
5. Probert.
6. "Memoir," 367.
7. Ibid., 366–68.
8. GC. There is a second very early poem by Alexander Gilchrist in the Gilchrist Collection. "Ode," a translation from German, was written on the back of a school exercise in astronomy in March 1844. Alex was almost sixteen.
9. GC. This fragment of a novel or short story consists of six pages (three sheets of pale blue notepaper written on both sides) numbered 17–22, n.d..
10. GC. A twelve-folder collection of poems—folders numbered 2–13—copied in a fine, precise hand on pale blue paper, both sides of each page completely filled. Of the fifty-one poems, thirty-five are sonnets and all are dated October–December 1848 (including revisions of poems written earlier).
11. In later years, rereading Alex's early poems, Anne could not have helped comparing, compassionately, his "A London Monologue" and "A London Lot," slightly different versions of the same poem, with two poems about prostitutes by two great poets whom she knew. The amateurish melodrama and attitudinizing in Alex's poem makes it clear that his knowledge of a prostitute was only as a character on stage or as a frowzy waif glimpsed from a distance on a city street. His poem has neither the haunting beauty of Dante Gabriel Rossetti's tender picture of "lazy laughing languid Jenny, / Fond of a kiss and fond of a guinea" nor Whitman's direct and sympathetic approach in "To a Common Prostitute"—"Not till the sun excludes you do I exclude you, / Not till the waters refuse to glisten for you and the leaves to rustle for you, do my words refuse to glisten and rustle for you."
12. GC. There are nine poems in this collection, written on two four-page blue paper folders

and undated. Clearly not intended for other eyes, these impassioned poems spill across the pages with many underlinings and corrections. Four are titled "Sonnet"; the titles of the others are "The Apparition," "To My Fair Idea," "Love's Baring," "Love Disdained," and "Life!"

13. GC. This untitled poem, unlike Alex's other private poems, is dated; and, unlike the others, it is the only poem on a single sheet of paper. This suggests that it may have been sent, or was intended to be sent, to Anne.

14. *Letters*, 58–59.

15. Ibid., 58, n. 2.

16. *Corr.* 2:135, n. 61.

17. HHG, 30.

18. Ibid., 29.

19. In the nineteenth century and earlier, men of means often employed a professional amanuensis, usually a young man. For example, Jonathan Swift served William Temple in this capacity. In this letter, which Probert concludes in his own hand, he writes: "Forgive the 'amanuensis' part—it has been my habit of 40 years, to write by dictation. When I employ my own fingers, my brains run ahead, and go 'woolgathering' in all directions."

20. GC. Letter to Anne Burrows from Thomas Probert, Newport, 13 February, 1849. Thomas Probert was a solicitor at Newport, a large village near Earls Colne. He was born in 1776, married in 1813, and died on 24 May, 1849, three months after writing this letter to Anne. His daughter, Anne Henrietta Probert, was born in 1818 and died in 1881. She never married, although in a letter to his sister Milly Thomas, written on 31 July, 1849, Alex, in describing a visit to Colne, mentions that Annie Probert, who was also visiting there, had recently had "an offer, which she refused, from a clergyman with a good living & moderate fortune" (GC). Annie was very religious. She was much loved by her brothers, especially the impecunious ones who had gone to Australia, to whom she would often send ten pounds and advice on moral living. I am indebted to Richard H. C. Probert for this information. Thomas Probert was his great-great-grandfather.

Was Johnny's "own dearest Annie Probert" the "tender and long cherished attachment," whose letters "in a well known hand" he asked Anne to destroy after his death? It seems very likely. She was older than he by about eight years and his first cousin.

21. *The Angel in the House*, a long work in four books by Coventry Patmore (1823–96), was one of the nineteenth century's most popular poems. It was published in its entirety in 1854 (reprint, London: George Bell and Sons, 1906). Its title has survived to become a term for a nineteenth-century woman's ideal position in society.

22. In *Beeton's Book of Household Management*, published in 1861 (reprint, New York: Farrar, Straus and Giroux, 1974), Isabella Beeton described the duties of the sick-nurse:

> Where serious illness visits a household . . . a professional nurse will probably be engaged . . . but in some families, and those not a few let us hope, the ladies of the family would oppose such an arrangement as a failure of duty on their part. . . . The sick-room should be quiet; no talking, no gossiping, and, above all, no whispering. . . . No rustling of dresses, nor creaking shoes either . . . Miss Nightingale denounces crinolines, and quotes Lord Melbourne on the subject of women in the sick-room, who said, "I would rather have men about me, when ill, than women; it requires very strong health to put up with women." Ungrateful man! (J. H. Murray, Strong-Minded Women, 94–95)

23. HHG, 31.

24. GC. Letter to Milly Thomas from Alexander Gilchrist, 31 July, 1849. Melicent Gilchrist, one of Alex's three older sisters, married William Thomas. Although the date of her birth has not been recorded (except that she was born on 13 May), according to the Probert family genealogical chart, she appears to have been older than her sister Margaret, born 23 June, 1819, and Elizabeth Ellen Champion, born 26 August, 1823. Milly was probably the elder sister under whose "gentle guidance" Alex received his early education.

25. Murray, *Strong-Minded Women*, 129.

26. Ibid., 128. The book by William Acton, M.D. (1814–75) from which these excerpts are taken—*The Functions and Disorders of the Reproductive Organs, in Childhood, Adult Age, and Advanced Life, Considered in Their Physiological, Social, and Moral Relations*—was published in 1875. It would seem to be a summing up of Dr. Acton's own opinions and those of his professional contemporaries, arrived at after many years of practice. Alex could not have read Dr. Acton's book, but he would have been exposed to its widely held tenets.

27. *Letters*, 59–60.

Chapter 5. Guildford

1. Herbert Harlakenden Gilchrist, "Anne Gilchrist," *Dictionary of National Biography*, ed. Leslie Stephen (London: Smith, Elder & Co., 1890), 21:340–41.
2. HHG, 36.
3. GC. Letter from Keswick, Cumberland, to Milly Thomas from Alexander Gilchrist, 28 July, 1851. The letter begins: "Dearest Sister: Annie being the slowest of letter-writers and 'best of wives,' we have entered into a compact to write our letters in common. I to act as [?], and sometimes, as in the present instance as amanuensis. Annie suggests our friends will not consider the latter part of the arrangement an improvement. She has the vanity to think her writing a little better than mine!" The last three pages are written by Anne and the letter is signed "Annie and Alick." The eight-page letter describes their honeymoon travels.
4. I am indebted to Canon James Gilchrist for this information.
5. HHG, 35.
6. *Letters*, 59–60.
7. *LG*, "Children of Adam," 102.
8. *Letters*, 59.
9. GC. In their letter to Milly Thomas on 28 July, 1851, Alex and Anne enthusiastically recommended lodgings they had enjoyed at Lyme Regis.
10. GC. Letter to Julia Mary Newton from Alexander Gilchrist, Lyme Regis, 28 December, 1851.
11. J. H. Murray, *Strong-Minded Women*, 82.
12. GC. Letter to Julia Mary Newton from Alexander Gilchrist, Lyme Regis, 5 January 1852.
13. "Memoir," 371.
14. Ibid., 372–73.
15. *Letters*, 60.
16. Ibid., 109–10. Anne had previously expressed these convictions in an essay, "A Neglected Art," *Macmillan's Magazine*, 12 October, 1865, 494–501.
17. I have not been able to positively identify William Haines. A William Henry Haines (1812–84) was a genre painter in London. However, the close friend of Alexander and Anne Gilchrist was living in 1886. In that year he was criticizing *Anne Gilchrist: Her Life and Writings* for Herbert, chapter by chapter (GC, letter to Herbert from William Haines, 31 March, 1886).
18. GC. Letter to Walter White from Alexander Gilchrist, 2 March, 1853. Walter White (1811–93), son of a cabinetmaker in Reading, left school at the age of fourteen to learn his father's trade. In 1834 he came to America with his wife and children and worked at cabinetmaking in New York and Poughkeepsie, hoping to earn more money there. He returned to England in 1839, gave up cabinetmaking, and began to write literary articles (between 1844 and 1849 two hundred were published in *Chambers's Journal*). Between 1854 and 1881 he published many travel books based on "holiday walks." He became assistant secretary of the Royal Society, resigning in 1884. His wife left him in 1845, his sons emigrated, and he lived alone for the last thirty years of his life ("Walter White," in the *Dictionary of National Biography*, 21:83–84).
19. GC. Letter to Walter White from Alexander Gilchrist, 18 September, 1854.
20. "Memoir," 372.
21. *The Life of William Etty* was republished in 1978, in one volume, by EP Publishing, East Ardsley, Wakefield, West Yorkshire, England.
22. Alexander Gilchrist, *Life of William Etty, R.A.* (London: David Bogue, 1855), 2:317–19. Gilchrist gives no source for the quotations in the text, although they seem to be from Etty's autobiography. Herbert tells us that "it was a tradition in the family to avoid notes; to recast the text rather than to use them" (HHG, 258).
23. Ibid., 319–20.
24. Ibid., 324–30.
25. *LG*, "Children of Adam," 96.
26. HHG, 41.
27. The Carlyles' house on Cheyne Row belongs to the National Trust and is open to the public. My sources of information about it are "Carlyle's House," the National Trust brochure, and a tour of the house.
28. HHG, 41–42.
29. Ibid., 46, 50.

30. In the Gilchrist Collection there is a letter to Alexander Gilchrist from William Calder Marshall, 12 May, 1885. A clipping is enclosed of a biographical sketch of Marshall, presumably from *Men of the Time*. In this rather huffy note, the sculptor makes several corrections about the sales and locations of his works.

31. "Memoir," 373. Aiso HHG, 55.

Chapter 6. 6 Cheyne Row

1. Elsie M. Lang, *Literary London* (Folcroft, Pa.: Folcroft Library Editions, 1973), 32.

2. Cheyne Row, just off Cheyne Walk, is close to the Thames. It consisted originally of a terrace of twelve red-brick houses. Ten now remain. The site once belonged to Lord Cheyne. (National Trust brochure, "Carlyle's House," 8).

3. "Robert Tait, who was about the house taking photographs for some time before he began on the picture, got very much on Mrs. Carlyle's nerves. She wrote of him as 'that weary artist who took the bright idea last spring that he would make a picture of our sitting room—to be amazingly interesting to Posterity a hundred years hence. . . . The dog is the only member of the family who has reason to be pleased with his likeness as yet' " (National Trust brochure, "Carlyle's House," 17).

4. Nero was a controversial member of the Carlyle household. Alex recorded in his notebook: "Carlyle said, 'Never dog had given trouble more disproportionate to its use and worth than Nero had to him.' (Mrs. Carlyle) 'It had been worth it all.' He denied it, and reiterated the absurdity of its existence. It would be a kindness to kill it. (Mrs. Carlyle) 'If he is to be believed, he shouldn't make affectionate speeches to Nero in the garden when he thought no one heard' " (HHG, 75). Alex later reported that when Nero died Carlyle "cried like a child" and told Jane that "he could not rebuke her; he felt so wretched himself" (HHG, 84).

5. National Trust brochure, "Carlyle's House," 31.

6. Ibid., 22.

7. Even in the old ark of a house at Guildford, Anne managed to create an attractive and cozy atmosphere. In a letter to Anne from Guildford on 23 September 1853—Anne was probably visiting her mother at Earls Colne—Alex wrote: "What a dear room, this drawing room is: *perfect*; an ideal inflence: perennially delightful and fresh. . . . The soul is deeply influenced, unconsciously and hourly by outward influences. I believe living in a room like *this* does a great deal for one. Last night I slept in our spare-room: a charming room. But I don't know that I like the featherbed as well as our mattress" (GC).

8. *WMR-Rem*, 305. Rossetti had met Alex before this evening that he describes, although he did not remember exactly when or where. He had reviewed *The Life of Etty* for *The Spectator* in 1855. This evening was Rossetti's first and last visit to Alex at No. 6. It took place in the autumn of 1861, not long before Alex's death on 30 November of that year.

9. Letters to Alexander Macmillan from Alex, 28 Dec. 1860; 20 Jan. 1861; 5 April 1861. In these letters Alex invites Macmillan to No. 6 to discuss the publication of the *Life of Blake*. Macmillan lived on Henrietta Street and Alex frequently attended his "Thursdays." Beinecke Rare Book and Manuscript Library, Yale University Library.

10. Letter to Alex from Palmer, September 1861, in which Palmer thanks Alex for his "kind offer of a bed as it will enable us to go well into the Blake Manuscripts." Letter is included in "Eleven Holograph Letters from Samuel Palmer to Alexander Gilchrist and Anne, his Widow, 1861-1862." Beinecke Rare Book and Manuscript Library, Yale University Library.

11. HHG, 67.

12. Ibid., 79.

13. Gertrude Himmelfarb, *Marriage and Morals Among the Victorians* (New York: Alfred A. Knopf, 1986), 14.

14. J. H. Murray, *Strong-Minded Women*, 111-12.

15. HHG, 79-80.

16. Entries from Alex's notebooks, HHG, 80-85. Alex was not entirely innocent of nosiness himself. He had the temerity to question Jane about Lady Ashburton: "I asked Mrs. Carlyle

about Lady Ashburton? 'Oh, she had been completely vanquished;' resolved not to like her, but had been obliged to; 'stood out five days.' It was not her fascination in the drawing-room, but when on 'the fifth day she came up to my room, and spoke like an unaffected Highland girl, that Lady Ashburton won my heart; she spoke so freely and unguardedly about persons and things; most persons in that station so guarded and careful'" (HHG, 82–83).

17. HHG, 73. Herbert supplies the helpful information, in brackets, that Skittles was a "courtezan."

18. HHG, 86. Letter to Alex from Jane, 31 July, 1861.

19. J. H. Murray, *Strong-Minded Women*, 111.

20. Anne Gilchrist, "A Glance at the Vegetable Kingdom," *Chambers's Journal of Popular Literature, Science and Arts* (London) 8, no. 197, (10 October 1857), 234–36.

21. Anne Gilchrist, "Whales and Whalemen," *Chambers's Journal of Popular Literature, Science and Arts* (London) 13, no. 328 (14 April 1860), 225–25. Anne's essay is the lead article in the issue.

22. Herman Melville, *Moby Dick* (1851; reprint, New York: W. W. Norton, 1967), 118.

23. Anne Gilchrist, "Whales and Whalemen," 227. Anne is pointedly differentiating between the "veracious" English Scoresby and Yankee Melville, who "befools" his readers, although she admits by instructs them as well. When Anne Gilchrist and Henry James met in the 1880s, they had more in common than they may have known. As youthful critics, each was guilty of a monumental underassessment. In 1860, thirty-two-year-old Anne loftily dismissed Melville as a clever Yankee. In 1865, twenty-two-year-old James brashly declared that Mr. Walt Whitman not only couldn't write poetry, he couldn't even write good prose. James retracted this judgment in later years, when he became an admirer of Walt and enthusiastically acknowledged his genius. Anne did not live long enough for the long-delayed appreciation of Melville to make her aware of her blunder.

24. Melville, *Moby Dick*, 117–18.

25. HHG, 64.

26. Himmelfarb, *Marriage and Morals*, 51–53.

27. Anne Gilchrist, "Our Nearest Relation," *All the Year Round* (London: Conducted by Charles Dickens, 1859–70) 1 (28 May 1859), 112–15.

28. Harold Aspiz, "The Body Electric," in *Walt Whitman and the Body Beautiful* (Urbana: University of Illinois Press, 1980), 143–79.

29. Anne Gilchrist, "What is Electricity?," *Once a Week* (London) 4 (2 February 1861), 163–65.

30. Anne Gilchrist, "The Parentage of a Sunbeam," *Once a Week* (London) 3 (22 September 1860), 348–51.

31. Anne Gilchrist, "The Indestructibility of Force," *Macmillan's Magazine* (London) 6, (August 1862), 337–44.

32. *The Magnet Stories: For Summer Days & Winter Nights* were published in London by Groombridge & Sons, 5 Paternoster Row, "and sold by all booksellers." They were advertised as "Seaside and Holiday Reading," with "a new story every month—each complete in itself." "Lost in the Wood" was no. 16 in the series.

33. Undated, untitled typescript of a memoir of her mother by Grace Gilchrist Frend, 8. Hereafter cited as Frend. Feinberg Collection, Library of Congress. In the Feinberg Catalog the manuscript is given the title "Anne Gilchrist and Walt Whitman," but there is no title or date on the actual typescript. In Grace's diaries, written in the 1920s, when she was in her sixties, she mentions this memoir many times: the months of work that she put into it; her hopes for it; her despondency at its repeated rejections. Her diaries are in the Gilchrist Collection.

34. A copy of the church record of the baptism of the four Gilchrist children was kindly sent to me by Canon A. S. J. Holden, vicar of St. Andrew's Church, Earls Colne. Canon Holden has confirmed my opinion that the only explanation of this unusual baptism is that it was done to keep the family peace.

35. GC. Letters to Anne from Alex: from Guildford, Friday afternoon, 23 September 1853—½ past 4, fragment; from Guildford, n.d., written in crosshatch; from Guildford, 22 May 1856, fragment; from 6 Cheyne Row, 13 May 1857; fragment, n.d., written in crosshatch. In crosshatch, the writer fills a page, turns it 180 degrees, then continues to write in lines at right angles with his first lines.

36. GC. Letter to Anne from Alex, Stoke-next-Guildford, Wednesday evening, 28 September 1853, 9 o'clock, fragment.
37. "Memoir," 373–74.
38. Letters to Alexander Macmillan from Alex, 6 Cheyne Row, 29 November 1859 and 24 December 1860. Berg Collection, New York Public Library.
39. Letters to Alexander Macmillan from Alex, 6 Cheyne Row, 15 and 17 April 1861; and from Mr. Mott's Abinger (?) Cottage near Dorking, 25 July 1861. Berg Collection, New York Public Library.
40. HHG, 95.
41. Stanley B. Burns, M.D., "Scarlet Fever," in *The British Gallery of Medical History* (New York: Bristol Laboratories, 1985), vol. 4, no. 2, n.p.
42. Letters to Alexander Macmillan from Alex, 6 Cheyne Row, 23 October and 20 November 1861. Berg Collection, New York Public Library.
43. HHG, 98–100.
44. Ibid., 101.
45. "Memoir," 375.
46. *Letters*, 60.
47. "Memoir," 375–76.
48. Alex is buried in an old section of Kensal Green, where decaying headstones, most of them illegible, tilt and lean in thickets of unmown grass. His handsome bronze tomb, designed by Philip Webb, has sunk so deep in the earth that one must kneel down and pull back the sod in order to read the inscription:

> Alexander Gilchrist Barrister and Author
> Born April 25, 1828. Died November 30, 1861
> O Love, O Silent and Invisible Friend

The common grave of John Parker Burrows and his son no longer has a headstone. "It's about there," the custodian says, pointing to a spot a few feet from Alex's tomb. "Just about there—opposite the front wheel of your car." In the Gilchrist Collection there is a photograph of the Gilchrist tomb taken when it was still aboveground.

Chapter 7. Brookbank

1. Letters to Anne from Gabriel Rossetti, Samuel Palmer, and Jane Carlyle, HHG, 103–10. Palmer's letter, written on 2 February 1862, is included in its entirety in *Eleven Holograph Letters from Samuel Palmer to Alexander Gilchrist and Anne his widow 1861–1862*, Beinecke Rare Book and Manuscript Library, Yale University Library. Samuel and Anne Palmer were devastated by the death of their son More, still a schoolboy, in July 1861. Alex was attentive and helpful during the funeral and afterward, and the *Eleven Holograph Letters* include five letters to Alex thanking him for his *"great kindness and tenderness"* at the awful time, & ever since" (letter 5, 26 July 1861). After Alex's death, Palmer wrote long letters of comfort and fatherly advice to Anne. Four of these letters are included in *Eleven Holograph Letters*. His advice ranges from professional directions for the completion of the *Life of Blake* to suggestions about bringing up children: "You are no doubt acquainted with the virtues of cocoa—especially for young people who take morning exercise—if the stomach will not at first take it, less cocoa & more milk will smooth the way" (letter 9, 27 April 1862). Palmer (1805–81), a disciple of Blake, was an etcher and landscape painter.
2. I have not been able to identify Isabella Erskine Ireland except as a friend of Anne who seems to have been about the same age. She lived at 4 Selwood Place, S.W., Brompton, London. Anne apparently stayed with her when she was working at the British Museum during the completion of the *Life of Blake*, since she wrote a letter to Macmillan from that address on 29 August 1862 (Berg Collection, New York Public Library). After Anne's death, Isabella wrote motherly letters to Grace—to "My dearest Giddy"—from the same address (GC).
3. GC. Notepaper folders 2, 3, and 4 of an undated letter to Grace from Isabella Erskine Ireland—folder 1 is missing. Written after Anne's death and before the publication of Herbert's biography, probably 1886.

4. HHG, 107.
5. Letter to Alexander Macmillan from Anne, 6 Great Cheyne Row, 1 February 1862. Berg Collection, New York Public Library.
6. GC. Letter to Grace from Isabella Ireland, n.d.
7. HHG, 114. The woman was Geraldine Jewsbury, a novelist (*Zoe, The Half-Sisters, Right or Wrong*) and Jane Carlyle's close friend. It was she who told Froude, Carlyle's biographer, that Carlyle had been "one of those persons who ought never to have married." By this she meant, and Froude understood her to mean, that Carlyle was impotent. See Phyllis Rose, *Parallel Lives: Five Victorian Marriages* (New York: Vintage, 1984), 60.
8. HHG, 114–15.
9. GC. Letter to Grace from Isabella Ireland, undated, In the Gilchrist Collection there is a copy of the catalogue of the sale of a collection of books to be sold at auction by Messrs. Puttick and Simpson, Auctioneers of Literary Property and Works of Art, at their gallery, No. 47, Leicester Square, W.C. (Formerly the Mansion of Sir Joshua Reynolds, P.R.A.), "on Tuesday, December 9th, 1873, and three following Days, at ten minutes past one o'clock precisely." The collection included the library of "the late Alexander Gilchrist, Esq., Author of 'The Life of William Blake,' and 'The Life of Wm. Etty, R.A.'" There are 1459 items listed, with no indication of which were from Alex's library. Some possibilities would seem to be: #3, Robert's *History of Lyme Regis* (14 vols.); #381, Cuvier's *La Regne Animal* (3 vols.); #387, Schleiden's *Principles of Botany*, 1849; and #80, "Blake's *Silver Drops, or Serious Things*, 4 curious plates, old morocco, n.d." One wonders why William Haines or Anne—who used both Cuvier and Schleiden as references in her scientific essays—would part with these, especially with the Blake plates.
10. I have determined the exact date of the move to Shottermill from information in a letter to Macmillan from Anne, 6 Cheyne Row, 31 March (a Monday) 1862. "We shall arrive at Shotter Mill on Thursday. . . . My children are pretty well. I think the change to the country will return them to a full measure of health. I trust so." Letter in Berg Collection, New York Public Library.
11. GC. Letter to Grace from Isabella Ireland, n.d.
12. For all of this information about Shottermill and the surrounding area I am indebted to Bronwen Tickner, She has sent me annotated maps, photocopies of old pictures, pictures that she has taken herself, reprints of magazine and newspaper articles, and pages of notes copied from books in the local library. In October 1985, I spent a day with her in Shottermill. We visited Brookbank Cottage and retraced Anne's steps in her long walks that she loved so much, standing on the summit of Hind Head and looking down on the magnificent scene below, as Anne must have done innumerable times.
13. Frend, 5.
14. HHG, 124.
15. Betty Coombs, "George Eliot in Surrey," *The Lady*, 20 November 1969, 806. Brookbank Cottage, privately owned, is a famous landmark in Shottermill, not because it once belonged to Anne Gilchrist, but because of George Eliot's occupancy. Since Anne's time, the house has been divided into two residences. The one on the right, as one faces the cottage, is called Middlemarch. The one on the left is Brookbank, with its name in bold letters on a sign on the gate leading to the front door.
16. Frend, 6.
17. George Eliot, *Daniel Deronda* (1876; reprint, New York: Penguin Books, 1967), 249–50.
18. Frend, 7.
19. HHG, 126. These lines are also quoted in *Corr.* 2:136, n. 62.
20. The Probert family chart does not show whether Mrs. Burnie was Alex's sister Elizabeth Ellen or his sister Eliza. His sister Melicent married William Thomas. His sister Margaret married Thomas Nicolls.
21. Letters from Anne to William Haines and Milly Thomas, HHG, 152, 154.
22. Letter to Alexander Macmillan from Anne, 6 Cheyne Row, 6 December 1861. Berg Collection, New York Public Library.
23. Letter to Alexander Macmillan from Anne, 6 Cheyne Row, 20 March 1862. Berg Collection, New York Public Library.
24. HHG, 132–33. Linnell had made the same offer to Alex, "the bare notion of which filled him with horror." In offering to read the proofs, Linnell told Anne frankly that "he might put in or take out what he did not agree with." The source of concern was that Linnell had had a

dispute with the painter Tatham about the ownership of some of Blake's work, and Linnell wanted to make certain that Alex had not taken Tatham's side.

25. Anne was chosen to write the biographical and critical sketch of Blake for Leslie Stephen's *Dictionary of National Biography* (London: Smith, Elder & Co., 1890), 2:643–46.

26. After the publication of the *Life of Blake*, a surprising incident occurred, which William Rossetti reports in *Rossetti Papers: 1862-1870*— Anne burned a Blake manuscript! "It was a long thing which I really believe even Mr. Swinburne will pronounce pure rubbish." Anne wrote to Rossetti on 18 November 1863. She sent it to Rossetti to read, he returned it to her, and she burned it. In a bracketed note, Rossetti comments ruefully: "The 'long thing' by Blake, which Mrs. Gilchrist regarded as 'pure rubbish,' was a prose narrative of a domestic, and also fantastic, sort, clearly intended by its author to count as humouristic or funny, and somewhat in the Shandean vein. I read this performance and heartily confirmed Mrs. Gilchrist in the conviction of its being rubbish; yet I was startled to learn soon afterwards that, on receiving my letter, she had burned the MS. The thing was stupid, but it was Blake's." It is indeed startling that usually prudent Anne, who was aware that Blake material was currently bringing substantial prices at Christie's, should have burned any scrap of Blake holograph. But she was not alone in her rashness. Gabriel Rossetti also burned a "residuum" of Blake MSS, including a leading passage from Blake's *French Revolution* (William Michael Rossetti, comp., *Rossetti Papers: 1862-1870* [London: Sands, 1903], 41–42; hereafter cited as *WMR-Papers*).

27. Letters from Anne to William Rossetti and from Gabriel Rossetti to Anne, HHG, 135–37.

28. Letter to Alexander Macmillan from Anne, Brookbank, 11 July 1862. Berg Collection, New York Public Library.

29. William Haines is a shadowy figure. Clarence Gohdes and Paull Franklin Baum, editors of *Letters of William Michael Rossetti*, identify him only as "a close friend of Alexander Gilchrist, assisted in preparing the biography of Blake" (9n). In a letter to his sister Milly Thomas on 31 July 1849 (GC), Alex spoke of "the Haines," of "William and Mrs. Haines." Mrs. Haines was probably his mother, since there is no mention anywhere of his having a wife. In the Gilchrist Collection there are two letters from Haines written to Herbert after Anne's death, when Haines was criticizing Herbert's biography chapter by chapter. The letters, dated 31 March and 1 April 1886, from "Iffley [?] Lodge," are addressed to "my dear Herbert" and signed "Yours affect'ly." In tone, they are letters from a father or an affectionate uncle. Judging from the frequency of his visits to Brookbank, he would seem to have lived nearby during Anne's residence there. In his letter to Milly Thomas, Alex mentions an essay by Haines, "The Revival of National Architecture," which had just appeared in *The Builder*. Whatever his background and profession may have been, William Haines was obviously a man of taste and culture, with a broad knowledge of the arts.

30. Letter to Alexander Macmillan from Anne, 6 Cheyne Row, 15 March 1862. Berg Collection, New York Public Library.

31. HHG, 125.

32. Anne's many letters to William Rossetti were frequently signed "Annie" Gilchrist. For one example, see *WMR-Papers*, 43.

33. Letter to Alexander Macmillan from Anne, Brookbank, 30 July 1862. Berg Collection, New York Public Library.

34. HHG, 128.

35. Letter to Alexander Macmillan from Anne, Brookbank, 29 August 1862. Berg Collection, New York Public Library.

36. Letter to Alexander Macmillan from Anne, Brookbank, 1 December 1862, Berg Collection, New York Public Library.

37. Letter to Alexander Macmillan from Anne, Brookbank, (?) December 1862. Berg Collection, New York Public Library.

38. Letters to Anne from Carlyle and Palmer, HHG, 141–43.

39. Review of Alexander Gilchrist's *Life of Blake*, *North American Review*, October 1864, 465–82.

40. HHG, 142. Letter written "to a relative."

41. Ibid., 151.

42. According to *The Wellesley Index to Victorian Periodicals, 1824–1900*, Anne's essay "A

Neglected Art" was published in *Macmillan's Magazine* in October 1865—and a photocopy of the essay verifies this date. However, according to Herbert (HHG, 153), it was "The Indestructibility of Force" that was published in that year, although it was actually published in *Macmillan's* in August 1862. As verification of the 1865 publication date for "Force," Herbert quotes from a letter from Anne to Haines on 24 July 1864, in which she wrote: "I have been trying to get together . . . materials for an article on Dr. Carpenter's writings. Chiefly on his very remarkable and philosophical views of life and the 'vital force,' but I have not succeeded—seem to have got together every book he has ever written but the right one" (HHG, 153). Since Dr. Carpenter is mentioned only once in "Force," briefly and near the end of the essay, it would seem that in 1864 Anne was planning an article dealing exclusively with Carpenter to follow an already published "Force." There is no evidence that the second article was ever written. But it does seem that, either carelessly or deliberately, Herbert gives the wrong date of publication for "Force," while ignoring "A Neglected Art" altogether.

43. Anne Gilchrist, "A Neglected Art," *Macmillan's Magazine*, 12 (October 1865), 494–501.
44. GC. Letter to Anne from Walter White. 24 March 1859.
45. Anne Gilchrist, "A Neglected Art," 495–96.
46. Ibid., 496.
47. Ibid.
48. Ibid., 497.
49. Ibid.
50. Ibid., 498.
51. Ibid.
52. Ibid., 499.
53. Ibid.
54. Ibid.
55. Ibid., 499–500.
56. Herbert may have been embarrassed by his mother's suggestion that ladies descend into their own kitchens wearing aprons, but he would not have been embarrassed by her socialist sympathies. After the Fabian Society was organized in 1884, Herbert and Grace attended meetings.
57. Anne Gilchrist, "A Neglected Art," 500–501.
58. Ibid., 501.
59. David Masson (1822–1907) started *Macmillan's Magazine* and edited it until 1867.
60. HHG, 153.
61. *LG*, "A Song of Joys," 178.
62. Frend, 5.
63. GC. Letter to Herbert from Walter White, 8 April 1887.
64. HHG, 160.
65. *LG*, "Song of Myself," 83.
66. HHG, 120.
67. Ibid., 145.
68. Ibid., 175. Anne Gilchrist's great-great-granddaughter, whose name is also Anne Gilchrist, has sent me a photograph of a small painting of Beatrice at the age of ten or twelve. It shows a delicate, oval, very serious young face, blond hair parted in the center and drawn severely back. She does indeed look more like a lily than a rose.
69. HHG, 162–63.
70. Greyshott Farm in the 1860s is described as a two-storyed stone-and-brick house with small, low rooms, windows with diamond panes, and doors with bolts and bars. The beautiful windows of the house overlook lawns that lead onto wide expanses of heath land. The Tennysons did not rent the entire house, but only enough rooms for the family and three servants. Greyshott Farm, now Greyshott Hall, is four or five miles from Brookbank. I am indebted to Bronwen Tickner for this information about Greyshott Farm from notes that she copied in the local library from *Greyshott*, J. H. Smith, 1978. In October 1985, I visited Greyshott Hall with her. To get there, we drove up "Tennyson's Lane," the lane that Anne used when she walked to the farm.
71. HHG, 165.
72. Emily Sellwood Tennyson, Baroness, *Lady Tennyson's Journal*, ed. James O. Hoge (Charlottesville: University of Virginia Press, 1981), 261.

73. Tennyson and Anne were friends for as long as she lived. Anne's grandson, Alexander Fitzmaurice Gilchrist, was born in 1878. His most vivid memory of his grandmother was having lunch at her house in the 1880s when Tennyson was a guest. The little boy put something very hot into his mouth—and spat it out! Anne rebuked him. But Tennyson took his part and said that he was very sensible. I am indebted to Canon James Gilchrist, Alexander's son, for this family anecdote.
74. HHG, 168-70.
75. Ibid., 168.
76. Frend, 8.
77. HHG, 171.
78. *Lady Tennyson's Journal*, 4. Tennyson's "slender-stalked tea rose" (1813–96) outlived her robust husband by four years. Her physical debility was probably due to a spinal disorder from which she had suffered since girlhood (Ibid., 4).
79. Ibid., 274.
80. *Letters of William Michael Rossetti: Concerning Whitman, Blake, and Shelley; to Anne Gilchrist and her son Herbert Gilchrist*, ed. Clarence Gohdes and Paull Franklin Baum (Durham, N.C.: Duke University Press, 1934), 74. Hereafter cited as *WMR-Letters*.
81. *Lady Tennyson's Journal*, 255.
82. HHG, 140.
83. *WMR-Papers*, 417.
84. HHG, 216-17. The "little Sir Joshuas" were Master Lord Burghersh and little Miss Theophilia Gwatkin.
85. One outing was a picnic with Mrs. Simmons, her neighbor, and another lady, a friend of Mrs. Simmons. The horse suddenly bolted and got out of control on the road at the top of Hind Head. He plunged into a ditch, threw them all into the hedge, and Anne felt the chaise go over her head, knocking her hat off. Mrs. Simmons's friend "was a stout old lady who had charge of the provisions (we were to have picniced at Churt). So she was landed in the hedge with the bottles and baskets all on her stomach, and the tenacity with which she afterwards clung to the same—called vehemently for corkscrews and insisted on our immediately beginning to eat bread and cheese—which after the excitement of being pitched out, one was of all things least inclined for—tickled me immensely" (HHG, 158-59). This outing took place in July 1865.
86. HHG, 126. Also see the obituary notice of Percy Carlyle Gilchrist in *Who Was Who: 1929-1940* (London: Adam & Charles Black, 1941), 3:511-12. The Felsted School, Felsted, Essex was founded in 1564 by Richard, Lord Riche, lord chancellor of England.
87. HHG, 203.
88. Ibid., 166.
89. Rossetti's *Poems of Walt Whitman* was published in February 1868—a year and a half before Madox Brown lent his copy to Anne.

Chapter 8. Godiva

1. HHG, 177.
2. William Rossetti, Elizabeth Porter Gould, and Arthur Stedman—whose *Selected Poems by Walt Whitman* was published in 1892, with an editor's note that "this edition of Mr. Whitman's poems is, on his part, a concession to friendship. He has not abandoned his position, but has yielded to urgent request"—were the only persons to whom Whitman ever gave permission to publish selections from *Leaves of Grass*. As in the case of Elizabeth Porter Gould and her *Gems from Walt Whitman*, Walt's permission to Rossetti was given reluctantly and later regretted. Through Moncure Conway, Rossetti was given permission to prepare and edit a volume of selections from Whitman's poems for publication in England—and, surprisingly, permission "to make verbal changes." What Conway had in mind was the deletion of words like *father-stuff, onanist,* and *veneralee,* which might offend British readers. On 17 November 1867, Rossetti wrote directly to Walt, thanking him for these privileges granted through Conway and remarking that, since he had Walt's permission to delete a few words or lines, perhaps a complete edition could be

published in England. On 3 December, Walt replied, in a letter courteously but adamantly firm, that the omissions he had agreed to were intended only for a book of selections, that he would never allow a complete edition to be printed with any deletions whatsoever, and that in the introduction to the book of selections he asked Rossetti to "make no allusion to me as authorizing, or not prohibiting &" (Allen, *Solitary Singer,* 386). "And now, my friend, having set myself right on that matter," Walt continued, "I proceed to say, on the other hand, . . . that if, before the arrival of this letter, you have practically invested in, or accomplished, or partially accomplished, any plan, even contrary to this letter, I do not expect you to abandon it, at loss of outlay; but shall *bona fide* consider you blameless if you let it go on. . . . For I feel, indeed know, that I am in the hands of a friend, and that my pieces will receive that truest, brightest of light and perception coming from love" (HHG, 181).

3. *WMR-Letters,* 23–24.
4. HHG, 288–89.
5. Frend, 1.
6. *WMR-Papers,* 403.
7. *Democratic Vistas,* in *Walt Whitman: Complete Poetry and Selected Prose,* ed. James E. Miller, Jr. (Boston: Houghton Mifflin, 1959), 500.
8. *LG,* "Song of Myself," 89.
9. *Democratic Vistas,* 500–501.
10. *WMR-Letters,* 23.
11. Although WW had assured Rossetti that he would hold him "blameless" if *Poems of Walt Whitman* was contrary in any way to the specifications that he had outlined in his letter, Walt resented Rossetti's meddling. "Damn the expurgated books! I say damn 'em! The dirtiest book in all the world is an expurgated book. Rossetti expurgated—avowed it in his preface: a sort of nod to Mrs. Grundy," he raged to Traubel (Horace Traubel, *With Walt Whitman in Camden,* vol. 1 [28 March–14 July 1888] [Boston: Small, Maynard & Co., 1906], 124; hereafter cited as *WWWC* 1). And on another occasion he fumed: "Expurgation is apology—yes, surrender that something or other was wrong. Emerson said expurgate—I said no, no. I have lived to regret my Rossetti yes—I have not lived to regret my Emerson no. Expurgate, expurgate—apologize, apologize: get down on your knees. . . . Did the Rossetti book ever do me any good? I am not sure of it: Rossetti's kindness did me good—but as for the rest, I am doubtful" (*WWWC* 1:151).
12. Paul J. Ferlazzo, "Anne Gilchrist, Critic of Walt Whitman," *South Dakota Reivew* 10, no. 4 (Winter 1972–73), 73.
13. It was Oliver Wendell Holmes's judgment that Whitman "takes into his hospitable vocabulary words which no English dictionary recognizes as belonging to the language" ("Introduction," in *Walt Whitman: Complete Poetry and Selected Prose,* ed. James E. Miller, Jr., li–lii).
14. HHG, 289.
15. Ibid.
16. *LG,* "Birds of Passage," 233.
17. *WWWC* 4:312.
18. Ibid., 313–14.
19. How Susan's letter reached WW is also a mystery, since the envelope was neither addressed nor stamped. Was it hand delivered? When Traubel asked him how the letter got into his hands, the poet evaded the question (*WWWC* 4:312).
20. Katherine Anthony, "A Normal Madness," 66 (11 January 1919), 16.
21. Douglas, *Feminization of American Culture,* 261.
22. *Letters,* 59.
23. *Corr.* 2:90, n. 52. Rossetti apparently believed that Anne had so little interest in poetry that he neither gave nor lent her a copy of *Poems of Walt Whitman* when it was published in 1868. It was not until June 1869, a year and a half later, that Madox Brown lent his copy to Anne.
24. Bucke, *Walt Whitman,* 215.
25. *WMR-Rem,* 404.
26. *WMR-Letters,* 28.
27. HHG, 183.
28. *WMR-Letters,* 29–31.
29. Ibid., 33–34.

30. *WMR-Papers*, 459. William O'Connor was employed in Washington by the Department of Treasury in the Light-house Division.
31. *WMR-Letters*, 35.
32. *WMR-Papers*, 459–60.
33. *WMR-Letters*, 35.
34. Ibid., 38.
35. *WMR-Papers*, 411.
36. *WMR-Letters*, 39. In thanking Rossetti for writing his introduction to the essay, Anne wrote: "I would not have a line otherwise in the beautiful sustaining words you have prefixed for me. I have indeed good cause to be grateful: for I do not see how I could have accomplished this which (whatever the immediate consequence to me) I shall never cease to rejoice in having accomplished, without your aid. Certainly I could not otherwise have had such favouring circumstances" (HHG, 191).
37. *WMR-Papers*, 415.
38. HHG, 187.
39. Allen, *Solitary Singer*, 416.
40. *Corr.* 2:91–92.
41. *WMR-Letters*, 44–45.
42. *Letters*, xxix–xxx.
43. Jerome Loving, *Walt Whitman's Champion: William Douglas O'Connor* (College Station and London: Texas A & M University Press, 1978), 92–93.
44. Anne Gilchrist, "A Woman's Estimate of Walt Whitman," *Radical* [Boston], May 1870, 345–59; hereafter cited as *EST*. Text used reprinted HHG, 287–307. For some reason, in his biography of his mother, Herbert changed the title of the essay to "An Englishwoman's Estimate of Walt Whitman." However, in his biographical sketch of his mother for the *Dictionary of National Biography* (vol. 21, 340–41), he used the original title.
45. Information from copy of May 1870 issue of the *Radical*, Berg Collection, New York Public Library.
46. Ferlazzo, *Gilchrist, Critic*, 67.
47. Allen, *Solitary Singer*, 177.
48. *WWWC* 3:167.
49. Justin Kaplan, *Walt Whitman: A Life* (New York: Simon and Schuster, 1980), 225.
50. *WWWC* 3:235.
51. There is evidence that from the start flirtatious, often-married, auburn-ringleted, forty-five-year-old Fanny cast her eye on Walt, as Justin Kaplan puts it, "in a cherishing way," Before she had read his book, she had seen him somewhere, probably in New York. On 19 April 1856, two months before she reviewed *Leaves of Grass*, she wrote a heavy-breathing description of Walt in her column in the *Ledger*. She openly admired his "muscular throat," his broad shoulders, and "that fine, ample chest of his." His voice, she wrote, was "rich, deep, and clear as a clarion note. In the most crowded thoroughfare, one would turn instinctively on hearing it, to seek out its owner." Two days later she sent a clipping of the article to Walt with a hand-delivered note that read:

"Leaves of Grass"
You are *delicious*! May my right hand wither if I don't tell the whole world before another week, what *one* woman thinks of you.
"Walt"? "what I assume you shall assume!" Some evening this week you are to spend with Jemmy [Parton] & me—Wednesday?—say (Kaplan, Whitman, 216–17).

52. Allen, *Solitary Singer,* 261.
53. Kaplan, *Whitman,* 242.
54. Allen, *Solitary Singer,* 261–62.
55. Ibid., 262.
56. Kaplan, *Whitman,* 243–44.
57. In listing the women who defended the 1860 edition of *Leaves of Grass* in print, Mary A. Chilton of Islip, Long Island, should be mentioned. On 5 June she sent a letter strongly endorsing the sex poems to the *Saturday Press*, and the letter was printed on 9 June. Reading

Whitman's poems, she found that "the simple grandeur of his expressed soul, filled mine with awe and reverence for the pages he had the genius to inspire." She did not find the poet's treatment of the human body and its functions offensive because in childhood "there is no blush of shame at sight of a nude form, and the serene wisdom of maturity covers this innocence with a halo of glory, by recognizing the divinity of humanity, and perceiving the unity of all the functions of the human body" (Allen, *Solitary Singer,* 262–63). Allen gives no clue to Mary's identity. But whoever she was, it took courage to write and mail that letter.

58. *Corr.* 2:2.
59. Ferlazzo, *Gilchrist, Critic,* 65–66.
60. Ibid., 71–72.
61. Ibid., 72. Anne had little patience with attempts to defend Whitman by comparing him with older, accepted writers. In July 1883, when she received Bucke's biography, she wrote to Walt:

> How do I hate all that unmeaning, irrelevant clatter about what Rabelais or Shakespeare or the ancients & their times tolerated in the way of coarseness or plainness of speech. As if you wanted apologizing for or could be apologized for on that ground! If these poems are to be *tolerated,* I, for one, could not tolerate them. If they are not the highest lesson that has yet been taught in refinement & purity, if they do not banish all possibility of coarseness of thought & feeling, there would be nothing to be said for them. But they do: I am as sure of that as of my own existence. When will men begin to understand them? (*Letters,* 217–18).

62. Ferlazzo, "Gilchrist, Critic," 79.
63. *EST,* 289–90.
64. Ibid., 292.
65. Ibid., 290.
66. Ibid., 291–92.
67. Ibid., 292–93.
68. Ibid., 294.
69. Ibid., 294–95.
70. Ibid., 296–97.
71. Ibid., 297.
72. Ibid., 297–98.
73. Ibid., 304.
74. Ibid., 304–6.
75. Ibid., 307.
76. Ibid., 299–300.
77. Ibid., 300.
78. Ibid., 301–2.
79. Ibid., 302.
80. HHG, 191.
81. In 1875, Longfellow, Lowell, and Holmes tried to discourage Lord Houghton from calling on "that awful Whitman" (Allen, *Solitary Singer,* 468).
82. Kaplan, *Whitman,* 328. Helen Price was the daughter of Mrs. Abby Price, an old friend of Louisa Van Velsor Whitman and WW.
83. *WWWC* 1:218.
84. *Corr.* 2:98, n. 20.
85. *WMR-Letters,* 56.
86. The paragraph that was omitted would have been on page 293, between the paragraph ending "of the free air and sunshine of to-day" and the paragraph beginning "But this poet" (HHG, 202). "It is both tiresome & stupid that they cut out the paragraph you refer to," Rossetti wrote to Anne in reply to the letter in which she pointed out the omission. "I was conscious of a certain abruptness in the printed article, tho' the precise facts were not present to my memory" (*WMR-Letters,* 56). What the missing paragraph was meant to show, Anne explains, was the unreasonableness of theologians on the one hand—who see nothing in the present but believe they will know everything in the hereafter—and poets, artists, and historians, who see nothing of beauty in the present but only in the distant past (HHG, 203).
87. *Letters,* 70.

Chapter 9. My Dearest Friend

1. *Letters*, 83.
2. *WMR-Letters*, 71.
3. *Letters*, 70.
4. *WMR-Letters*, 79-80.
5. Anne gave no address as part of the heading of her letter of 3 September 1871. However, since she tells WW near the close of the letter that after the 29th of the month she will be in her own home in Haslemere [the town a mile from the village of Shottermill], this first letter must have been written in the fields near Colne.
6. Anne's rather large writing careens across a page. It contrasts dramatically with the writing of two other women whose letters to him WW carefully preserved—the letters of Juliette Beach and the mysterious Ellen Eyre. The letters from both Juliette and Ellen are composed in perfectly straight and precisely parallel lines, as if their notepaper were ruled, and their writing, small and elegant, is like delicate lace. Their letters are in the Feinberg Collection, Library of Congress.
7. *Corr.* 2:134, n. 58.
8. Complete text of letter to Whitman from Anne, 3 September 1871: *Letters*, 58-64 and *Corr.* 2:134-38.
9. Anne's letter of 15 October to WW has been lost (*Letters*, 68, n. 2).
10. *Letters*, 65-66. Before writing this letter on 23 October, Anne sent WW copies of her first two letters (Ibid., 74).
11. Ibid., 67. Also, slightly different text, *Corr.* 2:140.
12. *Letters*, 68-70.
13. Ibid., 95. Gay Wilson Allen believes that the ring may have been Walt's mother's wedding ring and that "whether or not he intended this as a sort of token engagement, Mrs. Gilchrist could hardly be expected not to interpret it so" (Allen *Solitary Singer*, 453-54). When she received the ring, Anne wrote on 4 September 1873: "O the precious letter, bearing to me the living touch of your hand, vibrating through and through me as I feel the pressure of the ring that pressed your flesh—& now will press mine so long as I draw breath" (*Letters*, 96).
14. *LG*, "Calamus," 123.
15. *Corr.* 2:170. This letter is not included in *Letters*. Harned had never seen it until he read it in Grace Gilchrist Frend's unpublished memoir of her mother (Barrus, 158).
16. *Letters*, 78.
17. Ibid., 77-78.
18. Ibid., 80.
19. In 1874 forty-five-year-old William Rossetti married for the first time. His bride was Lucy Brown, daughter of Madox Brown by a first marriage. In her teens Lucy joined the Rossetti family for instruction by the women of the household—Maria, Christina, and Mrs. Rossetti—since her stepmother, Emma, who was very young, had her hands full with the care of other children. The Browns paid the Rossettis forty pounds a year for Lucy's maintenance and instruction. Lucy was frail and after her marriage seems to have spent most of her time either upstairs in the room outside her bedroom or at seaside resorts to improve her health. Their first child, Olivia Frances Madox Rossetti, was born in 1875. Gabriel Arthur Madox Rossetti was born in 1877. "Our two children are a great pleasure & interest to us both," Rossetti wrote to Anne in January 1878, "but at my present age, 48, & with income dependent upon my continuing to be alive in this world, we both think two of them enough, if only Destiny will so permit" (*WMR-Letters*, 109). But Destiny did not. Helen Maria was born in 1878 and occupied a cradle borrowed from Anne. It was probably also used by the twins, Mary Elizabeth and Michael Ford, born in 1881 (*WMR-Letters*, 105-11). For information about Lucy Brown see Winwar, *Poor Splendid Wings*, 102.
20. Joseph B. Marvin was a former owner and editor of the [Boston] *Radical*. When he called on Anne, he was employed in Washington in the Treasury Department and had gone to England on official business. In a note to Anne, WW introduced Marvin as "a valued friend of mine—a Yankee born & bred—democratic, literary, married" (*Corr.* 2:341).
21. Katherine Hillard (1839?-1915) was a friend of the Price family, Whitman's old

friends. She was a poet, translator of Dante's *Banquet* (1889), and editor of a scholarly work by Helena Petrovna Blavatsky (1907). Although she had enjoyed and appreciated WW's poetry for years, the two did not meet until February 1876. WW was much taken with her, and the two saw each other frequently when she was in Philadelphia (*Corr.* 2:224-25, n. 92).

22. In speaking of Moncure Conway to WW, Anne commented on walking in London: "I am half afraid Mr. Conway works too incessantly—that is, does not like well enough the indispensable supplement of close mental work—plenty of air & exercise &c.—hates walking, & indeed it is not to be wondered at in great, smoky London. . . . Unless one has a real passion for open air & the sense of sky overhead, like me" (*Letters*, 124).

23. *Letters*, 77. When Alex told a friend (Lucy Watson, granddaughter of James Gillman, biographer of Coleridge) that "I can rarely persuade Annie to take a holiday or to go into society," Anne replied with a smile, "Oh, yes! I do go out as much as I wish; but I do not need rest as some do; a change of work or occupation is rest for me" (HHG, 66).

24. *Corr.* 2:340-41, n. 65.

25. Barrus, 115.

26. Notice of Percy Carlyle Gilchrist, *Who Was Who: 1929-1940* 3:511-12.

27. *Letters*, 84, 117.

28. Percy was destined to be a distinguished and internationally known metallurgist. With his cousin, Sidney Gilchrist Thomas, he would be a cofounder of the Thomas-Gilchrist process of making steel from phosphoric pig iron. Sidney Thomas died in 1885 of emphysema at the age of thirty-five (*Dictionary of National Biography* 19:670-71). Percy would become vice president of the Iron and Steel Institute, a chevalier of the Legion of Honour, and a member of the Society of Chemical Industry, the Royal Society of the Arts, and other distinguished organizations.

29. *Letters*, 99-100, 106.

30. In the Gilchrist Collection there is a letter from the Admiralty dated 29 May 1840. It is addressed to the father of a Mr. Fitzmaurice, who was serving as mate on the *Beagle*. Fitzmaurice *père* had apparently written to inquire about his son's performance in that capacity. The report is glowing. Young Fitzmaurice was acting as a surveyor, and, in recognition of "the zealous and attentive manner in which he has performed every duty," a river that he had discovered and explored had been named for him. Where the river was is unclear. The first name of young Mr. Fitzmaurice is not given, but he may well have been Norah's father.

31. *Letters*, 126-28.

32. Ibid., 105-6. By her "letters" Anne meant "Estimate."

33. Ibid., 117, 120.

34. Ibid., 134-35.

35. GC. Letter to Anne from Alex, 13 May 1857.

36. Frend, 9.

37. *Letters*, 99.

38. Ibid., 123.

39. Ibid., 129. Anne's mother died on 15 August 1875. All of Anne's children were with her at the funeral, she told WW. Henrietta Carwardine Burrows is buried in the churchyard of Saint Andrew's Church in Colne. Her handsome stone tomb is close to the rear of the church building.

40. Ibid., 134. The London School of Medicine for Women was opened in 1874 by Sophia Jex-Blake, who had tried without success to obtain a medical education at the University of Edinburgh. She eventually received a medical degree at Berne, Switzerland, was reexamined in Dublin, and was eventually admitted to practice. On the staff of the London School of Medicine for Women when it opened were two distinguished women physicians. One was an American, Elizabeth Blackwell, the world's first woman doctor and the first woman in America to receive a diploma from a regular medical school—the Geneva Medical College in New York (Virginia G. Drachman, *Hospital with a Heart: Women Doctors and the Paradox of Separatism at the New England Hospital, 1867-1969* [Ithaca and London: Cornell University Press, 1984], 32). The other was Elizabeth Garrett Anderson, the first English woman doctor, who received her M.D. from the University of Paris in 1870 (J. H. Murray, *Strong-Minded Women*, 223, 311-12).

41. This photograph of Anne was on her *carte de visite*. On the back of the copy of the photograph in the Special Collections Department in the Van Pelt Library of the University of Pennsylvania is written: "From carte de visite of Anne Gilchrist taken at Halstead Essex, August

1874. Age 46—two years before her visit to America (Written by Mrs. Grace Gilchrist Frend—1926 for Harriet Sprague [Whitman collector].) Clara Barrus identifies this photograph (reproduced in *Whitman and Burroughs: Comrades*) as having been taken by "Miss Davison" in 1884. Dr. Barrus's date is either an error or a typographical mistake.

42. HHG, xiv–xv.
43. Barrus, 151. Also HHG, 283.
44. HHG, xv.
45. Ibid., 283.
46. *Letters*, 149.
47. Ibid., 137. In 1873, when Walt had his first stroke, Anne had written: "Perhaps if my hand were in yours, dear Walt, you would get along faster. Dearer and sweeter that lot than even to have been your bride in the full flush & strength and glory of your youth. I turn my face to the westward sky before I lie down to sleep, deep & steadfast within me the silent aspiration that every year, every month & week, may help something to prepare and make fitter me and mine to be your comfort and joy" (103).
48. Ibid., 144.
49. Ibid., 145. Also *Corr.* 3:30–31. In *Letters,* eight lines—"I do not approve. . . . we will talk about it yet in London"—are italicized; in *Corr.* they are not. I have chosen to use the *Letters* text since I believe that WW intended these lines to be as emphatic as possible. He may have kept two copies of this letter, one with these lines underscored, one without underlining—but either way his intention is very clear.
50. *Letters*, 134. Parting from her oldest child was painful for Anne. She hoped that perhaps he might join her in America after she had "been a little while in America & have made friends & had time to look about me . . . [for] a good certainty for him" (134). "Soon, soon as ever my boy has one to love & care for him all his own, I will come," Anne wrote to WW in December 1875. "I may not come before, not if it should break my heart to stop away from you, for his welfare is my sacred charge & nearer & dearer than all to me" (138). Parting was doubly hard for Anne because Percy resented her plan to go to America. "I think he never in his heart believed I really should go to America, and so it comes as a great blow to him now," she wrote to Walt in February 1876. "You must be very indulgent towards him for my sake, my dear friend" (141). Percy and Norah did not marry until 1877.
51. Ibid., 134, 136. Although it was not what Anne wanted to hear, Kate Hillard's advice to Herby was sound. In the nineteenth century young American artists were going to Europe for their training because of the dearth of good instruction at home.
52. Ibid., 135.
53. Ibid., 150.
54. I make this judgment from the tone of Rossetti's letters to Anne after she reached Philadelphia. "I suppose I may congratulate you in a general way on your American experiences & prospects," he began a letter in early January 1877 (*WMR-Letters,* 102). Anne sent him a brief card as soon as she landed in Philadelphia to assure him that she and the children had arrived safely (HHG, 227).
55. On 3 September 1874, Anne wrote to WW:

Did I ever tell you the cousin of mine who owns the priory here fought for two years in the Secession war in the army of the Potomac when Burnside & McClellan were at the head? John Carwardine was Major in a Cavalry regiment—was at Vicksburg, Fredericksburg, &c. Never wounded, or but slightly—had a good deal of outpost duty, being just the right sort of man for that, & has letters of approval from his generals of which he is not a little proud. Before that fought under the Stars & Stripes in Mexico. . . . I often think he was perhaps one of those your eyes rested on with pride & admiration—"handsome, tan-faced, dressed in blue." He is the very ideal of a soldier in appearance & bearing—has now some fine children, of whom he is very fond (*Letters,* 116–17).

John Carwardine (1829–89) was the son of the Reverend John Bryan Carwardine, a brother of Henrietta Carwardine Burrows. Although he was honorably discharged on 21 March 1863, Major Carwardine's medal for gallantry was not sent to his family until 1929! For this information I am indebted to Richard Harlakenden Carwardine Probert and his son Geoffrey.

56. In August 1875 Anne and her children had moved from 50 Marquis Road to 1 Torriano Gardens, Camden Road.

57. Advertisement listed under "Steamship Notices," *Phildelphia Public Ledger* 81, no. 143, Friday, 8 September 1876. Microfilm at Historical Society of Pennsylvania, 1300 Locust Street, Philadelphia.

Chapter 10. Mrs. G

1. Russell F. Weigley, ed., *Philadelphia: A 300-Year History* (New York: W. W. Norton, 1982), 466.
2. *The Gross Clinic* was rejected for the Memorial Hall Art Galleries by the Centennial's art jury because its realism shocked genteel Philadelphia. The magnificent canvas shows Dr. Gross explaining an operation—the removal of a diseased thigh bone—while his assistants do the work. Family-minded critics objected to the blood on Dr. Gross's scalpel, the exposure of usually unmentionable parts of the body, and the patient's mother, who is seated nearby, covering her face and recoiling in horror. They were outraged that society would think it proper to hang it "in a room where ladies, young and old, young girls and boys and little children, are expected to be visitors. It is a picture that even strong men find it difficult to look at long, if they can look at it at all" (Barbara Novak, *American Painting in the Nineteenth Century: Realism, Idealism, and the American Experience* [New York: Harper & Row, 1979], 199–200). When she visited the Exposition, Beatrice would surely have seen *The Gross Clinic*.
3. Weigley, *Philadelphia*, 459–70 for details of the Exposition.
4. *Letters,* 63.
5. HHG, 227.
6. *The Collected Writings of Walt Whitman: Daybooks and Notebooks,* ed. William White, 3 vols. (New York: New York University Press, 1978), vol. 1 Daybooks, 1876–1887, 42. Vol. 1 hereafter cited as *DBN.*
7. Barrus, 138.
8. *Corr.* 3:56, 60.
9. *DBN,* 42.
10. George Whitman, who had been a breveted lieutenant colonel in the Union Army (*Civil War Letters of George Washington Whitman*, ed. Jerome Loving [Durham, N.C.: Duke University Press, 1975], 27), was employed at Starr's Foundry in Camden (*Corr.* 2:203). There is no question that he and Louisa did all they could to make Walt happy and comfortable when he came to live with them in 1873, after he had suffered a stroke and lost his government post in Washington. Their first child, born while Walt was living with them, was named for him, Walter Orr Whitman. "I don't know a soul here—am entirely alone—sometimes sit alone & think, for two hours at a stretch—have not formed a single acquaintance here, any ways intimate," Walt wrote to Peter Doyle in September 1873. "My sister-in-law is very kind in all housekeeping things, cooks what I want, has first-rate coffee for me & something nice in the morning, & keeps me a good bed & room—All of which is very acceptable—(then, for a fellow of my size, the *friendly presence & magnetism needed*, somehow, is not here—I do not run foul of any)—Still I generally keep up a very good heart" (*Corr.* 2:245). While the Whitmans were living at 322 Stevens Street in Camden, Walt occupied the room that had been his mother's, and where she had died. He insisted on keeping everything exactly as it had been before her death, even to a favorite gray dress hanging in the wardrobe (Kaplan, *Whitman,* 347). In the fall of 1873, the Whitmans moved to a new house at 431 Stevens Street. On 3 October, Walt, who was complaining of a return of the "blurs" and dizziness after the excitement of the move, wrote to Pete: "My brother had a large room, very handsome, on 2nd floor, with large bay window fronting west built for me, but I moved up here instead [3rd floor], it is much more retired, & has the sun—I am very comfortable here indeed, but my *heart* is blank & lonesome utterly" (*Corr.* 2:248). The poet's independence—or obstinancy?—clearly made caring for him difficult for George and Lou. When she lived with them, Louisa Van Velsor Whitman—Walt's beloved "Mammy"—had also been a discontented guest. "i wouldent mind living here if i had a place of my own," she wrote to Helen Price in April 1873, "but this living with and not being boss of your own shanty ain't the cheese" (*Corr.* 2:201, n. 25).

11. Barrus, 138. WW's visits to the Montgomery House on 13, 14, and 15 September confirmed *DBN*, 42.
12. *LG,* "Calamus," 135.
13. *LG,* "Calamus," 115–16.
14. Edward Carpenter, *Some Friends of Walt Whitman: A Study in Sex-Psychology* (London: J. E. Francis, Athenaeum Press, 1924), 8.
15. *Corr.* 3:62, n. 94.
16. Wyatt, "Gilchrist and Whitman," 395.
17. WW sent Anne a copy of "Prayer of Columbus" when it was first published (*Harper's Magazine*, March 1874). She recognized at once that WW was portraying himself in the battered old mariner. "O august Columbus! whose sorrows, sufferings, struggles are more to be envied than any triumph of conquering warrior—as I see him in your poem his figure merges into yours, brother of Columbus," she wrote (*Letters*, 108).
18. When the Gilchrists rented 1929 North 22nd Street, its location was on the outskirts of the city. 1929 and the other houses that were eventually built beside it have been torn down. The Frederick Douglass Elementary School (North 22nd and Norris Streets) has been built on the site.
19. *DBN,* 42.
20. *Corr.* 3:62.
21. In 1862 the Woman's Medical College of Pennsylvania had moved from a few inconspicuous rooms, leased in a building at the rear of 627 Arch Street, to larger and more convenient rooms at North College Avenue and 21st Street (Clara Marshall, *The Woman's Medical College of Pennsylvania: An Historical Outline* [Philadelphia: P. Blakiston, Son & Co., 1897], 10, 14).
22. Barrus, 139. Joseph B. Marvin called on the Gilchrists at the Montgomery House shortly after their arrival (HHG, 228).
23. Barrus, 138.
24. *DBN,* 47–48.
25. *Corr.* 3:66.
26. Ibid., 74.
27. Ibid.
28. HHG, 227–28.
29. In his daybooks, WW recorded only one visit to the Exposition. On 24 October, 1876, he visited the fair with Mrs. Fannie Taylor, who had come to Camden to escort Mannahatta and Jessica Louisa Whitman, Jeff Whitman's daughters, back to St. Louis after a four-month stay with their uncles George and Walt. WW wrote: "the 2½ hours there wheel'd about in the chair—the Japanese summer-house—*the figure of Carlyle*—the visit to the Annex—the statuary—the crowd—the delightful ride along the Schuylkill, evening" (*DBN,* 47). WW had looked forward to the Centennial with eager anticipation, bringing out a new edition of *Leaves of Grass* in its honor, and hoping that the Exposition Committee would ask him to write the official poem for the opening. When Bayard Taylor, a former friend but now an open enemy, was asked instead, WW lost his enthusiasm for the fair but still brought out a Centennial edition.
30. Weigley, *Philadelphia,* 451–59.
31. *Philadelphia Public Ledger*, Monday, 11 September 1876. Microfilm at the Historical Society of Philadelphia, 1300 Locust Street, Philadelphia.
32. Register of matriculants for the twenty-seventh annual session (1876–1877). I am indebted to the Medical College of Pennsylvania for photocopies of records from their Archives and Special Collections on Women in Medicine.
33. *Minutes of the Faculty of the Woman's Medical College of Pennsylvania: July 10, 1876–April 30, 1881.* From The Medical College of Pennsylvania Archives, Collection 92. 74–75.
34. *Twenty-Ninth Annual Announcement of the Woman's Medical College of Pennsylvania (1878–1879).* Archives and Special Collections Medical College of Pennsylvania.
35. Ibid.
36. Marshall, *Woman's Medical College,* 17–20.
37. Ibid., 21–23. Dr. S. Hayes Agnew and Dr. S. D. Gross, subjects of two of Eakins's famous medical paintings, were conspicuous opponents of the recognition of women physicians in Philadelphia.
38. *Report of the Seventh Annual Meeting of the Alumnae Association of the Woman's Medical*

College of Pennsylvania, 17 March 1882, 17. Archives and Special Collections, Medical College of Pennsylvania.

39. "Caroline Virginia Anderson": Facts compiled by Miss Frances E. Still in a letter to Dean Fay of the medical college, dated 8 May 1948 (Archives and Special Collections, Medical College of Pennsylvania). In 1880, Dr. Wiley married the Reverend Matthew Anderson. In her long and distinguished career in medicine and education in Philadelphia, she was known as Dr. Caroline V. Still Anderson. She was the mother of five children and died in 1919 at the age of seventy-one.

40. Weigley, *Philadelphia,* 448.

41. Wendell Garrett, Paul Norton, Alan Gowans, and Joseph Butler, eds., *The Arts in America: The Nineteenth Century* (New York: Charles Scribner's Sons, 1969), 233, 245.

42. Weigley, *Philadelphia,* 449–50.

43. Alexander Eliot, *Three Hundred Years of American Painting* (New York: Time Incorporated, 1957), 143.

44. Although Herbert exhibited in the Royal Academy's Annual Summer Exhibitions as long as he lived, he was never elected a member of the Royal Academy. I am indebted to Constance-Anne Parker, librarian of the Royal Academy of Arts, for this information. Herbert's exhibited pictures were always ultraconventional in execution and subject matter. Two examples were *The Entrance of Cleopatra into Tarsus* and *Musgrave visits Lady Barnard at Buckelsford, Bury*. In 1886, he exhibited a portrait (probably one of his portraits of his mother) and another painting, *A London Rose* (Grace was his model), at the Glass Palace in Munich (*Dictionnaire critique et documentaires des Peintres, Sculpteurs, Dessinateurs et Graveurs*, 4:723).

45. Grace seems to have had a pleasing, if limited, voice. As a singer, she made three public appearances, according to records that still exist. After the Gilchrists returned to England, Grace sang at a meeting of the Fabian Society in May 1885 (*Letters,* 237). She sang at a concert (possibly after her mother's death) that Edward Carpenter attended. Afterward, in an undated note, he sent her some kindly criticism: "Thanks for a charming concert. . . . Your voice sounded very well, full & sweet. . . . [But] you must sing with more élan, go, fury, power. . . . Rich & full as your voice is you did not do it justice" (GC). Her third public appearance was as a member of the chorus in *Helena in Troas,* a play by Dr. John Todhunter produced in London in May 1886 (*WMR-Letters,* 171). In the 1920s. when she was in her sixties, Grace lived alone in Saffron Walden. Some of the older residents there remember her singing "Cherry Ripe" to entertain the village children at Christmas parties. I am indebted to Mr. H. C. Stacey of Saffron Walden for this information.

46. *WMR-Letters,* 102.

47. *Corr.* 3:65.

48. In August 1877, in a letter to Herby, who was on a camping trip with John Burroughs, Anne wrote from 1929: "Giddy is a good girl in doing the work. We are still without a girl and mean to be for the present, but in the winter, if we could meet with one, who was not a source of more discomfort than comfort, I should be glad to have one again" (Frend, 43). As a postscript to this letter, Anne added: "I have been doing a little needlework for Walt."

49. *Stoop* was one of the Americanisms that baffled Anne. "Mrs. Gilchrist told me that when she met a line, 'I went up the stoop, off the stoop,' some such use of the word, she put down her book, wondering for hours what could have been meant" (*WWWC* 4:243).

50. Horace Elisha Scudder, "Anne Gilchrist," in *Men and Letters: Essays in Characterization and Criticism* (Boston: Houghton, Mifflin and Co., 1887), 214. The same essay, with a change in the closing sentence, appeared as an unsigned review of Herbert's biography of his mother, *Atlantic Monthly* 60. (August 1887), 275–81.

51. Barrus, 139.

52. HHG, 228–29. Miss Maggie Lesley visited Anne at Hampstead in May 1881. At that time Maggie was studying art in Paris (*Letters,* 198).

53. Frend, 51. Also Weigley, *Philadelphia,* 520.

54. Horace Traubel, *With Walt Whitman in Camden,* vol. 2 (16 July, 1888–31 October, 1888) (1908; reprint, New York: Rowman and Littlefield, 1961), 335. Hereafter cited as *WWWC* 2.

55. *Corr.* 3:88.

56. Ibid., 86.

57. *WWWC* 2:292.

NOTES 257

58. *The Tea Party* was sold by Grace Gilchrist Frend to Harriet Chapman Sprague, whose Whitman collection is in the Rare Books Department of the Van Pelt Library of the University of Pennsylvania. The staff of the Rare Books Department kindly had the picture taken down from the wall so that I might study it in a good light.

There are fascinating details in the picture. Half-concealed in shadow, behind Anne's right shoulder there is a curious figure who appears to be a little maid. She is wearing a white cap; her hair, eyes, and brows are very dark; and her head is much too large for the rest of her. She is holding what looks like a wine bottle. Describing the picture to Walt in a letter on 6 May, 1883, Herbert wrote: "I am standing up bending over the tea-pot, with the kettle, filling it up" (*Letters*, 214). Did he invent a little maid because he found a self-portrait too difficult? Anne is wearing a black dress with a wide, white, ruffled organdy collar; her eyes are clearly hazel (Herbert says in his biography that his mother's eyes were hazel, although William Rossetti described them as dark and liquid); and, as Burroughs described her, she is indeed "a rosy woman." Grace has a lovely, alert young face and a graceful figure. There is an empty place at the table in the foreground and there are four cups on the tea tray in front of Anne. Did the artist leave the table to paint the picture? Or was Beatrice expected? Through an open window, green trees and another house a little distance away are visible. Herbert explained to Walt that this was a "pretty view of Cannon Place, Hampstead." He told Walt that he had titled the picture *The Good Gray Poet's Gift* because "you play a prominent part in this picture—seated at table bending over a nosegay of flowers, poetizing, before presenting them to mother." Anne wrote to Louisa Whitman and asked her for an old suit of Walt's for Herby to use in painting the picture, and in a letter to Herby on 12 February, 1884, Walt enclosed a piece of cloth from an old coat (*Corr.* 3:364).

59. Grace's magazine articles were "Chats with Walt Whitman," Temple Bar, February 1898, 200–212, and "Walt Whitman as I Remember Him," *Bookman*, July 1927, 203–5. I have found no record that Grace ever communicated with WW after her mother's death.

60. *Corr.* 3:87.

61. Frend, 82–83. Grace wrote her memoir of her mother during the 1920s, and, in her diaries for that period (GC), it is clear that she was desperately eager to have the memoir published. She seems to have believed that publication would not be possible unless she presented a favorable picture of Whitman. However, now and then in the memoir her real opinion of the poet bursts through. "Wayward" is surely a term of judgment that an older and more informed Grace—not young Giddy, no matter how much she disliked him—would choose to describe WW. Although the typescript of her memoir is untitled, in her diary for 1919–20 (GC) she notes that the title she had chosen was "Anne Gilchrist, Walt Whitman, and Their Circle: A Reminiscence and An Appreciation."

62. *Corr.* 3:87.

63. Ibid.

64. Ibid., 105.

65. Herbert was devoted to Whitman as long as the poet lived. When he was in England, he wrote regularly to Walt and helped collect funds for him; and he made two extended trips back to America. In 1887 he returned to paint Walt's portrait, which was exhibited in London at the Grovesnor Gallery the following year; and in 1888 he returned again to Philadelphia, where he leased a studio on Chestnut Street and taught for a short time at the Academy of Fine Arts. During this period, he visited Walt at 328 Mickle Street as faithfully as the Disciples, all of whom he knew. He was one of the speakers at Walt's seventieth birthday celebration.

66. *Corr.* 3:104.

67. *Letters*, 173.

68. Although Walt preferred Eakins's portrait, he refused to be too hard on Herbert's. In a conversation with Harned about Herbert's portrait, he said, "Don't make me say what I think about that. I love Herbert too much" (*WWWC* 1:156). And when David McKay called Herbert's picture a caricature, Walt protested: "That is too severe; take away the curls, the Italian curls, which I haven't, and it's not so bad; even of the curls they'd say: 'Damn 'im, if he ain't got 'em he'd ought to have 'em' " (*WWWC* 2:510).

69. In her diary for 1919–20 (GC), Grace recalled that Herbert had been deeply hurt by the caustic criticism of his portrait that he encountered firsthand in Philadelphia and later read in the first three volumes of Traubel's notes, published in 1906, 1907, and 1914. Herbert and Traubel

frequently clashed, and the usually impersonal Traubel openly expressed his dislike of the young Englishman and "his wretched and untrue presentment of W" (*WWWC* 5:332).

70. Barrus, 21.
71. Alma Calder Johnston, "Personal Memories of Walt Whitman," *Bookman* (London) 46, 404.
72. HHG, 229. Anne must have smiled to herself when she wrote that WW "fully realizes the ideal I had formed from his poems." But how could she have said anything less to Rossetti without revealing what her "ideal" had been?
73. *WWWC* 4:206.
74. *WWWC* 3:268.
75. *Corr.* 2:61.
76. William Sloane Kennedy, *Reminiscences of Walt Whitman* (1896; reprint, New York: Haskell House, 1973), 9.
77. *WWWC* 2:268.
78. *Letters,* 143.
79. *WWWC* 1:223.
80. HHG, 232–41. Herbert's notebook, "Memorandum of Conversations with Mr. Whitman during the latter part of 1876 & the commencement of 1877," is in the Rare Books Department of the Van Pelt Library of the University of Pennsylvania. The first entry is dated October 1876. On the page for Friday, 28 November, there is a sketch of WW seated in a chair, his right arm raised, clearly speaking emphatically. The notes contain accounts of many private conversations between Herbert and WW and a few brief comments by Anne when she was present. One of the early conversations between Herby and WW took place in the poet's small, third-floor room in Camden. The last entry is dated May 1877.
81. Horace Traubel, *With Walt Whitman in Camden*, vol. 5 (8 April–14 September, 1889), ed. Gertrude Traubel (Carbondale: Southern Illinois University Press, 1964), 150–51. Hereafter cited as *WWWC 5*.
82. Ibid., 12–13.
83. *WWWC* 4:134.
84. *WWWC* 2:238.
85. *WWWC* 4:93.
86. *WWWC* 5:509.
87. Barrus, 160.
88. Grace Gilchrist, "Chats with Walt Whitman." 201–02.
89. *Corr.* 3:91.
90. Ibid., 78.
91. *DBN,* 62. Also *Corr.* 3:98.
92. Frend, 22. When he left, Anne gave Carpenter a letter of introduction to William Rossetti, and, after the Gilchrists returned to England, Carpenter continued to be a close friend of the family.
93. Carpenter, *Days with Walt Whitman,* 16–17.
94. Carpenter, *Some Friends of Walt Whitman,* 8.
95. Letter to Mrs. Simmons from Anne Gilchrist, 23 December 1877. Feinberg Collection, Library of Congress.
96. *Corr.* 3:98.
97. *DBN,* 65, 68.
98. Grace Gilchrist, "Chats with Walt Whitman," 201.
99. Frend, 34. Walt disliked being disturbed when he was at the creek, and, according to Mrs. Stafford, Anne's surprise visit made him very angry (Allen, *Solitary Singer,* 479). This does not seem to tally with Anne's happy recollection of the day, or with Walt's in later years. In a letter to Mrs. Stafford on 6 January 1886, WW wrote: "Often think of Mrs. Gilchrist—(I have a good photo. of her)—Do you remember that day—last of May '77 I think—she & her two daughters came down to see us, & me down at the pond, under the old oak tree?" (*Corr.* 4:16).
100. Barrus, 164.
101. *Corr.* 3:4, 68.
102. Ibid., 5.
103. Ibid., 92, n. 63.
104. Ibid., 93.

105. In 1880, Colonel John R. Johnston, a Philadelphia artist and one of WW's close friends—the poet went to his home for supper every Sunday evening—was angered by something that WW said in a letter to his son and took the letter to another of WW's close friends, James Matlock Scovel, a Camden lawyer. Scovel urged WW to apologize to the Johnstons in order to "stop John[s]ton's blathering" (*Corr.* 3:177, n. 21).
106. *Corr.* 3:77, n. 11.
107. *DBN,* 75–76.
108. Letter to Mrs. Simmons from Anne Gilchrist, 23 December 1877. Feinberg Collection, Library of Congress.
109. Frend, 23.
110. *WWWC* 5:429.
111. *DBN,* 76.
112. Frend, 48.
113. Ibid., 48. Apparently the Gilchrists were not altogether taken with flamboyant Joaquin Miller. Herbert wrote: "Walt Whitman mentioned that his friend, Miller, delighted to trust strangers in posting letters and the like small commissions—to cultivate honesty through good-will: which is the prettiest trait we can now think of in connection with the author of *Songs of the Sierras*" (HHG, 231–32).
114. Letter to Mrs. Simmons from Anne Gilchrist, 23 December 1877. Feinberg Collection, Library of Congress.
115. Ibid.
116. I do not equate a professional guest and a freeloader. A freeloader accepts as much as possible and gives nothing in return. A professional guest repays hospitality with the pleasure of his presence.
117. *Twenty-Ninth Annual Announcement of the Woman's Medical College of Pennsylvania,* 4. Archives and Special Collections, Medical College of Pennsylvania.
118. *Caroline Virginia Anderson* (see n. 39).
119. *Corr.* 3:113.
120. Frend, 51.
121. Ibid. The New Century Club was founded in 1877 by Sarah C. F. Hallowell, who was its first president. It quickly outgrew its first quarters and a new clubhouse was built at Twelfth and Sansom. The club had a special interest in working women and held classes for them in dressmaking and typesetting. Many of Philadelphia's women leaders in the arts and politics were members (Weigley, *Philadelphia,* 520).
122. Barrus, 145–46.
123. Ibid.
124. *Letters,* 190.

Chapter 11. A British Lioness

1. Frend, 52.
2. On 9 May, Anne wrote to Herby from Round Hill: "We have much pleasant conversation with a Mr. Adams here, who was educated at Heidelberg & is lecturing on History at Smith College here. Also he does not disdain croquet for an hour after dinner, luckily for Giddy." Feinberg Collection, Library of Congress.
3. There is no record that Anne's translation of *La Legénde des Siècles* was ever published, although in her letter to Herby on 9 May she told him that she was thinking of sending it to Macmillan. According to Herbert, Anne was translating Hugo as early as 1868 (HHG, 174).
4. Anne Gilchrist, "Three Glimpses of a New England Village," HHG, 321, 328, 312–14.
5. HHG. 325.
6. Ibid., 325–28. Anne visited the Deaf and Dumb Institution, and in her essay gave a detailed account of the methods that Harriet Rogers and her assistants used to teach inflection, pitch, sound control, and finally actual speech to classes of about twenty children. Anne was fascinated with the process. While she was in Northampton, she also visited the state lunatic asylum.

She wrote to WW from Round Hill: "I went over the Lunatic Asylum here the other day & saw some strange, sad sights—some figures crouched down in attitudes of such profound dejection I shall never forget them—some very bright and talkative. It is said to be the best managed in America" (*Letters*, 155).

7. HHG, 328.

8. *Corr.* 3:118: Wyatt Eaton (1849–96), an American portrait and figure painter, organized the Society of American Artists in 1877.

9. GC. Letter to Beatrice from Herbert, George Rogers's farm near Chesterfield, 22 July 1878. Herby told Bee that in a few days he became acquainted with the village, "a charming cosey one." Chesterfield, on a mountaintop, seems to have been a summer retreat for city folk. Herby had met a Mr. Chadwick, "a distinguished preacher in Brooklyn," and a Mr. Bryant, "a rich jeweler in New York," both of whom, he told his sister, "have just taken tea with me & a very nice tea too prepared by [my] good landlady." The following winter, when Anne and Herbert and Grace were living in New York, they were entertained by both the Chadwick and Bryant families.

In the early 1880s, Herbert would retreat to another rural setting to paint. From 1890 until 1893, he lived alone in an old farmhouse that overlooked Centreport Cove on Long Island, raising his own vegetables, doing his own cooking, baking his own bread (and using Anne's recipe?). Dr. John Johnston and J. W. Wallace from Bolton, Lancashire visited him there when they came to America to see WW (Johnston and Wallace, *Visits to Walt Whitman in 1890–91: By Two Lancashire Friends* [1917; reprint, New York: Haskell House, 1970], 73–74, 125–128). Herbert painted his most ambitious picture, *Cleopatra Entering the Bay of Tarsus,* at Centreport. It was exhibited in New York at the Century Club and in Philadelphia at the Academy of Fine Arts in 1893 and at the Royal Academy in 1894.

10. Letter to Herbert from Anne Gilchrist, Round Hill Hotel, 9 May 1878. Feinberg Collection, Library of Congress. "Your luggage is come—I had to pay $1.13 for it. I am afraid you will find some pieces lost," Anne wrote, a note of exasperation briefly interrupting her usual loving tone. "The parcel came entirely to pieces & was a loose handful of sticks, etc. It ought to have been sewn up in canvas."

11. Marie Zakrzewska (1829–1902), daughter of a Berlin midwife, came to the United States in 1853, hoping to become a doctor of medicine. In New York, she met Dr. Elizabeth Blackwell, the first woman in America to obtain a medical degree (1849), who instructed her in English and helped her gain admission as a medical student at Western Reserve College. In 1857, Blackwell and Zakrzewska opened the New York Infirmary for Women and Children, financed largely by funds that Zakrzewska raised in Boston among that city's influential reformers in antislavery, women's rights, and other causes. For two years Zakrzewska was resident physician at the New York Infirmary. In 1859, with the infirmary firmly established, at the invitation of her friends in Boston, she organized her own clinical department at semicharlatan Dr. Samuel Gregory's New England Female Medical College in that city. In 1862, she left Gregory and, with the support of her Boston friends, founded the New England Hospital for Women and Children. Zakrzewska was an extremely homely woman, with a large nose that overshadowed her underdeveloped features—so homely that "almost as ugly as Marie" was a standard for comparison in her family (Drachman, *Hospital with a Heart,* 22–38).

12. *"Send Us a Lady Physician": Women Doctors in America, 1835–1920,* ed. Ruth J. Abram (New York: W. W. Norton, 1985), 191.

13. Drachman, *Hospital with a Heart,* 88

14. Ibid., 77, 156–57. Dr. Zak explained to the interns that the policy of using "Miss" and "Mrs." was based on concern for equality among them, since, at that time, not all had medical degrees. By 1877 and thereafter, all interns accepted at the New England Hospital had medical degrees.

15. *Letters,* 156–57.

16. Letter to Beatrice from Anne Gilchrist, Brooklyn, undated, but early December 1878. Feinberg Collection, Library of Congress.

17. *Letters,* 175–76. "Dr. Wiley is very popular with her patients," Bee told WW, "far more so than I."

18. Ibid., 180. Bee occasionally had other diversions as well. Joseph Marvin and his wife came to see her at the hospital, and on another day they took her to their house for lunch and a game

of lawn tennis (*Letters*, 157). One Sunday she heard Edward Everett Hale preach and went home to dinner with him. Bee liked his daughter, "a clever young artist," whom the Gilchrists had known in Philadelphia (176).

19. Frend, 9. Grace's private dislike of Whitman never lessened. On 22 October 1919, she wrote in her diary: "Dear, dear mother—Walt was not worthy of you—but that does only greaten & glorify your love—it does not make it less" (GC). She records in her diary that she tried unsuccessfully to block the publication by Fisher Unwin of her mother's letters—"Those divinely beautiful letters, dear Mother." And she notes that there was not a single review of *Letters* when it was published in England.

20. GC. Letter to Beatrice from Herbert, George Rogers's farm near Chesterfield, 22 July 1878.

21. *Corr.* 3:138.

22. *Letters*, 164.

23. Ibid., 155. Alexander Fitzmaurice Gilchrist was born at Blaenavon, Monmouthshire on 10 September 1878. He was educated at the Repton School and served in World War I, 1914–19, in the Queen's Westminster Rifles, retiring as a major. He married Beatrice Osborne in 1909. From 1932 until 1950, he was official solicitor to the Supreme Court of Judicature. He died on 9 March, 1956. Canon James Gilchrist was his only child (*Who Was Who: 1951–1960* [London: Adam and Charles Black], 5:420).

24. Letter to Herbert from Anne Gilchrist, Concord, 10 October, 1878. Feinberg Collection, Library of Congress.

25. *Letters*, 161.

26. It was Anne's friendships with the Carlyles, Rossettis, and Tennysons that opened doors for her in Concord, not her friendship with Whitman. When WW was in Boston in 1860, seeing his third edition through the press, he was not invited to Concord because Mrs. Emerson, Mrs. Alcott, and Mrs. Thoreau refused to have "that scandalous man" in their houses. It was not until 1881, when he was Franklin Sanborn's houseguest, that Mrs. Emerson and Mrs. Alcott agreed to meet him. Lidian Emerson was so charmed with the poet that she invited him to dinner at her house the next day (Gay Wilson Allen, *Waldo Emerson* [New York: The Viking Press, 1981], 666–67). In a newspaper essay on the *Letters*, 31 May 1919, Kate Buss wrote: "Recently I heard a New Englander, in whose house Mrs. Gilchrist stayed at length after she knew Whitman in Philadelphia, say that the published correspondence of Whitman and Mrs. Gilchrist was a great surprise to her. She explained that Mrs. Gilchrist rarely spoke of Whitman, her talk being more often of Carlyle and Emerson, and that the occasional mentions were casual and without stress" (Buss, *Boston Evening Transcript*, 31 May 1919 part. 3, col, 7.). The New Englander may have been Mrs. Jackson's daughter, whom Anne described in her letter to Herbert from Concord on 10 October as an "unmarried daughter, young, very Bostonish."

27. Letter to Herbert from Anne Gilchrist, Concord, 10 October 1878. Feinberg Collection, Library of Congress.

28. Frend, 64.

29. James R. Mellow, *Nathaniel Hawthorne in His Times* (Boston: Houghton Mifflin, 1980), 537.

30. *Letters*, 162.

31. HHG, 245.

32. Barrus, 181.

33. Frend, 62–63.

34. *Letters*, 161.

35. Letter to Beatrice from Anne Gilchrist, New York, undated, but winter of 1878–79. Feinberg Collection, Library of Congress.

36. *Corr.* 5:6.

37. In a letter to Jack Johnston from 1929 North 22nd St. on 20 June 1877, speaking of Herby, WW wrote that "he & I are very thick" (*Corr.* 3:88). One cannot assume that WW would have refrained from having a sexual relationship with Herby because he was Anne Gilchrist's son. Harry Stafford was the son of WW's kind hosts at Kirkwood. Edward Cattell was one of Harry's friends. Albert Johnston—"Dear Boy Al"—was the son of WW's generous friend J. H. Johnston, the New York jeweler at whose house on 5th Avenue WW was often a guest. On one occasion WW wrote to Al: "Send me word when the coast is clear, & everything lovely, & I will come on to Mott Haven [the Johnston's summer home] for a week's visit" (*Corr.* 3:271–72). Colonel John

R. Johnston of Philadelphia, another of WW's close friends, consulted his attorney about a letter that the poet wrote to his son—"Dear boy Jack" (See chap. 10, n. 105).

38. *Letters*, 105, 128.
39. HHG, 247.
40. Ibid., 242-43.
41. Ibid., 247.
42. *Letters*, 164-65.
43. HHG, 248.
44. *Letters*, 166.
45. "My dear Herby—Why do you not write, in answer to my earnest entreaties? it is a month at least since I have heard from you. I am very anxious to know how you are in health, how you are getting on with your work and what your wishes are as to the time of going to New York," Anne wrote from Concord on 10 October to Herby at Kirkwood. She added: "Pray write—there's a dear boy. My heart feels rather empty & I long for settled life all together again very much." Feinberg Collection, Library of Congress.
46. While the Gilchrists were staying at 177 Remsen Street in Brooklyn, in a letter to Bee in early December Anne wrote: "I had a long and interesting visit from Dr. Bucke—Walt's friend—the Englishman who is at the head of the Insane Asylum of New London, Canada. He is going to bring out a book about the physical basis of the moral & emotional nature & devote a chapter to Walt whom he regards as the highest development in this regard that has yet appeared" (Feinberg Collection, Library of Congress). This may have been the first time that Anne met Dr. Bucke.
47. Letter to Beatrice from Anne Gilchrist, Brooklyn, undated, but early December 1878. Feinberg Collection, Library of Congress.
48. Letter to Beatrice from Anne Gilchrist, New York, undated, but winter of 1878-79. Feinberg Collection, Library of Congress.
49. Letter to Beatrice from Anne Gilchrist, New York, 19 December, 1878. Feinberg Collection, Library of Congress.
50. Flamboyant William Merritt Chase (1849-1916), the great American impressionist, returned to the United States in 1878, after six years of study in Munich and Venice, and began to teach at the Art Students League. With his pointed beard and waxed mustache, he was one of the sights of New York when he appeared on Fifth Avenue, wearing a Munich student's cap and walking a huge white wolfhound on a leash. Although Herbert was a student at the league, there is no record that he ever visited Chase's famous Tenth Street Studio. It would have been an event to remember. A black servant in Turkish costume was kept standing outside; the interior was decorated with Bohemian bric-a-brac, colorful textiles, oriental screens, and musical instruments—in addition to a white cockatoo and two macaws (Richard J. Boyle, *American Impressionism* [Boston: New York Graphic Society (Little, Brown and Co.), 1974], 179-205). Chase worked with incredible speed. He told his students: "Take plenty of time for your picture; take two hours if you need it." Small wonder that, watching his maestro at work, Herby believed that someday he might paint WW's portrait in *one* sitting.
51. *Letters*, 178.
52. In a letter to Beatrice from Chesterfield, 22 July 1878, Herby told his sister that while he was at Round Hill he had made sketches for a picture of ladies bowling on the lawn (GC). The completed picture, eventually titled *A Game of Nine-Pins in New England*, would be exhibited at the Royal Academy in 1880 (*Catalogue of Royal Academy Exhibitors*). Is it possible that Herby had seen Winslow Homer's *The Croquet Match*, painted ca. 1869? In his letter to Bee, he described that painting that he was working on as "a somber picture, rather"—precisely the mood of Homer's picture of unsmiling, uncommunicating lady players.
53. *Letters*, 173. In his letter to WW, Herby included a charming picture of winter in Central Park:

> This morning being Sunday, I took my skates to the Park. The wind was high & whirled us about fantastically; ladies seated in wicker chairs were pushed rapidly along the Pond's smooth icy surface by their gentlemen escorts, tall men kissed the ice or sprawled full length on their backs, while others flew by like swallows; all this with a church spire peeping behind hills dappled with snow & sunshine: what more inspiriting than this.

54. Letter to Beatrice from Anne Gilchrist, New York, 29 December 1878. Feinberg Collection, Library of Congress.

55. Letter to Beatrice from Anne Gilchrist, New York, 29 January 1879. Feinberg Collection, Library of Congress.

56. Doing all the sewing by hand, Anne and Giddy made a black silk dress, trimmed with lace and fringe, for Giddy to wear to these festivities. "[It] is a very great success," Anne wrote to Bee from New York. "Giddy looks better than in anything else she has ever had" (undated letter, Feinberg Collection). Where did Anne and Giddy buy the fabric and trimmings? At the block-square department store of A. T. Stewart & Company on Ninth Street? At James McCreery & Company or Arnold Constable & Company on Eleventh Street? At Lord & Taylor's ornate new store at Broadway and Twentieth Street? Or at one of the many smaller shops on Broadway between Eighth and Twenty-third Streets that was known as the "Ladies' Mile" (Lloyd Morris *Incredible New York: High Life and Low Life of the Last Hundred Years 1850–1950* [New York: Random House, 1951], 111)?

57. GC. Letter to Anne Gilchrist from Herbert, New York, 18 November 1878.

58. Frend, 79.

59. The receptions that the Gilchrists went to and the names of those they met there: *Letters*, 173–74, 179–80. Additional information: Lloyd R. Morris, *Incredible New York*, 82, 175. While they were in New York, the Gilchrists saw a great deal of Kate Hillard, who often went to receptions with them and sometimes entertained the guests with recitations. Herby told WW that one evening at Mrs. Bigelow's "Miss H. was asked to recite & she recited the 'Swineherd' (Anderson's) charmingly, & 'The Faithful Lovers,' which took everyone" (*Letters*, 174). The Gilchrists also saw a great deal of General Edward Lee, organizer and first governor of the Territory of Wyoming (*Letters*, 180).

60. Mary Putnam Jacobi was one of America's most brilliant early women physicians. Like Bee, she had attended the Woman's Medical College and interned at the New England Hospital; when Anne met her she was affiliated with the New York Infirmary. WW seems to have known Dr. Jacobi too. "She talks well, doesn't she?" Anne wrote to him, "& has a face with plenty of individuality in it" (*Letters*, 171). "I have seen Mrs. Putnam Jacobi and shall see her again," Anne wrote to Bee on 28 January. "She seems friendly towards me, & is, I know, very anxious to gather women who will do credit to the profession in New York. She is very desirous to persuade Dr. Berlin to come here" (Feinberg Collection). In case it was necessary for Bee to postpone studying in Europe because of Percy's troubles, Anne was apparently looking for a temporary alternative for her.

61. GC. Letter to Beatrice from Herbert, New York, 25 December, 1878.

62. *Letters*, 167.

63. Ibid., 179. As she crossed on the Brooklyn ferry, Anne would have seen the Brooklyn Bridge under construction. Construction had begun in 1870 and would be completed in 1883.

64. Ibid.

65. Ibid., 167.

66. *Corr.* 3:148. What an ideal arrangement for WW this would have been! It is highly unlikely that Percy would have agreed to it. Bitterly opposed to his mother's exodus to America—and old enough when "Estimate" was published to fully understand it—he never ceased to resent his mother's attachment to the poet. WW was well aware of Percy's dislike. On 9 May 1889, Traubel recorded: "He spoke of Percy Gilchrist: 'He takes no stock in me—in fact, I doubt if he likes me. I have never seen him' " (*WWWC* 5:151). "Did I ever tell you about Percy Gilchrist?" Walt asked Traubel on 6 September 1888. "He's another son—invented some steel process—has made a million dollars or more by it, God help 'im. A million dollars is a lot of baggage to get in a man's way, ain't it?" (*WWWC* 2:270). After his mother's death, Percy came to the States on business but made no attempt to communicate with WW. "His [Herbert's] brother, the eldest, does not like me at all, and will not come to see me," Walt told Dr. John Johnston of Bolton, Lancashire in 1890. "He was in the States a year or two ago, with the English engineers" (Johnston and Wallace, *Visits to Whitman*, 143).

67. Frend, 78.

68. Ellen M. Calder (O'Connor), "Personal Recollections of Walt Whitman," *Atlantic Monthly*, June 1907, 828.

69. Frend, 78.
70. *DBN*, 141.
71. Allen, *Solitary Singer*, 485.
72. *Corr*. 3:155.
73. Frend, 78.
74. *Letters*, 166. When Anne told WW jubilantly that 112 Madison Avenue was "quite handy" to the Johnstons' house, she was still a newcomer to New York. The vicinity of Union Square is not exactly "handy" to Fifth Avenue near 86th Street. In 1879, the Johnstons' house was on the outer edge of the city's residential area. Alma Calder Johnston would recall that, when WW was visiting them in May 1879, "the residences on Fifth Avenue ended abruptly at Eighty-sixth Street; just beyond the grassy knolls of an old fruit farm had become a rural beer garden." WW enjoyed looking out of the window of his room "at the squatter settlement that reached to our vine-covered back-yard fence....Goats, geese, chickens, and innumerable children wandered over the grass about a whitewashed cabin, which was always being undone and made over." The terminus of the Fourth Avenue surface cars was only a block away, which made going downtown easy for WW (Alma Calder Johnston, "Personal memories of Walt Whitman," *Bookman* [London] 46:404–13). Alma Johnston, J. H. Johnston's second wife, was a writer and an officer of the Sorosis Club. She was a devoted friend of WW. Anne must have liked her very much, and vice versa.
75. Frend, 78.
76. *Corr*. 3:154.
77. *DBN*, 144–45.
78. *Corr*. 3:156. WW wrote to Harry Stafford from New York on 28 May that Anne told him she had been in Camden the Saturday before (24 May).
79. Frend, 82.
80. *Corr*. 3:154, 156–57.
81. Barrus, 146–47.
82. Frend, 82–83.

Chapter 12. Dark Mother

1. *Letters*, 181–182.
2. The Thomas-Gilchrist process for making steel from phosphoric pig iron, discovered in 1878–79 by Percy Gilchrist and his cousin Sidney Gilchrist Thomas, was a revolutionary invention in the field of metallurgy. Prior to this time it was believed that it was impossible to produce good steel from any but the purest ores and that the phosphoric ores abundant in England, France, Germany, and other countries were unsuitable for making steel of the best quality. In 1879, Percy and his cousin won lawsuits in Berlin against the Bessemer and Krupp Companies, who were trying to break their patent rights (*Letters*, 189). The Thomas-Gilchrist Converter was the leading process for converting pig iron for almost 100 years. Sidney Thomas died in 1885, at the age of thirty-four, after a long illness (obituary notice, *Graphic* [London], March 1885).
3. *Letters*, 183. Percy and Norah's second child, Eileen Fitzmaurice Gilchrist, was born after Anne's death—on 10 October 1891. She never married. She died in February 1989.
4. Ibid., 185.
5. GC. The small photograph was taken in Edinburgh. On the back is written in Anne's hand: "Beatrice Gilchrist, d. of Alexander and Anne."
6. GC. Letter to Beatrice in Wiesbaden from Grace, 11 September 1879.
7. Grace did not marry until 1897, nearly twenty years later. Her marriage to Alfred Henry Frend, an architect, ended quickly in a bitter divorce, prolonged because in England at that time a woman's right to own property was debatable under the law. Grace's diaries reveal her long struggle to keep whatever property had been hers—including the family silver, pictures, etc., that she had inherited (GC). In the Gilchrist Collection there is a letter from Percy to Grace expressing his disapproval of her plan to marry Frend and his intention of terminating the quarterly support payments that he had been sending her if the marriage took place. His stern letter includes no good wishes. A few days earlier, on 27 May, 1897, Herbert had written to "My dear Giddy": "I wish you all happiness my dear sister" (GC). Herbert was a witness at the wedding (GC-copy of marriage certificate).

8. *Letters*, 184–194. Letters to WW from Anne, 2 August and 5 December, 1879, 25 January and 22 August 1880.
9. HHG, 252. Emma Holland seems to have been Frederick Holland's daughter.
10. *Letters*, 192.
11. Ibid., 193.
12. Ibid., 188.
13. Ibid., 191.
14. HHG, 262–263
15. 12 Well Road is now 12 Well Walk. Although the interior has been remodeled into modern apartments, in 1985 the exterior looked very much as it must have when the Gilchrists lived there.
16. *Letters*, 197.
17. Ibid., 190–191.
18. Ibid.
19. HHG, 255–258.
20. *Corr.* 3: 178–179.
21. Ibid., 178, n.24.
22. *Letters*, 194. In Edinburgh, Bee was assistant to Dr. Sophia Jex-Blake, who had founded the London School of Medicine for Women in 1874. Dr. Jex-Blake and Bee may have met when Bee was a student there before she went to America.
23. Ibid., 193. Anne's kind friends were Mr. and Mrs. Pratt, a childless couple who lived a secluded life because Mr. Pratt was not well. Anne wrote to her "Dear Children" from Shottermill during this visit: "Got down all right though not without adventure. A wheel caught fire in the carriage next to ours & then it was discovered that there was no communication with the guard possible, & the train ½ mile long. Happily our train came to a stand to wait for one on ahead & then the gentlemen managed to make the guard hear" (Feinberg Collection, Library of Congress).
24. HHG, 255–258.
25. *Letters*, 195.
26. *Corr.* 3: 208.
27. *WWWC* 2: 382–83.
28. Letter to Whitman from Anne Gilchrist, Keats Corner, Well Road, Hampstead, 16 February, 1881. Special Collections, Van Pelt Library, University of Pennsylvania. Anne had sent WW a postal card in early January telling him that she was better (*Corr.* 3: 206), but this is her first extant letter to him since 22 August, 1880. Since she apologizes for being "so long silent," there were probably no other letters in the interim. She enclosed a photograph of her grandson in this letter.
29. *Letters*, 197.
30. Letter to Whitman from Anne Gilchrist, 4 Manor Place, Edinburgh, Scotland, 17 June, 1881. Special Collections, Van Pelt Library, University of Pennsylvania.
31. GC. Letter to Herbert from Anne Gilchrist, 4 Manor Place, Edinburgh, 30 June 1881.
32. GC. Letter to Walter White from Anne Gilchrist, 4 Manor Place, Edinburgh, 30 June, 1881.
33. Frend, 9.
34. Beatrice's death certificate, registered in the parish of Corstorphine in the county of Edinburgh, reads:

Beatrice Carwardine Gilchrist, Medical Attendant, single, 26.
Found dead on Corstorphine Bank Farm, August 15, 1881.
Supposed to have died July twentieth.
Cause of death: sudden, apparently syncope.
Identified by Percy C. Gilchrist, brother.
Cause of death as certified by Dr. Littlejohn, Edinburgh:
an overdose of hydrocyanic acid taken with suicidal intent.

35. Letter to Herbert and Grace from Anne Gilchrist, unsigned, undated, but from Edinburgh or Redcar, August 1881. Feinberg Collection, Library of Congress.
36. I am indebted to Cannon Gilchrist for a copy of the inscription on the headstone.
37. Alumnae Association of the Woman's Medical College of Pennsylvania, *Report of*

Proceedings of the Seventh Annual Meeting, March 17, 1882, Archives and Special Collections, Medical College of Pennsylvania 16–18.

Two newspaper notices of Beatrice's death were included in the Alumnae Association's *report*:

All who met Dr. Gilchrist in this country were struck by her devotion to science and her rare love of work. Self-reliant and strong, she seemed fitted for a prominent place in that hard-worked band of physicians to whose skill and tenderness we owe so much of our daily life and health. Fitted by her early inclination and high enthusiasm, she studied long and most faithfully, struggling under the impediments still thrown in a woman's way, and, with noble ambition, striving for the highest education and training obtainable.... Now that she had so nearly accomplished her purpose, it is sad that her young life should go out so suddenly, leaving us only an example (*Philadelphia Enquirer*, 23 September, 1881).

She had great self-reliance, with rare tenderness of nature, which fitted her eminently for success, and her death is felt to be a misfortune by all who are interested in woman's work. To her mother, who came with her to America, her loss is irreparable, and our deepest sympathies are hers. To medical science, the untimely end of a career so conscientiously begun is a great loss, for few women are at once so brilliant and so persistent (*Woman's Suffrage Journal*, Boston, 1 October, 1881).

38. *Letters*, 203.
39. *DBN*, 260.
40. *Corr.* 3:244, 246.
41. Ibid., 253–254.
42. *Letters*, 203.
43. GC. Anne Gilchrist's memorandum to her children copied by Herbert Gilchrist, 2 December, 1885.
44. *Letters*, 205.
45. *WMR-Letters*, 141.
46. HHG, 267.
47. Letter to John Ingram, Esq., Howard House, Stoke Newington Green, from Anne Gilchrist, 13 April, 1882. Manuscripts Department, Alderman Library, University of Virginia. When Rossetti wrote to Anne on 25 September, 1883 to acknowledge his copy of the newly published *Mary Lamb*, he added a postscript: "Speaking to Ingram the other day, I found him likewise more than pleased with your book. He says too that you gave him no trouble—being herein exceptional among his lady-contributors" (*WMR-Letters*, 143).
48. HHG, 269. William Haines, Anne's old friend who assisted her so faithfully with the first edition of the *Life of Blake*, helped her correct the proofs of *Mary Lamb*. With the work completed, Anne suffered a biographer's after-qualms: "Sometimes, in these last sheets I have feared diligently gathered scraps were not sufficiently *welded* and might read *scrappy*—but perhaps getting it in sheets enhances that defect. I was so bent on making the *dramatis personae* speak themselves whenever possible, that I sacrificed to that, the idea of a *flowing* narrative—which would no doubt have been a tame flow, after all, compared to their pungencies and delightful idiosyncrasies" (HHG, 270–71).

A review of *Mary Lamb* was the lead article in *the Academy*, 25 August, 1883, 121. The review was unreservedly favorable.

49. *Letters*, 221–22. Anne's careful research for *Mary Lamb* included extensive correspondence with Lucy E. Watson, granddaughter of James Gillman, Charles Lamb's close friend and a biographer of Coleridge. In the Gilchrist Collection there are two letters to Anne from Lucy Watson and the copyright agreement for *Mary Lamb*. A long "List of Authorities" is appended to the text of the book.
50. Anne Gilchrist, *Mary Lamb* (London: David Boguej Boston: Roberts Brothers, 1883), 243–44.
51. In England in the 1840s there were more than 150,000 women over twenty who did sewing at home for a living; by 1851 the number had risen to 388, 302 (J. H. Murray, *Strong-Minded Women,* 350). In the early nineteenth century, two male writers called attention to the plight of needleworkers: Thomas Hood's popular "The Song of the Shirt" was published in *Punch* in December 1843; Henry Mayhew's "Interviews with Needleworkers" was published in the *Morning Chronicle* in November 1849 (Ibid., 350–56).
52. Lamb, "Needlework," in Gilchrist, *Mary Lamb*, 243–255.
53. By supporting Mary Lamb's urgent plea that more opportunities to do remunerative work be made available to women, Anne was joining forces with an American author, Louisa May

Alcott. Alcott's plea, although oblique, was even more dramatic. In *Little Women* (1869), Jo March's sale of her one beauty—her long, luxuriant hair—as the only way that she could earn money for a family crisis is a symbolic act of prostitution.

54. Even in England in the 1870s and 1880s, WW was not widely accepted. When *Daniel Deronda* was published in 1876, George Eliot used two lines from a Whitman poem to head chapter 29. A slurring remark in the *Saturday Review* "about his 'nastiness' and uncritical English admirers" made her shy away and replace the lines in later editions (*Daniel Deronda* [1876; reprint New York: Penguin Books, 1967], 893).
55. HHG, 268, 270.
56. *Letters*, 226.
57. Ibid., 230.
58. Anne Gilchrist, "A Confession of Faith," *To-Day*, June 1885. Reprinted in HHG, 331-62.
59. HHG, 331, 334.
60. Ibid., 332-33.
61. Ibid., 339.
62. Ibid., 344.
63. Ibid., 349-50.
64. GC. Letter to Anne Gilchrist from William Wordsworth, Bombay, 10 August, 1884. William Wordsworth, son of the poet's son John, was born in 1836. In the Gilchrist Collection there is a packet of Dorothy Wordsworth's poems copied in Anne's hand.
65. GC. Letter to Anne Gilchrist from William Wordsworth, Bombay, 12 November, 1884.
66. In 1884 Anne wrote two biographical sketches for Leslie Stephen's *Dictionary of National Biography*—one of Blake, the other of Mary Matilda Betham, poet, miniature painter, and friend of the Lambs (2:643-46, 423). With the exception of these two sketches, "Confession" would be Anne's last published work. She began a study of Carlyle, hoping to repair some of the damage to his reputation by other biographers, but it was never finished (HHG, 282).
67. Allen, *Solitary Singer,* 432.
68. Margot Peters, *Bernard Shaw and the Actresses* (New York: Doubleday, 1980), 419, n.11. Between her almost-engagement to FB and her marriage, after her mother's death Grace had an almost-romance with the fascinating young Irishman. According to Shaw's biographers, his involvement with Grace amounted to nothing more than a mild flirtation carried on at the meetings of the Fabian Society and abruptly terminated by the interference of Emma Brooke, novelist, Fabian, and self-appointed protector of motherless Grace. Miss Brooke called on Shaw, accused him of being a philanderer, and demanded to know his intentions toward Grace; they exchanged letters on the subject and had another heated discussion in the hall of the British Museum. His biographers contend that Shaw, weary of her wrangling—and with affairs and flirtations with five other young women going at the same time—decided to bring the whole thing to an end (St. John Ervine, *Bernard Shaw: His Life, Work and Friends* [New York: William Morrow & Co., 1956], 156-59). However, there is an unpublished letter from Shaw to Herbert in the Gilchrist Collection that indicates that, even before Miss Brooke's visit to him on 1 April, 1888, Shaw had been attempting to break off his involvement with Grace. On 29 April, he wrote:

Dear Gilchrist
I avoided you yesterday at the Grosvenor because Miss Brooke gives me to understand that you may be in no mind to exchange recognitions with me. If so, I wish you would tell me exactly why, because there are things which I can explain to you which would worry Miss Brooke out of her senses if I were to spring them on her. Strained relations like ours are mortally disagreeable to me: and I suspect you can improve them by giving me a piece of your mind. I undertake not to fence with you; and I assure you I have no idea of defending my conduct throughout. I must have been idiotically thoughtless, to say the least of it; but the moment I saw the mischief I did my best to remedy it; and I believe I should have succeeded had not Miss Brooke, with the best intentions, interfered and disastrously beaten me. Pray let's have it out, if you don't mind.

Yrs.
G. Bernard Shaw

A letter to Shaw from a hurt and mystified Grace, smitten deeply enough to be jealous, verifies Shaw's explanation to Herbert—since it was written on 26 March, four days before Miss Brooke's visit to him.

Dear Mr. Shaw

I was too much pained by your altered manner to me to have energy enough left to shake off that gentleman who constituted himself my escort on the sole plea that he too came from Hampstead. I have felt myself these last few weeks socially estranged from you. I wish I had not parted so abruptly from you after that walk home from Mrs. Wilson's [Charlotte Wilson, anarchist wife of a London stockbroker and a founder of the Fabian Society]: I am sure it was all a misunderstanding: I was wrong to give way to childish jealousy of other women.... [omissions are Shaw's] I know I have everything to learn in socialism: my faults are not my destiny, though sometimes indeed one's faults create an adverse destiny for one.

Yours sincerely
Grace Gilchrist

Grace's letter, copied in Shaw's hand, is in the Special Collections of the Harry Ransom Humanities Research Center, University of Texas at Austin.

69. *Letters*, 225, 231, 237.
70. Ibid., 231.
71. Ibid., 223.
72. Ibid., 225, 237.
73. HHG, 281.
74. *WMR-Letters*, 147–62. WW's American friends did not neglect him by any means. In 1885, either Donaldson or Mary Davis suggested that a horse and buggy would give the poet much pleasure, since it was increasingly difficult for him to get out of doors. Thirty-five prominent men—including Richard Gilder, Mark Twain, Whittier, and Holmes—contributed ten dollars apiece for this purpose. Whittler hoped that "a kind, sober-paced roadster" would be more serviceable to WW in his lameness "than the untamed, rough-jolting Pegasus he has been accustomed to ride." A phaeton was built especially for the poet and a safe pony named Frank was found. WW drove Frank so furiously that the pony's knees gave out and he sold him for a faster horse. "This horse is a goer and delights me with his motion," WW told Donaldson. The poet drove him until 1888, when WW was no longer strong enough to continue (Allen, *Solitary Singer*, 522–23). In May 1886, the first installment of the funds collected in England—156, or about $850—was sent to WW by Rossetti. The list included Henry James, Robert Louis Stevenson, Havelock Ellis, and about eighty others (Allen, *Solitary Singer*, 524).
75. Letter to Edward Pease from Anne Gilchrist, Keats Corner, Well Road, Hampstead, 24 June, 1885. Manuscripts Department, Alderman Library, University of Virginia.
76. *Letters*, 241.
77. HHG, xi–xii.
78. *Corr.* 3:408, n.90.
79. GC. Anne Gilchrist's memorandum to her children.
80. *Corr.* 3:408, n.90.
81. Ibid., 408–9.
82. Ibid., 411.
83. Ibid., 408–9, n.90.
84. Ibid., 412–13.
85. Obituary of Anne Gilchrist, *Academy*, 5 December, 1885, 375–76.
86. HHG, 283–84.
87. *LG*, " 'Going Somewhere,' " 525.
88. *WWWC* 3:512, 97, 377. It has been pointed out that there is a similarity between the friendship of Walt Whitman and Anne Gilchrist and the friendship of Michelangelo and Vittoria Colonna. Both men were artists; both were homosexual; each was loved by a brilliant, well-born woman, widowed at an early age, who loved him and furthered his career; neither realized how much he too had loved until after her death.
89. *LG*, "Out of the Rolling Ocean the Crowd," 106.

BIBLIOGRAPHY

Abram, Ruth J., ed. *"Send Us a Lady Physician": Women Doctors in America, 1835-1920.* New York: W. W. Norton and Co., 1985.

Alcott, Bronson. *The Journals of Bronson Alcott.* Ed. Odell Shepard. 2 vols. Port Washington, New York: Kennikat Press, Inc., 1938.

Allen, Gay Wilson. *The Solitary Singer: A Critical Biography of Walt Whitman.* New York: Macmillan Co., 1960.

———. *Waldo Emerson.* New York: The Viking Press, 1981.

Alsop, Gulielma Fell, M.D. *History of the Woman's Medical College: Philadelphia, Pennsylvania, 1850-1950.* Philadelphia: J. B. Lippincott Co., 1950.

Anthony, Katherine. "A Normal Madness." *Dial,* 11 January 1919, 15-16.

Arvin, Newton. *Whitman.* New York: Macmillan Co., 1938

Aspiz, Harold. *Walt Whitman and the Body Beautiful.* Urbana: University of Illinois Press, 1980.

Barker, Felix, and John Gay, eds. *Highgate Cemetery: Victorian Valhalla.* Salem, N.H.: Salem House, 1984.

Barrus, Clara. *The Life and Letters of John Burroughs.* 2 vols. Boston: Houghton Mifflin Co., 1925.

———. *Whitman and Burroughs: Comrades.* Boston: Houghton Mifflin Co., 1931.

———, ed. *The Heart of Burroughs's Journals.* Boston: Houghton Mifflin Co., 1928.

Beaver, Joseph. *Walt Whitman—Poet of Science.* New York: Octagon Books, 1974.

Beeton, Isabella. *Beeton's Book of Household Management.* 1861. Reprint, New York: Farrar, Straus and Giroux, 1974

Bénézit, E., ed. *Dictionnaire critique et documentaire des Peintres, Sculpteurs, Dessinateurs et Graveurs (de tous les temps et de tous les pays par un groupe d'écrivains spécialists francais et etrangers).* New edition. Paris: Librairie Gründ, 1976.

Binns, Henry Bryan. *A Life of Walt Whitman.* London: Methuen and Co., 1905.

Blodgett, Harold. *Walt Whitman in England.* Ithaca: Cornell University Press, 1934; New York: Russell and Russell, 1973.

Boyle, Richard J. *American Impressionism.* Boston: New York Graphic Society (Little, Brown and Co.), 1974.

Briggs, Asa, ed. *The Nineteenth Century: The Contradictions of Progress.* New York: McGraw Hill, 1970.

Brion, Marcel. *Michelangelo.* Trans. James Whitall. New York: Bonanza Books, 1940.

Bucke, Richard Maurice. *Walt Whitman.* Philadelphia: David McKay, 1883; New York and London: Johnson Reprint Corporation, 1970.

Burns, Stanley B., M.D. "Scarlet Fever." Vol. 4, no. 2 of *The British Gallery of Medical History.* New York: Bristol Laboratories, 1985.

Burroughs, John. *Whitman: A Study.* Boston and New York: Houghton Mifflin Co., 1896.

Buss, Kate. "Anne Gilchrist to Walt Whitman—Some Comments on the Love Letters of a Woman to the Great American Poet, Whose Centenary is Now Being Observed." *Boston Evening Transcript,* 31 May 1919, pt. 3, col. 1.

Calder, Ellen M. "Personal Recollections of Walt Whitman." *Atlantic Monthly,* June 1907, 825-26.

Canby, Henry Seidel. *Walt Whitman, an American: A Study in Biography*. New York: Literary Classics, 1943.
Carpenter, Edward. *Days with Walt Whitman: With Some Notes on His Life and Work*. London: George Allen, Ruskin House, 1906.
———. *Some Friends of Walt Whitman: A Study in Sex-Psychology*. The British Society of Sex Psychology, no. 13. London: J. E. Francis, Atheneaum Press, 1924.
Carpenter, George Rice. *Walt Whitman*. New York: Macmillan Co., 1909.
Carter, Katy. *London and The Famous: An Historical Guide to Fifty Famous People and Their London Homes*. London: British Tourist Authority, 1982.
Concise Dictionary of National Biography: From Beginnings to 1921. Epitome of 1901–21. London: Oxford University Press, 1936.
Coombs, Betty. "George Eliot in Surrey." *Lady*, 20 November 1969, 806.
Curtis, Gerald. *The Story of the Sampfords*. Whitham, Essex: Mansell Bookbinders, 1981.
Deutsch, Babette. *Walt Whitman: Builder for America*. New York: Julian Messner, 1941.
Donaldson, Thomas Corwin. *Walt Whitman: The Man*. New York: Francis P. Harper, 1896.
Douglas, Ann. *The Feminization of American Culture*. New York: Alfred A. Knopf, 1977.
Drachman, Virginia G. *Hospital with a Heart: Women Doctors and the Paradox of Separatism at the New England Hospital, 1862–1969*. Ithaca and London: Cornell University Press, 1984.
Duyckinck, Evert A., and George L. Duyckinck, eds. *Cyclopedia of American Literature*. 2 vols. New York: Charles Scribner, 1856.
Eliot, Alexander. *Three Hundred Years of American Painting*. New York: Time Incorporated, 1957.
Eliot, George. *Daniel Deronda*. 1876. Reprint. New York: Penguin Books, 1967.
Ervine, St. John. *Bernard Shaw: His Life, Work and Friends*. New York: William Morrow and Co., 1956.
Faner, Robert D. *Walt Whitman and Opera*. Carbondale: Southern Illinois University Press, 1951.
Ferlazzo, Paul J. "Anne Gilchrist, Critic of Walt Whitman." *South Dakota Review* 10, no. 4 (Winter 1972–73): 63–79.
Frend, Grace Gilchrist. *See* Gilchrist (Frend), Grace.
Fuller, Margaret. *Woman in the Nineteenth Century*. 1845. Reprint. New York: W. W. Norton and Co., 1971.
Garrett, Wendell, and Paul Norton, Alan Gowans, Joseph Butler, eds. *The Arts in America: The Nineteenth Century*. New York: Charles Scribner's Sons, 1969.
Gilchrist, Alexander. *Life of William Etty, R.A.* London: David Bogue, 1855.
———. *Life of William Blake: With Selections from his Poems and Other Writings*. 1863. 2d ed. 2 vols. London: Macmillan and Co., 1880.
Gilchrist, Anne. *Anne Gilchrist: Her Life and Writings*. Ed. Herbert Harlakenden Gilchrist. London: T. Fisher Unwin, 1887.
———. *The Letters of Anne Gilchrist and Walt Whitman*. Ed. Thomas B. Harned. New York: Doubleday, Page; London: T. Fisher Unwin, 1918.
———. "A Glance at the Vegetable Kingdom." *Chambers's Journal of Popular Literature, Science and Arts* (London) 8, no. 197 (10 October 1957): 234–36.
———. "Our Nearest Relation." *All the Year Round* (London: Conducted by Charles Dickens, 1859–70) 1 (28 May 1859): 112–15.
———. "Whales and Whalemen." *Chambers's Journal of Popular Literature, Science and Arts* (London) 13, no. 328 (14 April 1860): 225–28.
———. "The Parentage of a Sunbeam." *Once a Week* (London) 3 (22 September 1860): 348–51.
———. "What is Electricity?" *Once a Week* (London) 4 (2 February 1861): 163–65.
———. "Lost in the Wood." *The Magnet Stories: For Summer Days and Winter Nights*, no. 16 (1861): 51–96.

_____. "The Indestructibility of Force." *Macmillan's Magazine* (London) 6 (August 1862): 337-44.

_____. "A Neglected Art." *Macmillan's Magazine* (London) 12 (October 1865): 494-501.

_____. "A Woman's Estimate of Walt Whitman." *Radical* (Boston), May 1870, 345-59. Reprinted as "An Englishwoman's Estimate of Walt Whitman" in *Anne Gilchrist: Her Life and Writings*, 287-307.

_____. "A Memoir of Alexander Gilchrist." In *Life of William Blake: With Selections from His Poems and Other Writings* by Alexander Gilchrist. 2d ed. 2 vols. (London: Macmillan and Co., 1880) 2: 359-76.

_____. *Mary Lamb*. London: David Bogue; Boston: Roberts Brothers, 1883.

_____. "Three Glimpses of a New England Village." *Blackwood's Edinburgh Magazine*, November 1884, Reprinted in *Anne Gilchrist: Her Life and Writings*, 309-30.

_____. "A Confession of Faith." *To-Day* (London), June 1885. Reprinted in *Anne Gilchrist: Her Life and Writings*, 331-62.

_____. "Mary Matilda Betham." In *Dictionary of National Biography*, 2: 423. Ed. Leslie Stephen. London: Smith, Elder and Co., 1890.

_____. "William Blake." In *Dictionary of National Biography*, 2: 643-46. Ed. Leslie Stephen. London: Smith, Elder and Co., 1890.

Gilchrist (Frend), Grace. "Chats with Walt Whitman." *Temple Bar Magazine* (London), February 1898, 200-212.

_____. "Walt Whitman as I Remember Him." *Bookman* (London), July 1927, 203-5.

_____. Typescript of unpublished memoir of her mother. Feinberg Collection, Library of Congress.

Gilchrist, Herbert Harlakenden. "Alexander Gilchrist." In *Dictionary of National Biography*, 2: 340. Ed. Leslie Stephen. London: Smith, Elder and Co., 1890.

_____. "Anne Gilchrist." In *Dictionary of National Biography*, 2: 340-41. Ed. Leslie Stephen. London: Smith, Elder and Co., 1890.

_____, ed. *Anne Gilchrist: Her Life and Writings*. London: T. Fisher Unwin, 1887.

Gould, Elizabeth Porter. *Anne Gilchrist and Walt Whitman*. Philadelphia: David McKay, 1900.

Gray, J. M. Review of Anne Gilchrist's *Mary Lamb. Academy* (London), 25 August 1883, 121.

Himmelfarb, Gertrude, *Marriage and Morals Among the Victorians*. New York: Alfred A. Knopf, 1986.

Holloway, Emory. *Free and Lonesome Heart: The Secret of Walt Whitman*. New York: Vantage Press, 1960.

Houghton, Walter E., ed. *The Wellesley Index to Victorian Periodicals, 1824-1900*. 2 vols. Toronto: University of Toronto Press, 1966.

Innes-Smith, Robert. "The Chapel-Barn of St. Stephen, Bures and the de Vere Monuments." Reprint from *East Anglia Life*, n.d., n.p.

_____. "The Earls of Oxford." Reprint from *East Anglia Life*, n.d., n.p.

Ireland, Mrs. Alexander. *Life of Jane Welsh Carlyle*. New York: Charles Webster and Co., 1891.

Irwin, Mabel MacCoy. *Whitman: The Poet-Liberator of Woman*. New York: Published by the author, 1905

Jacobi, Mary Putnam. "Women in Medicine." In *Woman's Work in America*, edited by Annie Nathan Meyer, 139-205. New York: Henry Holt, 1891.

James, Henry. "Mr. Walt Whitman." In *The Portable Henry James*, edited by Morton Dauwen Zabel, 422-29. New York: Viking Press, 1951.

Johnston, Alma Calder. "Personal Memories of Walt Whitman." *Bookman* (London) 46: 404-13.

Johnston, John. *Notes of a Visit to Walt Whitman, etc., in July 1890*. Bolton: T. Brimelow and Co., 1890.

Johnston, John and W. Wallace. *Visits to Walt Whitman in 1890-91; By Two Lancashire Friends*. 1917. Reprint, New York: Haskell House, 1970.

Kaplan, Justin. *Walt Whitman: A Life*. New York: Simon and Schuster, 1980.

Kazin, Alfred. *An American Procession.* New York: Alfred A. Knopf, 1984.
Keller, Elizabeth Leavitt. *Walt Whitman on Mickle Street.* New York: Mitchell Kennorley, 1921.
Kennedy, William Sloane. *Reminiscences of Walt Whitman.* 1896. Reprint. New York: Haskell House, 1973.
──────. *The Fight of a Book for the World: A Companion Volume to Leaves of Grass.* West Yarmouth, Mass.: Stonecroft, 1926.
Keynes, Geoffrey. *Blake Studies: Essays on his Life and Work.* Oxford: Clarendon Press, 1971.
Lang, Elsie M. *Literary London.* Folcroft, Pa.: Folcroft Library Editions, 1973.
Loving, Jerome. *Walt Whitman's Champion: William Douglas O'Connor.* College Station and London: Texas A & M University Press, 1978.
──────. ed. *The Civil War Letters of George Washington Whitman.* Durham, N.C.: Duke University Press, 1975.
MacKenzie, Norman, and Jeanne MacKenzie. *The Fabians.* New York: Simon and Schuster, 1977.
Marshall, Clara. *The Woman's Medical College of Pennsylvania: An Historical Outline.* Philadelphia: P. Blakiston Son and Co., 1897.
Matthiessen, F. O. *American Renaissance: Art and Expression in the Age of Emerson and Whitman.* New York: Oxford University Press, 1941.
McBriar, A. M. *Fabian Socialism and English Politics: 1884–1918.* Cambridge: Cambridge University Press, 1966.
Mellow, James R. *Nathniel Hawthorne in His Times.* Boston: Houghton Mifflin, 1980.
Melville, Herman. *Moby Dick.* 1851. Reprint. New York: W. W. Norton, 1967.
Miller, Edwin Haviland, ed. *A Century of Whitman Criticism.* Bloomington: Indiana University Press, 1969.
──────. ed. *The Artistic Legacy of Walt Whitman: A Tribute to Gay Wilson Allen.* New York: New York University Press, 1970.
Minutes of the Faculty of the Woman's Medical College of Pennsylvania: July 10, 1876–April 30, 1881. The Medical College of Pennsylvania Archives, collection 92, 74–75.
Morgan, Charles H. *The Life of Michelangelo.* New York: Reynal, 1960.
Morris, Harrison Smith. *Walt Whitman: A Brief Biography with Reminiscences.* Cambridge: Harvard University Press, 1929.
Morris, Lloyd. *Incredible New York: High Life and Low Life of the Last Hundred Years (1850–1950).* New York: Random House, 1951.
Murray, Janet Horowitz. *Strong-Minded Women and Other Lost Voices from Nineteenth-Century England.* New York: Pantheon, 1982.
Murray, Linda. *Michelangelo.* New York: Oxford University Press, 1980.
Novak, Barbara. *American Painting of the Nineteenth Century: Realism, Idealism, and the American Experience.* New York: Harper and Row, 1979.
──────. *Nature and Culture: American Landscape and Painting, 1825–1875.* New York: Oxford University Press, 1980.
Osborne, Harold, ed. *The Oxford Companion to Art.* London: Oxford University Press, 1970.
Palmer, Samuel. *Eleven Holograph Letters from Samuel Palmer to Alexander Gilchrist and Anne his widow 1861–1862.* Beinecke Rare Book and Manuscript Library, Yale University Library.
Patmore, Coventry. *The Angel in the House.* 1854. Reprint in *Poems.* London: George Bell and Sons, 1906.
Pease, Edward R. *The History of the Fabian Society.* 1916. Reprint. London: George Allen and Unwin, 1925.
Peters, Margot. *Bernard Shaw and the Actresses.* New York: Doubleday, 1980.
Review of Alexander Gilchrist's *The Life of William Blake: With Selections from his Poems and Other Writings. North American Review,* October 1864, 464–83. Unsigned.

Review of *Anne Gilchrist: Her Life and Writings*, edited by Herbert Harlakenden Gilchrist. *Athenaeum*, 26 March 1887, 409. Unsigned.
Review of *The Letters of Anne Gilchrist and Walt Whitman*, edited by Thomas B. Harned. "Walt Whitman and his Noblest Woman-Friend." *Current Opinion*, December 1918, 394–95. Unsigned.
Ridley, Hilda M. "Great Friendships: Anne Gilchrist and Walt Whitman." *Canadian Magazine* 61 (July 1923): 251–58.
Rose, Phyllis. *Parallel Lives: Five Victorian Marriages*. New York: Vintage Books, 1984.
Rossetti, Dante Gabriel. *Poems*. Leipzig: Bernhard Tauchnitz, 1873.
Rossetti, William Michael, ed. *Poems of Walt Whitman*. London: John Camden Hotten, 1868.
———, comp. *Rossetti Papers, 1862–1870*. London: Sands, 1903.
———. *Some Reminiscences of William Michael Rossetti*. 2 vols. New York: Charles Scribner's Sons, 1906.
———. *Letters of William Michael Rossetti: Concerning Whitman, Blake, and Shelley; to Anne Gilchrist and her son Herbert Gilchrist*. Ed. Clarence Gohdes and Paull Franklin Baum. Durham, N.C.: Duke University Press, 1934.
Schyberg, Frederik. *Walt Whitman*. 1933. Reprint. Trans. Evie Allison Allen. New York: Columbia University Press, 1951.
Scudder, Horace Elisha. "Anne Gilchrist." In *Men and Letters: Essays in Characterization and Criticism*, 195–214. Boston: Houghton Mifflin; Cambridge, Mass.: Riverside, 1887.
Stephen, Leslie, ed. *Dictionary of National Biography*. 26 vols. London: Smith, Elder and Co., 1890.
Stern, Madeleine B. *Louisa May Alcott*. Norman: University of Oklahoma Press, 1950.
Symonds, John Addington. *Walt Whitman: A Study*. London: John C. Nimmo, 1896.
Tennyson, Charles. *Alfred Tennyson*. New York: Macmillan Co., 1949.
Tennyson, Emily Sellwood, Baroness. *Lady Tennyson's Journal*. Ed. James O. Hoge. Charlottesville: University of Virginia Press, 1981.
Thieme, Ulrich, and Fred C. Willis, eds. *Allgemeiner Lexikon Der Bilden Ken Kuenstler*. Vol. 14. Leipzig: Verlag von E. A. Seemann, 1921.
Traubel, Horace. *With Walt Whitman in Camden*. Vol. 1 (28 March–14 July 1888). Boston: Small, Maynard and Co., 1906; vol. 2 (16 July–31 October 1888). 1908. Reprint. New York: Rowman and Littlefield, 1961; vol. 3 (1 November 1888–20 January 1889). 1914. Reprint. New York: Rowman and Littlefield, 1961); vol. 4 (21 January–7 April 1889). Ed. Sculley Bradley. Philadelphia: University of Pennsylvania, 1953; Carbondale: Southern Illinois University Press, 1959; vol. 5 (8 April–14 September 1889). Ed. Gertrude Traubel. Carbondale: Southern Illinois University Press, 1964; vol. 6 (15 September 1889–6 July 1890). Ed. Gertrude Traubel and William White. Carbondale: Southern Illinois University Press, 1982.
Twenty-ninth Annual Announcement of the Woman's Medical College of Pennsylvania (1878–1879). Archives and Special Collections, Medical College of Pennsylvania.
"Walter White." In *Dictionary of National Biography*, 21: 83–84. Ed. Leslie Stephen. London: Smith, Elder and Co., 1890.
Weigley, Russell F., ed. *Philadelphia: A Three Hundred-Year History*. New York: W. W. Norton, 1982.
Whitman, Walt. *Leaves of Grass*. In *Leaves of Grass: Comprehensive Reader's Edition*. Ed. Harold W. Blodgett and Scullery Bradley. New York: New York University Press, 1965; New York: W. W. Norton, 1973.
———. *Leaves of Grass*. In *Walt Whitman: Complete Poetry and Selected Prose*. 5–408. Ed. James E. Miller, Jr. Boston: Houghton Mifflin Co., 1959.
———. *Democratic Vistas*. In *Walt Whitman: Complete Poetry and Selected Prose*, 455–501. Ed. James E. Miller, Jr. Boston: Houghton Mifflin Co., 1959.
———. *Memoranda During the War [and] Death of Abraham Lincoln*. Ed. Roy P. Basler. Westport, Conn.: Greenwood Press, 1972.

———. *In Re Walt Whitman*. Ed. Horace L. Traubel, Richard Maurice Bucke, and Thomas B. Harned. Philadelphia: David McKay, 1893.

———. *Walt Whitman's Workshop: A Collection of Unpublished Manuscripts*. Ed. Clifton Joseph Furness. Cambridge: Harvard University Press, 1928.

———. *Faint Clews and Indirections: Manuscripts of Walt Whitman and His Family*. Ed. Clarence Gohdes and Rollo G. Silver. Durham, N.C.: Duke University Press, 1949.

———. *Prose Works, 1892*. Vol. 1, *Specimen Days*. Ed. Floyd Stovall. New York: New York University Press, 1963.

———. *Prose Works, 1892*. Vol. 2, *Collect and Other Prose*. Ed. Floyd Stovall. New York: New York University Press, 1964.

———. *The Correspondence of Walt Whitman*. Ed. Edwin Haviland Miller. 6 vols. New York: New York University Press, 1961–1977.

———. *The Tenderest Lover: The Erotic Poetry of Walt Whitman*. Ed. Walter Lowenfels. New York: Delacorte Press, 1970.

———. *The Collected Writings of Walt Whitman: Daybooks and Notebooks*. 3 vols. Vol 1, *Daybooks, 1876–1881*. Ed. William White. New York: New York University Press, 1978.

———. *Walt Whitman: The Measure of His Song*. Ed. Jim Perlman, Ed Folsom, and Dan Campion. Minneapolis: Holy Cow! Press, 1981.

Wilson, Rufus Rockwell, and Otilie Erickson Wilson. *New York in Literature: The Story Told in the Landmarks of Town and Country*. Elmira, New York: The Primavera Press, 1947.

Winwar (Grebanier), Frances. *Poor Splended Wings: The Rossettis and Their Circle*. Boston: Little, Brown, and Co., 1933.

———. *American Giant: Walt Whitman and His Times*. New York: Harper and Brothers, 1941.

Wood, Christopher, ed. *The Dictionary of Victorian Painters*. Research by Christopher Newall. Woodbridge, Suffolk, England: Antique Collectors' Club, 1978.

Wyatt, Edith Franklin. "Anne Gilchrist and Walt Whitman." *North American Review*, September 1919, 388–400.

Zweig, Paul. *Walt Whitman: The Making of the Poet*. New York: Basic Books, 1984.

Index

Acton, Dr. William, 61, 239 n.26
Agnew, Dr. S. Hayes, 255 n.37. *See also* Eakins, Thomas
Alcott, Abigail May (Mrs. Bronson), 261 n.26
Alcott, Bronson, 193
Alcott, Louisa May, 24, 193, 266 n.53
Aldrich, Charles, 224
Allen, Gay Wilson, 125, 128, 251 n.13
Anderson, Dr. Elizabeth Garrett, 252 n.40
"Anne Gilchrist, Critic of Walt Whitman" (Ferlazzo), 119, 128, 130-31
Anne Gilchrist: Her Life and Writings (ed. Herbert Gilchrist), 18, 19, 25-30, 33, 178-79, 235 n.1; review of, 25-26
Anthony, Katherine, 20-21, 121, 141
Art Students League of New York, 189, 197
Ashburton, Lady Harriet, 76, 241 n.16

Barrus, Clara, 21, 22, 141, 201-2, 234 n.21
Beach, Juliette Hayward, 129-30, 251 n.6
Beeton's Book of Household Management (Isabella Beeton), 239 n.22
Bell, Currer. *See* Brontë, Charlotte
Berlin, Dr. Fanny, 190, 191, 195, 263 n.60
Besant, Annie, 23
Betham, Mary Matilda, 267 n.66
Bigelow, Frank, 203, 205-6
Bigelow, Mrs. John, 198, 263 n.59
Binns, Henry Bryan, 19
Blackwell, Dr. Elizabeth, 252 n.40
Blake, Life of William (Alexander Gilchrist), 14, 72, 89; Carlyle on, 101; completion of by Anne, 98-101; Herbert Gilchrist on, 209; Samuel Palmer on, 101; review of, 101; second edition of, 208, 209-10; Whitman on, 210
Bloomer, Amelia, 23
Bodley, Dean Rachel (Woman's Medical College), 166
Bogue, David, 60, 68, 72, 217
Booth, Miss (editor of *Harper's Bazaar*), 198
Bradford, George, 193
Brontë, Charlotte (Currer Bell), 14, 24, 61, 102
Brookbank Cottage, 95-97; description of in *Daniel Deronda*, 97; George Eliot's tenancy of, 97, 114, 244 n.15
Brooke, Emma, 267 n.68

Brown, Emma (Mrs. Ford Madox), 75, 90, 110, 207, 251 n.19
Brown, Ford Madox, 55, 75, 92, 110, 207; lends Anne *Poems of Walt Whitman*, 15, 115, 116
Bucke, Dr. Richard Maurice, 16, 20, 262 n.46; Anne on biography of Whitman by, 234 n.7, 250 n.61
Burnie, Mrs. (Alexander Gilchrist's sister), 97-98, 100, 244 n.20
Burroughs, John, 16, 19, 23, 55, 118, 185-86, 192, 234 n.21; description of Gilchrists by, 159; as Anne's guest, 180, 219; letters from Anne to, 147, 194, 217; tributes to Anne by, 16, 227; on Whitman, 175-76, 179-80, 182, 200
Burrows, Henrietta Carwardine (Anne's mother), 32-33, 38, 40, 43, 56, 60; ancestry of, 26-30; descriptions of, 30, 39-40, 87, 88; illness and death of, 42, 45-46, 150, 252 n.39; letter to Anne from, 44-45
Burrows, Henry (Anne's uncle), 43, 238 n.32
Burrows, John Parker (Anne's father), 25, 32-33, 38, 236 n.14; ancestry of, 30-32; description of, 30; letters to Anne from, 37-38
Burrows, John Thomas (Anne's brother), 33, 37, 38, 43, 236 n.3, 236 n.16, 238 nn.32 and 33; and Anne, 34-35, 42-43; illness and death of, 43, 44; final letter to Anne from, 43-44
Buss, Kate, 21, 141, 261 n.26

Cahusac's School, the Misses, 36-37, 38, 40, 106
Calder, Ellen M. *See* O'Connor, Ellen
Call, Dr. Emma, 190
Carlyle, Jane Welsh, 55, 66, 80, 95, 170; described by Alexander Gilchrist, 71-72; letters to Alexander Gilchrist from, 76, 77-78; letters to Anne from, 77, 90, 92, 93, 95, 113-14; takes lessons in bread making from Anne, 77; on Lady Ashburton, 241 n.16; on marriage, 77
Carlyle, Thomas, 55, 73, 101, 114, 177, 178, 267 n.66; and Alexander Gilchrist, 71-72, 76, 91, 93; as a husband, 78, 244 n.7
Carlyles, the (Jane and Thomas), 23, 76-78,

275

94, 193, 261 n.26; at 5 Cheyne Row, 71–72, 73–75, 77, 241 nn.3 and 4; defended by Anne to Whitman, 178, 179; marital difficulties of, 76, 78
Carpenter, Edward, 16, 19, 118, 162, 206, 213, 258 n.92; as Anne's guest in Philadelphia, 16, 180–81, 258 n.92; letter to Grace Gilchrist from, 256 n.45
Carpenter, George Rice, 234 n.45
Carwardine, Ann Holgate (Anne's grandmother), 28–30, 33
Carwardine, Reverend Charles William (Anne's uncle), 34, 237 n.5
Carwardine, Henry Holgate (Anne's uncle), 38, 45–46, 55, 56, 60, 87, 238 n.37
Carwardine, Major John (Anne's cousin), 156, 253 n.55
Carwardine, Reverend Thomas (Anne's grandfather), 28–30, 238 n.31
Cattell, Edward, 183, 195, 261 n.37
Central Park (New York City), 200, 262 n.53
Chase, William Merritt, 197, 262 n.50
Cheyne Row (London): history of, 73, 241 n.2
Chilton, Mary A., 249 n.57
Clapp, Henry, 129
Comte, Auguste, 39, 55
"Confession of Faith, A" (Anne Gilchrist), 219–21
Constable, Arnold & Company, 263 n.56
Conway, Moncure, 19, 146, 159, 171, 207, 247 n.2, 252 n.22

Dana, Charles A., 130
Daniel Deronda (George Eliot), 97, 267 n.54
Darwin, Charles, 81, 220
Davis, Mary, 223, 268 n.74
Democratic Vistas (Whitman), 118, 220
Donaldson, Thomas, 16, 17, 268 n.74
Dorr, Dalton, 222
Douglas, Ann, 40
Dowden, Edward, 222, 227
Doyle, Peter, 19, 177, 182, 195, 254 n.10

Eakins, Thomas, 158, 168, 175, 254 n.2, 255 n.37
Earls Colne (Essex), 25, 26, 45–46, 86–87
Eaton, Wyatt, 189, 194, 197, 260 n.8
Edgeworth, Maria, 39
Eldridge, Charles, 174–75, 180
"Electricity, What Is?" (Anne Gilchrist), 82–83
Eliot, Charles William, 196
Eliot, George, 14, 77–78, 97, 178, 198, 206, 267 n.54; tenancy of Brookbank, 97, 114, 244 n.15
Ellis, Sarah Stickney, 23, 42, 43. See also *Women of England*

Elsie Dinsmore books (Finley), 40, 237 n.20
Emerson, Ellen, 193
Emerson, Lidian (Mrs. Ralph Waldo), 193, 261 n.26
Emerson, Ralph Waldo, 23, 39, 55, 128, 171, 177; Anne's opinion of, 39; Anne's visits to, 193–94; and Whitman, 130, 182, 248 n.11
"Estimate of Walt Whitman, A Woman's" (Anne Gilchrist), 15, 24, 39, 69, 127–28, 130, 131–39, 219, 220, 221, 250 n.86
Etty, Life of William (Alexander Gilchrist), 60, 66, 68–70; critical response to, 68
Eyre, Ellen, 251 n.6

Fabian Society, 223, 224, 246 n.56, 267 n.68
Felsted Grammar School, 114, 148, 247 n.86
Ferlazzo, Paul. See "Anne Gilchrist, Critic of Walt Whitman"
Fern, Fanny, 128–29, 249 n.51
"Force, The Indestructibility of" (Anne Gilchrist), 84–86, 102
Forster, John, 77
Frend, Alfred Henry, 264 n.7
Frend, Grace Gilchrist. See Gilchrist, Grace
Fuller, Margaret, 23, 24, 121
Furness, Horace Howard, 171
Furness, William Henry, 171

Galaxy, 127
Game of Nine-Pins in New England, A (Herbert Gilchrist), 197, 262 n.52
Gilchrist, Alexander (husband), 14, 97–98, 177, 220, 238 n.1, 244 n.9; and Alexander Macmillan, 89, 89–90, 241 n.9; as art critic, 58–60, 72, 89; childhood and early education of, 49–51; courtship of Anne by, 47, 52–53, 238 n.12; and Dante Gabriel Rossetti, 89; described by Anne, 54, 91; described by William Michael Rossetti, 47; drawing of by Herbert Gilchrist, 47; engagement and marriage to Anne of, 58–61; illness and death of, 90–91, 93, 227, 243n.48; and Jane Carlyle, 71–72, 76, 77–78, 241 n.16; legal education of, 47–49, 51–52; letters to Anne from, 87–88, 241 n.7; letters to Julia Newton from, 65–66; *Life of Blake* by, 72, 89; *Life of Etty* by 60, 63, 66; parents of, 49–51; poems and early writings of, 47, 51, 52–53, 73, 238 n.9; and Samuel Palmer, 75, 89, 243 n.1. See also *Blake, Life of William; Etty, Life of William*
Gilchrist, Alexander Fitzmaurice (grandson), 193, 203, 208, 210, 223, 261 n.23; and Tennyson, 247 n.73
Gilchrist, Anne Burrows: ancestry of, 26–33; arrival in America of, 159; and baptism of children of, 87; and Beatrice Gilchrist in

Edinburgh, 210–11; and Beatrice Gilchrist's studies in Switzerland, 203–5, 207, 208–9; *Blake, Life of,* completion of by, 98–101, 245 n.26; and *Blake, Life of*, 2nd. ed., 208, 209–10; in Boston, 195–96; at Brookbank, 95–96, 97–98, 247 n.85; in Chesterfield (Massachusetts), 192–93; childhood of, 25, 33, 34–36, 237 n.5; in Concord (Massachusetts), 193–94, 261 n.26; courted by Alexander Gilchrist, 47, 52–53; writes "Confession of Faith, A," 219–21; correspondence with Wordsworth's grandson of, 221–22; critical appraisals of, 14, 15–16, 17–19, 22; death of, 226; and death of Alexander Gilchrist, 91; and death of Beatrice Gilchrist, 211–13; departure for America of, 153–57; departure for England of, 201–2; departure from Philadelphia of, 185–86; describes America and Philadelphia, 164, 165, 184; early interest in science of, 78–79; educates her children, 108–10, 114; engagement to Alexander Gilchrist of, 53–54, 57–61; and *Etty, Life of*, 63–64, 68, 70–71; farewell of Whitman and, 201–2; and father, 33, 37–38; as feminist pioneer, 23–24, 67, 103–5, 108, 136–39, 217–19; first letter to Whitman from, 13, 47, 53–54, 61–62, 64, 65, 66–67, 91, 97, 122, 141–43; and Grace Gilchrist's shipboard romance, 205–6; guests in Philadelphia of, 168, 179–81, 183; increasing ill health of, 197, 210, 226; on housework, 67; illness of when no reply to "Estimate" from Whitman, 139, 140; and illness (scarlet fever) of husband and children, 89–91, 93; as literary ambassador, 22–23; letter to Herbert and Grace Gilchrist from, 211; letters to Beatrice Gilchrist from, 191, 194, 197, 198, 199–200; letters to Herbert Gilchrist from, 189–90, 260 n.10, 262 n.45; letters to Whitman (1871–1876) from, 144–51, 153, 153–56, 251 n.13, 253 n.47; letters to Whitman (post-Philadelphia) from, 191–92, 193, 197, 199, 201, 262 n.46; on marriage to Alexander Gilchrist, 61–62, 63–64; new friends in Philadelphia of, 170–71; in New York City, 196–202; in Northampton (Massachusetts), 187–89, 259 n.6; nostalgia for America of, 206–7; obituary of and tributes to, 227–28; operation and recovery of, 181; photograph of (1851), 58; photograph of (1874), 151, 252 n.41; raises funds for Whitman, 147, 224; reads *Leaves of Grass* and falls in love with Whitman, 115, 117–20; on religion, 39, 40–42; return to England of, 203, 207; schooldays, of, 36–38; self-education of, 39, 55, 78, 114–15; as socialist, 107; at 12 Well Road, Hampstead (London), 207–8, 219, 222, 265 n.15; translates Hugo, 171; visit to Whitman at Timber Creek, 181–82, 258 n.99; and Whitman in New York, 199–200, 200–201; and Whitman in Philadelphia, 177–80; writes "Estimate of Walt Whitman, A Woman's," 125, 249 n.36, 250 n.86; writes memorandum to her children, 214–15. *See also* "Confession of Faith, A"; "Electricity, What Is?"; "Estimate of Walt Whitman, A Woman's"; "Force, The Indestructibility of"; "Lost in the Wood"; *Mary Lamb*; "Memoir of Alexander Gilchrist"; "Neglected Art A"; "Relation, Our Nearest"; "Sunbeam, The Parentage of a"; "Three Glimpses of a New England Village"; "Vegetable Kingdom, A Glance at the"; "Whales and Whalemen"

Gilchrist, Beatrice Carwardine (daughter), 14, 67, 68, 89–90, 109, 113, 185, 194; death of, 211–13, 223, 265 nn. 34 and 37; described by Christina Rossetti, 110; education (medical) of, 24, 149–50, 154–56, 166–68, 184–85; internship of, 185, 190–91, 201, 260 n.18; painting of, 246 n.68; photograph of, 205; practice in Edinburgh of, 209, 210–11; studies in Switzerland of, 205, 207, 208–209; and Whitman, 174–75, 190–91. *See also* New England Hospital for Women and Children; Women's Medical College of Pennsylvania

Gilchrist, Deborah Champion (Alexander Gilchrist's mother), 43, 47, 49

Gilchrist, Eileen Fitzmaurice (granddaughter), 264 n.3

Gilchrist, Grace (later Grace Gilchrist Frend) (daughter), 14, 19, 75, 109, 181, 187, 223, 229, 259 n.2, 264 n.7; descriptions of, 110, 112, 149, 154, 256 n.48; and Frank Bigelow, 205–206; and Edward Carpenter, 180, 206, 256 n.45; memoir of her mother (unpublished) by, 87, 112–13, 117, 174, 180, 192, 201, 202, 242 n.33, 257 n.61; on publication of Anne's letters to Whitman, 20–21, 235 n.22, 261 n.19; and George Bernard Shaw, 223, 267 n.68; singing career of, 170, 208, 223, 256 n.45; and Whitman, 172–74, 180, 192, 202, 257 nn. 59 and 61; 262 n.19

Gilchrist, Herbert Harlakenden (son), 14, 18, 19, 20, 38, 42, 43, 45, 47, 75, 109, 185, 213, 223, 229, 237 n.9, 240 n.22, 264 n.7; and "A Neglected Art" (Anne Gilchrist), 102, 245 n.42; art career of, 208, 209, 215, 223, 256 n.44, 257 n.69, 260 n.9; art studies of, 149, 168, 189, 193, 194, 197–98, 262 n.50; described by Anne, 154; described by

Whitman, 26, 179; description of Anne by, 153; early education of, 108–10, 148; and "Estimate of Walt Whitman, A Woman's" (Anne Gilchrist), 249 n.44; and George Bernard Shaw, 267 n.68; and Harry Stafford, 182; on Henrietta Carwardine Burrows, 30; letter to John Burroughs from, 164, 171; letters from Whitman to, 164, 180, 199, 226; letters to Whitman from, 197–98, 208, 209, 226, 262 n.53; in Massachusetts, 189, 192–93, 260 n.9; and "Our Nearest Relation" (Anne Gilchrist), 81; and Tennyson, 112–13; and Horace Traubel, 257 n.69; and Whitman, 175, 178–79, 194–95, 224, 235 n.1, 257 n.65, 258 n.80. See also *Anne Gilchrist: Her Life and Writings; Game of Nine-Pins in New England, A; Portrait of Anne Gilchrist* (1882); *Portrait of Anne Gilchrist* (1885); *Portrait of Walt Whitman; Tea Party, The*

Gilchrist, James (Alexander Gilchrist's father), 49–51

Gilchrist, Norah Fitzmaurice (Mrs. Percy), 148, 154, 203, 208, 252 n.30

Gilchrist, Percy Carlyle (son), 15, 65–66, 90, 109, 211, 229, 235 n.22; and Anne's trip to America, 253 n.50; career of, 148, 198, 203, 208, 223, 252 n.28, 264 n.2; dislike of Whitman of, 264 n.7; education of, 114, 148; and Grace Gilchrist's marriage, 264 n.7; marriage of, 148, 154, 184

Gilchrists, the (Alexander and Anne), 63–64, 66–68, 72, 75, 229, 240 n.3

Gilder, Jeannette, 23, 55, 198

Gilder, Richard Watson, 23, 198, 268 n.74

Gillman, James, 45, 252 n.23, 266 n.49

Gould, Elizabeth Porter, 17, 18–19, 19, 22, 247 n.2; Whitman on (to Traubel), 18

Gross, Dr. S. D., 158, 254 n.2, 255 n.57. See also Eakins, Thomas

Haines, William, 68, 71, 95, 98, 102, 110, 115; and *Anne Gilchrist: Her Life and Writings*, 236 n.16, 240 n.17, 245 n.29; and *Life of Blake*, 100; and *Mary Lamb*, 266 n.48

Hale, Edward Everett, 130, 260 n.18

Harlakenden, Roger, 26

Harlakenden, William, 26

Harned, Thomas B., 16, 17, 19, 20, 54; defense of publication of *The Letters of Anne Gilchrist and Walt Whitman* by, 21, 192, 234 nn. 8 and 21

Hawthorne, Sophia (Mrs. Nathaniel), 193

Hayley, William, 28

Higginson, Colonel Thomas Wentworth, 195–96

Highgate Cemetery (London), 39, 138, 237 n.15

Hillard, Kate, 146, 154, 168, 198, 222, 251 n.21, 253 n.51, 263 n.59

Hoar, Elizabeth, 193

Hoar, Judge Rockwood, 193

Holland, Emma, 207, 265 n.9

Holland, Frederick May, 23, 193, 213

Holmes, Oliver Wendell, 128, 248 n.13, 250 n.81, 268 n.74

Homer, Winslow, 262 n.52

Hunt, Leigh, 73, 74, 217

Ingram, John H., 215, 266 n.47

"Interviews with Needleworkers" (Henry Mayhew), 266 n.51

Ireland, Isabella Erskine, 90, 92–93, 94–95, 114, 243 n.2

Jackson, Mrs. Charles (Lidian Emerson's sister-in-law), 193

Jacobi, Dr. Mary Putnam, 190, 198, 263 n.60

James, Henry, 73, 207, 242 n.23, 268 n.74

Jewsbury, Geraldine, 94, 244 n.7

Jex-Blake, Dr. Sophia, 209, 212, 252 n.40, 265 n.37

Johnston, Albert (son of John H.), 183, 195, 261 n.37

Johnston, Alma Calder (Mrs. John H.), 177, 264 n.74

Johnston, Jack (John R. Johnston, Jr.), 171, 174; and affair with Whitman, 183, 195, 259 n.105

Johnston, Dr. John (Bolton, England), 260 n.9, 263 n.66

Johnston, John H. (New York City), 177, 182, 200, 213, 264 n.74; Whitman and Anne's farewell at house of, 201–2

Johnston, Colonel John R. (Philadelphia), 259 n.105, 261 n.37

June, Jennie (Mrs. Croly), 198

Kaplan, Justin, 249 n.51

Kathie Stories (Amanda Douglas), 40, 237 n.20

Kennedy, William Sloane, 178, 234 n.21

Kensal Green Cemetery (London), 38, 44, 91, 227, 243 n.48

Ladies' Mile, The, 263 n.56

La Légende des Siècles (Victor Hugo, trans. Anne Gilchrist), 171, 259 n.3

Lamb, Charles, 217

Lamb, Mary, 24, 201. See also *Mary Lamb*

Lawrence, Sir Thomas, 30, 236 n.9

Lazarus, Emma, 23, 55, 198, 222

Leaves of Grass (Whitman), quotations from: "Birds of Passage," 119; "Calamus," 145, 160, 161; "Children of Adam," 64, 70–71; "Dalliance of the Eagles, The," 187; "Drum-

INDEX

Taps," 134; "Eidólons," 25; "Gods," 140; "'Going Somewhere,'" 227; "Lilacs Last in the Dooryard Bloom'd, When," 203; "Out of the Cradle Endlessly Rocking," 13, 34; "Out of the Rolling Ocean the Crowd," 228; "Song of Joys, A," 109; "Song of Myself," 39, 41-42, 110, 116, 118; "Songs of Parting," 92; "To a Common Prostitute," 238 n.11; "Whispers of Heavenly Death," 158; "Woman Waits for Me, A," 63
Lee, General Edward, 263 n.59
Lesley, Professor J. Peter (and family), 171, 185, 222, 256 n.52
Letters of Anne Gilchrist and Walt Whitman (ed. Thomas Harned), 19-21, 234 nn.19 and 21, 235 n.22, 261 n.19. *See also* Harned, Thomas
Lewes, George Henry, 77, 97, 114, 198
Little Women (Louisa Alcott), 266 n.53
London School of Medicine for Women, 150, 252 n.40, 265 n.22
Longfellow, Henry Wadsworth, 23, 128, 196, 250 n.81
Lord & Taylor, 263 n.56
"Lost in the Wood" (Anne Gilchrist), 34-36, 86
Loving, Jerome, 127
Lowell, James Russell, 128, 250 n.81

McCreery, James & Company, 263 n.56
Macmillan, Alexander 55, 75, 89, 92, 241 n.9; and Anne during completion of *Life of Blake*, 98-101; and Anne during second edition of *Life of Blake*, 208, 209
Marshall, William Calder, 241 n.30
Marvin, Joseph B., 146, 147, 164, 180, 251 n.20, 255 n.22, 260 n.18
Mary Lamb (Anne Gilchrist), 15, 24, 201, 215-19, 266 n.48
Masson, David, 108, 246 n.59
Melville, Herman, 80, 242 n.23
"Memoir of Alexander Gilchrist, A" (Anne Gilchrist), 49-52, 66, 68, 71, 72, 91, 209
Menken, Adah Isaacs, 129-30
Meredith, George, 89
Michelangelo and Vittoria Colonna, 19, 268 n.88
Miller, Edwin Haviland, 22, 54, 141, 195
Miller, Joaquin, 19, 23, 180, 183, 198, 259 n.113
Milnes, Richard Monckton (Lord Houghton), 77, 100, 250 n.81
Montgomery House (Philadelphia), 159, 163
Morris, Harrison, 16, 17
Moulton, Louise Chandler, 177, 198
Mrs. Leicester's School (Charles and Mary Lamb), 217

"Needlework" (Mary Lamb), 24, 217-19
"Neglected Art, A" (Anne Gilchrist), 102-8, 219
New Century Club (Philadelphia), 171, 185, 259 n.121
New England Hospital for Women and Childen, 184, 185, 190
Newton, Julia Mary, 92; letters from Alexander Gilchrist to, 65, 65-66; letters from Anne to, 39, 40-41, 42, 44, 54, 55, 60; reminiscences of Anne by, 37, 39, 42, 44
1929 North 22nd Street (Philadelphia), 163, 255 n.18; Christmas 1877 at, 183; description of by Anne, 164; description of by Herbert Gilchrist, 164; Russian visitors at, 183
Northampton (Massachusetts), 185, 187-89. *See also* "Three Glimpses of a New England Village" (Anne Gilchrist)
Norton, Eliot, 195

O'Connor, Ellen (later Ellen M. Calder), 129, 200
O'Connor, William Douglas, 118, 122, 130-31, 178, 249 n.30 and "A Woman's Estimate of Walt Whitman," 124-25, 127

Palmer, Samuel, 55, 187; and Alexander Gilchrist, 75, 89, 101, 243 n.1; and Anne, 92, 110, 243 n.1
Parton, James, 129
Parton, Sara Payson Willis. *See* Fern, Fanny
Patmore, Coventry, 239 n.21
Pease, Edward, 224
Pennsylvania Academy of Fine Arts, 168
Perry, Bliss, 17, 18, 19, 21, 234 n.10
Philadelphia in 1876, 158-59, 165-66
Pope, Dr. Augusta, 190, 222
Pope, Dr. Emily, 190, 222
Porter, Miss (Grace Gilchrist Fread's companion), 229
Portrait of Anne Gilchrist, 1882 (Herbert Gilchrist), 215
Portrait of Anne Gilchrist, 1885 (Herbert Gilchrist), 226
Portrait of Walt Whitman (Thomas Eakins), 175
Portrait of Walt Whitman (Herbert Gilchrist), 175; compared with Eakins's portrait, 175; Whitman's defense of, 257 n.68
Pound, Ezra, 131
Pratt, Mr. and Mrs. (friends of Anne), 209, 214, 265 n.23
Price, Helen, 139, 213, 250 n.82
Probert, Annie (Anne's cousin), 44, 238 n.33, 239 n.20
Probert, Thomas (Anne's uncle), 56-57, 177, 239 n.20

Radical (Boston), 127–28
"Relation, Our Nearest" (Anne Gilchrist), 80–82, 220
Rogers, Harriet, 188, 259 n.6
Romney, George, 28, 30
Rossetti, Christina, 23, 55, 110, 118, 205, 251 n.19
Rossetti, Dante Gabriel, 23, 55, 73, 114, 129, 207, 223, 237 n.15, 238 n.11, 245 n.26; assists Anne with *Life of Blake*, 14, 99, 101, 208, 209; friendship of Alexander Gilchrist and, 89, 90, 92
Rossetti, Lucy Brown (Mrs. William Michael), 146, 251 n.19
Rossetti, William Michael, 19, 23, 55, 110, 207, 215, 227, 241 n.8; and "A Woman's Estimate of Walt Whitman," 15, 116–19, 122–25, 127, 139, 250 n.86; assists Anne with *Life of Blake*, 14, 99–101, 208, 209; descriptions of Alexander Gilchrist by, 47, 75; descriptions of Anne by, 75, 79, 122, 151–53, 224; lends Anne *Leaves of Grass*, 116–18; letters from Anne to, 96, 109, 114, 116, 165, 249 n.36; letters to Anne from, 140–41, 170; marriage and children of, 146, 251 n.19; on Anne's move to Philadelphia, 156, 170, 253 n.54; *Poems of Walt Whitman* edited by, 15, 18, 115, 118, 247 n.2, 248 n.23; raises funds for Whitman, 224, 268 n.74
Rossettis, the (family), 193, 219, 251 n.19, 261 n.26
Round Hill Hotel (Northampton, Massachusetts), 185, 187, 189
Rousseau, Jean Jacques, 39, 55, 177

Saffron Walden (Essex), 30–32, 229
Sampfords, the (Essex), 30–32
Sanborn, Franklin B., 193, 261 n.26
Schyberg, Frederik, 22
Scovel, James Matlock, 259 n.105
Scudder, Horace Elisha, 23, 170, 195, 207
Sewall, Dr. Lucy, 190
Shaw, George Bernard, 223, 267 n.68
Simmons, Mrs. (Anne's neighbor in Shottermill), 181, 183, 184, 185, 187, 247 n.85
Smith College, 24, 188, 259 n.2
Smith, Susan Garnet, 120–21, 248 n.19
"Song of the Shirt, The" (Thomas Hood), 266 n.51
Sorosis Club, 198, 264 n.74
Stafford, Harry, 182, 261 n.37; descriptions of Gilchrists by Whitman to, 171–72, 174; dislike of Herbert Gilchrist of, 182; family of, 160, 213; Whitman's attachment to, 182, 195
Stafford, Susan (Mrs. Stafford), 213, 258 n.99
Stedman, Arthur, 247 n.2

Stewart, A. T. & Company, 263 n.56
Still, William and Letitia, 167
"Sunbeam, The Parentage of a" (Anne Gilchrist), 83–84
Swinburne, Charles Algernon, 73, 89, 129
Symonds, John Addington, 28

Tait, Robert, 74, 241 n.3
Tales from Shakespeare (Charles and Mary Lamb), 217
Tea Party, The (Herbert Gilchrist), 172 215, 257 n.58
Tennysons, the (Alfred and Emily), 246 n.70, friendship with, 110–13, 207, 247 n.73; remembered by Herbert and Grace Gilchrist, 112–13
Tennysons, The (Alfred and Emily), 246 n.70, 261 n.26
Tennyson, Emily, 112, 113, 247 n.78
Thomas, Melicent Gilchrist (Alexander Gilchrist's sister), 60, 63, 239 n.24, 240 n.3
Thomas, Sidney Gilchrist (Alexander Gilchrist's nephew), 203, 252 n.28, 264 n.2
Thoreau, Cynthia Dunbar (Henry Thoreau's mother), 261 n.26
"Three Glimpses of a New England Village" (Anne Gilchrist), 24, 187–89, 219, 259 n.6
Traubel, Horace, 16, 17, 19, 20, 120, 192, 228; and Herbert Gilchrist, 257 n.69. *See also* Whitman, Walt

"Vegetable Kingdom, A Glance at the" (Anne Gilchrist), 79
Victoria, Queen, 101; Anne's dislike of, 179

Wale, Mary, 28
Wallace, J. W., 21, 260 n.9
Watson, Lucy, 252 n.23, 266 n.49
"Whales and Whalemen" (Anne Gilchrist), 79–80
White, Walter, 68, 102–3, 109, 110, 210–11, 240 n.18
Whitman, George Washington (WW's brother), 160, 180, 181, 223, 254 n.10
Whitman, Jessica Louisa (WW's niece), 180, 255 n.29
Whitman, Louisa Orr (Mrs. George), 160, 180, 181, 213, 223, 254 n.10, 257 n.58
Whitman, Louisa Van Velsor (WW's mother), 139, 254 n.10
Whitman, Mannahatta (WW's niece), 180, 255 n.29
Whitman, Walt, 15, 19–20, 54, 118, 143, 153–54, 186, 208, 223, 255 n.29, 261 n.26, 268 n.74; and Anne's death, 17, 226, 227–28; on Anne Gilchrist (to Traubel), 139, 171, 172, 178–79, 228, 234

n.19; as Anne's guest in Philadelphia, 163, 164–65, 171–72, 177–80, 183, 185; on Anne's move to America, 153–54, 253 n.49; on Anne's visit to Timber Creek, 258 n.99; on Anne's voice, 151; and Beatrice Gilchrist, 174–75, 191, 208, 210, 213; defenses of 130–31; defenses of by women, 120–21, 129–30, 249 n.51, 249 n.57; disciples of, 16–17; on Elizabeth Porter Gould, 18; on "Estimate of Walt Whitman, A Woman's" (Anne Gilchrist), 139; on Fanny Fern, 128–29, 249 n.51; and Grace Gilchrist, 172–74, 180, 192, 202, 261 n.19; and Herbert Gilchrist, 175, 178–79, 194–95; on Herbert Gilchrist's portrait (of WW), 175, 257 n.68; homosexuality of, 182–83, 259 n.105; meets Gilchrists, 159–60; and parting with Gilchrists, 174, 201–2; letters to Anne from, 144, 145, 163, 164, 170, 181, 193, 213, 226; letters to Herbert Gilchrist from, 164, 180, 199, 226–27; on *Life of Blake* (2nd. ed.), 209–10; in New York City, 199–202; sends photograph to Anne, 127; sends ring to Anne, 145, 251 n.13; and William Michael Rossetti, 125–27, 247n.2, 248n.11. See also *Democratic Vistas; Leaves of Grass*

Whitman, Walter Orr (WW's nephew), 254 n.10
Whittier, John Greenleaf, 128, 268 n.74
Wiley, Dr. Caroline Still, 167–68, 185, 191, 256 n.39, 260 n.17
Williams, Talcott, 16, 17
Wilson, Charlotte, 267 n.68
Winwar, Frances (Grebanier), 22
Woman's Medical College of Pennsylvania, 156, 164, 166–67, 233 n.21. *See also* Gilchrist, Beatrice
Women of England. *See* Ellis, Sarah Stickney
Wordsworth, Dorothy, 221–22, 267 n.64
Wordsworth, William, 85, 220
Wordsworth, William (poet's grandson), 221–22, 267 n.64
Wyatt, Edith, 22, 141, 162

Zakrzewska, Dr. Marie, 190, 191, 195, 201, 208, 260 nn.11 and 14
Zweig, Paul, 22